Educating Second Language Children

The whole child, the whole curriculum, the whole community

Edited by

Fred Genesee
McGill University

CAMBRIDGE
UNIVERSITY PRESS

Published by the Press Syndicate of the University of Cambridge
The Pitt Building, Trumpington Street, Cambridge CB2 1RP
40 West 20th Street, New York, NY 10011-4211, USA
10 Stamford Road, Oakleigh, Melbourne 3166, Australia

© Cambridge University Press 1994

First published 1994

Printed in the United States of America

Library of Congress Cataloging-in-Publication Data

Educating second language children : the whole child, the whole
curriculum, the whole community / edited by Fred Genesee.
p.   cm. – (Cambridge language education)
Includes bibliographical references and index.
ISBN 0-521-45179-5. – ISBN 0-521-45797-1 (pbk.)
1. Linguistic minorities – Education (Elementary) 2. Children of
minorities – Education (Elementary) I. Genesee, Fred. II. Series.
LC3725.E38   1994
371.97 – dc20   93-8570
                                                                        CIP

A catalog record for this book is available from the British Library

ISBN 0-521-45179-5 hardback
ISBN 0-521-45797-1 paperback

Contents

Contributors

Nancy Cloud, Hofstra University, Hempstead, New York
Elizabeth Coelho, Brookbanks Centre, North York, Canada
Jim Cummins, Ontario Institute for Studies in Education, Toronto,
    Canada
Fred Genesee, McGill University, Montreal, Canada
Naomi S. Goodz, Dawson College, Montreal, Canada
Else V. Hamayan, Illinois Resource Center, Des Plaines, Illinois
Jean Handscombe, North York Board of Education, North York, Canada
Sarah Hudelson, Arizona State University, Tempe, Arizona
Donna M. Johnson, University of Arizona, Tucson, Arizona
Denise McKeon, American Educational Research Association,
    Washington, DC
Mimi Met, Montgomery County Public Schools, Rockville, Maryland
Cindy Pease-Alvarez, Stanford University, Stanford, California
Catherine E. Snow, Harvard Graduate School of Education, Cambridge,
    Massachusetts
Patton O. Tabors, Harvard Graduate School of Education, Cambridge,
    Massachusetts
Olga Vasquez, University of California – San Diego, La Jolla, Cali-
    fornia

Series editor's preface

Preparing children to cope with school instruction in a dominant but unfamiliar language is a major educational issue in those parts of the world experiencing a pattern of immigration across cultural and linguistic borders. Immigrant children are expected to acquire rapidly the skills needed to progress in regular school subjects at the same rate as children from the dominant language. Different approaches to education, including pull-out second language classes, sheltered content instruction, and bilingual education, have been designed to help children make the transition to learning through the medium of their second language.

In *Educating Second Language Children,* Fred Genesee has brought together a team of specialists to address the challenges of teaching immigrant children from a number of fresh perspectives. The result is a valuable and comprehensive introduction to this area of second language education.

Although the role of language is of major concern to the contributors, the book looks at far more than linguistic issues. It presents an integrated approach to education that encompasses social, cognitive, and academic, as well as linguistic, dimensions. The focus throughout is on making links across the various contexts of the learner's experience – the classroom, the school, the family, and the community – and what language means for the child in each of these contexts. The authors thus cover a broad range of issues as they outline approaches to the design of pre-school and school-based programs. The book will be a valuable resource for educators, teachers, and policymakers interested in the education of second language children.

Jack C. Richards

Editor's acknowledgments

The editing of this book has benefitted immensely from the assistance of many people. Most certainly, it has benefitted from the close collaboration that I have enjoyed with each and every author. Not only have they collaborated generously with me in the preparation of their individual chapters, but they have also provided me with invaluable guidance in the overall planning and development of the book. Thus, although I appear as the editor, this volume has in fact been jointly edited by us all. Only I, however, am responsible for those aspects of the book which may be wanting from the readers' points of view. I would like to thank the authors for their collaboration, hard work and insights. I would also like to express particular appreciation to the following people (listed alphabetically) for their extraordinary assistance to me: Scott Enright, Else Hamayan, and Jean Handscombe.

Introduction

Fred Genesee

Our concerns in this book are with children between approximately 4 and 12 years of age who have learned a language or languages other than English during their preschool years, who are living in predominantly English-speaking communities or countries and who are being educated primarily through English. In some countries, such as Canada and the United States, we would say that these children are in elementary school; elsewhere, the level of schooling for this age group is labelled differently. The precise terminology used to refer to their level of schooling is unimportant. What is important is that these children are in their formative, preadolescent years, and for them learning English is a necessity not only for becoming socially integrated into the life of the school and the community at large but also for academic success in school and ultimately for economic survival and well-being in adulthood.

Throughout the book these children are referred to as ESL or second language students and children, and in some cases as "language minority" children. These terms have been chosen because they lack the more serious shortcomings of alternatives that I and the other contributors considered. Some terms, such as *limited English proficient* (or LEP), are unacceptable because they focus on apparent deficiencies in these children's development. Others, such as *bilingual,* are avoided because they focus on a characteristic which may not apply to all students. This is not to say that we do not support the goal of bilingualism for ESL students or for English-speaking students, for that matter. To the contrary, we do. Furthermore, although we focus on working in largely English-medium school settings, this does not mean that we favor educational programs for ESL children that teach only through English. Nor does it mean we believe that these children's home language and culture should be ignored by schools and replaced by English and the majority culture. To the contrary, we believe that maintenance and development of the home language and culture are pedagogically sound and essential components of any effective educational program (Heath, 1986; Wells, 1986). Indeed, where possible and where desired by parents, use of the home language and incorporation of the home culture into the curriculum and activities of the school are to be strongly encouraged. Research has shown that language minority children who develop their first language skills fully during the preschool years often make the transition to schooling in English more easily and effectively than children who do not maintain the home language (Dolson, 1985).

Although the terms *ESL* and *second language* appear throughout the book, we have reservations about using them. The main one is that they focus attention on one aspect of the teaching and learning of these children – the second language aspect; our concerns are with the entire education of the child – academic, cognitive and social as well as linguistic. It is for this reason that the book is titled *Educating Second Language Children: The Whole Child, The Whole Curriculum, The Whole Community*. Effective education of second language children calls for a more integrative approach than that which has characterized professional thinking and practice in the field to date. When I speak of an integrative approach, I am referring to more than integrating language and content, although this is important. All too often, teaching children who are learning a second language and learning through a second language has not been integrated with other important aspects of education. Educating second language children has been kept separate from issues concerning their social integration in mainstream classrooms and the school at large. It has been consigned to second language teaching specialists, thereby keeping grade level and second language teachers from integrating their professional competencies and resources and from cooperating extensively in planning whole educational programs for second language students. Specialized and often esoteric methods of instruction have been prescribed to teach second languages – methods which in many cases make it difficult to integrate and coordinate instruction for second language and English-speaking students in the same classes. Moreover, instruction for second language students has even been kept separate from their "education" outside school – in their families and communities – so the formal education of the children is not integrated with their living and learning outside school.

The message in this book is quite different. It seeks to integrate the process of thinking about and the practice of teaching second language students from the perspective of the whole child, the whole curriculum and the whole community. The theoretical arguments and pedagogical recommendations presented apply no matter what language is the primary medium of instruction – be it the child's home language or a second language. Thus, much of what we have to say applies not only to second language teachers and specialists but also to grade level teachers, bilingual teachers, and first language development specialists.

A number of beliefs underlie this perspective and have figured prominently in planning this book. Some were clear and strong in the beginning; others were vague and ill-formed; all of them have been enriched and clarified for me as I worked with the contributors whose chapters you are about to read. It is important, and I hope useful, to discuss these beliefs briefly to make clear the general perspectives which motivated the organization of this book and the unifying themes which serve to integrate the diverse contributions that follow. As you read on, you can judge for yourself whether you share these beliefs and whether the theory and research reviewed in each chapter adequately substantiate the approaches and perspectives advanced by the writers.

The whole child

Effective instruction is developmental. It builds on the skills, knowledge and experiences that young children acquire prior to coming to school and while they are in school, and it extends and broadens their skills and experiences in developmentally meaningful ways throughout their school years. In other words, the starting point for planning and delivering instruction is the child – instruction for second language children should be first and foremost *child-centred*. From the teacher's point of view, planning and providing instruction on the basis of children's existing competencies and using experiences and knowledge that are familiar to the learner provides a solid foundation for extending children's skills and knowledge in new directions. From the second language student's point of view, learning on the basis of established skills and known experiences provides a reassuring context in which to acquire new skills and concepts.

It is axiomatic in development that, notwithstanding general patterns in the preschool and early school years, there is tremendous variation in the development of children even within the same sociocultural group. Such variation reflects the cumulative influences of both constitutional and experiential/background (social, nutritional, psychomotor, etc.) differences among children. To be developmentally meaningful, instruction for second language children must also be *individualized* to take account of important differences among young learners.

All too often, educational programs for these children focus on teaching language to the exclusion of other aspects of their development. And yet research on child language acquisition during the last four decades indicates decisively that authentic language learning does not take place in isolation from other aspects of children's development. Rather, it is intimately linked with, constrained by and a contributor to cognitive and social development. These interrelationships are numerous and complex, but some simple examples will illustrate the general point.

In the realm of early cognitive development, it is generally believed that children's first words emerge when they do (during the second year of life usually) because it is at this stage in their development that children can begin to think in terms of symbols. Thus, they are able to use words to symbolize the world around them. In fact, children's first words and utterances generally refer to concrete objects, social events and feelings that are part of their immediate experiences, probably because these are the facts of life that children know and can refer to using linguistic symbols, or words.

Children's acquisition and use of words as symbols ultimately frees their thinking and experience from the here-and-now and the concrete so that they are able to think about and refer to abstract ideas, feelings and possibilities (Bruner, 1964). Language gives life to abstract notions such as friendship, evolution and justice because of its symbolic properties. Whereas the early manifestations of language are constrained by the child's level of cognitive development, language contributes to the subsequent development of higher order, abstract levels of cognitive ability.

Among school-age children, language learning in school is initially constrained by their cognitive abilities, but it ultimately advances those abilities. Because second language students find it difficult to learn new language skills which refer to abstract concepts, cognitive operations or experiences which are not yet part of their intellectual repertoire, they should first be given opportunities to learn language in conjunction with experiences that are compatible with their current abilities and knowledge. In this way, learning new language skills to talk about what is already known or has already been experienced will be facilitated. Once learned, these new language skills can serve as tools to acquire and master other concepts and skills. The interdependence between language and cognition becomes especially important in the higher grades, where more and more of the academic goals become abstract and dependent on language for their acquisition (in mathematics, science and history, for example).

Research also indicates that learning a language involves more than learning a linguistic code to label the physical world or to refer to abstract concepts; it entails learning how to use the code in socially appropriate and effective ways (Hymes, 1971). Anyone who has learned a second or foreign language as an adult and has tried to use it with native speakers will appreciate that it is not enough to know the words and grammar of the language – you must also know how to use them in socially acceptable ways. This is a complex task. The specific values, beliefs and relationships which comprise the social life of the group whose language the child is learning shape the patterns of language usage in that community in complex and important ways (Schieffelin & Ochs, 1986). Thus, through the process of learning a language that is embedded in the social life of a community, the child learns the values, beliefs and ways of interacting in that community and in turn becomes a member in good standing in that social group. In other words, in learning a language the developing child becomes a fully functioning and valued member of the community of speakers of that language.

This is equally true for children learning a new language in school. It is now generally accepted that schools socialize children to the values, beliefs and goals of the dominant society. Research shows that this is accomplished to a large extent through the patterns of communication and interaction that characterize school life. Indeed, teaching and learning in school entail socially and culturally distinct forms of communication and interaction (Diaz, et al., 1986). Thus, the social environment of the school is important for second language students because it provides an interpersonal context for learning language that goes beyond language itself and beyond the academic curriculum. It gives social meaning to the patterns of language use in the school, and it offers social rewards to those who integrate into it successfully. To become fully functioning and valued members of the school community, second language students must learn the sociolinguistic norms of the school. Indeed, their academic success depends on their acquisition of both the social and linguistic codes which constitute language.

Taken together, these views from research mean that language learning and, therefore, language teaching in school cannot take place in isolation if they are to be useful and successful. They must be integrated with the other social and cognitive aspects of the child's development and of the child's schooling. From the student's point of view, learning a second language in school should be seen as a means to achieving social integration and academic success, not as an end in itself. Otherwise, the motivation to learn English in school will be seriously undermined. From the teacher's point of view, instruction for second language children must be seen as the means for achieving these goals in school. This means that teachers should facilitate the integration of second language students with native-English-speaking students and that the curriculum for second language students should be integrated (albeit perhaps with adaptations that will make it more accessible) with that of English-speaking students. By implication, the measure of our success at accomplishing this integration shall be found in the academic achievement of second language students and their social integration into the academic and nonacademic activities of the school.

The whole community

Researchers and educators have long argued that the academic success of children is influenced in significant ways by their linguistic and social backgrounds. This has been a common theme in explanations of the academic difficulties faced by and often disproportionate failure of children from minority sociocultural groups. However, they have had trouble understanding the precise nature of these children's backgrounds and, therefore, the exact reasons for their academic problems. Early theories focused on language skills and, in particular, characterized those skills as deficient in certain respects (see, for example, Bernstein, 1970). Furthermore, they interpreted these putative language deficits as symptomatic of underlying cognitive deficiencies that hampered childrens' achievement in school. The reported linguistic and cognitive deficits were attributed to deficiencies in the quality of the social relationships and intellectual climate in the childrens' homes.

Critics of this position – and there have been many – have pointed out that the language skills of language minority children are not deficient; it is as complex and rule-governed as that of children from middle-class majority groups (Labov, 1969). Critics have also noted that the patterns of language use and the cognitive abilities characteristic of middle-class language majority children and their families were being used to judge the competence of other children and their families, as if middle-class ways of using language are the only or best way and an absolute basis for assessing others. Finally, researchers interested in cross-cultural matters have argued convincingly that it is impossible to assess cognitive abilities in isolation without taking into consideration the social context in which intellectual skills have been learned and are routinely used (Bruner, 1964; Heath, 1986). Thus, to arrive at a valid assessment of the cognitive abilities of language minority students, it is necessary to understand the sociocultural context in which these abilities were acquired and are routinely used.

Subsequent and more informed views of this issue characterized the backgrounds of children from the minority group as simply *different* from those of children from the majority group. Such differences, it was argued, pose academic problems for these children because the schools they attend are based on and reflect the backgrounds of the dominant social group. Although advocates of this position did not characterize the children as deficient, they saw them as ill-prepared for schooling that emphasizes predominantly middle-class, majority group ways of doing things. This perspective is a definite improvement over the deficit view; however, it is still far from satisfactory. Despite its explicit intent, the "difference" hypothesis has all too often been used euphemistically by some educators and policymakers as a substitute for *deficit*. But, more important, even when it does not imply deficits in background, it calls for change in the children and their families if the mismatch between home and school is to be redressed or reduced. Moreover, the "difference perspective" fails to provide substantive insights into the specific characteristics of minority group children's family and community life that might have an impact on schooling. Thus, it is pedagogically empty.

Recent research in a variety of social and cultural communities has come a long way toward broadening our knowledge and understanding of specific patterns of language, social and cognitive development in families and communities with diverse sociocultural characteristics (Heath, 1986; Phillips, 1983; Schieffelin & Eisenberg, 1984; Schieffelin & Ochs, 1986). While generalizations of any sort are untenable when one looks at specific instances, the findings from this research have revealed rich and complex patterns of social interaction, language use and learning in these groups. Barring abnormal disabling circumstances, the evidence indicates that children from language minority backgrounds have often had linguistic and cultural experiences during the preschool years that, as Pease-Alvarez and Vasquez point out (see Chapter 4), have been enriched by the home culture, the dominant group culture in which they live, and the multiculturalism that inevitably results from contact and interaction between minority and majority groups in a pluralistic society. In other words, far from being impoverished, deficient, or merely different, the out-of-school experiences of second language children are immensely rich and complex. As a result, they acquire rich funds of knowledge that they bring to school.

It is foolish to advocate educational programs that seek to remediate or compensate for nonexistent developmental deficiencies in language minority children, as the earlier deficit view prescribed. And it is wasteful to talk about minimizing differences between the homes of language minority children and mainstream schools if this means ignoring the capabilities and knowledge that language minority children bring with them to school. To the contrary, the developmentally sound and "pedagogically optimistic" approach (to use Diaz, et al.'s term, 1986) is to encourage development of the home language and culture both in the homes of language minority children and, where possible, in their schools, and to use the linguistic, cognitive and sociocultural resources that language minority children bring to school as a basis for planning their formal education. This can only happen, however, if teachers become knowledgeable about and comfortable with the larger communities in which these children grow up and live.

Generally speaking, public education reflects the knowledge and assumptions held by educational authorities about the experiences and backgrounds of children from the majority group (McGroarty, 1986). In some cases, educational programs are even based on systematic research on the development and experiences of these children (Heath, 1986). Education, therefore, can be said to be developmentally sensitive to and culturally appropriate for majority group children. For education to be appropriate and sensitive to children who are learning a second language and through a second language, it is necessary for educators to refocus their attention to also take into account significant background and learning factors particular to the development of these children.

Variation in the background of second language children is likely to be extensive given the considerable diversity of their first languages, their level of second language proficiency, previous educational experiences, medical conditions, the circumstances in which they live or have come to live in an English-speaking community, and so on. Since second language students' backgrounds are so diverse and probably unfamiliar to educators who are not members of these groups, educators, especially teachers, who work with second language students must actively seek to know better the backgrounds of these students in order to plan effective instruction for them.

It is worth repeating that although a common theme throughout this book is second language learning and learning through a second language, this does not mean rejecting or neglecting the resources that language minority children have developed in their homes and communities; in particular, it does not mean replacing or minimizing the importance of the home language and culture in favor of the dominant language and culture. To the contrary, the perspective in this book is in favor of developmental additive bilingualism (Lambert, 1980). Schools, along with families and communities, share the responsibility for making the transition from the home to school successful and comfortable for second language children. Effective education calls especially for adaptation by schools so that the funds of knowledge that second language children bring with them are fully integrated into the curriculum along with those of English-speaking students.

The whole curriculum

The instructional needs of second language students are often fragmented under the assumption that children who come to school without full proficiency in the language of instruction must acquire proficiency before being given full access to instruction in academic domains. As a result, there has often been a preoccupation with providing students with special language instruction at the expense of instruction in other areas of the curriculum. Moreover, the very nature of the language instruction they receive often leaves their education fragmented since they are not receiving instruction in the kinds of academic language skills they need to cope in other areas of the curriculum.

During the last fifteen years, there have been major shifts in our thinking about the nature of language and language learning and its relationship to academic achievement. It is no longer believed that language learning and, therefore, language instruction are effective if they occur in isolation. As a result of extensive research on first language acquisition (some of which was reviewed earlier) and on language learning in immersion school programs (Genesee, 1987), it is now generally recognized that languages are acquired more effectively when they are learned in conjunction with meaningful content and purposive communication. Meaningful content provides a motivation for language learning that goes beyond language itself. Certainly, few school-aged children are interested in learning language for its own sake. Integrating language learning with meaningful and interesting content also provides a substantive basis for language learning. In other words, nonlinguistic content provides ''cognitive hangers'' on which new language structures and skills can be hung. Similarly, authentic communication provides a real social context for learning communicative functions of the new language. In the absence of such authentic communication, language can only be learned as an abstraction devoid of conceptual and communicative substance.

There is a growing appreciation, again based on research findings, that language is not monolithic and that language proficiency is not unidimensional. Researchers who study language in social context emphasize that there is considerable variation in the formal and functional characteristics of language from one context of use to another. What constitutes appropriate and effective language use depends on the particular situation. This is equally true within school itself. The language skills that students need for social interaction with their peers and teachers in class and in the school at large are different from those needed to function effectively during formal instructional periods. Moreover, it is now widely believed that language varies even across academic domains so that different language skills are needed in a mathematics classroom in comparison to a science or history classroom. The differences include not only specialized vocabulary but also special forms of expression related to specific academic domains, such as describing technical procedures or articulating hypotheses in science. This means that knowing how to use language in one context does not necessarily mean knowing how to use it effectively in another.

These insights about language and language learning have important implications for instructional planning for second language children. More specifically, ESL teachers are increasingly being encouraged to use meaningful content as a basis for planning and providing second language instruction. It makes sense, for the reasons noted here, that they use the academic content and goals outlined in the general curriculum as a basis for planning language instruction. Planning that incorporates the language skills that second language children need for dealing with instruction in specific academic domains is a way of respecting the specificity of functional language use, as well as of ensuring that the language skills taught to second language students are useful. If language skills are taught in isolation of the rest of the curriculum, they will not transfer or be useful for coping with academic instruction. Consequently, second language students will not benefit fully from academic instruction in their other classes.

In addition to these changes that have an impact on second language teachers, others are being called for which affect grade level teachers. More specifically, grade level teachers are being asked to modify their academic instruction using second language instructional strategies so that academic content is more accessible to their second language students. This makes good sense since grade level teachers have primary responsibility for the academic goals of the curriculum and, thus, a professional responsibility for and vested interest in maximizing the academic achievement of their whole class, including their second language students. Grade level teachers are also being called on to create opportunities for second language students to learn the language skills they need to cope with specific forms of academic instruction. In other words, they are being asked to share responsibility along with second language teachers for promoting the second language development of their students. This also makes sense considering that second language students spend extended periods of time with grade level teachers and, as we have already noted, academic content can be an effective basis for promoting second language proficiency. Teachers are in a unique position to gauge the academic language proficiency and the language learning needs of their students first-hand and to provide opportunities for extending their language skills in ways that are particularly relevant to the their overall education.

The challenge of developing a curriculum that is fully integrative, child-centred and individualized is not a part-time concern. It cannot be accomplished by second language teachers working alone with second language students on language development in isolation during circumscribed periods of the day. It calls for the involvement of grade level teachers working with second language teachers. Everything we know about language learning indicates that success is likely if it serves social and cognitive goals. This means extending language learning beyond the language classroom to include times of the school day which are largely social or cognitive in nature. Educational planning for second language students should be an integral part of all departments and units charged with planning and overseeing education within a community with children who are learning a second language and through a second language.

Children who come to school with no or limited proficiency in English are currently part of the educational landscape in virtually all urban public schools in most English-speaking countries, and this trend is likely to continue for the foreseeable future. It is no longer tenable to regard these children as a minority of the public school population and, on this basis, give them access to limited resources in the school. Educating second language children calls for the concerted involvement of all teachers and educational professionals working in such schools and for the utilization of all appropriate and available educational materials, technologies and approaches.

The book

Educational planning for second language students cannot be single-minded or predetermined. It must be responsive to diversity among children and change within children. It avoids "back to the basics" if *basic* means the same for all. And it incorporates and takes advantage of the social, intellectual and personal resources students have acquired in their homes and communities. Teachers must be sufficiently knowledgeable and confident to make their own instructional decisions – informed by scholarship, their reading of the professional literature and their own experiences and knowledge about their students, past and present. The chapters that follow are intended to give teachers guidance in making decisions about instruction for second language students. They are meant to assist you in discovering your own way of thinking about the development and education of these children so that you are able to make your own best instructional decisions. Each chapter presents a review of related theory and research findings along with discussions and recommendations about what the writers consider current best practice. Many chapters include a list of additional references for those who are interested in exploring particular issues further.

The book is organized into four main sections: "General Perspectives," "The Preschool Years," "The Classroom" and "Additional Challenges." These divisions are somewhat arbitrary, and you will probably find considerable overlap. This is as it should be since every chapter is concerned in some way with educating second language children. Brief introductions to the chapter are provided at the beginning of each section.

References

Bernstein, B. (1972). A sociolinguistic approach to socialization: With some reference to educability. In J. J. Gumperz & D. Hymes (Eds.), *Direc-*

tions in sociolinguistics: The ethnography of communication. NY: Holt, Rinehart & Winston, 465–497.

Bruner, J. S. (1964). The course of cognitive growth. *American Psychologists, 19,* 1–15.

Diaz, S., Moll, L. C., & Mehan, H. (1986). Sociocultural resources in instruction: a context-specific approach. In *Beyond language: Social and cultural factors in schooling language minority students* (pp. 187–230). Los Angeles, CA: Evaluation, Dissemination, and Assessment Center.

Dolson, D. (1985). The effects of Spanish home language use on the scholastic performance of Hispanic students. *Journal of Multilingual and Multicultural Development, 6,* 135–155.

Genesee, F. (1987). *Learning through two languages: Studies of immersion and bilingual education.* New York: Newbury House.

Heath, S. B. (1986). Sociocultural contexts of language development. In *Beyond language: Social and cultural factors in schooling language minority students* (pp. 143–186). Los Angeles, CA: Evaluation, Dissemination, and Assessment Center.

Hymes, D. H. (1971). Competence and performance in linguistic theory. In R. Huxley & E. Ingram (Eds.), *Language acquisition: Models and methods* (pp. 3–28). New York: Academic Press.

Labov, W. (1969). The logic of non-standard English. *Georgetown Monographs on Language and Linguistics, 22,* 1–22.

Lambert, W. E. (1980). The social psychology of language: A perspective for the 1980s. In H. Giles, W. P. Robinson, & P. M. Smiths (Eds.), *Language: Social psychological perspectives* (pp. 415–424). Oxford: Pergamon Press.

McGroarty, M. (1986). Educator's response to sociocultural diversity: Implications for practice. In *Beyond language: Social and cultural factors in schooling language minority students* (pp. 299–343). Los Angeles, CA: Evaluation, Dissemination, and Assessment Center.

Phillips, S. (1983). *The invisible culture.* New York: Longman.

Schieffelin, B. B., & Eisenberg, A. R. (1984). Cultural variation in children's conversations. In R. Schiefelbusch & J. Rickar (Eds.), *The acquisition of communicative competence* (pp. 379–418). Baltimore, MD: University Park Press.

Schieffelin, B. B., & Ochs, E. (1986). Language socialization. *Annual Review of Anthropology, 15,* 163–246.

Wells, G. (1986). The language experience of five-year-old children at home and at school. In J. Cook-Gumperz (Ed.), *The social construction of literacy* (pp. 69–93). Cambridge, England: Cambridge University Press, 69–93.

SECTION I:
GENERAL PERSPECTIVES

McKeon (Chapter 1) and Cummins (Chapter 2) present *general perspectives* on language, culture and schooling. Both authors argue that in order to create effective school environments for second language children, it is necessary to understand the broader sociocultural context in which schools function and in which children grow up. On the one hand, schools reflect, promote and are shaped by the social values, goals and ideologies of the dominant cultural group in society. On the other hand, schools are currently facing an unprecedented and increasing number of children who grow up in linguistic and cultural communities that fall outside the dominant cultural group. Consequently, many of the assumptions, principles and practices on which schools have traditionally relied are no longer the most appropriate. McKeon and Cummins call on us to reexamine some of the assumptions that have figured so prominently in traditional schooling; they review some of the "facts" about linguistic and cultural diversity that are relevant to an understanding of the language development of children from diverse backgrounds; they explore the implications of these facts for classroom practice; and they propose general ways in which teachers can stay informed about and respond to the needs of *all* their students.

1 Language, culture, and schooling

Denise McKeon

"A nation of immigrants" – the phrase used so often to describe the United States – has a romantic and exotic flavor. The phrase evokes images seen in tintype photographs. For some of us, it means scratchy black and white pictures of men with dark suits and women in long, dark dresses clutching children to their sides, with views of the New York skyline framing the scene from behind. For others, it means groupings of Chinese men in traditional dress standing alongside just-completed stretches of railroad tracks in the West. These images are also set in countries other than the United States – countries such as Australia, Canada, and Great Britain. No matter what the image, however, the time frame always seems to be in the past.

For teachers and schools, however, this vision of a nation of immigrants lives on. It is primarily in the public schools that current patterns of immigration come alive for all to see. The vision is one of children, children from every ethnic, cultural, and linguistic group.

Questions of language, culture, and schooling have existed as long as there have been immigrant children entering schools in their new countries of residence (Crawford, 1989). These questions are also raised in discussions of effective education for native peoples, such as Native American, Inuit, and aboriginal students. In fact, in almost every instance where a minority group interacts with a majority school system, the relationship of language, culture, and schooling merits discussion. The reason? In every country, certain groups of minority students have experienced what Ogbu and Matute-Bianchi (1986) refer to as "persistent disproportionate school failure."

Schools have recently begun to recognize that different types of students may require different types of programmatic responses. Students come to schools not only with a variety of languages but also with a variety of skills in their first languages. Some may have been outstanding students in their countries of origin; others may never have attended school or may have come from linguistic communities with strong oral, rather than literate, traditions.

Students with little formal schooling in their first language may be overwhelmed by a program of all-English instruction that assumes conceptual readiness which students may not possess. Students with high levels of proficiency in their first language who have well-developed academic and conceptual backgrounds may be stifled in language programs that fail to challenge them cognitively (Handscombe, 1989). Schools have begun to recognize on a programmatic level what teachers have long suspected: Acquiring a language for the purpose of succeeding in school is an extremely complex process.

How do schools and teachers deal with such diversity? How can schools be made more hospitable and welcoming to linguistically and culturally diverse groups? How can schools become places of learning and achievement for all students? The relationship of language, culture, and schooling is a critical one in the search for answers to these questions. Since it is now very likely that grade-level teachers will work with language-different children sometime in their career (Rigg & Allen, 1989), it makes sense for all teachers to understand the cultural and linguistic processes that influence a child's perspective on school and learning.

In order to foster just such an understanding, this chapter provides an overview of language acquisition processes for both first and second language learners. It includes a discussion of language use and variation, again in first and second language contexts. The chapter shows how a student's cultural background can influence not only the language learning process, but, more important, the way it can influence how a student views school and school achievement. Finally, the chapter shows the complexities of learning language in a school context and provides some strategies that teachers may implement in their classrooms to help foster the linguistic, affective, and cognitive growth of linguistically and culturally diverse students.

How children learn and use language

The first thing the research on language acquisition has taught us to remember about language learning, whether it is a first or second language, is that people learn language because they are in real situations communicating about important and interesting things. Furthermore, this communication is seen and perceived as something which is highly valued (Urzua, 1989). An initial look at the environments in which young children develop their language reveals a great deal of linguistic variety, yet virtually all children effortlessly and naturally learn the language of the home. Children's language development before they come to school takes place largely through conversations that they hear and have with members of their family.

At one time, it was thought that children learned to talk by imitating their parents. More recent research suggests, however, that children learn language by actively constructing principles for the regularities that they hear in the speech of others, such as parents, brothers, and sisters, and those they interact with on a regular basis (Brown, 1973; Chomsky, 1969). Evidence of these principles can be seen when children use forms such as *goed* (as in "My daddy goed to the store yesterday"), *foots,* and even *feets.* Such errors in children's speech provides us with clues that children are indeed constructing their own hypotheses of how the language functions since they haven't heard these particular forms in the speech of adults (Wells, 1986). As language develops, children become capable of dealing with greater degrees of complexity. They begin to recognize the inconsistencies of their own speech. They modify their hypotheses about the rules of language and gradually reorganize their language system so that their language approximates more complex adult forms – *goed* becomes *went.*

It may be comforting for teachers to know that learning the linguistic structures and rules of a second language occurs in much the same way (Dulay & Burt, 1974). The fact that children actively construct rules for language is evidence of their natural language learning ability, an ability that is present in the acquisition of both the first and subsequently acquired languages. Children who are acquiring a second language typically "try out" the language with equal creative fervor. Many of the errors made by children acquiring English as a second language are exactly the same errors made by young monolingual speakers of the language. Beginning students are as likely to say *goed* and *foots* as first language learners of English. They are using a process described as "creative construction" (Dulay, Burt, & Krashen, 1982; Lindfors, 1989).

Creative construction is a process similar to the one described by Wells (1986) but has certain additional features, the primary one being that second language learners tend to be more sophisticated language learners. Except for the case of those children who learn two languages from birth (Genesee, 1989), these second language learners already have some (if not most) of the components of one spoken language under their belts.

Children do not learn only linguistic structures and rules. They also learn *how* to communicate using the structures and rules that make up the language. The speech of parents and other members of the family provides evidence about language use, helps the child interpret objects and events, and provides feedback on the effectiveness of the child's communication skills (Wells, 1986). Language that emerges through shared activities with the child, usually in the form of conversation, appears to provide critical input to the young language learner about how to use language. One-to-one conversations which focus on topics of interest and concern to children maximize the opportunity to achieve shared understandings of the topics that are raised. Adults may attempt to enhance these understandings further by modifying or "fine-tuning" their speech in order to make meaning more accessible to the child. They speak in the "here and now," keep their sentences short and simple, emphasize key words, and frequently paraphrase and repeat what the child has said. In modifying their speech in this way, adults not only increase the chances that the child will understand what they say but also help children feel that conversation is worthwhile and enjoyable, an activity which enables them to be effective in understanding and controlling their surroundings.

Variation in language use

Language variation is a normal and pervasive feature of all languages. It occurs within particular geographical groups, socioeconomic groups, and certain cultural groups (e.g., Spanish spoken by Cubans versus that spoken by Mexicans), as well as across groups (middle versus working class; English spoken in Australia versus English spoken in Canada). It occurs as a function of the particular topic being discussed, the purpose for which language is being used, and the characteristics of the speakers who are engaged in conversation. Language variation may emerge in any or all aspects of language use: the lexicon, phonology, syntax, or general communication patterns of language.

Lexical variation concerns vocabulary choice. In New York, for example, one might use the word *soda* to request a flavored carbonated beverage, whereas in Illinois *pop* is the word most often heard. Variation occurs in the sounds of language as well. It is the type of variation that most people associate with the concept of "accent." For example, most North Americans would immediately recognize a "British accent" as one which is different from their own. " Southern accents," "Boston accents," and "New York accents" are examples of regional phonological variations that exist in the United States. Syntactic variation is evident in the choice of structural or grammatical patterns employed by groups of speakers. Examples of syntactic variation are the use of double negatives, as in "I can't get no satisfaction," or the substitution of one verb form for another, as in "I already done it," or "I be going." Communication patterns vary with regard to turn-taking in conversation or the way in which the speaker makes requests, offers criticism or advice, or expresses feelings. Tannen's (1990) work on the differences in men's and women's speech highlights these variations in communication patterns.

Not only do children acquire the structures of a given language, but they also learn the particular variety of language that is used by their caretakers and others around them. They learn conventions of language use which allow them to become members-in-good-standing of their particular linguistic community. Language variation plays an important role in establishing the racial, ethnic, or social identity of children; therefore, it is important that such variation be treated with respect.

Language variation, however, has been shown to elicit important social reactions from others, particularly when a specific variety of language is perceived as different from one's own (Ryan & Giles, 1982). The value placed on a certain way of saying something is very closely associated with the social status of people who say it that way. Judgments about whether a particular form of speech is "correct" are based on our attitudes about language and the different groups of people who use particular forms. Language variation may cause one to be seen as uneducated or highfalutin, that is, putting on airs. What is considered polite in one language community may be perceived differently by another. Such language varieties may rouse strong emotional, attitudinal, and behavioral responses. These responses become critically important in the education of children, as children from different speech communities begin to come into contact with the norms for language use which have been established by the school.

Children whose dialects are not deemed to be prestigious by society are usually aware of this evaluation and feel that their language is not as good as other people's. Wolfram and Christian (1989) point out that language variation may affect the quality of education received by the student in at least two ways. One is the possibility that a child's dialect may interfere with the acquisition of skills such as reading, on which later success might depend. The other is that teachers, school personnel, and other students who hear a dialect may make erroneous assumptions about the speaker's intelligence, motivation, and even morality. In some cases, a student may be "tracked" with the so-called slower groups or even placed in special classes because of a particular speech pattern.

A ten-year ethnographic study conducted in two speech communities, Roadville and Trackton, in the Piedmont Carolinas of the United States, points to some of the educational consequences and implications of such language variation (Heath, 1983). Heath describes the ways in which children from these two blue-collar communities are socialized as talkers, readers, and writers and how their language socialization differs from that of "middle-class mainstream" children.

What differs between these two groups of children and middle-class mainstream children appears to be not the quantity of talk but the kind of talk that children learn and use. Middle-class mainstream children generally learn not only how to label objects and answer questions but also how to create extended narratives, predict and maneuver events through imaginative storytelling, and build on and extend already existing schemata. It is precisely these types of language uses that children encounter as they enter and move through school. Neither Roadville nor Trackton children experience such home-grown linguistic learning and, therefore, experience difficulty in schools that do not understand or take their varieties of English into account when planning instruction. Roadville children initially experience success in school but soon fall behind. By junior high school (children 11 to 13 years of age), most are ready to get on with their lives and are simply waiting out school's end or their sixteenth birthday, the legal age for leaving school in the United States. Trackton students fall quickly into a pattern of failure and drift through their remaining years in school.

Just as there is variation in language use between different socioeconomic groups, there is also variation in both the language socialization patterns and the language usage fostered by linguistic minority communities. Heath (1986) argues that language learning is cultural learning based on three factors: assumptions of parents about their role as teacher, the ways in which oral and written language are used in the home and community, and the links that exist between the home and community and outside institutions, such as the school.

Evidence for differences in language learning and use in different ethnic groups comes from Heath's (1986) exploration of immigrant families. In Chinese-American families, for example, linguistic norms of parent-controlled conversations closely mirror the type of linguistic behavior expected in many traditional classrooms – parents ask children factual questions, and they monitor children's talk and activities through verbal correction, explication, and evaluation. Families see their role as complementing that of the school. Chinese-American parents see themselves as active agents in their children's language learning.

In relatively recent Mexican-American arrivals, parents, especially mothers, have primary caregiving responsibility while children are young, but the entire extended family may share some of the responsibility for rearing children. Parents model behavior they expect children to learn; they do not typically accompany their actions with step-by-step directions. They seldom ask children to verbalize what they are doing while they work, nor do they ask questions that require children to repeat facts or rehearse the sequence of events. Older children are expected to entertain younger ones; younger children are almost never alone with only one adult – they are surrounded by adults and children. Young children grow up in a rich verbal environment, and although relatively little talk is directed specifically to them, they hear language from other children and adults used for many functions. Adults talk to adults, and children talk to each other. Children are taught to be respectful of adults, answer talk directed to them, and not to initiate social conversations with their elders.

As demonstrated in Heath's Roadville and Trackton study, the customs of language use and the patterns of language learning in the homes and linguistic communities from which language minority children come may vary substantially from the conventions of school language use and learning. Where a mismatch occurs between what children bring from home and what is expected and taught in schools, the processes of language learning and academic learning may be just that much more difficult for language minority children.

Linguistic and cultural discontinuities

The cultural and linguistic barriers cited by Heath (1983, 1986) suggest that there are discontinuities that exist between the home and the school for many groups who are not part of the "mainstream middle class." While such discontinuities may create hardships for all groups, some groups clearly seem to experience more difficulty than others in making the transition from home to school.

Ogbu and Matute-Bianchi (1986) have examined variability in the school performance of different linguistic minority groups around the world. Although the specific linguistic minority groups that do well in school vary, each country appears to foster success in schooling some groups while other groups languish. In addition, there appears to be evidence that variability in performance is affected by the country in which a particular group finds itself. A group may do well in one country but poorly in another. One example of such variable performance is the case of Korean students, who have been shown to perform quite poorly in schools in Japan but quite well in schools in the United States (DeVos & Lee, 1981).

Researchers speculate that variability in the performance of linguistic minority students may be partly explained by examining the connection between education and other societal institutions and events affecting minorities (Cummins, 1989; Ogbu & Matute-Bianchi, 1986). In addition, they suggest that the social perceptions and experiences of particular minority groups can affect the outcome of their children's schooling. Ogbu and Matute-Bianchi distinguish between what they call immigrant minorities and castelike minorities. It is important not to stereotype the behavior of any individual according to the categories discussed by Ogbu and Matute-Bianchi since within each category there is a wide range of adaptations to life in a given culture. The categories do help, however, to build a framework in which minority achievement can be better understood.

Immigrant minorities include groups who have moved more or less voluntarily to their new country foɪ political, social, or economic reasons.

Examples of such minorities in the United States are Koreans-Americans, Japanese-Americans, Cuban-Americans, and Chinese-Americans. Immigrants in this group tend not to evaluate their success in the new country by comparing themselves with elite members of the host society; their frame of reference is still in the country from which they emigrated. They compare themselves either with their peers in the old country or with peers in the immigrant community.

Education is an important investment for such immigrant groups because it is perceived as the key to advancement, particularly for children. Immigrant children are taught to accept the school's rules for behavior and achievement; they learn to switch back and forth between two cultural frames of reference, that of the home and that of the school. Their ability to make these adjustments without feeling that they are losing their own culture enhances their ability to perform effectively in school.

Castelike minorities, according to Ogbu and Matute-Bianchi (1986), are minorities that have become incorporated into a society more or less permanently and involuntarily through such processes as conquest, colonization, or slavery, then relegated to a menial status within the larger group. Originally sent to Japan as colonial subjects in forced labor, the Koreans who perform poorly in school there function as a castelike minority in that setting. African-Americans, Mexican-Americans, Native Americans, and Puerto Ricans are examples of such minority groups in the United States.

Castelike minorities tend to believe that they cannot advance into the mainstream of society through individual efforts in school or by adopting the cultural beliefs and practices of the dominant group. The belief that they cannot "make it" leads these minorities to adopt survival strategies to cope with the conditions in which they find themselves and to make them distinct from the dominant group. Such strategies may eventually become cultural practices and beliefs in their own right, requiring their own norms, attitudes, and skills. These strategies might be incompatible with what is required for school success; thus, castelike minorities may tend to experience the conflict of two opposing cultural frames of reference – one appropriate for the dominant group and one appropriate for minorities. Castelike minorities are reluctant to shift between the two frames because they perceive the frame of the dominant group as clearly inappropriate for them. Since schooling tends to be bound up with the ideals and practices of the dominant group, it also tends to be seen as something less than appropriate for members of the minority group. Members of the minority community who try to behave like members of the majority community (i.e., learning English, striving for academic success and school credentials) may be ostracized by their peers. The dilemma for such minority students is that they must choose between two competing cultural frames: one which promotes school success and one which is considered appropriate for a good member of the minority group (Matute-Bianchi, 1986; Trueba, 1984).

The relationship of culture and schooling is one that requires further examination, but one fact becomes starkly apparent – although learning English is essential for success in school for all linguistic minority students, the acquisition of English alone in no way guarantees that every linguistic minority student will succeed academically. The question of school achievement is not solely a linguistic one; the cultural messages received by children from both the school and the larger society may influence their feelings about school as well as their feelings about themselves in relation to school. As Ferdman (1990, p. 184) states, ''[I]ndividual merit needs to be defined in a culturally relativistic way that takes group membership into account.''

Language variation in academic contexts

The language learning that takes place in early childhood sets the stage for more complex language learning and usage. Older children require more sophisticated language skills which help them maneuver through complex social situations and challenging academic situations. Language researchers and theoreticians have recently begun to explore the ways in which these more complex forms of language vary and, in turn, how that variation affects the ability of students to learn and use language in academic settings (Bialystok, 1991; Collier, 1987, 1989; Chamot and O'Malley, 1985; Crandall, 1987; Cummins, 1981a; Mohan, 1986). The context of language use and the conceptual content of communication are two possible sources of variation which have been explored.

The context of language use refers to the degree to which the environment is rich with meaningful clues that help the language learner decipher and interpret the language being used. Face-to-face conversations, for example, provide the opportunity to observe nonverbal cues such as facial expressions and gestures. Tone of voice conveys meaning far beyond what mere words can express, as any child listening to a frustrated parent demand that toys be picked up *now* can attest. Children learning to play a game not only have the verbal directions to rely on in helping them figure the game out, they can also actually watch others playing. Language used in environments which contain plentiful clues to its meaning are described as context-embedded (Cummins, 1981b). Context-embedded or contextualized language is evident in some types of school activities as well. In a science demonstration, for example, as the teacher explains the steps in performing an experiment, students can actually watch the actions, tying the language to something in the ''here and now.'' (See Chapter 7 by

Met in this volume for suggestions on how to make new academic content context-embedded.)

Decontextualized or context-reduced language use, on the other hand, occurs when there is little in the immediate environment, other than the language itself, which helps learners derive meaning from the language being used. Oral language that is decontextualized can be exemplified by telephone conversations, when a listener no longer can rely on facial expressions or gestures to infer meaning. Reading, especially in books with no pictures, requires that the learner depend strictly on the story text to derive meaning. Lectures, such as those given in the upper elementary grades (where students are 8 to 12 years of age), dealing with topics like the American Revolution or the greenhouse effect provide little in the way of nonlinguistic clues to support meaning.

For children who are learning English as a second language, the implications of such language variation are significant. While children may be able to deduce meaning from context-embedded language, the process of understanding and mastering decontextualized language use is much more difficult. Since much of school language tends to be context-reduced once one moves beyond the earliest grades, ESL children often find themselves lost in a world of meaningless words.

The content of communication (i.e., what the language is about or relates to) is also important to consider. Variation in the content of linguistic messages can result in different levels of cognitive demand being made on learners. Language used to communicate about familiar objects and concepts generally places less of a cognitive load on learners than language about complex notions or unfamiliar abstract ideas. Linguistic messages about topics one already knows and understands are less cognitively demanding than messages about a new concept or principle.

In addition, researchers are now beginning to suggest that specific content domains, such as math, science, and history, are associated with specific varieties of language (Dale & Cuevas, 1987; Kessler & Quinn, 1987; King, Fagan, Bratt, & Baer, 1987). The use of distinctive words, structures, and communicative functions has been found to vary with the particular content area being taught. Therefore, students need to master different language varieties in order to master particular academic content areas. Language-sensitive content teaching, therefore, is required for students who are learning content material while trying to learn a second language (see also Chapter 7 in this volume).

It has been shown that school language becomes more complex and less contextualized in successively higher grades (Collier, 1989; Cummins & Swain, 1986). Thus, the ability to learn content area material becomes increasingly dependent on interaction with and mastery of the language connected to such material. The ability to demonstrate what one has learned also increasingly requires extensive use of oral and written forms of language. The academic consequences of such increased language demands on students are readily apparent. Careful planning of instruction is needed in order to help students develop the decontextualized language skills they will need to master the cognitively demanding content in the higher grades.

Language use in school settings

The length of time which second language students appear to need in order to master language for academic purposes accounts for some of the confusion experienced by teachers working with second language learners (Cummins, 1981b). Many children puzzle their teachers with displays of relatively proficient English in social settings such as the playground and the cafeteria, where contextualized language skills are sufficient. When these students move back into the classroom, however, their teachers are sometimes heard to muse, "I think he knows more than he's letting on . . . I hear him using English in the playground, and yet when it's time to do social studies, his English suddenly disappears. Is he trying to fool me into thinking he doesn't understand so that he can get out of work?" Probably not. In many cases, children who have achieved modest levels of contextualized English proficiency find themselves "mainstreamed out" of support programs which are needed to help them continue the process of acquiring the decontextualized language skills they need to cope with higher order concepts that are language dependent. The disparity between children's linguistic capabilities in social settings compared to their capabilities in academic settings often results in children being asked to handle a larger linguistic load than they are ready to carry.

An additional matter to be considered with regard to children's language use in school settings is that of teacher-student interaction. The ways in which teachers use language with students appear to be influenced by teachers' perceptions of children's linguistic abilities. These perceptions, in turn, may affect not only the quantity and quality of cognitively challenging language that a teacher provides, they may also affect a child's access to learning.

In this regard, Schinke-Llano (1983) observed twelve monolingual English-speaking teachers working at the fifth and sixth grade levels. All had classes with both native English speakers and ESL learners. Her observations revealed that the teachers interacted less frequently with the ESL students than with their native-English-speaking counterparts. She also observed that when interactions did occur with the ESL students, they were significantly different in type – the interactions with ESL students tended to be managerial in nature rather than instructional. Finally, she found that even when the same type of interaction occurred for both groups of students, the teachers' interactions were briefer with ESL students than with the native-English-speaking students.

Although Schinke-Llano (1983) offers several explanations for these observations, two are particularly noteworthy. First, she speculates that the pattern of interactions may be due to the seating arrangements in the classrooms she observed. In over half of the classrooms, ESL students were seated in the rear of the room. She suggests further that there may have been a relationship between the students' seating position and the teachers' perceptions of the ESL students' ability to participate in the class. That is, those students who are perceived by teachers as most able to participate are generally placed closer to the instructional heart of the classroom, near the teacher.

The second and perhaps more compelling explanation offered by Schinke-Llano is that the teachers avoided interacting with the students for fear of embarrassing them. Implied in this explanation, however, is the fact that the teachers assumed that the students would be unable to answer or do well; their perceptions of the students influenced the way in which they interacted with them.

Schinke-Llano's research leads to two intriguing questions. First, if teachers' perceptions of students' linguistic and cognitive abilities are inaccurate, what are the possible consequences for the students? Many studies of teacher perceptions and expectations can be found in the literature on school achievement (Brophy & Good, 1974; Rist, 1970; Rosenthal & Jacobson, 1968). While these studies were not concerned specifically with ESL learners, they suggest that teachers' perceptions and expectations play a significant role in the education of all students. The effect of these perceptions and expectations remains unclear, but it seems likely that inaccurate perceptions on the part of teachers make it that much harder to plan appropriate instruction that meets children's needs.

Second, given the fact that teachers' interactions with second language students appear to be different, can these interactions be modified so that they facilitate linguistic and cognitive development? Much research and many curriculum development efforts recently have centered on this second question. The promotion of whole language, content-based second language instruction, and whole-school environments which foster the achievement of students appear to show great promise for facilitating such language and cognitive growth (see also Chapter 7 and "Putting It All Together").

What teachers can do

Given the complexities of the relationships between language, culture, and schooling, teachers might wonder if there is anything that an individual teacher can do to help second language learners in their efforts to achieve linguistic and academic proficiency. The answer is an emphatic "Yes!"

First, *examine and recognize your own perceptions and behaviors toward children from different linguistic and cultural backgrounds.* Teachers, like their students, are cultural beings. Learn to see yourself as an agent and transmitter of culture, a role that you fulfill with respect to conceptual and linguistic learning as well as interactional style (McGroarty, 1986). Be a self-observer as well as an observer of the children in your classroom. Teachers are sometimes not aware of the implicit teaching going on in their own classroom (Carew & Lightfoot, 1979). Reflect on your own teaching practice, particularly with regard to the ways in which you interact with students from different linguistic and cultural groups. As Heath (1986, p. 181) states, "Teachers must be culturally and linguistically sensitive to the kinds of language uses they are offering students and the cognitive and academic, as well as linguistic, demands they are making of students." Recognize that many of the types of language skills and patterns of language usage taught in the home may be quite appropriate for inclusion in the classroom; these skills and usage patterns become the scaffolding upon which school language skills and uses are built.

Recognize also that there is considerable variation among speech communities regarding language use. None of these variations is to be considered "better" than any other; certain variations more closely match the model of language use which is employed and fostered by the school.

Second, *teachers can make their classrooms authentic.* Since language learning thrives in settings where language is used to communicate about real ideas to real people, using the second language for authentic communication in the classroom will help to foster an atmosphere conducive to language development. As Lindfors (1989) points out, "filling in blanks on a worksheet or writing text 'using as many of this week's spelling words as you can' isn't language outside of the classroom, and it isn't language inside the classroom either."

Promoting authentic communication means that language will be used in meaningful and purposeful ways. It also means that activities will be planned that include speaking, reading, and writing. Urzua (1989) refers to teaching in this type of setting as "milieu teaching." Instead of the question-answer interchanges that are so common in conventional school settings, milieu teaching assumes a more conversational tone between teacher and student. In conventional classrooms, teachers provide most of the language used in the exchange, commenting on a task the child may be doing or describing their own actions. Milieu teaching extends the language contributed by children to the classroom conversation. If the child points to a picture and says, "Boat," the teacher may respond by saying, "Oh, I see you're pointing at the boat. You know, when I was little, I used to have a little red boat that I would play with in the sink. You put soap powder in the boat and it made bubbles in the water." This type of milieu teaching closely matches what caregivers in first language situations do – they carry on both sides of the conversation, and in doing so, they provide language input from which children construct hypotheses about the language; they teach children the rules for interacting through language.

Third, *integrate language teaching with content learning*. Researchers and educators have recently begun to explore Canadian models of language immersion for potential application to second language learning (Genesee, 1987, ch. 11; see also Chapter 7 in this volume). One such approach, content-based second language instruction, offers an integrated model for language and academic skills development (Chamot & O'Malley, 1987; Mohan, 1986; Snow, Met, & Genesee, 1989). In a content-based model, the content provides both a "motivational and cognitive basis for language learning" (Snow, Met, & Genesee, 1989). Content objectives and language skills compatible with those objectives are taught concurrently, providing students with the opportunity for continued academic growth while they are learning the language.

Fourth, *realize that not all second language learners are alike*. Just as we recognize individual differences among native-English-speaking students, we must recognize that linguistic minority children are different from one another. They come not only with different languages, academic experiences, and cultural backgrounds but also with different expectations about the nature and purpose of school. Children from a particular language and cultural group must also be seen as individuals as well as members of that cultural group. Not all children who come from castelike groups exhibit a castelike mentality in their response to the demands of schools. Not all "immigrant" students in Ogbu's terms are successful in school. There is great variation within groups.

In this regard, teachers can create classrooms that eliminate cultural barriers. Approaches such as cooperative learning have been shown to exhibit potential for improving the academic achievement of culturally and linguistically different students, as well improving intergroup relations (Kagan, 1986; see also Chapter 8).

Finally, *find someone to help you acquire the skills and knowledge that will allow you to facilitate learning*. It could be that some formal training such as a workshop or course might be helpful to you. It might also be that talking with a colleague you respect who seems to have good success with students might be a source of inspiration and insight. Observing other teachers is another way of learning; it helps to see someone else cope with situations that parallel your own. However you choose to learn, you can be sure that you won't be in this alone. The number of second language students grows larger every day.

Teachers face many challenges; students face challenges as well. Both can be well served if teachers understand the following points which have been presented in this chapter:

- The ability to acquire language, whether it is the first or a second language, is a natural ability which takes place over time. Classroom practices that promote authentic language use enhance children's acquisition of language.
- Academic success and achievement do not depend on language proficiency alone. Content-sensitive language teaching facilitates academic language and content learning.
- Language variation exists as a natural feature of all languages. Children's language, an essential part of their social and cultural identity, must be respected.
- Schools and teachers may exhibit cultural values different from those brought by children from their homes and communities. Recognition of these differences and the cultural bind which they may create for children is an important awareness for teachers to achieve.
- A great variety of instructional strategies and techniques which will help teachers have been developed. These strategies and techniques make school more rewarding for both second language students and those who teach them.

References

Bialystok, E. (Ed.). (1991). *Language processing in bilingual children.* New York: Cambridge University Press.

Brophy, J. E. & Good, T. L. (1974). *Teacher-student relationships: Causes and consequences.* New York: Holt, Rinehart and Winston.

Brown, R. (1973). *A first language: The early stages.* Cambridge, MA: Harvard University Press.

Carew, J. V. & Lightfoot, S. L. (1979). *Beyond bias: Perspectives on classrooms.* Cambridge, MA: Harvard University Press.

Chamot, A. U. & O'Malley, J. M. (1985). *A cognitive academic language learning approach.* Rosslyn, VA: National Clearinghouse for Bilingual Education.

Chomsky, C. (1969). *The acquisition of syntax in children from 5 to 10.* Cambridge, MA: MIT Press.

Collier, V. P. (1987). Age and rate of acquisition of a second language for academic purposes. *TESOL Quarterly, 21,* 227–249.

Collier, V. P. (1989). How long? A synthesis of research on academic achievement in a second language. *TESOL Quarterly, 23,* 509–531.

Crandall, J. (Ed.). (1987). *ESL through content area instruction: Mathematics, science, social studies.* Englewood Cliffs, NJ: Prentice Hall.

Crawford, J. (1989). *Bilingual education: History, politics, theory, and practice.* Trenton, NJ: Crane Publishing Co.

Cummins, J. (1981a). The role of primary language development in promoting educational success for language minority students. *Schooling and language minority students: A theoretical framework.* Los Angeles: Evaluation, Dissemination, & Assessment Center.

Cummins, J. (1981b). Four misconceptions about language proficiency in bilingual education. *NABE Journal, V,* 3: 31–45.

Cummins, J. (1989). *Empowering minority students.* Sacramento, CA: California Association for Bilingual Education.

Cummins, J. & Swain, M. (1986). *Bilingualism in education.* New York: Longman.

Dale, T. C. & Cuevas, G. (1987). Integrating language and mathematics learning. In J. Crandall (Ed.), *ESL through content-area instruction: Mathematics, science, social studies* (pp. 9–54). Englewood Cliffs, NJ: Prentice Hall.

DeVos, G. A. & Lee, C. (1981). *Koreans in Japan.* Berkeley, CA: University of California Press.

Dulay, H. C., & Burt, M. K. (1974). Natural sequences in child second language acquisition. *Language Learning, 24,* 37–53.

Dulay, H. C., Burt, M. K. & Krashen, S. D. (1982). *Language two.* New York: Oxford University Press.

Ferdman, B. M. (1990). Literacy and cultural identity. *Harvard Educational Review, 60,* 2: 181–204.

Genesee, F. (1987). *Learning through two languages: Studies of immersion and bilingual education.* Rowley, MA: Newbury House.

Genesee, F. (1989). Early bilingual development: One language or two? *Journal of Child Language, 16,* 161–179.

Handscombe, J. (1989). A quality program for learners of English as a second language. In P. Rigg & V. G. Allen (Eds.), *When they don't all speak English.* Urbana, IL: National Council of Teachers of English.

Heath, S. B. (1983). *Ways with words.* Cambridge, England: Cambridge University Press.

Heath, S. B. (1986). Sociocultural contexts of language development. *Beyond language: Social and cultural factors in schooling language minority students* (pp. 143–186). Los Angeles: Evaluation, Dissemination & Assessment Center.

Kagan, S. (1986). Cooperative learning and sociocultural factors in schooling. *Beyond language: Social and cultural factors in schooling language minority students* (pp. 231–298). Los Angeles: Evaluation, Dissemination & Assessment Center.

Kessler, C. & Quinn, M. E. (1987). ESL and science learning. In J. Crandall (Ed.). *ESL through content-area instruction: Mathematics, science, social studies* (pp. 55–88). Englewood Cliffs, NJ: Prentice Hall.

King, M., Fagan, B., Bratt, T., & Baer, R. (1987). ESL and social studies instruction. In J. Crandall (Ed.). *ESL through content-area instruction: Mathematics, science, social studies* (pp. 89–121). Englewood Cliffs, NJ: Prentice Hall.

Lindfors, J. W. (1989). The classroom: A good environment for language learning. In P. Rigg & V. G. Allen (Eds.). *When they don't all speak English.* Urbana, IL: National Council of Teachers of English.

Matute-Bianchi, M. E. (1986). Ethnic identities and patterns of school success among Mexican-descent and Japanese-American students in a California high school: An ethnographic analysis. *American Journal of Education, 95,* 233–255.

McGroarty, M. (1986). Educators' responses to sociocultural diversity: Implications for practice. *Beyond language: Social and cultural factors in schooling language minority students* (pp. 299–343). Los Angeles: Evaluation, Dissemination & Assessment Center.

Mohan, B. A. (1986). *Language and content.* Reading, MA: Addison-Wesley.

Ogbu, J. U., & Matute-Bianchi, M. E. (1986). Understanding socio-cultural factors: Knowledge, identity, and school adjustment. *Beyond language: Social and cultural factors in schooling language minority students* (pp. 73–142). Los Angeles: Evaluation, Dissemination & Assessment Center.

Rigg, P. & Allen, V. G. (Eds.) (1989). *When they don't all speak English.* Urbana, IL: National Council of Teachers of English.

Rist, R. C. (1970). Student social class and teacher expectations: The self-fulfilling prophecy in ghetto education. *Harvard Educational Review, 40,* 3: 411–451.

Rosenthal, R. & Jacobson, L. (1968). *Pygmalion in the classroom.* New York: Holt, Rinehart and Winston.

Ryan, E. B. & Giles, H. (1982). *Attitudes toward language variation.* London: Edward Arnold.

Schinke-Llano, L. (1983). Foreigner talk in content classrooms. In H. Seliger & M. H. Long (Eds.), *Classroom centered research in second language acquisition* (pp. 146–165). Rowley, MA: Newbury House.

Snow, M. A., Met, M., & Genesee, F. (1989). A conceptual framework for the integration of language and content in second/foreign language instruction. *TESOL Quarterly, 23,* 2: 201–217.

Tannen, D. (1990). *You just don't understand: Talk between the sexes.* New York: William Morrow.

Trueba, H. T. (1984). The forms, functions, and values of literacy: Reading for survival in a barrio as a student. *NABE Journal, 9,* 21–38.

Urzua, C. (1989). I grow for a living. In P. Rigg & V. G. Allen (Eds.), *When they don't all speak English* (pp. 15–18). Urbana, IL: National Council of Teachers of English.

Wells, G. (1986). *The meaning makers: Children learning language and using language to learn.* Portsmouth, NH: Heinemann.

Wolfram, W. & Christian, D. (1989). *Dialects and education: Issues and answers.* Englewood Cliffs, NJ: Prentice Hall/Regents.

Additional readings

Cantoni-Harvey, G. (1987). *Content-area language instruction: Approaches and strategies.* Reading, MA: Addison-Wesley.

Guthrie, G. P. (1985). *A school divided: An ethnography of bilingual education in a Chinese community.* Hillsdale, NJ: Lawrence Erlbaum.

Hakuta, K. (1986). *Mirror of language: The debate on bilingualism.* New York: Basic Books.

Ovando, C. J., & Collier, V. P. (1985). *Bilingual and ESL classrooms: Teaching in multicultural contexts.* New York: McGraw-Hill.

Padilla, A. M., Fairchild, H. H., & Valadez, C. M. (Eds.). (1990). *Bilingual education: Issues and strategies.* Newbury Park, CA: Sage.

Scarcella, R. (1990). *Teaching language minority students in the multicultural classroom.* Englewood Cliffs, NJ: Prentice Hall/Regents.

Ventriglia, L. (1982). *Conversations of Miguel and Maria: How children learn a second language.* Reading, MA: Addison-Wesley.

2 *Knowledge, power, and identity in teaching English as a second language*

Jim Cummins

This chapter outlines the knowledge base and pedagogical options available to educators and policy-makers in addressing the education of children from English as a second language (ESL) backgrounds. In an increasing number of urban centers in the United States and Canada, ESL children represent the majority school population; in other words, the ESL student is the norm rather than the exception. This reality has important implications for school boards and teacher education institutions. Specifically, it suggests that all teachers should be knowledgeable about patterns of language and social development among ESL students and also be capable of implementing pedagogical strategies in the mainstream classroom that are effective for both ESL and native-English-speaking students.

The issue of what constitutes "effective" pedagogical strategies raises broader questions related to the purpose of schooling. Clearly, one component of what constitutes "effectiveness" entails the development of proficiency in using the English language in both oral and written modes. However, language is always used for some purpose, and thus, we must examine what purposes of language use are promoted in the classroom interactions that students experience. Language is also never devoid of content, so the nature of the content that students are exposed to in learning English must be considered. In short, in addressing the extent to which pedagogical strategies for teaching English as a second language can be considered "effective," we must also address the question "effective for what?" (Peirce, 1989; Pennycook, 1989).

I shall argue that in most North American contexts, the education of ESL students (whether in mainstream or withdrawal classes) takes place within structures that limit the possibilities for students' personal, intel-

I would like to thank Fred Genesee, Nanci Goldman, Paul Rowney, Sudia Paloma McCaleb, Brigette Roberge and Joan Wink for helpful comments on a previous version of this chapter. Also, some of the ideas in the chapter were developed collaboratively with Mary Ashworth and Jean Handscombe in the context of carrying out a review of the Vancouver School Board's ESL program.

lectual and social development. Despite the fact that most educators and policy-makers are undoubtedly well intentioned and committed to helping students succeed academically, they have generally failed to challenge and transform structures that systematically discriminate against students. Among the structures that limit students' development are the following:

- Policies at federal, state/provincial or local levels that fail to take account of the knowledge base that exists regarding students; for example, policies in the areas of special education, psychological assessment, streaming/tracking, entry and exit criteria for bilingual or ESL programs all systematically discriminate against ESL students (Cummins, 1984, 1989).
- Teacher education institutions that continue to treat issues related to ESL students as marginal and that send new teachers into the classroom with minimal information regarding patterns of language and emotional development among students and few pedagogical strategies for helping students learn (Henley & Young, 1989).
- Curriculum that reflects only the experiences and values of the middle-class white native-English-speaking population and effectively suppresses the experiences and values of ESL students.
- The absence from most schools of professionals capable of communicating in the languages of students and their parents; such professionals could assist in functions such as home language instruction, literacy tutoring, home language assessment for purposes of placement and intervention, and parent/school liaison.
- Criteria for promotion to positions of responsibility (e.g., principals) that take no account of the individual's experience with or potential for leadership in the education of ESL students.

In addition to structures such as these that systematically limit the possibilities for students to develop both personally and academically, the disabling process is further entrenched by educators who define their roles in a narrow mechanistic way as transmitting a body of knowledge and skills to students. Within this role definition, classroom interactions are not oriented to the expression, sharing and critical examination of students' experiences nor to analysis of issues that pertain to the division of wealth and status both within the specific society and the global context. I shall argue that failure on the part of educators to focus classroom interactions on the interpretation of student experience and on the critical analysis of issues related to social justice compounds the effects of the discriminatory structures within which the education of ESL students unfolds.

In the next section, I provide an overview of demographic changes that have affected western industrialized countries in recent years and which form the context for the educational issues discussed in this chapter.

Then, I sketch some aspects of the knowledge base that does exist with respect to ESL students and review principles that have been suggested as central to an equitable education for these students. Finally, the issue of critical literacy for students is discussed, and a framework for implementing this type of pedagogical approach is outlined.

The demographic context of ESL instruction

In most western industrialized countries the proportions of students from linguistically and culturally diverse backgrounds have increased rapidly during the past twenty years. The increased proportions result both from continued high rates of immigration in many countries together with declining birthrates among the native-born populations of these countries.

In the United States, for example, it is estimated that documented and undocumented immigrant children represent about 6 percent of the American school population (National Coalition of Advocates for Students [NCAS], 1988). However, geographic concentration of immigration has resulted in major influxes in several states and urban centers. For example, in the year 2001, the NCAS report estimates that minority enrolment levels will range from 70 to 96 per cent in the nation's fifteen largest school systems. In California, by that time, so-called minority groups (e.g., Latin-Americans, African-Americans, Asian-Americans) will represent a greater proportion of the school population than will students from the so-called majority group.

Many minority students in the United States experience a much higher secondary school drop-out rate than do majority students and are frequently streamed into low-ability groups. According to the NCAS report,

inflexible assessment practices can lead to very low expectations of immigrant students by school personnel. Many young newcomers are placed in low expectation tracks or ability groups, where inadequate educational experiences may result in alienation from school, dropping out, and the impossibility of attaining higher education. (1988, p. 48)

Similar patterns have emerged from reports in Britain (Swann, 1985) and Canada (Wright & Tsuji, 1984). Immigrants to Canada, for example, numbered 84,302 in 1985 but have increased steadily since then to a projected level of 250,000 annually from 1992 through 1996. These increases have been implemented as part of the federal (Conservative) government strategy to combat the combined effects of low birth rates and a rapidly aging population. Within the schools of major urban centres, linguistic and cultural diversity have increased substantially in recent years. For example, in Toronto and Vancouver, more than half the school population comes from a non-English-speaking background (Ashworth, Cummins & Handscombe, 1989). Clearly, these proportions are likely to rise substantially in view of the fact that immigration levels in the 1990s will be triple what they were in the mid-1980s.

Data from several European countries surveyed by the Organization for Economic Cooperation and Development's (OECD) Centre for Educational Research and Innovation (CERI, 1987) reveal a similar pattern. CERI reported that the average foreign enrolment at the primary level varied from 4.8 per cent in the Netherlands to 18 per cent in Switzerland and 38 per cent in Luxembourg. The proportions for Belgium (13.5 per cent), France (10.1 per cent), Germany (11.9 per cent) and Sweden (8.7 per cent) were also substantial.[1] With respect to foreign student placement, two clear patterns were observed in the OECD data: first, the overrepresentation of foreign children in special education classes, and second, the overrepresentation of foreign students in low academic streams at the secondary level. The report notes that the disproportionate placement of foreign children in special education classes

persists over the years without any apparent significant improvement [and] affects primarily certain of the nationalities that are more recent arrivals and/ or whose cultural values are further removed from those of the host country. (1987, p. 32)

The report notes that these children find themselves relegated to special classes, not because their condition warrants this but because they are for the moment unable to follow a normal course of education as a result of insufficient command of the language of instruction. This approach may provide a convenient solution over the short term but, according to CERI (1987, p. 33), "over the longer term seriously jeopardizes the school careers of the children concerned."

With respect to streaming at the secondary level, the data show that "when there are a number of alternative streams available, the enrolment rate of foreign children is always higher than that of nationals in those streams or cycles which either require only minimal qualifications or provide only a short course of instruction" (1987, p. 33). Lack of minimal school qualifications, according to CERI, is closely associated with long-term unemployment, and the social consequences of these trends are significant; specifically,

it is clear that exclusion from the education system constitutes the first stage in a process of marginalization, culminating in exclusion from the system of

1 These figures do not take account of the substantial number of students who, although of foreign origin, have acquired the nationality of the host country. Thus, they underestimate the real extent of linguistic and cultural diversity in the school systems of these countries.

production and – since social integration depends on integration within the labour force – in exclusion from society itself. (1987, p. 35)

In conclusion, linguistic and cultural diversity is the norm in many urban western school systems and will continue to be so for the foreseeable future. From the data previously sketched, it is clear that school systems are still struggling to adapt to this changing multilingual/multicultural educational reality, with varying degrees of success. There is considerable variation in the educational policies adopted in different countries. This is partly a result of the volatile sociopolitical context within which issues related to immigrants and minority groups are analyzed. For example, the fact that particular interventions (e.g., bilingual education in the United States) involve the institutionalization of minority languages and confer status and power (e.g., white-collar jobs) on previously subordinated minority groups means that research findings and theoretical interpretations are not neutral with respect to the societal power structure. Thus, while advocates for very different forms of education usually proclaim that their primary concern is the right of minority children to a quality and equitable education, the suggested interventions and their rationales vary widely.

In view of the diversity of policies and the sociopolitical tensions associated with the education of immigrant students, it becomes important to establish the knowledge base that does exist to guide policies in this area.

A knowledge base for educational policies

What I am terming a "knowledge base" represents my perception of research findings that have important implications for policy and pedagogy in the education of ESL students. The patterns highlighted here appear to me to be generally consistent with other reviews of the literature (e.g., Collier, 1989), although the focus and audience of particular reviews will affect which aspects of the research are highlighted (see, e.g., Larsen-Freeman, 1991, for a review focused on second language acquisition research). My major concern is with persistent misconceptions on the part of educators, policy-makers and the general public that continue to be used to rationalize structures and pedagogical practices that disable students. These misconceptions reinforce particular role definitions which educators adopt that mediate their interactions with ESL students (Cummins, 1989). For example, in the past, the belief that bilingualism was a negative force in children's development reinforced educators' determination to eradicate children's bilingualism, resulting in considerable physical and psychological violence against children and ultimately massive educational failure. The constellation of institutional structures, role definitions and patterns of educator-student interaction formed part of a broader process of political and economic subordination of particular minority groups. This process of subordination continues in most countries, although now it is frequently clothed in the discourse of equity, effectiveness and multiculturalism.

The following research findings have been elaborated elsewhere (Cummins, 1984, 1989) and therefore will not be discussed in detail.

The effects of bilingualism

There is considerable evidence that the acquisition of two or more languages entails positive consequences for metalinguistic development (Bialystok, 1991; Goncz & Kodzopeljic, 1991; Ricciardelli, 1989). It has also been reported that children who had acquired literacy in two languages performed significantly better in the acquisition of a third language than did children from monolingual backgrounds or those from bilingual backgrounds who had not acquired literacy in their home language (Swain & Lapkin, 1991). These latter comparisons are particularly convincing in that the biliterate group had considerably lower socioeconomic status than the monolingual background group.

A large number of additional studies point in the direction of cognitive advantages associated with bilingualism, although caution must be exercised in making strong claims for bilingual advantages because of the difficulties of controlling background variables in some of the studies. What is clear, however, is that the development of home language literacy skills by students entails no negative consequences for their overall academic or cognitive growth, and, in some situations, there may be significant educational benefits for students in addition to the obvious personal benefits of bilingualism.

One pedagogical and policy implication is that rather than attempting to eradicate children's bilingualism "in order to help them learn English," educators should encourage students to develop their linguistic talents and also provide parents with advice and resources (e.g., first language [L1] books) to enable them to promote the L1 in the home.

The relationship between L1 and L2

There is considerable evidence of interdependence of literacy-related or academic skills across languages (see Cummins, 1991, for a review) such that the better developed children's L1 conceptual foundation, the more likely they are to develop similarly high levels of conceptual abilities in their L2. The moderate to strong correlation between academic skills in L1 and L2 suggests that L1 and L2 abilities are manifestations of a common underlying proficiency. The interdependence of academic aspects of proficiency across languages has been used to interpret the fact that in bilingual programs, either for minority or majority students, instruction through a minority language results in no academic loss in the majority language. In fact, frequently for minority students an inverse relationship between amount of instruction in English and English academic achievement is observed. For example, Ramirez, Yuen and Ramey (1991) in a large-scale longitudinal study reported that Latin-American students who had received at least 40 per cent of their instruction through Spanish throughout elementary school appeared to have better prospects of catching up academically in English with their native-English-speaking peers than similar students who had received all their instruction through English or who had been exited to an all-English program in the early grades (around grade 2).

The implication of these data is that bilingual programs that strongly promote students' L1 literacy skills are viable means to promote academic development in English. The positive results of programs that continue to promote literacy in L1 throughout elementary school can be attributed to the combined effects of reinforcing students' cultural identity and their conceptual growth as well as to the greater likelihood of parental involvement in such programs, as reported by Ramirez, et al. (1991). In contexts where extended bilingual programs are not possible owing to large numbers of students from diverse backgrounds in the same schools, educators can still communicate to students the value of developing their L1 abilities and reinforce students' and parents' efforts to do so (e.g., in after-school or Saturday morning classes).

The acquisition of conversational and academic aspects of English proficiency

Research studies by Collier (1987) and Cummins (1981) suggest that very different time periods are required for students to attain peer-appropriate levels in conversational skills in English as compared to academic skills. Specifically, while there will be major individual differences (Wong Fillmore, 1991), conversational skills often approach nativelike levels within about two years of exposure to English, whereas a period of four to nine years (Collier, 1987, 1989) or five to seven years (Cummins, 1981) of school exposure has been reported as necessary for second language students to achieve as well as native speakers in academic aspects of English.

These trends have considerable relevance for a number of policy and pedagogical issues. For example, they show that ESL support will still be beneficial (and frequently necessary) even after students have attained conversational fluency in English. Exiting children prematurely from ESL or bilingual support programs may jeopardize their academic development, particularly if the mainstream classroom does not provide an environment that is supportive of language acquisition. It is also clear that psycho-educational assessment of ESL students is likely to underestimate students' academic potential to a significant extent if any credence is placed in the test norms which are derived predominantly from native-English-speaking students.

While the research findings that have been outlined are strongly supportive of bilingual instruction for students, they also entail implications for the education of students in culturally diverse contexts where bilingual programs may not be possible. The pedagogical principles outlined in the section that follows (adapted from Ashworth, Cummins & Handscombe, 1989) focus on these contexts.

Pedagogical principles

1. The educational and personal experiences students bring to schools constitute the foundation for all their future learning; schools should therefore attempt to amplify rather than replace these experiences.   Schools communicate subtle (and sometimes not so subtle) messages to students regarding the value of their prior experiences and the appropriateness of their language and culture within the broader societal context. Research suggests that students who are valued by the wider society (and by the schools that inevitably tend to reflect that society) succeed to a greater extent than students whose backgrounds are devalued (see Ogbu, 1978). Thus, students' cultural identities are likely to be validated by instructional programs that attempt to *add* English to the language(s) that students bring to school while encouraging them to continue developing their first language oral and written skills. On the other hand, programs that attempt to replace students' first language with English may undermine the personal and cultural confidence that is essential to students' academic progress.

In addition, as suggested by the interdependence principle, the conceptual knowledge that students possess in their first language constitutes a major component of the "cognitive power" that they bring to the language learning situation. It thus makes sense to value, and where possible, continue to cultivate these abilities both for their own sake and to facilitate transfer to English (see also Chapter 4).

2. The fact that upwards of five years may be required for students to reach a level of academic proficiency in English comparable to their native-English-speaking peers suggests that schools must be pre-

pared to make a long-term commitment to support the academic development of students. There are several implications of the different time periods required to develop peer-appropriate levels of conversational and academic language skills. First, it is clearly not sufficient just to get students over the initial difficulties of acquiring English. Student progress must be monitored for several years after they appear to be comfortable in English to ensure that they are coping with, and acquiring an ability to manipulate the more formal abstract language that becomes increasingly important for school success as students advance through the grades.

Another implication is that second language provision cannot be conceptualized as a separate program that exists apart from the mainstream of the educational system. Withdrawal of students from the regular classroom may sometimes be necessary and appropriate in the early stages of learning, but it is not a viable option for the length of time that the student may need support in mastering the academic aspects of English. Thus, it is likely that *all* teachers in a school will be required to address the learning needs of second language students by individualizing their instruction to take account of the very different levels of English proficiency and the different rates of learning represented among these students.

3. Together with the attributes (e.g., L1 literacy) that students bring to the learning situation, access to interaction with users of English is a major causal variable underlying both the acquisition of English and students' sense of belonging to the mainstream society; the entire school is therefore responsible for supporting the learning and interactional needs of students, and second language provision should integrate students into the social and academic mainstream to the extent possible. Enright and McCloskey (1988) have clearly expressed the importance of genuine interaction in the classroom and the relationship between this point and the first principle outlined:

Students fully develop second language and literacy through using the second language in many different settings, with a wide variety of respondents and audiences (including themselves), and for a wide variety of purposes. . . . Students' language and literacy development is facilitated by a comfortable atmosphere: one that values, encourages and celebrates efforts to use language; that focuses primarily on the meaning and intention of utterances and messages rather than on their form; and that treats ''errors'' as a normal part of becoming increasingly better thinkers and communicators. (p. 21)

An emphasis on interaction in the classroom is clearly related to an instructional orientation that values and attempts to amplify students' prior experiences.

Following Handscombe (1989), it is important to emphasize that a focus on promoting interaction with native speakers does not imply placement of students into regular classrooms without provision of additional support for both students and their teachers. Nor does it imply a pull-out program that offers support in a segregated setting for part of the day and mainstreaming for the rest. What tends to happen in this case is that many students flounder in the mainstream part of the day because no support has been provided to student or teacher in that context. At the same time, both teacher and student tend to assume that the short period of pull-out assistance is *the* learning for the day and the rest is a kind of marking time until increased proficiency is acquired through the language program.

What is required is the provision of instructional strategies within the mainstream classroom that are appropriate for all students, for example, peer tutoring, cooperative learning, creative writing and project-oriented activities. Such activities are effective for academic and language development as well as for intercultural understanding. A frequently neglected aspect of culturally and linguistically diverse classrooms is the opportunity provided to teachers to explore curricular topics from many different cultural perspectives. By recognizing diversity as an educationally valuable resource, teachers not only validate the cultural backgrounds of students but also offer all students expanded possibilities for cultural enrichment.

4. If students are to catch up academically with their native-English-speaking peers, their cognitive growth and mastery of academic content must continue while English is being learned. Thus, the teaching of English as a second language should be integrated with the teaching of other academic content that is appropriate to students' cognitive level. By the same token, all content teachers are also teachers of language.   As has been discussed, language learning is a process that takes time; students may require at least five years to catch up with their native-English-speaking peers in academic aspects of English. Clearly, students' cognitive growth and their learning of subject matter content cannot be postponed until their English language skills are developed to the level of their classmates. In recognition of this reality, educators have increasingly emphasized the importance of integrating language teaching with the teaching of academic content (see also Chapter 7). Thus, effective instruction, whether in mainstreamed or pull-out classes, will simultaneously promote language, cognition and content mastery. In the absence of this integration, the already formidable task that students face in catching up to their native-English-speaking peers will be rendered considerably more difficult.

The modifications to the instructional program required to integrate language and content in a manner appropriate for students do *not* entail a dilution in the conceptual or academic content of the instruction, but rather require the adoption of instructional strategies that take account of students' academic background and ensure comprehension of the material being presented. For example, Mohan (1986) and Early (1990) have emphasized the role of *key visuals* (e.g., diagrams, graphs, timelines, etc.) as a means of adapting content for second language learners and making new information at least partially understandable.

In short, content-based language instruction is particularly appropriate to address the learning needs of ESL students and help them bridge the linguistic and academic gap between themselves and native-English-speaking students.

5. The academic and linguistic growth of students is significantly increased when parents see themselves, and are seen by school staff, as co-educators of their children along with the school. Schools should therefore actively seek to establish a collaborative relationship with minority parents that encourages them to participate with the school in promoting their children's academic progress.   The most clear-cut evidence of the academic benefits that can accrue to students as a result of the establishment of a collaborative relationship between the school and parents is found in the two-year educational experiment conducted in the borough of Haringey, a working-class area of London, England, by Tizard, Schofield and Hewison (1982). The experiment consisted in having parents listen on a regular basis to their children read books sent home from school. These children's reading progress was compared to that of children who were given additional reading instruction in small groups several times a week by a trained reading specialist. Many parents in the district spoke little or no English and many were illiterate in both English and their first language (Greek and Bengali, for the most part). Despite these factors, parents almost without exception welcomed the project and agreed to listen to their children read as requested and to complete a record card showing what had been read.

It was found that children who read to their parents made significantly greater progress in reading than those who were given additional reading instruction, and this was particularly so for children who, at the beginning of the project, were experiencing difficulty learning to read. In addition, most parents expressed great satisfaction at being involved in this way by the schools, and teachers reported that the children showed an increased interest in school learning and were better behaved. Lack of literacy or English fluency did not detract from parents' willingness to collaborate with the school, nor did it prevent improvement in these children's reading.

In general, successful parental involvement is likely to depend on the extent to which parents see the school as a welcoming environment rather than the intimidating environment it often is for many parents with limited knowledge of English. Clearly, the presence in the school of staff who speak the language of the parents will greatly facilitate parental involvement. The persistent exclusion of bilingual and multilingual professionals from school staffs conveys an unambigous message to parents and students about the power relations that are operating in the school and society.

School staffs and individual teachers, however, also have the potential (and responsibility) to begin the process of establishing partnerships with parents of second language students. When educators define their roles in terms of challenging the discrimination embodied in institutionalized structures, then there are many possibilities for involving parents in their children's education and providing a welcoming atmosphere in the school. The initiative explored in the Tizard, et al. (1982) study is just one example; there are many more ranging from family literacy and social history projects (e.g., Ada, 1988; Lopes & Lopes, 1991) to stocking the library with books in the languages of the community or the simple strategy of providing bilingual or multilingual signs in the school (Enright & McCloskey, 1988).

Such projects and activities will only be successful when they reflect an underlying role definition that challenges the societal power structure that has historically excluded parents from subordinated groups from genuine participation. The initiative for the dismantling of barriers to participation may come from parents and students rather than from educators (see Skutnabb-Kangas, 1988, for an account of a strike by Finnish parents and students in Sweden), but regardless of where the initiative originates, the goal for educators, individually and collectively, should be to strive towards a genuine two-way collaboration where parent and student voice can confidently find expression within the school. Clearly, this process is more likely to occur when the entire school community is committed to social justice and actively reflects and values the diversity of languages and cultures represented in the school; however, this type of consensus within schools is rarely the case, and thus it is incumbent on *individual* educators to initiate collaborative relationships between school and community.

These principles have stressed respecting parents' and students' language and culture and building instruction on their previous experience and L1 abilities (see also Chapter 4). The importance of communicative interaction and of the integration of language and content has also been stressed. It is important, however, to inquire more fully into the nature of the interaction and content that will form the basis of students' educational experiences.

Critical literacy and knowledge generation in ESL

There is a considerable degree of consensus among psycholinguists that both first language acquisition and cognitive development are active, constructive processes whereby children generate their knowledge of the world and their linguistic knowledge within a matrix of social interaction (Wells, 1986). While input that children can make sense of is clearly essential, children are not passive recipients of knowledge and language but rather partners with adults in the co-construction of their realities. Through their interaction with children, adults (and older children) mediate the construction of meaning by helping to create with children the interpersonal conditions within which learning can occur.

The influence of Vygotsky's (1978) notion of the *zone of proximal development* (ZPD) is very evident in current applications of this general view of learning to the classroom. Vygotsky viewed the ZPD as the distance between children's developmental level as determined by individual problem solving without adult guidance and the level of potential development as determined by children's problem solving under the influence of, or in collaboration with, more capable adults or peers. Expressed simply, the ZPD is the interpersonal space where minds meet and new understandings can arise through collaborative interaction and inquiry. Newman, Griffin, and Cole (1989) label this interpersonal space *the construction zone*. Moll (1989, p. 59) points out that central to Vygotsky's notion of the ZPD are "the specific ways that adults (or peers) socially mediate or interactionally create circumstances for learning," and he emphasizes that the child is not passive but "an active organism helping create the very circumstances for his or her own learning."

This view of the learning process is clearly consistent with the emphasis in the previous section on interaction with users of English as a central component of students' academic development. However, the notion of the ZPD assumes even more significance for understanding students' development when extended to the conceptualization of students' personal development, specifically to the negotiation and construction of identity among ESL students.

I have argued that a focus on identity is crucial in understanding the educational difficulties of many second language students. Specifically, groups that tend to experience academic difficulty frequently manifest a pattern of insecurity or ambivalence about the value of their own cultural identity as a result of their interactions with the dominant group (Cummins, 1989; Ogbu, 1978). The rules of the social mobility (or educational achievement) game reflect the status of subordinated groups as "internal colonies" (Blauner, 1969). Dominant group institutions and representatives of those institutions (e.g., teachers) require that subordinated groups deny their cultural identity as a necessary condition for success in the mainstream society where the gatekeepers are invariably representatives of the dominant group, or at lower levels, compliant subordinated group members who have accepted the rules of the game. Many students resist this process of subordination through "disruptive" behaviour, often culminating in dropping out of school (Fordham, 1990; Willis, 1977). Others modify their cultural identity by "acting white" (Fordham, 1990), often buying educational success at the expense of rejection by their peers and ambivalence about their identity. Still others are never given the opportunity in school to gain either academic confidence or pride in identity and, over time, internalize the negative attributions of the dominant group and live down to their teachers' expectations.

The point being made here is that many subordinated group students are disabled educationally and rendered "voiceless" (Giroux, 1991) or silenced (Fine, 1987; Walsh, 1991) in very much the same way that their communities have been disempowered (often for centuries) through their interactions with societal institutions. The converse of this proposition is that students from communities that have historically been subordinated will succeed educationally and amplify their "voice" or their expression of personal identity to the extent that the patterns of interaction in school reverse those that prevail in the society at large; in other words, the extent to which these patterns of interaction actively challenge societal power relations. The ways in which educators attempt to orchestrate the pattern of interactions with students will reflect the role definitions that they have assumed with respect to these societal power relations.

The development of identities in school can be viewed within the framework of the ZPD. The historical pattern of dominant-subordinated group interactions has been one where educators have constricted the zone in an attempt to sanitize deviant cultural identities. For educators to agree to become partners in the transmission of "knowledge," minority students were required to acquiesce in the subordination of their cultural identities and to celebrate as "truth" the "cultural literacy" of the dominant group. The constriction of the ZPD by educators reflected a process whereby they defined their role as "civilizing," "saving," "assimilating" or "educating" students whose culture and values they viewed as inherently deficient. Through this exercise of power over others (Galtung, 1980), they reproduced societal patterns and limited students' possibilities to develop their own power over self and to define and interpret their own realities and identities.

A starting point in constructing an alternative interactional process in schools is to recognize that educator-student interactions constitute a process of negotiating identities. Through our interactions with students (and colleagues), we are constantly sketching an image not just of our own identities and those we envisage for our students, but also of the society we hope our students will form. Our actions and interactions both reflect and contribute to the formation of our identities. Our identities encompass multiple and frequently contradictory voices which find differential possibilities for expression depending on the institutional and interpersonal context (Laing, 1969; Simon, 1987; Walsh, 1991).

The ZPD represents a useful metaphor for describing the dual process of reciprocal negotiation of identity and collaborative generation of knowledge. Educators whose role definition encompasses challenging discriminatory institutional structures will attempt to create conditions for interaction which expand students' possibilities for identity formation and critical inquiry (knowledge generation). Rather than constricting the ZPD so that students' voices are silenced, educators who adopt this type of role definition will attempt to initially constitute the ZPD in such a way that students' voices can be expressed, shared and amplified within the interactional process. Under these conditions, the ZPD will then be co-constructed by students and educators as, through their interactions, they script their own identities and that of the society they envisage.

This framework addresses the question posed at the beginning of this chapter relating to the effectiveness of pedagogical strategies for ESL students, namely, "effective for what?" The content of instruction and the focus of language interaction in the classroom always reflect educators' role definitions and their vision of societal realities and goals. For example, it has been argued by many theorists that the vision of our future society, implied by the dominant transmission models of pedagogy, is a society of compliant consumers who passively accept rather than critically analyze the forces that impinge on their lives. Thus, Sirotnik (1983), on the basis of the data from Goodlad's (1984) major study of American classrooms, points to the hidden curriculum that is being communicated to students in the typical classroom; this classroom contains

a lot of teacher talk and a lot of student listening . . . almost invariably closed and factual questions . . . and predominantly total class instructional configurations around traditional activities – all in a virtually affectless environment. It is but a short inferential leap to suggest that we are implicitly teaching dependence upon authority, linear thinking, social apathy, passive involvement, and hands-off learning. (p. 29)

The same perspective has been forcefully argued by Henry Giroux and his colleagues (Giroux & McLaren, 1986) who maintain that the critical

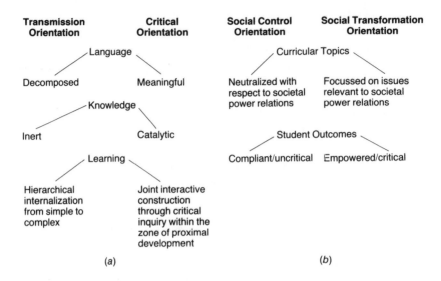

Figure 1   Pedagogical and social assumptions underlying educator role definitions. **(a)** Educator pedagogical assumptions. **(b)** Educator social assumptions.

thinking skills necessary for meaningful participation in a democratic society are being eradicated by our current models of schooling.

Figure 1 attempts to map the pedagogical and social assumptions that reflect particular forms of institutional and individual educator role definitions. Conservative approaches to education that are reflected in much of the current focus on "educational reform" in North America will tend to combine a transmission orientation to pedagogy with a social control orientation to curricular topics and student outcomes. The patterns of classroom interaction and their social implications are similar to Sirotnik's description previously cited.

Within a transmission orientation to pedagogy, task analysis is typically used to break language down to its component parts (phonics, vocabulary, grammatical rules) and transmit these parts in isolation from each other. Knowledge is viewed as static or inert, to be internalized and reproduced when required. Approaches to learning associated with a transmission orientation reflect these views of language and knowledge in that learning is assumed to progress in a hierarchical manner from simple content to complex.

By contrast, within a critical pedagogical orientation, educators encourage the development of student voice through critical reflection on experiential and social issues. Language and meaning are viewed as inseparable, and knowledge is seen as a catalyst for further inquiry and action. This is consistent with a Vygotskian view of learning that emphasizes the centrality of the ZPD where knowledge is generated through collaborative interaction and critical inquiry (Vygotsky, 1978). Language use and interaction in the classroom reflect and extend students' experience and are focused on *generating* knowledge rather than on the transmission and consumption of socially sanitized information more typical of most North American classrooms.

With respect to social outcomes of schooling and ways of achieving these outcomes, conservative approaches aim to (re)produce compliant and uncritical students, and, to this end, they ensure that all curricular content that might challenge the view of reality favoured by the societal power structure is expunged. By contrast, critical educators are focused on creating conditions that open possibilities for student empowerment and transformation of oppressive social structures. Thus, they attempt to select curricular topics that relate directly to societal power relations and encourage students to analyze these topics/issues from multiple perspectives.[2]

As one example of the very different pedagogical implications of conservative versus critical approaches, consider the ways in which the issue of Columbus's "discovery" of America might be treated. Traditional curricula have celebrated Columbus as a hero whose arrival brought "civilization" and "salvation" to the indigenous population. In fact, as Bigelow (1991) points out, few North American texts mention that Columbus initiated the slave trade and cut off the hands of any indigenous people who failed to bring him sufficient gold. The "discovery" of America resulted within a few years in the genocide of the indigenous populations in the islands where Spanish rule was established. Critical educators would encourage students to explore the reality omitted from

---

2 Within the continua sketched in Figure 1, there are clearly many intermediate positions. For example, "whole language" approaches highlight the importance of meaningful language use and two-way interaction within the classroom; however, critical analysis of issues related to social justice tends not to be a focus of instruction in many "whole language" classrooms and has not been strongly emphasized by most "whole language" theorists. Thus, while "whole language" approaches are quite compatible with the critical and social transformation orientations sketched in Figure 1, in practice they sometimes remain at the level of uncritical celebration of individual narratives and neglect issues of power and social justice (see Delpit, 1988, for a critique of whole language approaches applied to inner-city African-American children).

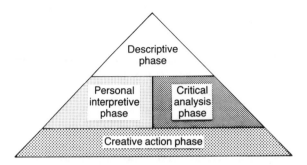

Figure 2   Comprehensible input and critical literacy.

the sanitized accounts in traditional texts, critically inquire as to why the texts present the type of picture they do and to explore the parallels with current issues relating to power in our society. They would also explore the possibilities for taking action in relation to the issues raised through critical inquiry, as outlined by Bigelow (1991).

One framework which elaborates a critical literacy approach to the education of ESL students is presented by Ada (1988a, 1988b) on the basis of Paulo Freire's work (see Figure 2). Ada's framework outlines how zones of proximal development can be created that encourage students to share and amplify their experience within a collaborative process of critical inquiry. She distinguishes four phases in what she terms "the creative reading act."[3] Each of the phases distinguished by Ada is characterized by an interactional process (either between the teacher and students or among peers) that progressively opens up possibilities for the articulation and amplification of student voice. The "texts" that are the focus of the interaction can derive from any curricular area or from newspapers or current events. The process is equally applicable to students at any grade level. Ada (1988a, p. 103) stresses that although the phases are discussed separately, "in a creative reading act they may happen concurrently and be interwoven."

---

3 I have slightly modified the labels given by Ada for the four phases in order to try and highlight certain aspects of the process. Although presented here in a linear format, the phases should not be thought of as requiring a linear or sequential approach. In other words, the process of collaborative critical inquiry can begin at any of the four phases and be incorporated in any manner into the instructional process. It is not in any sense formulaic but should be reinvented by individual teachers according to their perceptions and circumstances. The essential components are that students' experience and critical inquiry constitute the curriculum as much as any "text" since in the absence of students' experience and critical inquiry no text can become truly meaningful.

- *Descriptive phase.* In this phase the focus of interaction is on the information contained in the text. Typical questions at this level might be: Where/when/how did it happen? Who did it? Why? These are the type of questions for which answers can be found in the text itself. Ada points out that these are the usual reading comprehension questions and that "a discussion that stays at this level suggests that reading is a passive, receptive, and in a sense, domesticating process" (1988a, p. 104).

- *Personal interpretative phase.* After the basic information in the text has been discussed, students are encouraged to relate it to their own experiences and feelings. Questions that might be asked by the teacher at this phase are: Have you ever seen/felt/experienced something like this? Have you ever wanted something similar? How did what you read make you feel? Did you like it? Did it make you happy? Frighten you? What about your family? Ada (1988a) points out that this process helps develop children's self-esteem by showing children that their experiences and feelings are valued by the teacher and classmates. It also helps children understand that "true learning occurs only when the information received is analyzed in the light of one's own experiences and emotions" (p. 104). An atmosphere of acceptance and trust in the classroom is a prerequisite for students (and teachers) to risk sharing their feelings, emotions, and experiences. It is clear how this process of sharing and critically reflecting on their own and other students' experiences opens up identity options for students that are typically suppressed within a transmission approach to pedagogy where the interpretation of texts is nonnegotiable and reflective of the dominant group's notions of cultural literacy.

- *Critical analysis phase.* After children have compared and contrasted what is presented in the text with their personal experiences, they are ready to engage in a more abstract process of critically analyzing the issues or problems that are raised in the text. This process involves relating what has been presented in the text to broader social issues as well as drawing inferences and exploring what generalizations can be made. Appropriate questions might be: Is it valid? Always? When? Does it benefit everyone alike? Are there any alternatives to this situation? Would people of different cultures/classes/genders have acted differently? How? Why? Ada emphasizes that school children of all ages can engage in this type of critical process, although the analysis will always reflect children's experiences and level of maturity. It should be emphasized that this process of critical inquiry is not focussed only on negative social phenomena. It essentially involves students using higher-order thinking processes to deepen their comprehension of events (or phenomena) and to explore the social implications of these events.

• *Creative action phase.* This is a stage of translating the results of the previous phases into concrete action. The dialogue is oriented towards discovering what changes individuals can make to improve their lives or resolve the problem that has been presented. Let us suppose that students have been researching (in the local newspaper, in periodicals such as *National Geographic, Greenpeace,* etc.) problems relating to environmental pollution. After relating the issues to their own experience and critically analyzing causes and possible solutions, they might decide to write letters to congressional representatives or members of parliament, highlight the issue in their class/school newsletter in order to sensitize other students, write and circulate a petition in the neighborhood, write and perform a play that analyzes the issue, and so on.

The processes described in Ada's framework are clearly compatible with the five pedagogical principles for effective ESL teaching suggested by Ashworth, et al. (1989). A context (or ZPD) is created where students can voice their experience; meaningful and socially relevant content is integrated with active use of language in written and oral modalities; and students are challenged to use their developing language skills for higher-order thinking. However, Ada's phases of critical literacy go beyond the principles articulated by Ashworth, et al., by addressing directly the question "effective for what?" The possibilities for identity formation and knowledge generation reflected in the types of interactions highlighted by Ada are integral to any notion of empowerment. This point is clearly expressed by McLeod (1986) in an article entitled "Critical Literacy: Taking Control of Our Own Lives," in which he documents how a focus on complex issues such as racism, colonialism and war led working-class students (in London, England) to explore the forces that affected their existence. He points out that

Being literate in the 1980's means having the power to use language – writing and reading, speaking and listening – for our own purposes, as well as those that the institutions of our society require of us. The classroom processes by which that power is achieved include the first exercise of that power. (p. 37)

Comprehensible input and critical inquiry

While Ada's critical literacy framework is clearly relevant to all students, it has specific implications for the education of students within both the mainstream classroom and ESL and bilingual classes. The process of critical literacy outlined by Ada is essentially a process of constructing a zone of proximal development that expands students' conceptual possibilities and their options for identity formation.

The expansion of conceptual possibilities can be seen by relating the framework to the notion of "comprehensible input." Although most applied linguists acknowledge that the understanding of messages (comprehensible input) is a central aspect of second language acquisition, few concur with Krashen's (1989) claim that comprehensible input is *the* major causal variable in this process. Most would assign more weight than Krashen does to active use of the target language (what Swain [1986] has termed "comprehensible output"). A further disadvantage of the term "comprehensible input" is that it implies that language learning is largely a passive process of merely receiving input (although Krashen himself has emphasized the active constructive nature of the process of making input comprehensible).

Thus, communicative interaction (which includes input and output) is seen as a more useful variable to emphasize in the second language acquisition process than comprehensible input in isolation. The notion of "communicative interaction" is also clearly more compatible with the emphasis in this chapter on the ZPD as the interpersonal matrix, co-constructed through interaction, within which learning takes place.

The representation of Ada's framework in Figure 2 highlights the fact that "comprehension" is not an "all-or-nothing" phenomenon; rather, it can take place at different levels, and the process outlined by Ada represents phases in the progressive deepening of comprehension. This deepening of comprehension represents a progressive expansion of conceptual horizons. Thus, the more we process input or information, the more potential there is for deepening our understanding of the phenomena in question. The process of making input comprehensible is an active constructive process that can be facilitated or inhibited by those we are interacting with (or by characteristics of texts we are reading).

In short, we cannot understand messages without acting on them. Initially, the action is usually internalized (Piaget's cognitive operations) but external actions will also contribute to the process of understanding. At the tip of the pyramid in Figure 2 is the descriptive phase where students' comprehension of the text (or phenomenon) is quite limited in that students have processed or acted on the text only to the extent that they are capable of reproducing the basic information it contains. Minimal cognitive action is involved. If the process is arrested at this phase (as it is in most classrooms), the knowledge will remain inert rather than becoming a catalyst for further exploration.

The personal interpretive and critical analysis phases represent internalized action on the text. Although this internalized action can be carried out by individuals, the process will usually be enhanced when the action is collaboratively constructed in the context of social interaction. The personal interpretive phase deepens the individual's comprehension by grounding the knowledge in the personal and collective narratives that make up our experience and history. The critical analysis phase further extends the comprehension process by examining both the internal logical coherence of the information or propositions and their consistency with other knowledge or perspectives. Finally, the creative action phase constitutes concrete action that aims to transform aspects of our social realities. This external action to transform reality also serves to deepen our comprehension of the issues.

With respect to expansion of possibilities for identity formation, students engaging in the critical literacy process outlined in Figure 2 have the possibility of actively voicing their own realities and their analyses of issues rather than being constricted to the identity definitions and constructions of "truth" implicitly or explicitly transmitted in the prescribed curriculum. When classroom interaction progresses beyond the descriptive phase, students engage in a process of *self-expression;* in other words, by sharing and critically reflecting on their experience, they collaboratively construct a ZPD that expands options for identity formation.

Conclusion

I have argued that a framework for critical literacy in ESL must go beyond technical issues of how to transmit the language code effectively to broader issues of the social purposes for which language is used and the social relevance of the instructional content. Vygotsky's notion of the ZPD and Ada's phases of critical literacy highlight the fact that knowledge is socially constructed, as are personal and cultural identities. The construction of both knowledge and identity is jointly enacted by students and educators within the zone of proximal development. The ways in which educators define their roles with respect to second language students and minority communities will determine the extent to which they constrict the ZPD to limit students' possibilities for identity development and knowledge generation or, alternatively, expand the ZPD to ground the curriculum in students' experiences so that a much broader range of possibilities for identity formation and knowledge generation are available to students. Educators' role definitions reflect their vision of society, and implicated in that societal vision are their own identities and those of the students with whom they interact. The outcome of this process for both educator and student can be described in terms of *empowerment.* Empowerment can thus be regarded as the collaborative creation of power insofar as it constitutes the process whereby students and educators collaboratively create knowledge and identity through action focused on personal and social transformation.

References

Ada, A. F. (1988a). Creative reading: A relevant methodology for language minority children. In L. M. Malave (Ed.), *NABE '87. Theory, research and application: Selected papers*. Buffalo: State University of New York.

Ada, A. F. (1988b). The Pajaro Valley experience: Working with Spanish-speaking parents to develop children's reading and writing skills in the home through the use of children's literature. In T. Skutnabb-Kangas & J. Cummins (Eds.), *Minority education: From shame to struggle*. Clevedon, England: Multilingual Matters.

Ashworth, M., Cummins, J., & Handscombe, J. (1989). *Report on the Vancouver School Board's ESL Program*. Report submitted to the Vancouver School Board, January 1989.

Bialystok, E. (1991). Metalinguistic dimensions of bilingual language proficiency. In E. Bialystok (Ed.), *Language processing in bilingual children*. Cambridge, England: Cambridge University Press.

Bigelow, B. (1991). Discovering Columbus: Re-reading the past. *Our Schools, Our Selves, 3*, 1: 22–38.

Blauner, R. (1969). Internal colonialism and ghetto revolt. *Social Problems, 16*, 393–408.

Centre for Educational Research and Innovation (1987). *Immigrants' children at school*. Paris: OECD.

Collier, V. P. (1987). Age and rate of acquisition of second language for academic purposes. *TESOL Quarterly, 21*, 617–641.

Collier, V. P. (1989). How long? A synthesis of research on academic achievement in a second language. *TESOL Quarterly, 23*, 509–531.

Cummins, J. (1981). Age on arrival and immigrant second language learning in Canada: A reassessment. *Applied Linguistics, 2*, 132–149.

Cummins, J. (1984). *Bilingualism and special education: Issues in assessment and pedagogy*. Clevedon, England: Multilingual Matters.

Cummins, J. (1989). *Empowering minority students*. Sacramento: California Association for Bilingual Education.

Cummins, J. (1991). Interdependence of first- and second-language proficiency in bilingual children. In E. Bialystok (Ed.), *Language processing in bilingual children*. Cambridge, England: Cambridge University Press.

Delpit, L. (1988). The silenced dialogue: Power and pedagogy in educating other peoples's children. *Harvard Educational Review, 58*, 280–298.

Early, M. (1990). Enabling first and second language learners in the class-room. *Language Arts, 67*, 567–575.

Enright, D. S. & McCloskey, M. L. (1988). *Integrating English: Developing English language and literacy in the multilingual classroom.* Reading, MA: Addison-Wesley.

Fine, M. (1987). Silence and nurturing voice in an improbable context: Urban adolescents in public school. *Language Arts, 64*, 2: 157–174.

Fordham, S. (1990). Racelessness as a factor in black students' school success: Pragmatic strategy or pyrrhic victory? In N. M. Hidalgo, C. L. McDowell, & E. V. Siddle (Eds.), *Facing racism in education* (pp. 232–262). Reprint series No. 21, Harvard Educational Review.

Galtung, J. (1980). *The true worlds: A transnational perspective.* New York: The Free Press.

Giroux, H. A. (1991). Series introduction: Rethinking the pedagogy of voice, difference and cultural struggle. In C. E. Walsh, *Pedagogy and the struggle for voice: Issues of language, power, and schooling for Puerto Ricans* (pp. xv–xxvii). Toronto: OISE Press.

Giroux, H. A. & McLaren, P. (1986). Teacher education and the politics of engagement: The case for democratic schooling. *Harvard Educational Review, 56*, 213–238.

Goncz, L. & Kodzopeljic, J. (1991). Exposure to two languages in the preschool period. *Journal of Multilingual and Multicultural Development, 12*, 3: 137–163.

Goodlad, J. I. (1984). *A place called school: Prospects for the future.* New York: McGraw-Hill.

Handscombe, J. (1989). Mainstreaming: Who needs it? In J. Esling (Ed.), *Multicultural education and policy: ESL in the 1990s. A tribute to Mary Ashworth* (pp. 18–35). Toronto: OISE Press.

Henley, R. & Young, J. (1989). Multicultural teacher education. Part 4: Revitalizing faculties of education. *Multiculturalism, 12* (3): 40–41.

Krashen, S. (1989). *Language acquisition and language education.* New York: Prentice-Hall International.

Laing, R. D. (1969). *Self and others.* London: Tavistock Publications.

Larsen-Freeman, D. (1991). Second language acquisition research: Staking out the territory. *TESOL Quarterly, 25*, 2: 3–350.

Lopes, J. M., & Lopes, M. (1991). Bridging the generation gap: The collection of social histories in the Portuguese heritage language program. *The Canadian Modern Language Review, 47*, 708–711.

McLeod, A. (1986). Critical literacy: Taking control of our own lives. *Language Arts, 63*, 37–50.

Mohan, B. (1986). *Language and content.* Reading, MA: Addison-Wesley.

Moll, L. (1989). Teaching second language students: A Vygotskian perspective. In D. Johnston & D. Roen (Eds.), *Richness in writing: Empowering ESL students* (pp. 55–69). New York: Longman.

National Coalition of Advocates for Students. (1988). *New voices: Immigrant students in U.S. public schools.* Boston: National Coalition of Advocates for Students.

Newman, D., Griffin, P., & Cole, M. (1989). *The construction zone: Working for cognitive change in school.* Cambridge, England: Cambridge University Press.

Ogbu, J. (1978). *Minority education and caste.* New York: Academic Press.

Peirce, B. N. (1989). Toward a pedagogy of possibility in the teaching of English internationally. *TESOl Quarterly, 23,* 3: 401–420.

Pennycook, A. (1989). The concept of method, interested knowledge, and the politics of language teaching. *TESOL Quarterly, 23,* 4: 589–617.

Ramirez, J. D., Yuen, S. D., & Ramey, D. R. (1991). *Executive summary. Final report: Longitudinal study of structured English immersion strategy, early-exit and late-exit transitional bilingual education programs for language-minority children.* Contract No. 300-87-0156. Submitted to the U.S. Department of Education. San Mateo: Aguirre International.

Ricciardelli, L. (1989). *Childhood bilingualism: Metalinguistic awareness and creativity.* Unpublished dissertation submitted to the University of Adelaide, Australia.

Simon, R. (1987). Empowerment as a pedagogy of possibility. *Language Arts, 64,* 370–380.

Sirotnik, K. A. (1983). What you see is what you get – consistency, persistence, and mediocrity in classrooms. *Harvard Educational Review, 53,* 16–31.

Skutnabb-Kangas, T. (1984). *Bilingualism or not: The education of minorities.* Clevedon, England: Multilingual Matters.

Skutnabb-Kangas, T. (1988). Resource power and autonomy through discourse in conflict – a Finnish migrant school strike in Sweden. In T. Skutnabb-Kangas & J. Cummins (eds.), *Minority education: From shame to struggle* (pp. 251–277). Clevedon, England: Multilingual Matters.

Swain, M. (1986). Communicative competence: Some roles of comprehensible input and comprehensible output in its development. In J. Cummins and M. Swain (Eds.), *Bilingualism in education: Aspects of theory, research and practice.* London: Longman.

Swain, M. & Lapkin, S. (1991). Heritage language children in an English-French bilingual program. *Canadian Modern Language Review, 47,* 4: 635–641.

Swann Report, (1985). *Education for all.* London: HMSO.

Tizard, J., Schofield, W. N., & Hewison, J. (1982). Collaboration between teachers and parents in assisting children's reading. *British Journal of Educational Psychology* 52: 1–15.

Vygotsky, L. S. (1978). In M. Cole, V. John-Steiner, S. Scribner, & E. Souberman (Eds.), *Mind in society: The development of higher psychological processes.* Cambridge, MA: Harvard University Press.

58   *Jim Cummins*

Walsh, C. E. (1991). *Pedagogy and the struggle for voice: Issues of language, power, and schooling for Puerto Ricans.* Toronto: OISE Press.

Wells, G. (1986). *The meaning makers.* Portsmouth, NH: Heinemann.

Willis, P. (1977). *Learning to labor: How working class kids get working class jobs.* Lexington: D. C. Heath.

Wong Fillmore, L. (1991). Second-language learning in children: A model of language learning in social context. In E. Bialystok (Ed.), *Language processing in bilingual children* (pp. 49–69). Cambridge, England: Cambridge University Press.

Wright, E. N. & Tsuji, G. K. (1984). *The grade nine student survey: Fall 1983.* Toronto: Toronto Board of Education.

SECTION II:
THE PRESCHOOL YEARS

Effective education is developmental – it builds on the skills, knowledge, and experiences that young children acquire in their homes and communities prior to coming to school and while they are in school; it extends and broadens those skills and knowledge in developmentally meaningful ways. The writing of the chapters in Section II, ''The Preschool Years,'' has been motivated with this general perspective in mind. The chapters explore the experiences of three different groups of children – children who grow up learning two languages from birth (Goodz, Chapter 3); children who grow up in a minority language community learning a language other than English (Pease-Alvarez & Vasquez, Chapter 4); and children learning English as a second language in preschool programs (Tabors & Snow, Chapter 5). The childhood experiences depicted in these chapters are representative of the family and community experiences of many second language students. But these experiences are often unfamiliar to monolingual English-speaking educators from the majority group. By reviewing what we know about language learning and development in these diverse situations, the chapters in this section seek to provide the reader with a knowledge base for understanding the development of second language students better and, consequently, for planning developmentally appropriate classroom instruction for them.

3 Interactions between parents and children in bilingual families

Naomi S. Goodz

This chapter is concerned with simultaneous bilingual language acquisition or "bilingualism as a first language" (Swain, 1972). Such development can be distinguished from sequential or successive bilingual acquisition, a process that occurs when one language is established before a second is introduced. Since the criteria for deciding that a language is "established" are far from clear, most researchers in childhood bilingualism have adopted the convention that children who are introduced to a second language during their first three years are engaged in simultaneous bilingualism; children who are exposed to a second language only after the age of three are said to be engaged in sequential bilingualism (Hakuta, 1986; McLaughlin, 1984; Taeschner, 1983; Vaid, 1986). At first glance, the focus of this chapter appears to be different from others in this book, which focus on school-age children learning a second language after the first has been established. However, it is generally well accepted that children's development during the preschool years is an important basis for their subsequent development in school. Language is an important medium of communication in school, and language for academic purposes is an important skill that children must learn. The transition to school and children's ultimate success in school depend very much on the continuity of language development. Researchers have shown that the transition to school and children's acquisition of academic language skills do not depend on which particular language is used in the home. Rather, a successful experience in an academic setting is linked to the quality of language experiences that children have in the home and how these are extended in school (Heath, 1986; Wells, 1986).

Most educators are knowledgeable about the language development of English-speaking children because these children have been studied extensively, and research findings about their preschool development are often included in professional programs for teachers (see Chapter 6 for a discussion of language experiences relevant to literacy development). There is much less research on children raised bilingually, and the information that is available does not often figure in professional education for teachers. Therefore, knowledge about the preschool development of such

61

children is less likely to be part of a teachers' knowledge base. As a result, there can be misconceptions about these children and their linguistic competence. It is important for educators to understand the kinds of language experiences children have had and the processes that underlie their language learning so that they can help them build on these skills and experiences. This chapter aims to dispel possible misconceptions about bilingual development and to provide some of the knowledge needed to understand bilingual children better.

Many questions about simultaneous bilingualism are similar to those asked about second language acquisition. Examples include whether the first language should be firmly established before a second is introduced, the best age to expose a child to a second language, and the optimal method of presenting the second language. Related concerns include whether children exposed to two languages will begin to talk at the same age as monolingual children, whether they will show a developmental sequence that is similar to monolingual children, and whether bilingual children will acquire their languages with the same speed and ease as monolingual children.

These are questions that parents also often ask educators. Answers to these questions can thus help educators working with second language and bilingual children to formulate more effective educational programs and advise parents with respect to appropriate language strategies in the home. In this chapter, I will focus on concerns about possible linguistic confusion and rate of acquisition in the early stages of simultaneous bilingual development. I will begin with a brief review of previous research and then continue with a discussion of my own longitudinal study of French-English bilingual families. Throughout the chapter I will argue that monolingual and bilingual children approach the task of language acquisition in the same way and that their early utterances can be understood as the expression of cognitive, affective, and social notions that are important to them, using the linguistic resources available to them at any particular point in their development.

Language differentiation in bilingual children

It is often believed in North America and other predominantly English-speaking countries that early exposure to two languages, either simultaneously or sequentially, is detrimental to language acquisition. This belief rests on an implicit assumption that learning more than one language in early childhood necessarily produces confusion and interference between the languages. This assumption has had a great influence on the thinking of parents, educators, and researchers and has stimulated controversy on both theoretical and practical levels. On a practical level, it has manifested itself in the worries of linguistically mixed couples who wish to raise their children bilingually but wonder whether it would be better to establish one language firmly before exposing the child to a second in order to avoid confusing the child and perhaps slowing the overall rate of language acquisition. Moreover, parents are worried that their children will never be as competent in either of their two languages as monolingual children are in one. Concerns such as these may also be expressed in educational policies; for example, in the province of Quebec, francophone children are not exposed to a second language in school before the fourth grade to ensure that no disruption in establishing the first language occurs. Another striking example of the expression of such concerns is found in countries, such as the United States, where minority language parents are encouraged to use the majority language with their children as early as possible under the false assumption that the sooner the children are exposed to English, the faster and better they will learn it.

The assumption that linguistic confusion is an inevitable consequence of early exposure to two languages has engendered much discussion on a theoretical level as well. Among researchers the focus of the discussion is on the ability of bilingual children to differentiate two language systems. The majority of researchers, as well as parents and educators, consider that language differentiation is a gradual process that unfolds in a series of stages over several years (Redlinger & Park, 1980; Taeschner, 1983; Volterra & Taeschner, 1978). According to this view, children begin with a single system that incorporates the two languages and only gradually do they differentiate them. In one such theory (Volterra & Taeschner, 1978), the bilingual-to-be child is said to begin with one lexical system that includes words from both languages. During the second stage, the child distinguishes two different lexicons but continues to use one set of syntactic rules. Finally, in the third stage, the child has two separate linguistic codes, differentiated in both lexicon and in syntax, but each language is associated exclusively with the person who uses that language. According to this theory, true bilingualism is only present at the end of the third stage, when children no longer categorize people in terms of the language they speak. Proponents of this view do not consider the possibility that the child may be aware that he or she is being presented with two languages from the beginning.

In comparison with the one-system view, some investigators believe that the task of language differentiation is accomplished much earlier and less gradually than the process just described (Bergman, 1976; de Houwer, 1990; Genesee, 1989; Goodz, 1989; Padilla & Leibman, 1975). These researchers have suggested that prelinguistic infants easily differentiate their two languages, and they do this using differences in the prosody of each language, such as intonation, stress, and rhythm as cues (Genesee, 1989; Goodz, 1986). In fact, I would argue that from the beginning infants hear each language as a different melody and that different languages may be as distinct for infants as different songs. The distinctiveness of such prosodic "melodies" in communicating effective messages to infants within a single language has been noted by other investigators (Fernald, 1989; Trehub, Trainor, & Unyk, 1993). Indeed, according to Fernald (1989), the melody – meaning individual intonation contours that are specifically associated with a variety of affective states – is the message.

Research on the early stages of simultaneous bilingual language acquisition, for the most part, has consisted of studies involving small numbers of children, typically one or two, who have been exposed to a wide variety of dual language combinations of varying similarity. Further, these language combinations have been presented to the children in many different ways. Some children have heard two or more languages in the home. In these situations, some children have heard each parent speaking only his or her own native language; some have heard both parents speaking each language some of the time; some have heard the second language spoken by a grandparent, governess, housekeeper, or friend of the family. Some children have been exposed to one language in the home and to a second language in a nursery school, day-care setting, or by peers. In some cases, the two languages to which children are exposed are spoken by large numbers of people in the surrounding society or neighborhood whereas in other cases, only one of the languages is spoken outside the family.

These different situations obviously create very different language learning environments for the child and very different challenges, both for parents attempting to raise their children as bilinguals and for teachers who receive these children in their classrooms. These examples represent only a few of the possibilities, and often children are exposed to a combination of more than one scenario. Researchers have seldom given detailed information about the manner in which young children are exposed to "bilingualism as a first language," and they seldom take such variation into account when interpreting their data. It is not surprising then that the observations reported often contain contradictions and inconsistencies.

One point on which there is agreement is that some mixing at the lexical level occurs during the early stages of language development in virtually all bilingual children (Bergman, 1976; Goodz, 1989; Imedadze, 1967; Leopold, 1939–1949; Lindholm, 1980; Lindholm & Padilla, 1978; Padilla & Leibman, 1975; Redlinger & Park, 1980; Ronjat, 1913; Swain, 1972; Volterra & Taeschner, 1978). There is, however, controversy about the extent of such mixing. As Genesee (1989) has noted, different studies have reported very different rates of mixing. However, most investigators report that mixed utterances appear more frequently in the early stages of acquisition and diminish gradually with ages. For example, Vihman (1982) reported a steady decline in the proportion of mixed utterances by her Estonian/English bilingual son, with the highest rate, 34 per cent, at age 1;8 descending through 22 per cent at 1;9, 20 per cent at 1;10, 11 per cent at 1;11, and 4 per cent at 2;0. Redlinger and Park (1980) reported mixing ranging from 20 per cent to 30 per cent during Brown's Stage I (Brown 1973), 12 to 20 per cent during Stage II, 6 to 12 per cent during Stage III, and 2 to 6 per cent during Stages IV and V.

There is also controversy about what language mixing means. Some researchers regard language mixing as a manifestation of children's failure to differentiate the two systems (e.g., Volterra & Taeschner, 1978; Redlinger & Park, 1980), some even interpret it as language confusion, and others argue that children at this early stage have no linguistic system at all (Leopold, 1939–1949). Despite strongly held opinions that early dual language exposure almost inevitably produces negative consequences, there are reasons to believe that such interpretations are not supported by the extant data. The general purpose of my research, therefore, has been to resolve some of these contradictions by studying a larger number of children who were learning the same two languages. And, since previous work has provided very little information about the conditions of bilingual exposure, a related goal was to provide a detailed description of the way in which the parents of bilingual-to-be children present their languages and then to relate the type of exposure to children's bilingual acquisition.

The findings I will discuss are drawn from an ongoing longitudinal study of French-English bilingual families. The term *bilingual family* is used to describe a family in which one parent speaks French as a first language and one parent speaks English as a first language. Either or both parents may speak two languages. The subjects discussed in this chapter were thirteen first-born children and their parents. The children were from 13 to 15 months old at the beginning of the study. Their mothers had at least one year of university education, and their fathers, with one exception, had at least one university degree. The parents' occupations included teaching, engineering, social work, and accounting. Thus, the families' socioeconomic status can be classified as middle to upper middle class. All parents declared themselves to be firmly committed to speaking only their own native language when addressing their children.

The language samples were collected during home visits occurring at fairly regular intervals over a period of three to four years. Although an attempt was made to visit each mother-child and father-child dyad every six weeks, one or both parents were sometimes unavailable due to work commitments or holidays, occasionally necessitating intervals of longer than six weeks between observations. Each session consisted of naturalistic observation of either the mother and child or the father and child while

Table 1. *Proportion of language mixing in child-to-parent speech*

Age groups	Mother$_E$[a]	Father$_F$[b]	Mother$_F$	Father$_E$
5–12 months	.0000	.000	.000	—
13–18 months	.0008	.000	.000	.000
19–24 months	.0040	.006	.006	.004
25–30 months	.0150	.050	.024	.013
31–36 months	.0270	.062	.030	.006
37–42 months	.0180	.030	.004	.008

[a] E – Denotes English-speaking parent
[b] F – Denotes French-speaking parent

they were involved in a variety of activities such as block building, puzzle solving, and discussing picture books. The sessions were audio-taped while a bilingual observer kept a written record of the children's utterances as well as detailed notes on the contexts of the parent-child interactions. Transcripts of the audiotapes were coded for mean length of utterance (MLU) for parents and children, frequency of language switching (i.e., a total switch from one code to another), and frequency of language mixing (i.e., the use of two languages within a single utterance) for both parents and children. Separate records were kept of all new lexical items used by children in each session as well.

Language mixing in bilingual children

In keeping with previous reports of language mixing in the speech of young bilinguals, my data show some language mixing in the spontaneous productions of all of the young bilinguals I observed. The proportion of language mixing by children in each age group addressing their mothers and fathers separately is presented in Table 1. The table provides a separate breakdown for children addressing francophone and anglophone parents. It is evident that the proportion of language mixing was very small, ranging from 0 to 5 per cent. Interestingly, these data indicate that language mixing increased gradually over most of the age range under consideration. Thus, mixing at the very youngest ages was almost nonexistent but showed an increase in the 19 to 24 month old age group that continued in the 25 to 30 month group and peaked at ages 31 to 36 months. At 37 to 42 months, the proportion of language mixing decreased but continued at a higher rate than that shown by the three youngest groups.

The finding that language mixing showed an increase with children's age is different from previous reports but is not really surprising given two considerations. First, in the bilingual families I studied, the children were exposed to a different language from each parent. Unless the child makes equal progress in each language, duplicates every experience with both parents, and unless each parent ensures that conversations about similar events, objects, and experiences take place, the child is unlikely to acquire corresponding or equivalent lexical items in each language. Thus, as the child seeks to express more and more ideas, he or she may need to borrow more and more lexical items from the parent's non-native language or even switch entirely to the parent's non-native language if the child has not had equivalent experiences in both languages.

Second, I would argue that bilingual children approach the language acquisition task in the same way as monolingual children in different language communities around the world. That is, they express the cognitive notions they have developed toward the end of the sensorimotor period, using whatever vocabulary is available to them, combining their one-, two-, and three-word utterances according to the rules of the apparently universal language known as "childrenese" (Bloom, 1970; Braine, 1963; Brown, 1973). According to this view, early lexical mixing does not reflect confusion of the two languages, but rather that the child, wishing to communicate and lacking the necessary vocabulary, borrows either an inappropriate word from the same language, as in overextension (Clark, 1971), or an appropriate word from the second language. As their thoughts and experiences become more complex, they may be compelled to use more items from the other parent's language in order to fill in gaps in their vocabulary knowledge.

There are several lines of evidence in my research that indicate that children may use items from one language when conversing in the other, even though they are aware of the differences in the systems. One line of evidence comes from the many examples of children's requests for equivalents in the language that is not being used in a current conversation. "How do you say that in French (or English)?" is a commonly heard utterance by children, beginning as early as 18 months of age in some cases. A second kind of evidence for linguistic awareness comes from children's differential use of a lexical item depending on whether the linguistic context of the conversation is English or French. For example, one child in my study in commenting to his anglophone mother about the observer said, "Mommy, he has such long *cheveuxs*,"[1] with strong emphasis on the English plural morpheme. However, later in the same session, when addressing his francophone father and using *les cheveux* in a French sentence, there was no attempt to mark the plural by adding an

---

1 The translation for *les cheveux* is hair. *Les,* the plural form of French articles, indicates that the noun is plural.

Table 2. *Mean number of vocabulary types used by child with parents*

Age groups	C→M_E[a]	C→F_F[b]	C→M_F[c]	C→F_E[d]
5–12 months	7	3	8	—
13–18 months	27	10	5	33
19–24 months	46	51	66	85
25–30 months	174	47	70	159
31–36 months	192	80	87	186
37–42 months	270	119	96	173

[a] C→M_E Denotes speech addressed by child to English-speaking mother
[b] C→F_F Denotes speech addressed by child to French-speaking father
[c] C→M_F Denotes speech addressed by child to French-speaking mother
[d] C→M_E Denotes speech addressed by child to English-speaking father

English morpheme. Examples of this kind, together with instances in which children use French pronunciation when introducing an English lexical item into a French utterance, and vice versa, strongly suggest that children's language mixing should not be attributed to failure to differentiate the two systems or confusion between them. Rather, it appears that children are borrowing either an equivalent item because a term in the host language is unknown or even because it is the term that is most commonly used by both parents. Perhaps the most striking example of children's linguistic awareness comes from four-and-a-half-year-old Lexi. After viewing hieroglyphics at an Egyptian exhibit, Lexi asked her mother, "How do you translate that square talk into French, Mommy?" This example not only provides evidence of Lexi's awareness of different language systems, but also of a precocious awareness of the relationship between the symbolic representation of a language in writing and the language as it is spoken.

Rate of bilingual development

Both the vocabulary and MLU data, presented in Tables 2 and 3, indicate clearly that acquisition did not proceed at the same rate in each of the children's languages. The group data show that for families in which mothers are anglophones, both MLU and lexical development were more rapid in English than in French. Also, although the majority of children with anglophone mothers showed more rapid progress in English, this was not the case for all of the children in this group.

One common expectation is that when disparities in children's acquisition rates occur, they will show more rapid progress in their mothers' language. However, my findings fail to confirm this view. I would

Table 3. *Children's mean length of utterance in English and French*

Age groups	C→M$_A$[a]	C→F$_F$[b]	C→M$_F$	C→F$_A$
5–12 months	1.02	1.00	1.00	—
13–18 months	1.12	1.14	1.00	1.24
19–24 months	1.16	1.33	1.19	1.38
25–30 months	2.18	1.26	1.59	2.19
31–36 months	2.78	2.06	1.69	2.72
37–42 months	3.71	3.00	2.74	2.35

[a] C→M$_A$ Denotes speech addressed by child to anglophone mother
[b] C→F$_F$ Denotes speech addressed by child to francophone father

suggest instead that such disparities are influenced by differences in the characteristics of the child-directed speech of each parent – differences that may serve to make one language more salient for the child, even in the prelinguistic stage. These characteristics may include prosodic features such as elevated pitch, which is effective in attracting the child's attention; a slower rate of speech, which enhances the child's ability to process parental utterances; and emphasis and repetition of important words, which facilitates their extraction from the speech stream. Other important variables may include the parents' ability to understand the child, their sensitivity to the child's level of semantic and syntactic development, and their ability to elicit and maintain communicative interactions with the child. Such variations may change parental input in ways that lead to differences in the child's ability to extract words and meaning from the speech directed to them, differences in the amount of attention elicited from the child, and other variables that have been shown to influence early language acquisition (see Hoff-Ginsberg & Shatz, 1982, for a review). Further research is needed to pinpoint the reasons for the different rates of acquisition in each language. It is evident, however, that there is no simple relationship between a child's proficiency in each language and the language of daycare, maternal language, or the language of the neighbourhood.

It seems clear from the vocabulary data that, contrary to the claims of some investigators and the fears of many parents, early simultaneous bilingualism does not result in a delay in the appearance of first words, nor does it retard subsequent vocabulary development. Despite unequal progress in the two languages, the data show that in each age category, in at least one language, vocabulary development of young bilinguals compares favourably with the development of monolingual children as reported by other researchers (Brown, 1973). However, a more complete answer to questions about the rate of acquisition, as well as language differentiation, must await the detailed examination of the acquisition of specific linguistic structures, such as the acquisition of interrogative forms, negation, the possessive, and so on.

Parent-language mixing in bilingual families

It is generally thought that language mixing in young bilinguals can be minimized or eliminated by strict adherence to a parent/language separation. However, very little research has systematically evaluated this claim by direct observation of parent-child conversations in bilingual families. Before concluding that children's language mixing reflects their lack of language differentiation, it is important to examine parental speech in bilingual families to determine the extent to which parents use only their own native language in addressing their children. With one exception (Lanza, 1992), previous researchers have relied on parental reports to obtain such information (Doyle, Champagne, & Segalowitz, 1978). As will be seen, however, parental reports may not always accurately represent their interactions with their children.

The findings from my study suggest that the actual language behaviour of parents in bilingual families is not determined by a simple decision to present the languages in a prespecified way. In general, the data indicate little evidence to support a de facto parent/language separation, and although there was some variation among the participating families, all parents spoke both French and English to their children under some conditions. This was true even when parents described themselves as firmly committed to the idea of a parent/language separation. The absolute frequency of parental language switching or mixing was quite low in some cases and usually appeared to be influenced by factors that varied with the children's age, and above all, with their acquisition status in each language. In addition, language switching by parents may have been influenced by the parent's level of fluency in each language as well as by such situational factors as the need to attract the child's attention, for emphasis, and to discipline the child.

My findings indicate that before children began to say their first words, parents used the non-native language relatively infrequently. When they did use it, it seemed to be because of extralinguistic variables such as the number of other people who were present while the parent was addressing the infant, the languages they spoke, the linguistic context in which a given conversational topic occurred, and the parent's degree of fluency in each language. For example, a French-speaking father, alone with his infant, typically spoke entirely in French, switching to English only if English speakers were present. This was particularly the case if the father's fluency in English was superior to the French ability of the others present. However, as infants entered the last quarter of the first year and showed signs of becoming ever more active participants in the communicative interaction, the parent's determination to stick to the native language seemed to become even stronger. Thus, for most of the infant's first year, a time when the infant may be described as prelinguistic, parental use of the non-native language was very rarely seen.

As the children began to say their first words and then two- and three-word utterances, their parents used more non-native language in child-directed speech. There may be several reasons for this change in behaviour (Goodz, 1989). First, mother-to-child (and father-to-child) speech has been shown to be particularly sensitive and tuned in to changing characteristics of child speech. As shown by Garnica (1977), mothers feel a strong desire to communicate with their children and tend to use whatever device captures their children's attention most effectively. Thus, in order to encourage conversation, bilingual family parents may tend to choose words and linguistic structures that they are fairly sure the child will understand, even if these words are drawn from the vocabulary of the other parent's language.

Second, if the child uses a word from the parent's non-native language, the parent may repeat the word and continue in his or her own native language. This may occur because at this stage in the children's language development, when parents are anxious for their children to begin to talk, the primary goal is to encourage language behaviour irrespective of its form. In monolingual families, this motivation is shown by the parents' tolerance of a variety of linguistic errors. In fact, according to Brown (1973), in monolingual families, it is fairly well documented that when parents do make direct corrections, they are usually about the truth value of the children's utterances, as shown in the following example:

Child: Doggie flied out the window!
Mother: Doggies don't fly.

A third reason why the parent may switch languages in response to a child's utterance in the non-native language is to indicate to the child that his or her intention to communicate has been noted and that it has been understood. In fact, one reason for the wide prevalence of adult expansions of child speech at this point in development may be to indicate that a communication has been received and understood. It is abundantly clear, from observing the behaviour of children at this stage, that they are not satisfied until an expansion or at least a repetition has been provided. When no expansion is given, the child usually repeats the utterance until the adult finally responds. The need to repeat and expand a child's utterance is probably another major contributor to parental language mixing. My data contain many examples of such expansion sequences; they typically include parental repetition of the child's word in the non-native language along with the missing function words in the native language. Following the initial parental *mixed* expansion, the child's original utterance may be recast while still retaining the child's original words in the parent's non-native language, resulting in yet another parental mixed utterance. The following example illustrates a repetition-expansion-recast sequence:

Patrick holds out a truck to his anglophone father and says *"Camion."* The father's response is *"Camion!"* That's right, that's a *camion.* It's a big, blue *camion."*

Rarely will a parent provide a translation of the non-native item used by the child or request a translation. In fact, corrections of any kind are seldom given. When they are, they tend to be concerned with other aspects of the language learning situation, while attention to the separation of languages appears to be forgotten, as seen in the next example:

Patrick points to a pineapple and says "pinetree"! to his francophone mother. His mother's response is *"Non, ce n'est pas un pinetree, Patrick, c'est un pineapple. Dis pineapple, Patrick!"*

After failing to convince Patrick that the *pinetree* was a *pineapple,* this mother switched completely to English. It is clear that her main concern in this exchange was to correct her son's overextension. Further, in her eagerness to provide Patrick with the correct English term, she not only failed to maintain the parent/language distinction, but modelled language mixing for her child. She never attempted to provide the appropriate vocabulary item, *ananas,* in French.

These examples demonstrate that repetition, recasting, and expansion, all important characteristics of child-directed speech in general, may serve to stimulate a great deal of parental language mixing in bilingual families. Since, as I have indicated, children tend to pay special attention to parental repetitions and expansions, and even to demand them when they are not immediately forthcoming, such parental mixing, together with parents' tendencies to switch languages for emphasis or to gain children's attention, combine to produce a situation in which parents model language mixing at a time when their children are particularly attentive to what they are saying. Thus, even if the absolute number of such mixes is small, they tend to occur in interactions that are highly salient for the children.

It has been shown that as monolingual children acquire facility in speaking and begin to use full sentences, parental expansions, repetitions, and recasts slowly decrease while the complexity of their language to their children increases (Brown & Fraser, 1964). At this stage, parents begin to make more linguistic demands of their children and may even correct some of their errors. In bilingual families, this is paralleled by parents' ability to resist responding to children's non-native language use by using the non-native language themselves. Instead, the larger lexicons and greater grammatical complexity of children's utterances in at least one of the two languages are accompanied by a smaller proportion of parental linguistically mixed utterances, and thus a more complete separation of the languages can be observed.

Another factor that seems to influence parental language mixing at this stage is the appearance of disparities in the children's ability to produce each language. Thus, if children make more progress in one language than the other, as is the case in many of the families, parents appear to become strongly motivated to "clean up their language act," especially in the language that is slower to develop, to ensure that their children learn to communicate effectively in that language.

A finding of particular interest in my research was that mothers are more flexible in their adherence to the principle of a strict parent/language separation than were fathers with children at all ages studied. Also, mothers' use of the non-native language tended to increase specifically in response to their children's language switching behaviour. The impression of greater maternal flexibility was further reinforced by the spontaneous reports of some fathers that their wives were more likely to repeat utterances by children in the non-native language than they were. One father confided that resisting the temptation to repeat his child's preceding utterance in whatever language was used by the child was often very difficult indeed. The tendency of fathers to be more demanding of children with respect to language separation was also evident in other ways, such as earlier shifts in the direction of greater complexity in other characteristics of the language they addressed to their children. These results support the proposal that parental adherence to a language separation depends, to a substantial extent, on feedback from children. However, this finding is particularly true for mothers. Further, the results suggest that since parents may provide a model for language mixing in speech addressed to their children, interpretations of child language mixing as a reflection of linguistic confusion are unconvincing.

Mothers' and fathers' language in bilingual families

Studies comparing the characteristics of mother-to-child and father-to-child speech in monolingual families have reported some similarities. However, these characteristics have not been found to be related to children's progress in language acquisition (Hoff-Ginsberg, 1985). At the same time, differences between maternal and paternal language to children have also been reported. It is significant that where differences have been found, they are on characteristics that have been found to be related to the rate of appearance of specific structures in children's speech (Hoff-Ginsberg, 1985). In particular, it has been argued that children's involvement in conversations contributes to their language development (Hoff-Ginsberg & Shatz, 1982; Hoff-Ginsberg, 1985). According to Hoff-Ginsberg, involving the child in conversation not only provides an opportunity for the child to be exposed to parental input, but also motivates the child to attend more closely to the conversational topic. Furthermore, since the child is actively interested in the topic of conversation, comprehension should be easier, thus allowing the child to devote more attention to the linguistic structures the parent is presenting. However, some researchers have found that fathers are more controlling, involve the child less, interrupt more frequently, and use more imperatives (Bellinger & Gleason, 1980; Burrows, 1980; Giattino & Hogan, 1976; Gleason, 1975; Malone & Guy, 1982). Such behaviours tend to reduce the spontaneous productions of children and, in fact, have been found to predominate in maternal speech to language delayed children (Leifer & Lewis, 1983). These findings, together with reports that fathers and children have fewer and shorter conversations and that children are less persistent in repairing conversational breakdowns with fathers than with mothers (Tomasello, Conti-Ramsden, & Ewart, 1990), suggest that these characteristics of paternal speech may have negative consequences for children's language development.

This possibility is of particular significance for the bilingual family since the bilingual family father is entirely responsible for teaching his native language to his child and the language behaviours described above may decrease both the salience of his native language and his effectiveness as a language teacher. One hypothesis underlying my research is that because they have the role of primary transmitter of their native language, fathers would show a greater degree of fine-tuning in paternal speech than has been reported in previous studies of fathers in monolingual families.

In contrast with earlier research, the fathers and mothers in my study differed on only three of the sixteen "motherese" variables I examined. I also observed that the bilingual family fathers tended to discard adjustments in their speech earlier than the mothers and, at the same time, they increased the complexity of their speech to their children earlier than did the mothers. For example, the fathers used more tag questions with their 3-year-old children and recast consistently fewer of the older children's utterances than did the mothers. Fathers translated their children's nonnative utterances more often than did mothers, indicating their stronger tendency to maintain a language separation. Further, fathers differentiated their speech when addressing different age groups, while mothers tended to maintain their "motherese" adjustments over the entire age range studied.

Findings for variables related to repair of conversational breakdowns provide additional indications of enhanced sensitivity in the child-directed speech of bilingual family fathers. They appeared to understand their children as well as mothers, to have the ability to elicit, maintain, and extend conversational topics as well as mothers, and to be able to repair conversational breakdowns as well as mothers (Goodz, Goodz, & Green, 1991). In addition, in contrast to children of monolingual family fathers, bilingual children were as persistent and successful in repairing conversational breakdowns with their fathers as they were with their mothers (Goodz, Goodz, & Green, 1991). In addition, in contrast to children of monolingual family fathers, bilingual children were as persistent and successful in repairing conversational breakdowns with their fathers as they were with their mothers (Goodz, Goodz & Green, 1991).

Taken together, these results suggest that the bilingual family situation facilitates "fine tuning" in paternal speech, particularly speech addressed to the youngest children. They also support previous observations of fathers in monolingual families; that these changes are quickly given up by fathers, both as their children reach the age of three and as they observe increases in their children's linguistic proficiency. These findings are also in accord with expectations of other investigators that increased participation by fathers in general caretaking activities leads to changes in a variety of paternal behaviours. These changes serve to make fathers more similar to mothers (Pedersen, Zaslow, Cain & Anderson, 1981). Like monolingual family fathers, however, it would appear that as their children progress beyond the two- and three-word utterance stage, bilingual family fathers begin to be somewhat less sensitive and more demanding, as suggested by Gleason (1975), serving as a bridge between the child and the world outside the family.

Conclusions

The major focus of this chapter has been the overriding concern about whether "bilingualism as a first language" (Swain, 1972) is beneficial for children. As is often the case when systematic information is not readily available, strong and rigidly held opinions abound. Many predict long-lasting and dire consequences, whereas others, albeit fewer, promise benefits ranging from the obvious advantages of being able to function effectively in more than one language to enhanced perspective taking and social skills (Genesee, Tucker, & Lambert, 1975), and precocious linguistic awareness and metalinguistic abilities (Ben Zeev, 1977; Cummins & Mulcahy, 1978; Ianco-Worrall, 1972). Notwithstanding some positive biases, there is a persistent tendency to blame any missteps by bilingual children on early exposure to two languages. Thus, if some bilingual-to-be children say their first words a little later than their monolingual-to-be neighbours or cousins, dual-language exposure is immediately considered to be the culprit. Well-known variations in the onset and rate of language acquisition among monolingual children are ignored. Similarly, if an older bilingual child is even somewhat slow in beginning to read, or if writing skills are not equally developed in each language, even if the child has not had instruction in both languages, bilingualism is considered to have failed. The general decline in literacy skills, the object of so much concern and discussion at every educational level, is forgotten when even slightly substandard performance in these areas is given by bilingual children. Unfortunately, because bilingualism is almost always considered a major contributor to such difficulties and may even be considered a source of a range of behaviour problems, parents and educators alike tend to be very quick in deciding to eliminate one of the languages when such problems arise. The fact that a majority of the world's population in a variety of societies arguably achieve facility in at least two languages is usually either ignored or forgotten (Mackey, 1967). It is worth remembering that in many parts of the world, bilingualism is the rule rather than the esoteric exception it is often considered to be in North America.

I believe that my findings provide strong reassurance that early dual-language exposure does not have a negative effect on language acquisition. At the most basic level, my data clearly indicate that young bilingual-to-be children begin to say their first words and multiword combinations at the same time as monolinguals. Further, although most of the children do not progress at equal rates in each language, their subsequent vocabulary development in at least one language progresses at rates comparable to those found for monolinguals (Brown, 1973). In addition, other research I have conducted that I have not described here has shown that bilingual children show consistently greater and earlier awareness of language structure, for example, in judging adjective placements in French and English sentences, than do their monolingual French and English counterparts (Goodz, Legare, & Bilodeau, 1987).

With respect to questions of linguistic confusion and differentiation, I believe the data provide reassurance as well. Relatively little language mixing occurred in the utterances of the thirteen children who were observed at frequent intervals over a three-year period. Although there was variation in the proportion of mixed utterances observed in the children's speech, the range of variation was very small indeed. Inspection of the mixed utterances revealed that most language mixing resulted from the need to borrow lexical items that had not yet been acquired in the language being used at the time of the mix. As previously mentioned, borrowed items were used in ways that indicated the children were aware that they came from another language system. Further, most mixing occurred when the language of the conversation was the child's less proficient language.

It is intriguing that on a task requiring children to judge whether mixed utterances were acceptable when spoken by puppets, bilingual preschoolers consistently judged mixed utterances to be less acceptable and made their judgements at consistently younger ages than did monolingual controls (see Goodz, Legare, & Bilodeau, 1987). That they made these judgements while using mixed utterances in their own speech makes the argument for early language differentiation in competence, if not in performance, all the more compelling. These findings, together with the unexpected appearance of mixed utterances in parental child-directed speech, lead to the conclusion that such mixing should not be interpreted as being due to linguistic confusion or failure to differentiate the language systems, but rather as partly due to performance constraints and partly due to parental models that do not lead children to conclude that a strict separation of languages is the best or only way to communicate.

In making the decision to raise children with two languages, parents need to give explicit consideration to their goals and to the methods that might be used to accomplish them. For example, will they be content if their children can speak each language easily and effectively? Do they wish to ensure that their children can read and write in each language? Once their children have become bilingual, how will they ensure that both languages continue to develop beyond the initial basic ability to communicate?

The assumption that simultaneous bilingualism necessarily produces linguistic confusion is accompanied by an equally prevalent and confident belief that the only way to avoid such confusion is by adherence to a parent/language separation. This means that parents must speak only their own native language in the child's presence even if this means that parents speak to each other using different languages. Most parents claim to follow this one parent/one language principle. Some even claim to maintain the distinction when conversing with one another. My findings, however, suggest that despite their dedication, most parents are not able to achieve this goal. The practical problems involved in doing so are simply too many and too difficult. These include, as mentioned earlier, the difficulty of resisting the tendency to repeat and expand their children's early utterances and also the necessity to speak to relatives and friends, whether children or adults, who may not speak the native language of the parent.

The critical question that must be asked is: How important is it that the parent/language distinction be maintained? The answer depends on the aspects of acquisition with which one is concerned. It is fairly obvious that if a child is to acquire a given language, he or she must have ample opportunity to hear that language. He or she must also be able to engage in communicative interactions with an interlocutor who can modify his or her speech so that young children can extract important words from the speech stream. The interlocutor must also be able to elicit and maintain children's participation in a conversation. With regard to the importance of a parent/language separation, judging by the low rate of children's language mixing, both in my own research and in many previous studies, it seems reasonable to suggest that the maintenance of such a distinction does not appear to be crucial. Rather, what seems more important is that parents engage their children in conversations, that they provide the opportunity for children to take their turns as active participants in conversational exchanges in a variety of contexts, and that they respond to and encourage their children's linguistic efforts.

This conclusion is supported by a body of research indicating that arguably the most significant modifications of child-directed speech for influencing children's language acquisition are those that are effective in eliciting and maintaining communicative participation by children from the earliest stages of infancy. Most important and helpful is a relaxed and unself-conscious parent who does not insist that every linguistic effort be in the parent's language. It is also important to keep in mind that children in a wide variety of cultures around the world, whose parents do or do not make the modifications characteristic of child-directed speech, learn to speak their own native language or languages at approximately the same ages, passing through similar stages and achieving comparable degrees of facility.

References

Bellinger, D., & Gleason, J. (1980). Differences in parental directives to young children. Paper presented at the annual meeting of the American Psychological Association, Montreal.

Ben Zeev, S. (1977). The influence of bilingualism on cognitive strategy and cognitive development. *Child Development, 48,* 1009–1018.

Bergman, C. R. (1976). Interference vs. independent development in infant bilingualism. In G. D. Keller, R. V. Taeschner, & S. Viera (Eds.), *Bilingualism in the bicentennial and beyond* (pp. 86–95). New York: Bilingual Press/Editorial Bilingüe.

Bloom, L. (1970). *Language development: Form and function in emerging grammars.* Cambridge, MA: MIT Press.

Braine, M. D. S. (1963). The ontogeny of English phrase structure: The first phase. *Language, 39,* 1–14.

Brown, R., & Fraser, C. (1964). The acquisition of syntax. In U. Bellugi &

R. Brown (Eds.), The acquisition of language. *Monographs of the Society for Research in Child Development, 29,* 43–79.

Brown, R. A. (1973). *A first language: The early stages.* Cambridge, MA: Harvard University Press.

Burrows, P. B. (1980). Mother-father differences in behavior to children: The Mexican family. Paper presented at the annual meeting of the American Psychological Association, Montreal.

Clark, E. V. (1971). On the acquisition of the meaning of *before* and *after. Journal of Verbal Learning and Verbal Behaviour, 10,* 266–275.

Cummins, J., & Mulcahy, R. (1978). Orientation to language in Ukranian-English bilingual children. *Child Development, 49,* 1239–1242.

de Houwer, A. (1990). *The acquisition of two languages from birth: A case study.* Cambridge, England: Cambridge University Press.

Doyle, A. B., Champagne, M. & Segalowitz, N. (1978). Some issues in the assessment of linguistic consequences of early bilingualism. In M. Paradis (Ed.) *Aspects of bilingualism* (pp. 13–20). Columbia, SC: Hornbeam Press.

Fernald, A. (1989). Intonation and communicative intent in mothers' speech to infants: Is the melody the message? *Child Development, 60,* 1497–1510.

Garnica, O. (1977). Some prosodic and paralinguistic features of speech to young children. In C. Snow and C. A. Ferguson (Eds.), *Talking to children* (pp. 63–88). New York: Cambridge University Press.

Genesee, F. (1989). Early bilingual development. *Journal of Child Language, 16,* 161–179.

Genesee, F., Tucker, G. R., & Lambert, W. E. (1975). Communication skills of bilingual children. *Child Development, 46,* 110–114.

Giattino, J., & Hogan, J. C. (1976). Analysis of a father's speech to his language learning child. *Journal of Speech and Hearing Disorders, 40,* 524–537.

Gleason, J. B. (1975). Fathers and other strangers: Men's speech to young children. In D. P. Dato (Ed.), *Developmental Psycholinguistics: Theory and Applications* (pp. 289–297). Washington, DC: Georgetown University Press.

Goodz, N. S. (1986). Parental language to children in bilingual families: A model and some data. Paper presented at the Third Congress of the World Association for Infant Psychiatry and Allied Disciplines, Stockholm, Sweden.

Goodz, N. S. (1989). Parental language mixing to children in bilingual families. *Infant Mental Health Journal, 10,* 22–25.

Goodz, N. S., Goodz, E., & Green, D. (1991). Mothers' and fathers' conversations with their young bilingual children. Presented at the biennial meeting of the Society for Research in Child Development, Seattle, Washington.

Goodz, N. S., Legare, M. C., & Bilodeau, L. (1987). The influence of bilingualism in preschool children. *Canadian Psychology, 28,* 218.

Hakuta, K. (1986). *Mirror of language: The debate on bilingualism.* New York: Basic Books, Inc.

Heath, S. B. (1986). Sociocultural contexts of language development. In *Beyond language: Social and cultural factors in schooling language minority children.* Los Angeles, CA: Evaluation, Dissemination, and Assessment Center, 143–186.

Hoff-Ginsberg, E. (1985). Some contributions of mothers' speech to their children's syntax growth. *Journal of Child Language, 12,* 367–85.

Hoff-Ginsberg, E., & Schatz, M. (1982). Linguistic input and the child's acquisition of language. *Psychological Bulletin, 92,* 3–26.

Ianco-Worrall, A. (1972). Bilingualism and cognitive development. *Child Development, 43,* 1390–1400.

Imedadze, N. V. O. (1967). The psychological nature of child speech formation under conditions of exposure to two languages. *International Journal of Psychology, 2,* 129–132.

Lanza, E. (1992). Can bilingual two-year-olds code-switch? *Journal of Child Language, 19,* 633–658.

Leifer, J. S., & Lewis, M. (1983). Maternal speech to normal and handicapped children. *Infant Behavior and Development, 6,* 175–188.

Leopold, W. F. (1939–1949). *Speech development of a bilingual child: A linguist's record* (Vols. 1–4). Evanston, Illinois: Northwestern University Press.

Lindholm, K. J. (1980). Bilingual children: Some interpretations of cognitive development. In K. E. Nelson (Ed.), *Children's Language* (Vol. 2) (pp. 215–266). New York: Gardner Press.

Lindholm, K. J., & Padilla, A. M. (1978). Language mixing in bilingual children. *Journal of Child Language, 5,* 327–336.

Mackey, W. F. (1967). *Bilingualism as a world problem/Le bilinguisme: phenomene mondial.* Montreal: Harvest House.

Malone, M. J., & Guy, R. F. (1982). A comparison of mothers' and fathers' speech to their 3-year-old sons. *Journal of Psycholinguistic Research, 2,* 599–608.

McLaughlin, B. (1984). *Second language acquisition in childhood.* (Vol. 1: Preschool children). Hillsdale, NJ: Lawrence Erlbaum Associates.

Padilla, A. H., & Leibman, E. (1975). Language acquisition in the bilingual child. *The Bilingual Review/La Revista Bilingüe, 2,* 34–55.

Pedersen, F. A., Zaslow, M. J., Cain, R. L., & Anderson, B. J. (1981). Caesarean childbirth: Psychological implications for mothers and fathers, *Infant Mental Health Journal, 2,* 259–263.

Redlinger, W. E., & Park, T. Z. (1980). Language mixing in young bilinguals. *Journal of Child Language, 7,* 337–352.

Ronjat, J. (1913). *Le développement du langage observé chez un enfant bilingue.* Paris: Champion.

Swain, M. (1972). *Bilingualism as a first language.* Unpublished doctoral dissertation, University of California at Irvine.

Taeschner, T. (1983). *The sun is feminine: A study on language acquisition in bilingual children.* Berlin: Springer-Verlag.

Tomasello, M., Conti-Ramsden, G., & Ewart, B. (1990). Young children's conversations with their mothers and fathers: Differences in breakdown and repairs. *Journal of Child Language, 17,* 115–130.

Trehub, S. E., Trainor, L. J., & Unyk, A. M. (1993). Music and speech processing in the first year of life. In H. W. Reese (Ed.), *Advances in child development and behavior* (pp. 1–35). San Diego: Academic.

Vaid, J. (1986). *Language processing in bilinguals: Psycholinguistic and neuropsychological perspectives.* Hillsdale, NJ: Laurence Erlbaum Associates.

Vihman, M. M. (1982). The acquisition of morphology by a bilingual child: The whole-word approach. *Applied Psycholinguistics, 3,* 141–160.

Volterra, V., & Taeschner, T. (1978). The acquisition and development of language by bilingual children. *Journal of Child Language, 5,* 311–326.

Wells, G. (1986). The language experience of five-year-old children at home and at school. In J. Cook-Gumperz (Ed.), *The social construction of literacy* (pp. 69–93). Cambridge, England: Cambridge University Press.

4 Language socialization in ethnic minority communities

Cindy Pease-Alvarez and
Olga Vasquez

For the last three decades a growing number of researchers and educators interested in language development have focused on the connections that exist between language and culture. This interest has, in part, been influenced by the realization that when young children learn language in their homes and communities they learn more than the grammar, vocabulary, and sociolinguistic rules of a given language. Through their participation in the language milieu that is part of their everyday lives, they also learn the beliefs, values, and ways of the group into which they are born. As Heath (1986, p. 145) states, ''language learning is cultural learning.'' Thus, the language that surrounds and involves children plays a critical role in their overall development – it is the means by which children are socialized and culturized as well as the raw data they draw upon for acquiring language.

People from different cultures have access to very different language socialization experiences. Several factors that vary across cultures have been identified as sources of these differences. For example, studies by Ochs (1988), Schiefffelin and Ochs (1986), and Heath (1983) indicate that culture-specific views about child raising and language learning influence the ways parents and other adults interact verbally with children. Middle-class Anglo parents who believe that language learning is facilitated by adapting the situation to their child tend to assist their children's language-learning endeavors by engaging them in conversations and by accommodating their own talk in a variety of ways. They talk about topics in ways that take into account the child's ability and interest. They often use a more simplified, repetitive, and affect-laden register, known as baby talk or motherese. They elicit clarifications and elaborations, expand and extend children's utterances, and regularly engage children in predictable conversational routines.

These patterns of verbal behavior have not been observed in some nonwestern and working-class communities where parents believe that children learn best by adapting to their surroundings. Heath, Ochs, and Schieffelin claim that adults in these societies do not view young children as suitable or competent conversation partners. Instead, they expect children to seek out their own opportunities to learn language by listening to and observing others. Models may be provided or cues used to help direct a child's attention, but attempts to scaffold children's verbal contributions within the context of a conversation are not part of these groups' language socialization experiences.

For language-minority children who must learn English as a second language for schooling and for integration into the larger community, the complexities associated with living in a multicultural world also shape their language socialization experiences. Because these children come into contact with a variety of social and cultural influences and interact with people from many backgrounds, a range of experiences affects the language milieu that contributes to the way they view the world and their place in it. More often than not, these experiences and world views are unfamiliar to their teachers, who tend to be middle class, white, and English speaking. The goal of this chapter is to enhance teachers' knowledge about the language socialization experiences available to these children so that teachers can use them to inform their instructional practice.

We begin our discussion by describing the language experiences of language-minority children who live in Eastside – a Mexican immigrant community located in the San Francisco Bay area. Our description of this community is based on our own ethnographic study of language and literacy development in Eastside homes and schools (Pease-Alvarez, 1986; Vasquez, 1989; Pease-Alvarez & Vasquez, 1990; Pease-Alvarez & Mangiola, in press; Vasquez, Pease-Alvarez, & Shannon, in press).[1] After describing what we have learned about some of the language socialization experiences available to Eastsiders, we briefly describe language socialization in school settings. Finally, we suggest some ways that teachers can learn about their students' language socialization experiences at home and in the community so that this knowledge becomes a basis for planning effective instruction.

A thumbnail sketch of Eastside

Eastside is more than 500 miles north of the U.S.–Mexican border, yet its commercial life is similar to that of Mexican neighborhoods in cities throughout the Southwest. Atlantic Avenue, a main street at the southernmost end of the community, is lined with small shops and businesses.

---

1 Over the past ten years, we have engaged in a variety of relationships with Eastsiders. We have been teachers, students, interpreters, advisors, and friends of many individuals in the community. On many occasions, we have been cultural brokers for one another, each trying to help the other understand the intricacies of a culture foreign to her own.

Local grocery store windows are plastered with advertisements for such products as *tortillas, queso, leche, chiles, bistec,* and so on (tortillas, cheese, milk, chiles, beef). Shops like *la zapateria* (the shoe store), *las tienditas* [mom and pop markets], *restaurantes* (Mexican restaurants), and other Mexicano/Latino establishments – *las joyerias, discotecas* (jewelry stores, record stores) – all advertise in Spanish. Many businesses in the area cater to the regional tastes of immigrants from the central Mexican highlands state of *Michoacan,* which is the homeland for a substantial number of Eastside's Mexicano immigrants (Fonseca & Moreno, 1984). For example, *catarinas* (catering vans), stationed strategically along Atlantic Avenue, sell grilled meat tacos served with onions, chile peppers, and slices of lime, *al estilo Michoacan* or *Jalisco* (Michoacan or Jalisco style). Other businesses, like the barber shop, the billiard hall, the car upholstery, painting, and repair shops, and the bargain furniture stores, supply products and services catering especially to a Spanish-speaking clientele.

Although even a casual observer cannot fail to note the Mexican presence that permeates Eastside, a close look at the ethnic composition of the community reveals that other groups – including Anglos, African-Americans, Latin-Americans and immigrants from Asia and the Pacific Rim – are present as well. Other languages besides Spanish are spoken in the restaurants and public places along Atlantic Avenue; Eastside offers Chinese, Vietnamese, and Salvadoran food in addition to Mexican cuisine. The ethnic diversity of Eastside's neighborhoods dissolves as one travels out of the community towards neighboring areas.

There is a dynamic exchange across cultures, languages, and social classes in the community of Eastside. While maintaining their own cultural and linguistic repertoire, families at the same time incorporate and develop (with modifications) new ways of speaking and acting garnered from their day-to-day cross-cultural experiences. At home and in the community, relatives and friends engage in lengthy discussions about events in their multicultural world. In these discussions, family members demonstrate the oral virtuosity that the Mexican culture encourages (Ybarra-Frausto, 1984). Individuals compose new or retell old stories, jokes, and poetry for the entertainment of others. Topics of conversations center on family history, personal incidents, folklore, community characters, and media events. Community members rely on one another to meet their needs in an unfamiliar country. In the context of social relations, and in the performance of their routine daily chores and activities, individuals regularly exchange knowledge and skills of various kinds (Moll, Veléz-Ibanez, & Greenberg, 1988; Veléz-Ibanez, 1988).

Information about the world outside the community is brought into the home through the media, by adult family members with experiences in the work place, and by children through their experiences at school. These links with outside groups provide new sources of knowledge and uses of language for Eastsiders. For example, like radio and television, school provides a steady flow of information about values, clothing styles, and new forms of language. School children acquire knowledge about dressing, speaking, and relating to members of the opposite sex that sometimes comes directly into conflict with what they have been taught in their home and community. At work, adults routinely engage in intercultural communication as they execute their job responsibilities and satisfy their own personal needs. It is through this complex set of transactions that this Mexicano community becomes fluent in the dominant Anglo culture while simultaneously participating in local Mexican culture (Rosaldo, 1985).

This brief sketch gives only a very general sense of the complex but rich cultural and linguistic contexts in which Eastside children live and grow. Although they share the experience of having to negotiate two cultures and languages during the course of their everyday lives, these Mexican immigrants come from all walks of life and social classes. The ways they adapt to life in the United States and socialize their children vary widely. Their social and economic conditions foster stable as well as dysfunctional home life in which acculturation to mainstream middle-class values and norms often spurs stressful cross-generational tensions. Gender roles, American popular culture, and the loss of Spanish are common issues inciting conflicts in parent-child relationships. Unemployment and underemployment are constant concerns of many Eastsiders. The Mexicano community also has to contend with campaigns by alcohol and tobacco companies that contribute to alcohol use and abuse as well as violence (Cuellar et al., 1992). This nexus of cultures and social and economic realities makes up the broader context surrounding the language socialization experiences that we will describe.

Using and learning language in Eastside

Eastsiders' use of language clearly reflects their rich and complex social reality. Some of the uses of language in the home and in the community are reminiscent of those brought from the old country; others are similar to the way language is used by middle-class English speakers; and some language uses reflect Eastsiders' unique life experiences in a multicultural world. Those uses of language originating in Mexico are clearly different and not shared by the middle-class English speakers who live nearby. For example, family members in many Eastside homes share traditional Mexican folktales and family histories. The rhetorical patterns that accompany this oral entertainment resemble the kind of extemporaneous speechmaking that takes place in many communities throughout Mexico (Guerra, 1991).

Although differences exist, there are also similarities in the ways that Mexicano and middle-class English speaking parents talk with their children. Pease-Alvarez (1986) found, for example, that Eastside parents scaffold children's talk in the same ways as parents in the majority language community (Brown, 1968; Holzman, 1972; Moerk, 1972; Corsaro, 1977; Garvey, 1977, 1979; Cherry, 1979a, 1979b). She illustrates many occasions when Mexicano parents regularly used clarification and elaboration requests that succeeded in getting their children to extend their verbal contributions. One mother (M), routinely used these kinds of question-answer interactions in the context of conversations about her son's (N) experiences at school. As in the following exchange, it was always the mother who initiated these conversations:

M: ¿Más estaba en tu mesa, hijo?
N: ¿Maestra? ¿De maestra mami?
M: No, de niños.
N: Alejandro, Demis . . . ¿Y quién más estaba en tu mesa, hijo?
N: ¿Maestra? ¿ De maestra mami?
M: No, de niños.
N: Alejandro, Demis . . . Este Fernando me dió un pedazo de tortilla.
M: ¿Sí?
N: Sí. El lo que quiere ser mi amigo mami.
M: ¿El lo quiere ser tu amigo?
N: Uh, huh.
M: ¿Y'l te dió la tortilla para eso mijo?
N: Sí. Y luego dió un pedazo a Demis. Mira el pedazo. Ese vato se comió un pedazo grandote de taco.
M: ¿ Y tu comías la tortilla que te dió?
N: De taco. Demis se comó y luego dijo no quiero. Dijo . . . te sirves tortilla entera. ¿Verdad, que sí?
M: Van a ser amigos, ¿verdad?
N: Sí. Y también las niñas van a ser amigas todas.

M: Who else was at your table, son?
N: Teacher? Teacher, mami?
M: No, (which) children (were at the table)?
N: Alejandro, Demis . . . Fernando gave me a piece of tortilla.
M: Yes?
N: Yes, he wants to be my friend, mami.
M: He wants to be your friend?
N: Uh, huh.
M: And he gave you a tortilla for that, son?

N: Yes, and he gave a piece to Demis. A piece this size (using his hands to illustrate the size). That guy ate a big piece of taco.
M: And did you eat the tortilla that he gave you?
N: Taco. Demis ate it and then he said he didn't want it. He said . . . serve yourself a whole tortilla. Really.
M: They're going to be friends, right?
N: Yes. And the girls are all going to be friends.

In the preceding example, the child – with his mother's encouragement – describes a past experience. Her questions help him provide more explicit information as well as details about the series of events that made up this experience and the consequences of the events. The result is a sequentially organized narrative account with a beginning, middle, and end.

Recently we have been trying to identify the source of this kind of scaffolding behavior and the extent to which it characterizes the conversations that other Eastside adults have with their children. With this in mind, we asked over fifty Eastside parents the question, "How do children learn to talk?" When responding to this questions, all but a handful of parents talked about what they have done to help their children learn. Some explained how they relied on modeling and repetition to teach their children language. Mrs. Garrido described this process in the following interview excerpt:

Nosotros los enseñamos. Cuando ellos empiecan hacer ruidos con su boquita ah ah, empezamos a decirles, Maaa Maaa. Y que ellos nos iran a la boca. Maa Maa . . . Entonces cuando ellos aprenden decir "Maa Maa," les decimos "Paa Paa" y asi eventualmente hasta que ellos empiecen. . . . Nosotros ayudamos a ellos.

We teach them. When they learn to make noises with the mouth, "ah ah," we begin to tell them, "maa maa." And they look at our mouth. "Maa Maa." Then when they learn to say, "Maa Maa," we say, "Paa Paa" until they say it. We help them.

Mrs. Barraza, who also emphasized her role in the language-learning process, told us that she began to support her children's language when they were newborns. As she sees it, her efforts also help her children develop other abilities (e.g., learning to crawl and to walk). However, unlike Mrs. Garrido, who focused on the role of direct instruction, Mrs. Barraza emphasized the role of conversation. As she notes in the following passage from our interview, she felt that the conversations that she had with her two-month old helped the baby take on the role of conversational partner:

Esta niña no tiene más que dos meses y le platica uno y ella quiere platicar para atrás. Ella le hace barulla a contestar para atrás y a mi se me hace chiste porque estaba bien chiquita tenía como mes y medio y le platicaba uno y ella hasta se esforzaba porque quería platicar o sea que quería platicar . . . Si se enseñan a hablar pronto se enseñan ellas a hacer todo más rápido porque ya saben comunicarse y sin embargo si son mas tardías para hablar se tardan para todo. Para caminar porque como no saben si uno no les platica no les pone a hacer las cosas ellas. No se enseñan. Entonces necesita uno enseñar al niño a que platique a que se mantenga parado para que se amacise a que se enseñen a gatear y todo eso.

This girl isn't more than two-months old and when one talks to her, she wants to talk back. She makes noises at you to answer back. I think it's funny because she is so little. She was about a month-and-a-half old and if someone spoke to her, she made faces as if she wanted to talk, she wanted to talk. . . . If they learn to talk early they learn to do everything more quickly because they know how to communicate and if they take longer to talk they take longer at [learning] everything. [They take longer] to walk, because since they don't know, one [an adult] doesn't talk with them and doesn't make them do things on their own. They don't learn by themselves. So one needs to teach the child to talk with you, to stand alone so he can get strong, to learn to crawl and all those things.

As these excerpts indicate, many Eastside parents see themselves as responsible and deliberate participants in their children's language learning. Like middle-class Anglo parents, they accommodate their speech to their children. Some also claim to involve their children in language teaching exchanges. Moreover, many of the individuals we interviewed also described how they taught a child or younger sibling to read and write. Many recounted how they had provided experiences and obtained materials that they felt would lead to or enhance their children's literacy development (e.g., providing trips to the library, purchasing crayons and paper, reading aloud to their children, engaging a third party to tutor their children). In short, it is evident from the parents' perspectives that they are active participants in their children's language development.

In Eastside, language socialization is also shaped by the need for children to learn to negotiate and help others negotiate two or more languages and cultures. Most notable are those occasions when bilingual children are called upon to translate and interpret for adults. Vasquez (1989) and Shannon (1987) found that the role of family translator places children as language and culture brokers for adults, a role that shifts the power and knowledge of family dynamics at the same time that it provides unique opportunities for child language use and language learning. While translating and interpreting for adults, children must often make important decisions about the meaning of specialized vocabulary and even the rights and privileges of relatives and friends. These experiences also provide children with the unique opportunity to develop their second language at the same time that they maintain a high degree of fluency in Spanish. Recent research suggests further that interpreting real-life situations and translating written materials can enhance the children's metalinguistic awareness and language proficiency (Malakoff & Hakuta, 1991).

The following example of one bilingual child's first experience as family translator illustrates the critical role a child can play in negotiating her mother's health care (Shannon, 1987). This short segment of a longer conversation depicts the initial stages of the development of a conscious positioning of the interpreter vis-à-vis language and social interaction. The fledging efforts of 11-year-old Leti to translate for her mother, Mrs. Macias, and her mother's doctor, are as follows:

Doctor:	Good, better? Terrific. Progress examination today.
Leti:	Privacy?
Doctor:	Progress exam.
Leti:	Oh. (giggles)
Doctor:	How do you feel about returning to work on the first of September?
Leti:	First of September? That's when we're going to school?
Doctor:	No. **I want your mom to respond.** How does she feel about returning to work?
Leti:	Oh . . . *¿Que cómo se sentiría si va a trabajar el primero de septiembre?* [How would you feel if you go to work the first of September?]
Doctor:	(Addressing Mrs. Macias as he begins the examination) *A la derecha, por favor* [(Turn) to the right (side), please.]
Mrs. Macias:	*Dile que yo no me siento bien pero si el quiere mandarme que . . .* [**Tell him** that I don't feel well but if he wants to send me that . . .]
Leti:	She doesn't feel well, but if you want to send her, it's OK with her.
Doctor:	Well, we don't want to send her if she's not going to be able to work.
Mrs. Macias:	*¿Qué dice,* Leti? [**What did he say,** Leti?]
Leti:	*Que no la quiere mandar si no puede trabajar.* [That he doesn't want to send her if she can't work.]
Doctor:	But I would like to see her get back and we'll work hard and fast in these next couple of weeks.

Although Leti made mistakes when translating and had to be prompted (boldface), she succeeded in adequately conveying each participant's meaning to the other. The prompts provided by her mother and the doctor help her satisfy the expectations ascribed to the role of interpreter. After repeated experiences translating, Leti developed the expertise needed to assume the role of official translator for her family, a position formerly occupied by an older brother.

In Eastside homes, children also frequently translate printed materials for their parents and other members of the family's social network. Young children are often asked to translate letters from school as well as from other institutions; they sometimes translate excerpts from English textbooks and storybooks that are assigned as homework; and some Eastside elementary teachers encourage students to regularly read aloud and, if necessary, translate English books for parents and other family members. Often teenagers are responsible for translating information on bills, income tax forms, and job applications. In her study of the relationship between oral language and literacy in Eastside family interactions, Vasquez (1989) describes several occasions when adolescents were responsible for translating written documents. On these occasions, the adolescents often needed assistance to determine the texts' meaning. This need for mediation commonly led to an elaborate collaborative effort and a pooling of resources. For example, in the following exchange, 17-year-old Rosa seeks help from Vasquez and others present to negotiate the meaning of the U.S. Internal Revenue Service's SU 32 form so that she can elicit the appropriate responses from her Spanish-speaking relative.

Rosa: Total the number of allowances you are claiming. That means the dependents, right?
Vasquez: No, including yourself.
Rosa: Including yourself. *¿Eres tu y tu niño, verdad?*
            [It is you and your child, right?]
Relative: Uh-huh.
Rosa: *¿No más?*
            [Only?]
Relative: Uh-huh.
Rosa: I claim exemption from withholding because this year I do not expect a full refund. Should we do that?
Vasquez: That . . . always.
Rosa: I think we should do that *porque mira* [because look] "last year I did not owe any Federal." (reading the form) . . . She didn't work, she doesn't work, so she can't be that.
Vasquez: So that's out.
Rosa: She can't be an exempt because she is not a full-time student.
Vasquez: Right!
Rosa: It's got to be this year. I don't expect to owe any federal income tax except to have a right to a full refund.

As evident in this exchange, children, and especially family translators, rehearse functional language skills other than those of the home culture. In collaborative encounters such as the preceding one, they uncover the meaning and social functions inherent in a piece of written text. For example, Rosa realizes that understanding the function of the SU 32 form is essential to helping her relative provide the information requested in the form. Later in the conversation, she advises her relative when and where to use the form during the job interview. Thus, Rosa is required to provide more than a superficial translation of the statements if she is to adequately convey the meaning of the form's technical language – for example, allowances, claim, withholding, exemption. When she finds that her own knowledge and experience are insufficient, she calls upon the experience of others, in this case Vasquez, to augment her own. Like other family translators we know, Rosa meets the demands of the second language and culture by pooling available resources.

To summarize, Eastsiders draw upon a broad range of cultural and linguistic resources as they negotiate their daily lives. Some of their abilities and experiences are grounded in uniquely Mexicano patterns of knowing and interacting. Some ways of using and thinking about language, however, are shared by other cultures. Yet others are shaped by the users' experience of living and working in bilingual/multicultural communities. Children and parents are key players in one another's language socialization – parents perceive themselves to be deliberate and central participants in their children's language development, but children, too, are responsible for helping adults negotiate transactions with outside institutions. Thus, language socialization is a mutual endeavor, with adults and children taking responsibility for one another as they negotiate language and culture.

Language socialization in school

What happens when the school bell rings and language minority children like those we have described enter the world of the classroom for the first time? Many enter an unfamiliar world where they encounter a set of language-use practices that differ markedly from the way language is used in their homes and communities. English, their second language, is likely to be the primary medium of instruction. Teachers tend to do most of the talking, and their talk often focuses on a predetermined and decontextualized inventory of skills and topics. As a number of researchers have shown, student opportunities to talk often occur within the context of the recitation script – a teacher-dominated discourse sequence that bears little resemblance to the modes of talk that prevail in students' homes and communities (Goodlad, 1984; Ramirez, 1991). Teachers initiate this discourse sequence by either lecturing or having students produce or read a written text that eventually becomes the basis for a series of teacher questions that test students' knowledge of facts or skills (Tharp & Gallimore, 1989; Mehan, 1979). In most cases, teachers follow students' responses with a short evaluatory comment or another test question. As a number of researchers have described, the practice of asking for information that the questioner already possesses seldom occurs in the homes of many ethnic minority children (Philips, 1983; Heath, 1983). In Eastside homes, questions tend to focus on information that the questioner does not possess.

Despite the popularity of instructional approaches such as cooperative learning and peer tutoring that encourage greater student talk, the preceding recitation script continues to prevail in many North American classrooms that serve language-minority students. In our own observations of Eastside classrooms, we have noted occasions when recitation has crept into learning events that were intended to provide students with alternative ways of using language. For example, children's writing conferences or book discussion groups often become occasions when children use known-answer questions with one another. Even the teachers participating in these events frequently revert to this same kind of questioning. For example, the following conversation between a fifth-grade teacher and her bilingual students was her first attempt to engage students in an open-ended discussion of the book *Johnny Appleseed*. Prior to this, the teacher had participated in a teacher-training workshop that emphasized the role of student-centered discussion. Nevertheless, as the following excerpt from their discussion illustrates, the teacher directed and controlled the flow of the discourse as she fired known-answer questions at the students.

Teacher: So who can tell me what the book's about?
Student 1: Johnny Appleseed.
Teacher: Okay, who was Johnny Appleseed?
Student 2: About a – a kid who went around planting apple seeds.
Teacher: Planting apple seeds. Where did he plant 'em?
Student 2: All over the world.
Teacher: All over the world – or what . . .
Student 3: All over the country.
Student 4: Yeah.
Teacher: What country is that?
Student 3: Massachusetts.
Teacher: Okay, and where else?
Student 4: Ohio.
Student 3: Ohio.
Student 4: Indiana.

Teacher: All over the United States, huh? OK . . . How is it that he
            got to be called Johnny Appleseed?
Student 3: 'Cause he's . . .
Student 2: He was a real man.

Teachers' attempts to force students to adhere to unfamiliar patterns of
interaction like the one just described may ultimately lead to teacher-
student conflicts. Eventually these conflicts may impede students' academic achievement. For example, Piestrup (1973) found that when teachers in first-grade classrooms corrected and negatively sanctioned African-
American children's nonstandard pronunciations, children increased their
use of nonstandard English over the course of the school year. The
opposite was the case for African-American children enrolled in classrooms where the teachers did not correct the children's language. Erickson (1987) argues that this kind of conflict fosters a teacher-student
relationship devoid of trust. As he explains,

Teachers and students in such regressive relationships do not bond with each
other. Mutual trust is sacrificed. Over time students become increasingly
alienated from school . . . The more alienated the student becomes, the less
they persist in doing schoolwork. Thus, they fall further and further behind
in academic achievement. The student becomes either actively resistant –
seen as alienated and incorrigible or passively resistant – fading into the
woodwork as a well-behaved, low-achieving student (p. 348).

Thus, when the patterns of language use or the patterns of social interactions that children bring to the school are ignored or denigrated by their
teachers, the ensuing relationship may threaten the students' academic development.

To make matters worse, language use practices that originate in the
school can also contribute to problems at home. In some cases, conflicts
arise between parents and children over the values they feel are conveyed
by language use practices that their children bring from the school into
the home. For example, many Eastside parents disapprove of teachers
who emphasize the individual rights of students over the collective rights
of the family. From their vantage point, the critical discussion of family
matters by children and teachers at school represents a threat to the family
structure and parents' authority. They worry that teachers will encourage
their children to reveal information that may threaten their family's security (e.g., information about their immigration status, discipline practices).

Wong Fillmore (1991) provides a poignant discussion of the way
language policies in some schools have threatened the socialization environment available to children at home. In a recent study that focused on
the language-use practices in the homes of over 300 children of immigrant

parents, she found that preschool aged children who were enrolled in English-only or bilingual programs are particularly vulnerable to the loss of their primary language. As these children acquired English at school, they tended to rely more and more on English in their interactions with parents at home. In the case of parents who did not speak or understand English, communication between parents and children was impaired. Thus, the means by which parents socialized and enculturated their children was lost. As Wong Fillmore puts it,

When parents are unable to talk to their children, they cannot easily convey to them their values, beliefs, understandings, or wisdom about how to cope with their experiences. They cannot teach them about the meaning of work, or about personal responsibility, or what it means to be a moral or ethical person in a world with too many choices and too few guide posts to follow . . . When parents lose the means for socializing and influencing their children, rifts develop and families lose the intimacy that comes from shared beliefs and understandings (p. 343).

Connecting the worlds of schools, homes, and communities

Language minority children bring a rich variety of linguistic and cultural resources to the classroom. Some of these are very different from resources found at school. When schools don't incorporate or build upon the language-use patterns that have contributed to successful learning in students' homes and communities, they waste the resources that children bring to school. The results can be devastating. Conflicts may arise at home and at school that threaten students', parents', and teachers' ability to interact and learn from one another. In contrast, by acknowledging and building upon the meanings and experiences that students bring to school, teachers and administrators help foster healthy relationships between parents, teachers, and students. They also make schools places where students can benefit from experiences that have contributed to their learning in other settings. However, before this can happen, teachers and administrators need to learn about their students' lives outside of school. In doing this, they cannot simply rely on generalizations about the socialization experiences available to a group of children that shares the same language or cultural affiliation as their students. In the United States and Canada, groups classified under a single ethnic or linguistic label (e.g., Mexican-American, Spanish-speaking) have developed different values and interaction patterns. Even Mexican-origin students who live in the same community and share the same socioeconomic standing have access to very different learning experiences because of the variability in their linguistic, regional, and generational backgrounds. Teachers need to know about and understand the sociocultural backgrounds of *their* own students.

One way in which this can be accomplished is by having teachers and university-based researchers collaborate on ethnographic studies of students' communities. This in turn can lead to meaningful connections between curriculum and community. For example, Luis Moll (1992) and his colleagues at the University of Arizona have spent several years collaborating with teachers so that they can better understand and utilize students' cultural resources in classroom settings. Underlying this work is the principle that "the students" community represents a resource of enormous importance for educational change and improvement" (p. 21). Together, teachers and researchers have interviewed parents and other community members to identify the information and skills that are available to Mexicano households through an elaborate set of social networks that connects these households to other households and institutions. This set of information and skills, that Moll and his colleagues term *funds of knowledge,* consists of the "cultural practices and bodies of knowledge and information that households use to survive, to get ahead or to thrive" (p. 21). Examples of funds of knowledge available to families that were uncovered by the research team include information about the cultivation of plants, seeding, water distribution and management, animal husbandry, veterinary medicine, ranch economy, mechanics, carpentry, masonry, electrical wiring, fencing, folk remedies, herbal cures, midwifery, archaeology, biology, and mathematics.

Teacher-researchers participating in this work have organized their curriculum around these funds of knowledge. They have sought out and used the expertise of community members to teach them and their students about the specific areas of specialization that they have then built into their lessons. For example, Moll (1992) describes a teacher who developed a social network within her students' community of experts who contributed to a curriculum unit on construction. Experts included the students, who had participated in various research projects about construction, their parents and relatives, the parents of other students in the school, and resources that were available to the teacher through her own set of social networks (e.g., other school staff members, community members, university personnel). These experts shared their experiences in construction, participated in student-led interviews, and helped students design and implement their own construction project. In essence, this teacher worked to develop an approach to schooling that Moll describes as "teaching through the community" (p. 23).

Such research collaboration can be an important component of teacher-education programs. Under Vasquez's supervision, university students, some of whom will go on to become grade-level teachers, who are enrolled in a research methods practicum become involved in projects investigating the literacy and language-use practices available to Mexicano/Latino children in home and community contexts. As participant observers at an after-school computer literacy program, the students assist children with their activities – computer games and telecommunication dialogues with an electronic entity known as *El Maga* – and conduct research projects on such topics as children's problem-solving strategies, language choices, and uses of literacy. Data sources for these projects include the students' ethnographic fieldnotes, interviews, and audiorecordings of the children's interactions at the computer.

Throughout the practicum, culture, language, and learning are key topics of student-led seminars and teleconference discussions between Vasquez's student and other university students participating in similar research in East Lansing, Michigan. During these discussions, the university students share and critically examine their own and others' assumptions and generalizations about minority group members and their communities from a safe distance. Over electronic mail they openly respond to each other's comments when the topic is of a sensitive nature, such as pointing out each other's reliance on cultural stereotypes. On several occasions, students have publicly confronted their own narrow and unexamined perceptions about Mexicano/Latinos. For example, Lena, the 22-year-old daughter of a Mexican businessman, came to terms with her own negative characterization of Mexican-Americans. As she worked with the children and their families, she realized that her experience as a successful student in U.S. schools could not be generalized to all students of Mexican descent. For her, the realization that effort alone does not guarantee success was particularly painful. As she aptly stated, *"Mis compañeros de clase sabian más que yo, de las situación social de los mequico-americanos. Yo siempre he creido que era su culpa porque eran unos flojos y analphabetos."* [My own classmates knew better than I the social conditions of Mexican-Americans. I've always thought that it was their fault because they were lazy and illiterate.]

Teachers and school administrators can also learn about their students' families and communities without the help of researchers or university professors. Visiting students' homes, community centers, and community-based organizations and institutions may be an important first step. Like ethnographers, teachers can develop a set of interview questions and/or issues to discuss with parents and community members during these visits. The following list of interview topics and questions touches upon aspects of family and community life that may enhance teachers' understanding of their students.

- **Information sources in the community.**
  How do you find out about community events?

What community events do you participate in?

When you need information (e.g., about health care, jobs, social services), who do you go to?

- **Areas of expertise.**

What abilities and talents do you have?

What hobbies do you have?

What do you enjoy doing in your spare time?

Who do you know who brings special talents from your homeland? Describe those talents.

- **Family history.**

Tell me about your family background. Where do you come from?

How long have you lived in the area?

How did life in your home country differ from your life here?

- **Language use practices.**

Do you or others in your family share stories with your children?

What are your children's favorite stories?

What kinds of things does the family talk about (e.g., around the dinner table, at bedtime, at family gatherings)?

- **Children's everyday life at home.**

Describe a typical day in your child's life.

How do children express themselves (i.e., their needs, feelings, humor, worries)?

Do your children participate in activities that you feel are educational (e.g., *ballet folklórico,* Brownies, catechism)?

- **Parents' theories about learning.**

How do children learn (i.e., to talk, read, write, do math)?

What kinds of experiences help children learn?

What kinds of things do you do with your children that helps them learn these different things?

What do others in your family do to help them learn?

What can I do as a teacher to help your child learn in the classroom?

- **Parents' views on schooling.**

How will your children benefit from school?

How does your schooling compare to the schooling your children are receiving?

What are your major concerns about the education your children are receiving?

Teachers can use other ways to find out about their students' lives outside of school. Teachers who are hesitant to venture into their students' communities may find it less threatening to invite parents and representatives of different community groups to share their views and experiences with school members during formal meetings or panel discussions. One teacher we know regularly shares an interactive journal with his students' parents. In this journal he writes about his concerns and elicits information about a variety of topics. In addition to responding to his queries, parents voice their concerns about their children and the teacher's instruction. Teachers can also elicit the help of community members when it comes to interpreting events or phenomena that teachers don't understand or find troubling. For example, Cynthia Ballenger (1992), a preschool teacher who works with Haitian children, describes the conversations she has had with Haitian teachers, parents, and community members about the way they use language to discipline and reprimand children. Through these conversations, she has learned about the beliefs that underlie the way Haitian adults interact verbally with children and how these beliefs differ from her own. As she explains in the following excerpt from a recent article:

I also value greatly the extent to which these conversations, by forcing me to attempt to emphathize with and understand a view of the world that is in many ways very different from my customary one, have put me in a position to reexamine values and principles that had become inaccessible under layers of assumptions.'' (p. 207)

Community-based research involving teachers and students themselves can become an important part of the curriculum. For thirty years, the curriculum in Elliot Wiggington's high school English class has revolved around students' efforts to learn about the mountain community where they live (Wiggington, 1985). Frustrated by his students' lack of interest and engagement with a traditional grammar-oriented approach to language arts, Wiggington embarked upon a period of self-reflection and experimentation in the early 1960s that has continued unabated. Spurred by a colleague's reminder that ''the beauty into which you were born is often the beauty you never see,'' Wiggington and his students decided to investigate the resources that surrounded them in their own community. Over the years their research, mostly captured through oral interviews and films, has focused on the knowledge, practical abilities, and aesthetic accomplishments of different community members. A sampling of topics that have been the focus of their research is contained in the following list of chapter titles that are included in the books that Wiggington and his students have written:

Hide tanning

Hunting lore

Turkey shoots

Haint tales

Other scary stories

Banjos and dulcimers

Beekeeping

Conclusions

The United States, Canada, and other English-speaking countries are enjoying a period of increasing linguistic and cultural diversity. In many urban schools, students who speak languages other than English are now in the majority. As this chapter has sought to indicate, students from non-English language backgrounds are talented and resourceful participants in complex and dynamic communities. The linguistic, social, and cultural resources that these children have acquired in their families and communities are a natural developmental basis on which to plan and build their formal education. Building on students' existing funds of skills and knowledge cannot only serve to maintain these precious resources but at the same time is an effective means for extending their resources to include skills and knowledge in and about a new language and a new culture. Unfortunately, however, the linguistic and sociocultural resources that second language learners bring with them to school are often unknown and unfamiliar to grade level and even second language teachers who are charged with their education. They, therefore, go unsupported and untapped.

If contemporary schools are to develop appropriate and effective educational programs for the diverse students in their charge, then concerted efforts will need to be undertaken to understand and become familiar with the sociocultural-linguistic backgrounds of all students. To the extent that educators are part of the majority cultural group, they will have direct access to and most certainly intuitions about the backgrounds and therefore, the needs of majority group children. Indeed, it is widely accepted that schools reflect, impart, and contribute to the social values and ways of the majority group (McGroarty, 1986). What is called for in contemporary education is an extension of the bases for formulating educational programs to include knowledge about the backgrounds and needs of minority as well as majority group students. This is not a task to be undertaken only by university researchers for the sake of scholarship or by curriculum specialists who will make the fruits of their work available to teachers at some later and usually belated date. Rather, it is a task for teachers who have direct contact with minority language students and who are in most need of this information. A number of alternative strategies that teachers can use to extend their bases for planning the education of minority language students, on their own or with the collaboration of others, have been described in this chapter.

References

Ballenger, C. (1992). Because you like us: The language of control. *Harvard Educational Review, 62,* 2: 199–208.

Brown, R. (1968). The development of the wh questions in child speech. *Journal of Verbal Learning and Verbal Behavior, 7,* 279–290.

Cherry, L. J. (1979a). A sociocognitive approach to language development and its implications for education. In O. K. Garnica & M. L. King (Eds.), *Language, children, and society* (pp. 115–134). Oxford: Pergamon Press.

Cherry, L. J. (1979b). The role of adult's requests for clarification in the language development of children. In R. O. Freedel (Ed.), *Discourse processing: A multi-disciplinary approach II* (pp. 273–286). NJ: Ablex.

Corsaro, W. A. (1977). The clarification request as a feature of adult interactive styles with young children. *Language in Society, 6,* 183–207.

Cuéllar, J. B., Alaniz, M. L., Stephens, D., De Lucio, A., Martinez, G., & Jarvis, N. (March, 1992). *Environmental factors affecting alcohol use: An ethnographic study.* Paper presented at the annual meeting of the National Association for Chicano Studies. San Antonio, Texas.

Erickson, F. D. (1987). Transformation and school success: The politics and culture of educational achievement. *Anthropology & Education Quarterly, 18,* 4: 335–356.

Fonseca, O., & Moreno, L. (1984). *Jaripo, Pueblo de Migrantes,* Lázaro Cárdenas, A. C.: Centro de Estudios de la Revolución Mexicana.

Garvey, C. (1977). The contingent query: A dependent act in conversation. M. Lewis & L. Rosenblum (Eds.), *Interaction, conversation, and the development of language: The origin of behavior* (pp. 63–73). New York: Wiley.

Goodlad, J. (1984). *A place called school.* New York: McGraw-Hill.

Guerra, J. (1991). *The acquisition and use of literacy skills and literate behaviors in families of Mexican origin.* Unpublished doctoral dissertation, University of Illinois, Chicago.

Heath, S. B. (1983). *Ways with words: Language, life and work in communities and classrooms.* Cambridge: Cambridge University Press.

Heath, S. B. (1986). Sociocultural contexts of language development. In *Beyond language: Social and cultural factors in schooling language minority students* (pp. 143–186). Los Angeles: Evaluation, Dissemination, and Assessment Center.

Holzman, M. (1972). The use of interrogative forms in the verbal interaction of three mothers and their children. *Journal of Psycholinguistic Research, 1,* 4: 311–336.

Malakoff, M., & Hakuta, K. (1991). Translation skill and metalinguistic awareness in bilinguals. In E. Bialystok (Ed.), *Language processing in bilingual children* (pp. 141–167). Cambridge: Cambridge University Press.

McGroarty, M. (1986). Educator's response to sociocultural diversity: Implications for practice. In *Beyond language: Social and cultural factors in schooling language minority students* (pp. 299–343). Los Angeles: Evaluation, Dissemination and Assessment Center.

Mehan, H. (1979). What time is it, Denise?: Asking known information questions in classroom discourse. *Theory into practice, 18,* 4: pp. 285–294.

Moerk, E. (1972). Principles of interaction in language learning. *Merrill-Palmer Quarterly, 8*(3), 229–257.

Moll, L. C. (1992). Bilingual studies and community analysis: Some recent trends. In K. Hakuta & L. Pease-Alvarez (Eds.), *Educational Researcher, 21,* 2: 20–24.

Moll, L. C., Vélez-Ibanez, C. G., & Greenberg, J. (1988). *Project implementation plan. Community knowledge and classroom practice: Combining resources for literacy instruction* (Tech. Rep. No. L-10). Tucson: University of Arizona, College of Education and Bureau of Applied Research in Anthropology.

Ochs, E. (1988). *Culture and language development.* Cambridge: Cambridge University Press.

Pease-Alvarez, L., (1986). *Home and school contexts for language learning: A case study of two Mexican-American bilingual preschoolers.* Unpublished doctoral dissertation, Stanford University, Stanford.

Pease-Alvarez, L., & Mangiola, L. (in press). Learning and teaching together. In S. Hudelson & J. Lindfors (Eds.), *Working together: Collaborative research in language education.* Urbana, IL: National Council of Teachers of English.

Pease-Alvarez, L., & Vasquez, O. A. (1990). Sharing language and technical expertise around the computer. *Computers in the Schools, 7,* 91–107.

Philips, S. U. (1983). *The invisible culture: Communication in classroom and community on the Warm Springs Indian Reservation.* New York: Longman.

Piestrup, A. (1973). *Black dialect interference and accommodation of reading instruction first grade.* Monograph No. 4. Berkeley: Language-Behavior Research Laboratory.

Ramirez, D. J. (1991). *Final report: Longitudinal study of structured English immersion strategy, early-exit and late-exit transitional bilingual education programs for language minority children.* Washington, DC: Office of Bilingual Education.

Rosaldo, R. (1985). *Assimilation revisited* (Working Paper Series No. 9). Stanford University: Stanford Center for Chicano Research.

Schieffelin, B. B., & Ochs, E. (1986). Language socialization. *The Annual Review of Anthropology, 15,* 163–191.

Shannon, S. M. (1987). *English in el barrio: A sociolinguistic study of second language contact.* Unpublished doctoral dissertation, Stanford University, Stanford.

Tharp, R., & Gallimore, R. (1989). *Rousing minds to life: Teaching, learning, and schooling in social context.* New York: Cambridge University Press.

Vasquez, O. A. (1989). *Connecting oral language strategies to literacy: An ethnographic study among four Mexican immigrant families.* Unpublished doctoral dissertation, Stanford University, Stanford.

Vasquez, O. A., Pease-Alvarez, L., & Shannon, S. M. (in press). *Language learning and language socialization in a Mexicano community.* Cambridge: Cambridge University Press.

Veléz-Ibanez, C. (1988). Networks of exchange among Mexicans in the U.S. and Mexico: Local level mediating responses to national and international transformations. *Urban Anthropology and Studies of Cultural Systems and World Economic Development, 17,* 1: 27–52.

Wiggington, E. (1985). *Sometimes a shining moment: The foxfire experience, twenty years teaching in a high school classroom.* Anchor Books: Garden City, NY.

Wong Fillmore, L. (1991). When learning a second language means losing the first. *Early Childhood Research Quarter, 6,* 3: 323–346.

Ybarra-Frausto, T. (1984). I can still hear the applause. *La farandula chicana: Carpas y tandas de variedad.* In N. Kanelos (Ed.), *Hispanic theatre in the United States.* Houston: Arte Publica Press.

5 English as a second language in preschool programs

Patton O. Tabors and
Catherine E. Snow

In the past decade, a large number of non-English-speaking immigrant families, many with young children, have arrived in countries such as the United States, Canada, and Australia, where English is the primary language of schooling.[1] As a result, many children in these countries are beginning school with little or no established proficiency in English. Successfully educating these children is now a major challenge for educators in these nations. Further, where once assimilation was the predominant language policy in these countries, sensitivity to the importance of maintaining alternative languages and cultures has replaced the old ''sink or swim'' mentality. In fact, official policy for public education in these nations now calls for specialized educational services of some variety for children who do not speak English when they enter school. These policies and their implementation take many different forms, but the prevailing attitude is that successful schooling in a second language requires that programmatic adjustments be made in the educational setting.

Not surprisingly, the arrival of large numbers of immigrant families has not only had an impact on public education in English-speaking countries, but has had an effect on preschool education as well. In the United States, for example, Head Start and other types of preschools have experienced a sharp increase in the number of children enrolled from non-English-speaking homes.[2] Children from families whose home language is not English represent both a challenge and an opportunity for preschool educators: The challenge is to develop preschool programs that

---

1 For instance, during the 1980s, an estimated 9 million immigrants came to the United States, slightly more than in the great wave of immigration between 1901 and 1910. As a result, the U.S. Department of Education estimates that at least two million children, or 5 percent of the present school age population, have limited English proficiency. Further, an additional 3.5 million children of immigrants from families whose first language is not English are expected to enter the public schools in the 1990s (*Newsweek,* February 1, 1991).
2 One analysis of Head Start enrollment figures shows that of Head Start's total student population of 466,000 children in 1990, approximately 20 percent (93,000) were non-English dominant (Kresh, 1990).

can provide appropriate cognitive and linguistic enrichment for these children; the opportunity is to give them an early start in the process of learning a second language before they enter school.

By concentrating on the question of how a second language is acquired, however, we do not mean to imply that a second language should supplant or replace the child's first language; in fact, if learning a new language at this young age means the loss of the first language, then the process may well be counterproductive for the child's future success, both in school and out (Hakuta, 1986). Preschool educators, therefore, should be prepared to encourage parents to maintain the home language throughout this period, so their children can develop world knowledge, vocabulary, and discourse strategies in their first language at home while developing expertise in the new language at school.

The purpose of this chapter is to investigate the challenges and the opportunities that arise when preschool-aged children from homes where English is not the first language are placed in a setting where they have the option of learning English as a second language. The chapter is divided into three sections: (1) a discussion of the course of language development in the preschool period; (2) a discussion of the developmental sequence that has been observed when preschool-aged children are exposed to a second language; and (3) a discussion of how preschool classrooms can function as second language learning environments for these children.

Language development of young children

Preschool-aged children already have substantial, although not complete, control over their first language. Normally developing children of 3, 4, and 5 already understand what language is for and know a good deal about how their first language works. They have developed an extensive vocabulary, they can use all of the basic grammatical structures, and they have begun to learn when, where, and with whom it is appropriate to use certain language forms. Further, they have begun to gain control over a variety of discourse forms as well: scripts (''You go to someone's house, eat cake, and open presents.''), personal reports (''Yesterday I saw a tiger at the zoo.''), descriptions (''It was the baby teddy bear who was on the tree limb.''), event casts (''And now he's flying through the air.''), plans (''When I get to Grandma's house, I'm going to bake a pie.''), explanations (''I know Kristin had gym 'cause I saw her outside.''), and arguments (''I need to go now 'cause Mom is waiting.''). All of these linguistic skills will, of course, continue to increase in sophistication during the school years, but the foundations have already been developed by the time a child is of preschool age.

Some preschool-aged children have not only developed these linguistic skills in a first language, but have developed them in two languages simultaneously. As Goodz (see Chapter 3) points out, *simultaneous acquisition* of two languages is now a well-documented phenomenon; children who are exposed to two linguistic systems from a very early age demonstrate a capacity to keep their two languages separate and display an early understanding of the different situations when one or the other of their languages is appropriate (see Fantini, 1985; Genesee, 1989; Saunders, 1988; Taeschner, 1983, for case studies; see Meisel, 1989, concerning evidence against language confusion). Far from being a handicap, the process of acquiring two languages from a very early age is now seen to have cognitive as well as social benefits.

Yet other children acquire a second language after the basis for their first language has been established. This *sequential acquisition* of a second language occurs, for instance, when a young child enters preschool where the home language is not the language used in the classroom. This is the form of language acquisition that will be discussed in this chapter.

Second language development in preschool settings

When a preschool-aged child enters an environment where a second language is used, it is necessary for that child to adjust to this new situation. At this time, the child must realize that an entirely new language is required with a new vocabulary, a new set of rules for grammar and morphology, and a new set of social conventions. This realization, and the resulting effort that must then be expended to acquire the new language, present the child with both social and cognitive challenges. In this section we will discuss the general developmental sequence for young second language learners and then the factors that may influence that developmental sequence.

The developmental sequence

Researchers have noted a consistent developmental sequence for young children acquiring a second language: First, there may be a period of time when the child continues to use the home language even in second language situations; second, most children then enter a nonverbal period; following this period, children begin to use telegraphic and formulaic phrases in the new language; and, finally, children begin to develop productive use of the second language.

HOME LANGUAGE USE

When young children find themselves in a social situation where those around them speak a different language, there are really only two options: They can continue to speak the language they already know or they can stop talking altogether.

Some children initially pursue the first of these options. In a study of preschool-aged children from a variety of linguistic backgrounds attending an English-speaking nursery school program, Tabors (1987) observed a Brazilian boy, Joaquim, during his first day in the classroom where no one else spoke Portuguese, his home language:

At lunch: Joaquim tried some yogurt from his lunch, then pushed it away telling me something in Portuguese (which must have involved an explanation for why he wasn't going to eat it). After lunch he asked Johanna [one of the teachers] a definite question in Portuguese. She shook her head and said she didn't understand. Later he tried it on me. I also said I didn't understand. He didn't seem distressed but he didn't get an answer either.

Yasushi, a Japanese child in the same classroom, chose to try to speak Japanese only to the other Asian children in the classroom. Unfortunately, the two children he spoke to were Taiwanese and Korean and could not respond to him in Japanese. In each of these cases, unsuccessful initial efforts convinced these children that they would not be understood if they used their home language, and therefore, each discontinued the attempt to speak it in the classroom.

Some children, however, have been observed to persist in the use of their home language in similar situations. In a study involving forty second language learning children ranging in age from 18 months to 12 years, Saville-Troike (1987) found that 3- to 7-year-old children were willing to engage in what she terms "dilingual discourse" for some time after arriving in a setting where a different language was spoken. By dilingual discourse, Saville-Troike means that the children continued to speak their home language as if those around them could understand them. In fact, those around them often did answer them, using, of course, the language that the new arrivals could not understand. Saville-Troike reports that this form of communication "was generally effective for achieving desired ends when the children were involved in play, especially when there were objects to be manipulated. When context alone did not suffice for meaning to be inferred, however, the response to an unintelligible verbalization was frequently a blank look."

The older children in Saville-Troike's study came to realize quite quickly that this form of communication would not work; however, two younger children, Chinese brothers of 3 and 4, continued to use their home language for several months when communicating with anyone in their English-speaking nursery school classroom. When the older child was asked by a Chinese interviewer why he had finally stopped using Chinese in the classroom after two months of dilingual discourse, he replied that he "knew that they could not understand him, and he realized that they were not going to learn Chinese. He said that since he was learning English, he would use that language instead."

THE NONVERBAL PERIOD

Sooner or later, then, children faced with a social situation in which their home language is not useful for communication will abandon attempts to communicate in that language and enter a period when they do not talk at all. This period has been observed by a number of previous researchers who have termed it the "silent or mute period."

In Ervin-Tripp's (1974) study of American children learning French in Geneva, for instance, the researcher found that many of the children "said nothing for many months" and that her own children, ages 5 and 6½, "began speaking after six and eight weeks of immersion in the school setting." Itoh and Hatch (1978) observed a 2½-year-old Japanese child, Takahiro, who was not only silent but also socially isolated. During his first three months at nursery school, he spent most of his time on a tricycle as far away as possible from the other children. Itoh and Hatch called this a "rejection period" for Takahiro. Hakuta (1974) also observed a mute period with the Japanese girl he studied. Although he called her Uguisu, which means *nightingale* in Japanese, it took from October, when she arrived in the United States from Japan, until the following April for the nightingale to begin to sing in English. During the intervening time, she was attending kindergarten and playing with neighborhood English-speaking friends, but, much to the researcher's chagrin, she was not producing any English.

For all of these children, the realization that they could not communicate with those around them in their home language meant that they stopped *talking*. But this did not necessarily mean that they stopped *communicating*. Except for Takahiro, who isolated himself from his classmates, most of the young children who have been studied in these circumstances found alternative ways of trying to communicate with those around them. This is why we are calling this the nonverbal, rather than the silent, period. Although the children do not produce utterances during this time, most engage in various forms of nonverbal communication with others in their classrooms.

Tabors (1987) found that the use of nonverbal tactics by the second language learners was most common in the first few months. When in distress, the children would cry out or whimper, attracting the attention of an adult to come and help. When they wanted to procure an object or wanted to get help doing something, they would point and often mime their requests until the message got across. And when they wanted the name for an object in English, the second language learners would hold it up in front of someone else, usually an adult. In order for this behavior to be successful, of course, the communicative partner had to be perceptive about what the children wanted and willing to follow through on the request.

Interestingly, this form of communication was so pervasive at the beginning of the school year in this classroom – where more than half of the students were non-English speakers – that even one English-speaking child, Amanda, seemed to adopt the behavior:

During snack, Amanda came over to Johanna [one of the teachers] and started mugging and miming and pointing towards the table where a bowl of grated cheese was located. During this mugging she squinched up her face into a grimace/smile while closing her eyes and gesturing strongly with her arm. Johanna refused to "play the game" of guessing what Amanda wanted. Rachael kindly interpreted that Amanda wanted cheese. Johanna explained that there was already cheese on the pizza. Several more times during snack, Amanda "mimed" a request – but Johanna ignored her, seeming a bit perplexed by the behavior. Later, at lunch time, Amanda used the same "helpless act" with me, needing extra encouragement to get her lunch and pull in her chair.

After this one day, however, Amanda ceased producing this kind of behavior, perhaps because it didn't receive the kind of deference she had hoped it would. Nonetheless, it seems likely that the exaggerated gesturing and facial expressions were an overdramatized version of behaviors that Amanda saw around her among the second language learning children, behaviors that she felt got special attention from the adults in the classroom.

Trying to get a message across nonverbally is an appropriate early strategy in second language settings; most young children in these circumstances seem to be able unself-consciously to call this strategy into play when necessary. There are, however, social consequences to persisting in such behaviors. In this classroom, the second language learning children had to depend upon the help of the adults in the classroom during this period; as long as they remained nonverbal they were ignored or were treated like infants by the English-speaking children.[3] Obviously, in order

3 In this classroom there was one child, Takashi, who remained predominantly nonverbal during the year. One of the English-speaking children, Micah, tried everything he could to communicate with Takashi. Micah's activities included kissing Takashi, sticking his tongue out at him, flapping his lips at him, spinning himself around in front of him, chasing and wrestling with him, lifting him up from be-

to truly join in the classroom activities as social equals, second language learning children need to begin to produce utterances in the new language. In other words, they have to begin to crack the linguistic code.

Two studies, by Tabors (1987) and Saville-Troike (1988), have specifically looked at the behaviors of second language learning preschool children in this nonverbal period which demonstrated that they were cognitively engaged in beginning to crack the code. Tabors noted two strategies – spectating and rehearsing. *Spectating* refers to active observations by the second language learning children when they were in proximity to English speakers and were focusing on the language that was being used. Frequently, these behaviors occurred during joint activities like play dough manipulation at one of the tables or group activities like circle time. For example:

Jin Whie took the knife and went over to the play dough table, sitting down at an empty seat where there was a large glob of play dough and a roller. He began to roll out the play dough with the roller. The other children at the table were Kim, Rachael, and Gloria. They were still working on the birthday cake project, talking about what they were doing as they played. Jin Whie did not join in their discussions, but looked down at the play dough in front of him as he rolled it out . . . Then he *looked up and listened* to the other children at the table as they talked, holding a ball of play dough in his hand.

and:

At circle time: most of the children are now joining in well with the songs and games . . . Joaquim was slow to copy right away, but was beginning to get involved near the end. He was *watching* my face intently during the songs (I was across the circle from him).

hind, handing play objects to him, tickling him, and pulling his hood up on his sweatshirt. This behavior on Micah's part seemed most strongly reminiscent of how an older child might play with a much younger baby.

An instance of how the English-speaking children regarded a slightly older linguistically different child occurred at the end of the school year when a new student, Sam, came into the classroom. Sam was bilingual in Spanish and French, but he did not know any English. He was extensively ignored by the other children although he did make attempts to join in the run-and-chase games requiring no verbal ability that were sometimes played in the classroom. When one of the teachers took a series of slides of the children in the classroom and then showed them during circle time, a routine developed of naming all the children shown in each slide. Whenever a slide was shown that included a picture of Sam, all of the other children's names were called out, but never Sam's, in spite of the fact that it was used daily in the classroom by the teachers and was, therefore, known to the other children. Because he did not yet speak any English, Sam was apparently invisible to the rest of the children.

In each of these instances, the second language learning child seemed to be beginning to collect data about the new language being used around him. The intensity of this spectating behavior on the part of the children is what set it apart from simple noninvolved listening behavior.

Rehearsing refers to those behaviors by the learners that did not appear to be communicative but indicated that they were working on producing English. Much rehearsing was done extremely quietly as they played near English speakers and was, therefore, difficult to hear. Sometimes, however, it was possible to tune in to the rehearsal as it occurred:

Then Johanna came by and remarked, "Look at that nice play dough" and Jin Whie echoed, "Play dough."

and:

Then Micah said something which contained the phrase "have to . . ." and Jin Whie, who had again been watching Micah intently, mouthed the words "have to."

In these instances, Jin Whie is not trying to communicate with Johanna or Micah; he is rehearsing the sounds that he has just heard by repeating them out loud.

In Saville-Troike's study, the nature of this rehearsing process was more extensively revealed as she used directional microphones to capture and record the vocalizations of the young second language learners. Saville-Troike noted that much of this rehearsing was done at such a low volume that even those near the children could not hear what they were saying. Apparently, they were not yet ready to go public with their talk this early in the second language learning process.

As in Tabors' study, Saville-Troike found that the children used repetition as part of the rehearsing process, the younger children usually repeating the end of an utterance that they heard near them, but the older children sometimes repeating medial phrases or topics of the utterances. She also found other uses for this type of private speech, including connecting English words with appropriate objects, actions, or situations or incorporating English in dual language utterances as if explaining the meanings to themselves. Further, the children used this rehearsal time to play with the sounds of English and to begin to construct pattern drills for themselves in their new language. For example, a 5-year-old Japanese boy constructed the following:

I finished.

I have finished.

I am finished.

I'm finished.

and:

I want.

I paper. Paper. Paper.

I want paper.

During this nonverbal period, then, the young second language learners in these two studies were beginning to quietly unravel the sounds, meanings, and patterns of the new language in their environment. Although those around them may not have been aware of it, the process of cracking the code had begun.

TELEGRAPHIC AND FORMULAIC SPEECH

When young second language learners finally go public with their new language, observers have noted two consistent features: the use of *telegraphic speech* and the use of *formulaic speech*.

Telegraphic speech refers to the use of a few content words as an entire utterance without function words or morphological markers. This type of speech is also typical of a period of acquisition by very young children learning their first language. In Tabors' study, much of the telegraphic language used in the classroom during the first months revolved around the identification and naming of objects in English. An almost ritualized form was used in soliciting and providing this information. The most basic version of this form involved an adult asking a child "What's this/that?" and then, if the answer was not readily available, supplying the child with the noun. For example:

Then Gloria built a bridge as Johanna had done before. I asked "What's that?" She shrugged. I said, "Bridge." She repeated, "Bridge" then paused and said it again.

If the child was able to answer the "What's this/that?" question, then the next step in this process involved an elaboration or extension by the adult:

In the block area, Joaquim put a car up near my face. I said, "What's that?" He answered, "Car." I elaborated for him, "A racing car."

Quite quickly, the children began to answer the question before it was even asked, showing off and confirming what they already knew how to say:

At snack time, Yasushi indicated the crackers and told me, "Crackers," pointed to his crackers and announced, "Three" (there were), and showed me his juice and announced, "Apple juice." Each time he got a confirmation from me.

Using these strategies, the second language learning children in this classroom began to develop a vocabulary of object names in English that they could use in their interactions with the English speakers around them. Other early accomplishments also included counting, naming the ABCs, and identifying colors in English, all basic skills that the English-speaking children in the classroom were also working on at the same time.

The use of formulaic speech has also been documented by researchers studying young second language learners. This strategy, most extensively detailed by Wong Fillmore (1976), consists of young children using unanalyzed chunks or formulaic phrases in situations in which others have been observed to use them. These formulas often help children to get into play situations with the second language speakers around them. Phrases like "I wanna play wi' dese" (Nora in Wong Fillmore's study), "Get out of here" (Paul in Huang and Hatch's study), and "I'm a good idea" (Yasushi in Tabors' study) were used frequently and pervasively long before anything more than their most general connotation could have been understood by the children.

This strategy is often revealed when mistakes occur. Tabors observed such an incident one day when Jin Whie was on the ladder to the loft and, meaning to invite Micah to come up and join him, confidently directed, "Shut up!" Micah looked surprised and then rather hurt and backed down off the ladder instead of continuing his play with Jin Whie. In this case, Jin Whie was taking the chance that a phrase he had often heard in the classroom that contained the word *up* would work in this situation. Unfortunately, this time he had it wrong. More frequently, however, the use of formulaic phrases allowed the second language learning children to begin to participate in classroom activities in socially appropriate ways. Their use of formulaic utterances indicated to their English-speaking classmates that they could be interesting social partners.

PRODUCTIVE LANGUAGE USE

Eventually, however, in order to become full-fledged members of the social groups around them, second language learning children have to begin to use English productively, going beyond simple utterances and memorized chunks. In Tabors' study, the second language learning children began to construct novel utterances by combining formulaic beginnings like "I wanna," "I do," and "Lookit" with names for objects in order to construct simple utterances like "Lookit dunkin' donut," and "I do a ice cream.'' Only 5-year-old Joaquim, the oldest second language learner in the classroom, was able to move beyond this point during the study. In the spring months, he worked his way through some of the classic dilemmas in early language learning like the I/me distinction, the placement of the negative, and the construction of the past tense and questions in English. Utterances like ''Me sick, ''You no my mommy,'' ''What you putting in here?'' and ''You don't gotted me'' indicated that he was moving beyond his previous strategy of using grammatically correct but unanalyzed, chunks and was beginning to develop an understanding of the syntactic system in English. Wong Fillmore (1976, 1979) has documented this process extensively, showing how young second language learners, through comparison and breakdown of formulaic terms together with development and application of syntactic rules, arrive at productive control over their new language.

By outlining a particular developmental sequence of second language learning for young children, we do not mean to imply that these are discrete stages. At each point in this sequence, previously used strategies may still be pressed into service in an attempt to get a message across. The same child who is practicing verb declensions under her breath while playing alone may also be shouting out all the words to a favorite song at circle time, asking the teachers to ''push me'' when she is in a swing in the playground, and indicating with a gesture that she wants the top removed from a jar. In these ways she is demonstrating a range of strategies for responding to the problem of effective communication and social participation prior to complete acquisition of a second language.

Individual differences

As in all learning processes, individual differences have been observed to occur in how children proceed through the developmental sequence. In this section, individual differences that have been noted in studies of second language learning preschool-aged children will be discussed.

In the developmental sequence already outlined, the first step in the process was the use of the child's first language in the second language setting. But many children never use their first language this way, having been told by their parents, perhaps, that no one will be able to understand them. Awareness of the uselessness of speaking a language that no one understands may be age related: Younger children may persist in this effort longer than older children. Eventually, however, as we have seen, all children discover who can and who cannot understand what they are saying.

At this point children must decide whether or not to make the effort to acquire a second language. In Saville-Troike's study, there was a 5-year-old Japanese girl who informed a Japanese interviewer that English was too hard so she was not going to speak to people who spoke English. She actually followed through with this plan and did not learn any English during the course of the year-long study. Similarly, if children in a second language setting can find appropriate playmates who speak their first language, they can form their own social group and be selective about whom they choose as communicative partners beyond that group, most often concentrating on communication with their teachers rather than with their English-speaking peers (Meyer, 1989). Young children certainly seem to understand that learning a second language is a cognitively challenging and time-consuming activity. If they can find other means of communicating effectively within their environment, they may well choose to do so. Being exposed to a second language is obviously not enough; wanting to communicate with people who speak that language is crucial if acquisition is to occur.

Of course, the final goal of the acquisition process is productive control over the second language. We know that there are enormous individual differences among young children, as among adults, in how soon and how well productive control of a second language is achieved. In her study of five young Spanish speakers, Wong Fillmore (1979) found a wide differential in how much productive language the five children had by the end of the year in spite of the fact that they had all arrived from Mexico at the same time, all had parents with the same backgrounds, and all attended the same school. Wong Fillmore concluded that these differences "had to do with the interaction between the nature of the task of learning a new language, the strategies that needed to be applied to the task, and the personal characteristics of the individuals involved." The child who learned the most, Nora, was extremely outgoing, associated herself with English-speaking children by preference, and used every opportunity available to her to engage in meaningful conversation in her new language. The child who learned the least, Juan, in contrast, refused to have anything to do with English speakers and spent his free time with Spanish-speaking or bilingual friends. Wong Fillmore's evidence points to the fact that all of these children had the cognitive capacity to learn a new language, but they had a variety of social strategies that influenced how far they had progressed by the end of the study.

As the previous discussion indicates, second language acquisition is a natural, if complex, process that occurs when young children are placed in second language environments where they choose to develop the necessary communicative skills for that environment. Individual differences, however, are common owing to the fact that the process is both cognitively and socially challenging for young children.

Preschool classrooms as second language learning environments

The preceding discussion has focused on the general pattern of second language development by children in preschool settings. But what influence does that setting itself have on the learning process for these children? Are there specific aspects of the learning environment that have an impact on the process, and, if so, what particular aspects of the process or outcome are affected? In order to answer these questions, we will discuss three case studies of preschool classrooms where different approaches have been used to provide support for second language learning. The chapter concludes with a summary of what has been learned from these three studies about effective second language learning environments for preschool-aged children.

Case 1: Social support in a nursery school environment

In the nursery school classroom at the Tech Children's Center at the Massachusetts Institute of Technology which was studied by Tabors (1984, 1987), there were no overt efforts made to tailor the curriculum to the second language learning children. The teachers proceeded with a general developmental curriculum that included considerable free time, time in small group activities, as well as circle time when all the children gathered together with the teachers to listen to stories, sing songs, and discuss events of interest. In spite of this fact, there were both organizational and linguistic aspects of the classroom that provided support to the second language learners from the beginning.

The organizational aspect of the classroom that proved most helpful for the second language learners was the fact that the teachers had established a consistent set of routines for the children. These routines meant that, with a little observation, the second language learning children could pick up cues as to what to do and when, using the English-speaking children as models. The daily schedule of arrival, free play, clean-up, snack time, outside play, and circle time gave the second language learners a set of activity structures to acquire (i.e., put jackets in cubby, go to rug, find a place at a table for snack, help put toys away) that immediately allowed them to act like members of the group. Once absorbed into the context of the group, they were able to pick up on the available social cues to continue to act appropriately. For example:

Marion [one of the teachers] began to organize the soup making operation at one of the tables. Jean Ah was standing nearby watching. Marion asked her "Would you like to help, too, Jean Ah?" Jean Ah nodded her head. Marion

then announced, "O.K., there will be five helpers." Jean Ah sat down at
the table as Marion named the five helpers, including Jean Ah.

In this example, Jean Ah is addressed by the teacher in a questioning tone
that includes her name. This routine is similar in general format to
routines that occur again and again in the classroom: The teacher begins
to display particular types of materials for a project and invites students
to engage in the project. From previous experiences, Jean Ah can guess
that Marion has asked if she wishes to join the group. Then when she
hears her name and sees the other children start to sit down at the table,
Jean Ah does the same, indicating that she understands that she has been
included. Even without knowing anything more than her own name, Jean
Ah could look like she knew what was being asked of her in this situation.
Again, because the children were so good at using contextual cues to
guess what an appropriate action might be in a given situation, it was only
when a child guessed incorrectly that this strategy was fully revealed:

Yasushi and Rachael were sitting side by side working independently with
the story pieces. I sat down next to Rachael who was having a hard time setting up the pieces on the plastic stands that came with them. Yasushi, on the
other hand, had figured out how to set the pieces up and was putting some together. Rachael said to me, "I want to do what Yasushi did." I answered,
"Go ahead." She said, "I don't know how." I said, "Ask Yasushi to help
you." Rachael turned to Yasushi and said, "Can you help me to do that?"
He handed her one of the plastic pieces. She asked again, "How do you do
it?" He gave her the plastic bag that still had one extra piece in the bottom.

In this example, Yasushi's best guess is that Rachael has asked him to
provide her with pieces that she cannot reach, a typical request in this
situation; not actually understanding what she has said, he still responds
with an action in an attempt to be helpful.

In this case, Yasushi's best guess about what Rachael wanted did not
happen to be right, but she and Yasushi still continued their play side-by-
side. In other situations, looking as if you know what's being said when
you don't, can have more serious consequences. Snow (1983) observed a
5-year-old English girl, Nicola, in a kindergarten classroom in Amster-
dam who:

functioned perfectly in her class. She participated in art projects, listened at-
tentively during story reading, executed all the steps to the dance during music class. Her only failure came one day when the teacher announced, while
passing out snack, "Today we're going to wait until everyone is back at his
seat before we open our milk." Nicola failed to observe this deviation from
the standard routine, since she understood not a single word of Dutch, and
she was soundly scolded for having disobeyed. Nicola had done such a good

job of acting as if she spoke Dutch that betrayal of her ignorance was treated as obstinacy rather than poor language learning.

Fortunately, most teachers of young children in second language learning situations are more sensitive to the possibility of a child's not understanding verbal instructions than the teacher was in this situation.

A second source of support for these children came from the linguistic environment and can be divided into support for the acquisition of comprehension skills in English and support for production skills in English. Support for the development of comprehension skills involved a number of specific modifications that the adults in the classroom made when speaking to the second language learning children. These modifications were similar to ones that have been identified as facilitative in first language acquisition, such as emphasis placed on key words in a sentence, coordination of gesture and naming of objects, repetition of important words in context, and moving content words to the end of sentences. For example,

. . . As Fumi took the vegetables out of the bag and handed them to Orie to put in the guinea pig cage, Rosa [the teacher] said, "Another carrot, and lettuce (naming each vegetable as it was placed in the cage)." Then Rosa remarked, "Look at her, she's eating the *lettuce*. I think she likes the lettuce best."

In this example, Rosa coordinates the naming of the object with its being handled by one of the Japanese sisters. She also emphasizes the word *lettuce* as it is being consumed and then repeats it in the following utterance. Another example:

When Aram finished her project, Marion [the teacher] asked her, "Can I put your name on this? Can I put your *name?*" Aram nodded her head enthusiastically and Marion wrote Aram's name.

In this example, Marion uses repetition and emphasis to get her message across. She also moves the word *name* to the end of the sentence, possibly another modification for comprehension.

In this classroom, then, the language used by the teachers when working with the second language learners was heavily directed to present circumstances, involved objects and activities in plain view, and was often accompanied by coordinated gestures. In this way, the children were given a chance to derive meaning from more than one source of information.

Support for the development of English production skills began very early for the second language learners in this classroom because the teachers tried to respond to every effort that the children made to communicate in English, even if the message was unclear. By providing a supportive environment for the children's attempts to produce their new language, the teachers encouraged the children to keep trying. For example:

At the drawing table Aram showed her project to Marion [the teacher] and said something to her that was indistinguishable, i.e. her utterance sounded like a sentence, but it was not possible to understand what she said. Marion replied, "Oh, are you making that?"

Even after the children had begun to acquire some English, the teachers continued to do a great deal of work to keep a conversation going. At this stage, however, they required the children to make some efforts at verbal communication:

Ruben approached Marion with a suspender which had come loose. The following interaction occurred:

Marion: You're trying to tell me something.
Ruben: (no reply)
Marion: Do you want me to do something?
Ruben: (no reply)
Marion: Do you want me to do something with your suspender? Put it on my nose? (starts to do so)
Ruben: Red (showing her his pants)
Marion: Yes, red . . . red what?
Ruben: Red pants.
Marion: Do you want me to attach this to your red pants?
Ruben: Yes.
Marion: O.K. I'll do that for you.

And finally, the adults in the classroom made every effort to use the utterances of the second language learning children as points of departure for further communication, extending and expanding on what the children could say:

When I arrived there were already five or six children working with play dough at one of the work tables. I sat down at the table to join them. Jean Ah held up a round piece of play dough to me and said, "Cookie." I replied, "Is this a chocolate-chip cookie? May I eat it?" Jean Ah nodded and I pretended to eat the cookie. I then told Jean Ah, "That's a good cookie." Later, Jean Ah held up a cube shaped piece of play dough and said, "Chocolate." We followed the same procedure as before as I ate the piece of chocolate and commented on how good it was.

In general, then, the adult language used with the second language learners in this classroom helped the children understand what was being talked about and helped them begin to produce utterances in the new language as well. Once the children reached that point, they began to communicate with the English-speaking children in the classroom and to join into the social activities of the classroom more fully.

Case 2: Social engineering in a demonstration school classroom

In the classroom studied by Tabors, the support that was provided to the second language learning children came almost entirely from the adults; the English-speaking children chose to play with English-speaking play-mates in the classroom until the second language learning children began to communicate in English. This meant that the second language learning children had to wait for months to acquire English-speaking friends and to get involved in activities like sociodramatic play that are heavily dependent on language. A relevant question is: Is it possible to get non-English-speaking preschool-aged children into contact with English speakers more quickly? And if so, would this enhance the acquisition of the second language for these children?

These questions were the basis for an intervention study by Hirschler (1991) in a preschool classroom serving 3-, 4-, and 5-year-old Khmer-, Spanish-, and English-speaking children at the Demonstration School of the University of Massachusetts, Lowell. This school, developed specifi-cally in reaction to the large numbers of non-English-speakers entering the Lowell public schools, is based on a multilingual and multicultural model. In this model, children's preliteracy development in their first language is supported during language periods taught by native-speaking teachers. At other times of the day, however, the children join into group activities that are conducted in English. Hirschler believed that the English-speaking children in this classroom could act as valuable lan-guage resources for the second language learning children, if they could be persuaded to interact effectively with them.

Recognizing that children are capable of modifying their speech to less able speakers (Shatz & Gelman, 1977), Hirschler designed an interven-tion in which she trained five English-speaking children in a variety of strategies for approaching and sustaining interaction with the non-English speakers in the classroom. These strategies were ones that Hirschler developed from a review of the literature on input which has been shown to be most beneficial for second language learners. They are summarized in Table 1.

In order to introduce these techniques, Hirschler and a helper used role playing to model the desired behaviors before the entire group of children and then individually with the five target children. All of the strategies were understood by the children, and all but recasts were successfully

Table 1. *Strategies for interaction used in training*

Initiation: Children were taught to approach other children, establish eye contact, and ask the children to play with them or with a particular toy.

General linguistic aspects: Children were taught to speak slowly with good enunciation.

Reinitiation: Children were taught to repeat the initiation if it met with non-response.

Request clarification: Children were taught to request clarification of a response by the second language learner if the response was not understood.

Recast/expansion: Children were taught to repeat an utterance with slightly different wording when the second language learner indicated a lack of comprehension through nonresponse, noncontingent response, or other nonverbal signs.

---

elicited during the training sessions. In order to remind the children of these strategies, each was equipped with a reminder bracelet, and posters were placed in the classroom as well.

Interactional data collected pre- and post-intervention indicated that rates of initiations to second language learners increased two-and-a-half to three times for four of the five children. Rates of turn-taking and utterances per turn also increased, as did language modifications. The overall effect of the training, then, was to increase contact between the English-speaking target children and the second language learners earlier than would have been the case otherwise.

After the intervention, one particular English-speaking child took on a protective and teaching role with several of the Khmer speakers, consequently greatly increasing her interaction with them. In the following example, Tiffany is showing Therry some shells on the science table, delivering a highly contextualized and repetitive English lesson at the same time:

Tiffany: O.K. have to smell this. O.K.? That don't smell, does it? Ha! That don't smell. That don't smell.
Therry: (giggles)
Tiffany: Hear the ocean? Hear the ocean? Hear it? Oh, this one is loud! You can hear this one. Can you hear it? Wait, come here. Come here. Want to hear it? Look, hear this. Hear the ocean?

In this example Tiffany is functioning much like a teacher working with a second language learner, using repetition and modification to deliver her message. By helping the target children understand that the second language learners needed help and by providing information about how they might help, Hirschler made it possible for the second language learners to hear more contextualized language than would have been possible if their only conversational partners were the teachers in the classroom.

In these circumstances, the second language learning children did not have to wait until they could begin to produce English in order to be included in social groupings with their English-speaking peers. Hirschler speculates that "this benign form of social engineering could act as a catalyst to language development" for the second language learners. She suggests that it would be useful to integrate into the multi-cultural classroom, through discussion and group activities, the idea that some children are learning to speak English and there are ways that we can help them.

Although we know that children can modify their speech and are aware of the need to do so in certain circumstances, with younger children in particular, they are not as likely to understand this need when faced with same-age mates. In these circumstances, nonresponse is viewed as social rejection rather than lack of comprehension. Pointing out to children that other children speak different languages, that it will take time for them to begin to speak a new language, and that there are some ways that they can help in this process, could make the process a more positive one for all concerned.

Case 3: Curricular planning for language facilitation in a language acquisition preschool

In the preschool classroom studied by Tabors there were no overt curricular modifications made for the sake of the second language learning children; however, as we have seen, there were features of the classroom environment that tended to support language learning nonetheless. Taking this idea one step further, what would a preschool classroom look like where language acquisition was the main goal guiding curriculum planning and classroom activities?

Such a classroom has been developed at the Language Acquisition Preschool (LAP) at the University of Kansas. This school serves normally developing, specific-language impaired, and second language learning children (Rice, 1991; Rice & Wilcox, 1990, in preparation). The LAP classroom shares many of the features of other preschools, providing activities aimed at the development of social skills and school readiness. What differentiates this classroom is an emphasis on language development throughout the curriculum, the presence of a variety of children with limited language skills but age-appropriate social and intellectual

Table 2. *Intervention strategies for language facilitation*

Provide opportunities for language use and interaction:
- Provide rich and interesting activities "worth talking about"
- Allow quiet times when teachers are not talking and children can initiate conversation
- Arrange the environment so that not all materials are readily accessible in order to promote discussion

Provide focused stimulation on particular language features:
- Model target sounds or words for children; encourage (but do not require) repetition of models
- Recast children's utterances to maintain semantic information but extend syntactic use
- Recast adult utterances in the same way

Develop routines to help children connect events and language:
- Establish familiar daily routines like arrival time, circle time, snack time
- Develop scripts related to sociodramatic play activities including discussion/demonstration about roles, props, and activities
- Use event casting ("talking while doing") to model problem-solving strategies

Stimulate social interaction between children:
- Redirect children's requests to other children; provide a model if necessary

---

skills, the consistent emphasis on verbal activities, and encouragement of verbal interactions among the children.

Beginning with the premise that language is learned in socially interactive settings and that children construct their linguistic systems from the language they hear from adults and more capable peers, the architects of the Language Acquisition Preschool have developed intervention strategies to facilitate language development. These strategies are outlined in Table 2.

Many of these strategies are in common use in other preschool classrooms already; many of them are included in the examples from the Tech Children's Center, mentioned in connection with Tabors' study. But at the Language Acquisition Preschool these techniques have been brought to the forefront of the curriculum effort where they provide the framework for daily planning and for interaction between teachers and children. By highlighting the use of these techniques for language facilitation, the teachers at LAP have been able to help children with language difficulties make significant progress within the context of the classroom, while providing an optimum environment for the native-speaking and second language learning children as well.

English as a second language in preschools: What works?

From these case studies has emerged the model of the type of preschool classroom that works best for second language learning children; it is one in which the adults in the classroom provide opportunities for children to engage in useful and purposeful language interactions with sensitive interlocutors, both adults and peers. In order to achieve this, teachers should consider providing the following types of opportunities in their classrooms:

1. a routine and consistent organizational structure in which activities happen at regular intervals and in predictable ways;
2. a language rich environment in which teachers use language that encourages both comprehension and production skills;
3. discussions with, or perhaps training of, English-speaking children in the classroom to help provide socially appropriate language partners.

By providing an environment that includes these opportunities and by encouraging children to take advantage of them, preschool teachers can help individual second language learning children progress through the developmental sequence outlined earlier at the rate and in the way that best fits with their social capabilities and cognitive strengths.

References

Classrooms of Babel. (1991, February). *Newsweek,* pp. 56–57.

Ervin-Tripp, S. (1974). Is second language learning like the first? *TESOL Quarterly, 8,* June: 111–127.

Fantini, A. (1985). *Language acquisition of a bilingual child.* San Diego, CA: College-Hill Press.

Genesee, F. (1989). Early bilingual development: One language or two? *Journal of Child Language, 16,* February: 161–180.

Hakuta, K. (1974). A report on the development of grammatical morphemes in a Japanese girl learning English as a second language. *Working Papers in Bilingualism,* Vol. 4 (pp. 18–44). Toronto: OISE Press.

Hakuta, K. (1986). *Mirror of language: The debate on bilingualism.* New York, NY: Basic Books.

Hirschler, J. (1991). Preschool children's help to second language learners. Unpublished doctoral dissertation, Harvard University, Boston.

Huang, J. & Hatch, E. (1978). A Chinese child's acquisition of English. In E. Hatch (Ed.), *Second language acquisition: A book of readings.* Rowley, MA: Newbury House Publishers.

Itoh, H. & Hatch, E. (1978). A Chinese child's acquisition of English. In E. Hatch (Ed.), *Second language acquisition: A book of readings*. Rowley, MA: Newbury House Publishers.

Kresh, E. (1990). *Families in Head Start*. Unpublished manuscript. Prepared for the Panel of the Head Start Evaluation Design Project.

Meisel, J. (1989). Early differentiation of languages in bilingual children. In K. Hylterstam & L. Obler (Eds.), *Bilingualism across the lifespan: Aspects of acquisition, maturity, and loss*. Cambridge: Cambridge University Press.

Meyer, C. (1989). The role of peer relationships in the socialization of children to preschool: A Korean example. Unpublished doctoral dissertation, Ohio State University, Columbus.

Rice, M. (1991). Children with specific language impairment: Toward a model of teachability. In N. Krasnegor, D. Rumbaugh, R. Schiefelbusch, & M. Studdert-Kennedy (Eds.), *Biological and behavioral determinants of language development*. Hillsdale, NJ: Lawrence Erlbaum.

Rice, M., & Wilcox, K. (1990). *Language Acquisition Preschool: A model preschool for language disordered and ESL children*. (Grant No. G008630279). Washington, DC: Final report to the U.S. Department of Education, Office of Special Education Programs.

Rice, M., & Wilcox, K. (in preparation). *The Language Acquisition Preschool: A classroom program for language facilitation*. Baltimore, MD: Brookes Publishing.

Saunders, G. (1988). *Bilingual children: From birth to teens*. Clevedon, UK and Philadelphia, PA: Multilingual Matters.

Saville-Troike, M. (1987). Dilingual discourse: The negotiation of meaning without a common code. *Linguistics, 25,* 81–106.

Saville-Troike, M. (1988). Private speech: Evidence for second language learning strategies during the 'silent period.' *Journal of Child Language, 15,* 567–590.

Shatz, M., & Gelman, R. (1977). Beyond syntax: The influence of conversational constraints on speech modifications. In C. Snow & C. Ferguson (Eds.), *Talking to children: Language input and acquisition*. Cambridge, England: Cambridge University Press.

Snow, C. (1983). Age differences in second language acquisition: Research findings and folk psychology. In K. Bailey, M. Long, & S. Peck (Eds.), *Second language acquisition studies*. Rowley, MA: Newbury House Publishers.

Tabors, P. (1984). The identification of categories of environmental support available for second language acquisition in a nursery school classroom. Unpublished qualifying paper, Harvard University, Boston.

Tabors, P. (1987). The development of communicative competence by second language learners in a nursery school classroom: An ethnolinguistic study. Unpublished doctoral dissertation, Harvard University, Boston.

Taeschner, T. (1983). *The sun is feminine: A study of language acquisition in bilingual children.* Berlin, Heidelberg, New York, Tokyo: Springer-Verlag.

Wong Fillmore, L. (1976). The second time around: Cognitive and social strategies in second language acquisition. Unpublished doctoral dissertation, Stanford University, Stanford.

Wong Fillmore, L. (1979). Individual differences in second language acquisition. In C. Fillmore, D. Kempler, & W. Wang (Eds.), *Individual differences in language ability and language behavior.* New York: Academic Press.

SECTION III:
THE CLASSROOM

The chapters in this section turn to matters of direct relevance to the *classroom* – issues concerning the development of literacy in a second language (Chapter 6), teaching and learning content through a second language (Chapter 7), grouping strategies that promote learning in school (Chapter 8), and assessment in the classroom (Chapter 9). Preparation of these chapters has been motivated by dual concerns. First of all, the authors seek to be relevant and practical – these chapters are meant to assist teachers in planning, delivering, and assessing instruction. The authors cannot tell the reader exactly what to do since there is no single predetermined way to do this in all classrooms. Rather, they seek to provide frameworks and general guidelines that provide the individual practitioner with ways of thinking about the specific tasks they face so that they can make decisions that are maximally suited for themselves. The authors in this section have grounded their suggestions for classroom practice in current theory and research and, of course, in their own professional experiences. Their suggestions are necessarily open ended and subject to your critical application.

6 Literacy development of second language children

Sarah Hudelson

Recently, I received a telephone call from a local educator. She had been asked to organize a workshop for her school on "dealing with" English as a second language learners. The situation, she explained to me, was that significant numbers of non-English speakers were enrolling in the school in which she taught. In some classrooms nearly all the children were non-native speakers of English; in other rooms the percentages varied. Many of the teachers were asking for assistance in working with these learners. They did not know what to do, how to approach the children, how to teach them, and particularly, how to help them become more literate. She had been given my name as someone who knew something about the topic. Would I please come and speak?

The scenario I have just summarized is a common one for many of us in bilingual and second language education. The reality in many areas is that the number of non-English-speaking students in our schools is increasing. The questions that educators have are genuine. As responsible adults, we struggle with how to meet the educational needs of learners whose languages and cultures are different from what the schools may have assumed. For the learners' sakes, and for our own welfare, we need to determine how most effectively to assist students linguistically and stimulate them intellectually. And literacy development is a major component of what we must do. So what would I say with regard to this issue?

Defining literacy

For me personally, a response must begin with an examination of what literacy is (a definition of *literacy*) and a consideration of literacy goals that I might propose for learners in elementary school settings, whether they be native speakers of English or second language learners. *Webster's Ninth New Collegiate Dictionary* defines literacy as "the quality or state of being literate." The dictionary then defines *literate* either as an adjective, "able to read and write," or as a noun, "one who can read and write." Since literacy means more to me than knowing *how* to read and write or being *able* to read and write, these minimal explanations are not sufficient and force me to come to grips with my own definition.

At the core of my definition is meaning or the construction of meaning. I might define reading as a language process in which an individual constructs meaning through a transaction with written text that has been created by symbols that represent language. The transaction involves the reader's acting upon or interpreting the text, and the interpretation is influenced by the reader's past experiences, language background, and cultural framework, as well as the reader's purpose for reading. Similarly, I might define writing as a language process in which an individual creates meaning by using symbols to construct a written text. The text that the individual constructs will be influenced by the writer's language background, personal experiences, and cultural framework, as well as by the purpose for writing and the audience for the piece.

In addition to asking the general question "What is literacy?" I would also ask "What are the functions of literacy?" and "What is literacy for?" From a general perspective, literacy serves people by providing one medium through which individuals can learn about the world and share their understandings with others, accomplish some of the daily tasks of living, make and maintain connections with other people, express both uniqueness and commonality with others, reflect upon and try to act upon individual and community problems, make some changes in the world, enjoy the richness of language, understand their cultural heritages and the heritages of others, and struggle with the human condition and what it means to be human.

In moving from these broad notions of literacy I would then ask "What goals might be proposed for children in elementary school settings?" I would propose not only that children be *able* to read and write (i.e., be able to construct meaning from their own texts and the texts of others), but also that they *choose* to read and write, that they want to engage in these activities. This suggests to me that children would enjoy reading and writing and view reading and writing both as pleasurable and useful to them. They would use reading and writing to learn about and interpret the world and to reflect upon themselves in relation to people and events around them; they would use reading and writing to explain, analyze, argue about, and act upon the world (Freire, 1970; Heath & Hoffman, 1986). Thus literacy would be viewed as having the potential not only for changing the individual learner but also for changing the world. All of these views go beyond literacy as a set of skills – literacy as performance – to literacy as having the potential to open up new ways of viewing the world and transforming it (Wells, 1990). From my own perspective this view of literacy applies to both native speakers of English and learners for whom English is not their native language.

If one were to accept this view of literacy, the next logical question might be: How should literacy be promoted? Since the focus of this volume is second language learners, how should literacy be promoted for second language learners? My answer begins with a perspective on or philosophy of literacy development that leads to ways of working with children in classroom settings. My perspective comes from an examination of some of the research that has been done on children's (both native speakers and ESL learners) acquisition of literacy (being able to read and write), sometimes in the settings of home and community and sometimes in school. So I will begin with a consideration of what we know about how young children become readers and writers. From there I will move to the issue of what this means for daily work in classrooms with second language learners.

How children become literate

Using print in the environment

For at least the last fifteen years, research has demonstrated unequivocally that children in print-saturated or print-oriented societies are engaged, from very early in their lives, in making sense of the printed word, in figuring out the symbolic nature of print, in discovering that print may serve a variety of functions. Children also are engaged in experimenting with that print, whether they are interpreting print written by someone else or creating their own written texts.

One of the first contexts in which many children grapple with the meaning and function of print is the print in the world around them. This has come to be termed *environmental print*. Work with preschoolers has demonstrated that children 3 years of age or younger are able to identify familiar signs such as McDonald's and STOP and product labels such as Coca-Cola and Crest (Baghban, 1984; Goodman & Altwerger, 1981; Harste, Woodward, & Burke, 1984). Some young children may identify these labels initially based on their functionality rather than their exact name (e.g., Crest is labeled as "toothpaste" or "brush your teeth"). As their knowledge about reading and writing becomes more developed, children begin to use the actual name to identify the label. But more important, in terms of children coming to understand written language, is the realization of the symbolic nature of the written language – that the label stands for something else.

While most studies of environmental print knowledge have been conducted with native speakers of English, Yetta Goodman and her colleagues (Goodman, Goodman, & Flores, 1979) have pointed out that even young Navajo children, who are not native English speakers and who live in isolated parts of the Navajo nation, can identify English print from the environment and the names of cartoon characters such as Spider

Man. Catherine Wallace (1988) has found that ESL elementary school children in London are aware of the English print in the world around them and want to be able to read it. The fact that children act upon these symbols suggests that they are at work constructing hypotheses about how written language functions in both their native language and in another language (Hudelson, 1984).

Storybook reading

Another context for examining children's acquisition of literacy is that of storybook reading, where an adult or older fluent reader reads to a child and, specifically, where adult and child read the same story several times. In general this research has shown that, through storybook reading, young children come to know both an overall schema of story structure and the specific language used to tell stories (Baghban, 1984; Doake, 1985; Teale & Sulzby, 1986). They also come to understand that both the illustrations and the print are significant – that the illustrations help convey the story's meaning, and that the print (the squiggles on the page) symbolizes the language of the story. They come to know how to handle books and understand the concept of directionality. And, as written stories are shared with them, children begin to pay increasing attention to the print (Clay, 1985).

Children's hypotheses of how to read a familiar story change over time, beginning globally by considering the overall plot and using the pictures to provide a general reconstruction of the story (Weaver, 1988). As the story becomes more familiar, children focus on the story's sentences and lexicon; they give more attention to the text or print of the story and attend to syntactic and semantic aspects of it. As children pay more attention to the text, they cue in on individual words and letters, focusing on the graphophonic system. Many children go through a period of time, having broken code and realizing that they *can* sound out the words in the text, when they use the sound-letter system (graphophonemic) to the exclusion of other systems. Eventually, however, in order to become fluent independent readers, young learners make use of all the language systems (i.e., semantic, syntactic, graphophonic) simultaneously. The overall process of natural acquisition of reading appears, then, to be a top-down process, with children beginning with global notions of what reading is and gradually refining their notions (Weaver, 1988). That is, children begin with the whole story and gradually work their way down to the parts.

Some researchers (Doake, 1985; Teale & Sulzby, 1986) have referred to these phenomena as emerging reading or readinglike behavior. However, Baghban (1984) argues that these behaviors *are* reading if reading is viewed from a developmental perspective. In a fascinating case study of her own daughter's natural reading acquisition from birth to age 3, Baghban documents her daughter's gradual approximation of adult notions of reading and writing. Particularly significant for those of us working in second language settings is her explication of the parallel, simultaneous development of her daughter's speech, reading, and writing Baghban demonstrates that as her daughter's speech became more sophisticated and complete, so did her reading of storybooks. Giti, the little girl, began by echoing what she heard read to her so that her book babbling sounded as though she were reading in English. She moved from this to labeling the pictures and from there to using the plot schema of stories to provide more complete renditions of stories. All of this Baghban termed reading.

In addition to work done with native English speakers, we also have evidence that reading may emerge gradually from whole to part in languages other than English and among children for whom English is not their native language. Seawell (1985) has documented Spanish-English bilingual and English as a second language speaking Mexican-American children's construction of reading over a twelve-week period of sustained interactions with predictable books in both languages. For the past two years, two colleagues (Irene Serna and Yvonne Montiel) and I, through a series of longitudinal case studies, have been documenting the Spanish language literacy development of children enrolled in a whole-language bilingual program in Phoenix, Arizona. The case study data collection has included taperecording the kindergarten, first, and second grade children as they read both familiar and unfamiliar children's books. As we analyze the data from two years, we have been able to see their reading strategies change (although there are significant individual differences among the children, particularly with regard to rate of acquisition of literacy).

In the first tapings, when they read familiar books, the children reconstructed the stories using the illustrations and their recollection of the language of the author. The children did not tend to focus on the print in the stories, as there was neither pointing to particular words as they read nor voice-print match. In fact, one of the children, who reconstructed a story from memory, told us proudly, *"Yo puedo leer sin ver"* (I can read without looking). When asked to read an unfamiliar story (meaning one that had not been read to them and that they had not seen in the classroom), the common strategy was to construct a plot using the illustrations and not to deal with the print in terms of trying to decode specific words (see also Chapter 11).

Gradually, with familiar books, the children attended more to the actual print, attempting to match the words that they said to the words on the page. Still later, with both familiar and unfamiliar books, they cued in on each word on the page, focusing on each letter in turn and sounding out the words letter by letter and syllable by syllable. Thus, while earlier reading that focused semantically and syntactically had been fluent, the renderings of text that emphasized almost exclusively the graphophonic system became disfluent. We believe that this occurred because the children had figured out that they could sound out the words; they could use the sound-letter correspondences they were acquiring both to examine closely words that were already familiar to them and to figure out new words (Serna & Hudelson, 1993).

Children's construction of literacy through writing

The children acquired the sound-letter correspondences as they engaged in creating their own written texts (i.e., as they wrote in journals, created personal narratives, and constructed informational pieces related to content that they were studying). It is through their own original writing that they figured out sound-letter correspondences and applied these both to their own texts and to texts written by others. This context of children's acquisition of writing, then, is another that informs us and provides implications for classroom practice. A significant amount of research has been conducted, and it makes clear that children, long before they produce written text that conforms to adult standards or conventions, produce written texts for a variety of purposes (e.g., a birthday card or letter sent to one's grandparents, a list for the grocery shopping trip, a notice warning against entry into a private room, or a label indicating ownership, and so on). Long before they can write conventionally, children understand that written language is functional and that they can use it to accomplish their own purposes.

Early on, children also begin to experiment with how to express their purposes using written symbols (Clay, 1975). Much earlier than age 3, children may use scribbles similar to cursive to represent labels, names, or ideas. As motor control gradually increases, the scribbles more closely resemble adult cursive writing. By the age of 3, many children already have distinguished between drawing and writing as two different symbol systems for expressing one's meaning (Baghban, 1984; Weaver, 1988). Early letter forms that children produce, whether in strings or in certain combinations, resemble the letters of the alphabetic system that surrounds them even though they do not realize that these letter forms have any relationship to particular sounds in the language (Ferreiro, 1990; Weaver, 1988). Children may even ask an adult to interpret what they have written (Clay, 1975).

Although these efforts may be dismissed by some as children simply playing around or copying those around them, what they really indicate is learners struggling to figure out how the written language works. Young child writers are active constructors of the written language, and their representations of written language reflect their ideas, at any point in time, about how written language is structured. As their ideas or hypotheses change, so do the texts that they produce.

For many researchers, significant changes in children's writing occur when they figure out that the squiggles or forms are related to (and must in some way symbolize) the sounds of the language they are writing. At this point, in alphabetic languages such as English, children begin to relate the letters they are writing to the words they are creating and use invented spellings. Studies of invented spelling have made it clear that children's attempts at orthography are logical and reasoned although they do not conform to standard adult forms (Chomsky, 1971; Hudelson, 1981–1982; Read, 1975). In addition, invented spelling changes over time. Temple, Nathan, and Burris (1982), describing several stages of invented spelling in English, begin with an early *phonemic stage.* They note that children typically represent each word in a message by one or at most two letters, for example RCRBKD representing ''Our car broke down.'' Note, too, that conventional segmentation between words has not yet appeared.

In the next stage, *letter-name,* children usually represent more than one or two sounds in the word; they begin using some vowels as well as consonants, and they typically utilize a strategy of using the names of some of the letters rather than the sounds the letters make in their spelling. Thus a child might represent the sentence ''A kid sawed (saw) a red and pink house'' as A KCID SOD A RAD AND PEC HWS (Dobson, 1986).

From the letter-naming stage children gradually move into what Temple, Nathan, and Burris call *transitional spelling.* Spelling at this stage incorporates both the correct spellings of words from print and invented spellings that reflect the use of spelling patterns found in print. Thus a first grader writes, ''I have a ducke. She has baby ducklings. Theye foloe her in a strat line. Thaye are yellow.'' (I have a duck. She has baby ducklings. They follow her in a straight line. They are yellow.) Finally, children arrive at standard spelling.

While the delineation of these stages may suggest a linearity and unidirectionality, a careful examination of children's inventions makes it clear that different children use different patterns and combinations of patterns, and that the progression is not the neat linear one that these stages would imply. (It should also be noted that different researchers have developed somewhat varied categories to describe the stages of invented spelling.) What is most significant is that young writers solve their spelling problems by using what they know about English at a particular point in time. They are constructing for themselves the ortho-graphic rules of English as they work to create meaning.

Work on children's construction of written language also has taken place in languages other than English. Perhaps the best-known research is that of Emilia Ferreiro and Ana Teberosky, who investigated Spanish-speaking children's development as writers in Spanish. They coined the term *psychogenesis* to describe the gradual evolution of children's literacy development. Ferreiro and Teberosky (1982) suggest that children move through three developmentally ordered levels as they construct the written system of Spanish. At each level children create certain theories about how writing works. At the first level of development, children figure out that drawing and writing are two distinct symbol systems. They attend to the written language of the society in which they find themselves and adapt the letter forms to their own writing. They also decide that they must use a minimum of three-letter forms to write a word.

At the second level of development, children struggle both with quantitative and qualitative variations in the letter forms they use to express meaning. Children conclude that they can use the stock of letter forms available to them to express meaning by (1) using different letter forms for different words, (2) changing one or two letter forms in a sequence to create a different word, and (3) changing the order of the letter forms to create a different word. Both of these developmental levels involve the children in constructing written language without relating letter forms to specific sounds of the Spanish language.

The final stage of development involves the child considering how letter forms relate to the sounds of the language, in what Ferreiro (1990) calls the *phonetization of writing*. The first step in this stage involves children in the syllabic hypothesis, that is, in hypothesizing that each part of a word (each syllable) must be represented by a letter. Often, in Spanish, the more perceptible parts of each syllable are the vowel sounds, so the word *osito* (little bear) may be written OIO. At the second step, children begin to try out a new hypothesis, the syllabic alphabetic, where some of the written letters stand for syllable units but where some additional sounds are represented, so that *osito* might be represented as OSIO. Finally, children arrive at the alphabetic step, where they understand that every sound in a word needs to be represented by a letter. Invented spelling that reflects a variety of ideas about how Spanish orthography works occurs when children write alphabetically (Hudelson, 1981–1982) and standard segmentation still needs to emerge, but children have figured out that sounds are represented by letters.

In our ongoing research, we have noted similar hypothesis-generating and testing by our Spanish-speaking case study children. Our case study children's earliest journal entries were often drawings with strings of letters or letterlike forms underneath. Several of the young writers went through a phase where they copied words from books and from print around the room into their journals. When the learners began to associate words, sounds, and letters, they either hypothesized that each word was represented by one letter (usually the letter that represented the last sound in the word) or they represented each syllable in the word by one letter. At the word and syllabic levels, the sounds that were represented more often were the vowels rather than the consonants. From the syllabic hypothesis, our case study children gradually began to fill in more of the sounds of each of the words that they were writing until every sound was represented by a letter.

Standard segmentation between words also developed gradually. It was very common for the earliest writing to be one string of letter-sound correspondences, with no spacing at all. Other hypotheses about segmentation were that spaces were needed between every syllable or between phrase or clause units (Hudelson, 1991; Serna, 1991; Serna & Hudelson, 1993). As the children became more proficient writers, what they produced moved toward the more conventional, both in terms of segmentation and in terms of spelling.

Similarly, children growing up in cultures where different writing systems are used begin to create texts that resemble the written language of their cultures (Harste, Woodward, & Burke, 1984), and they exhibit patterns of development similar to those described earlier. Landsmann (1990) has demonstrated this with children becoming literate in Hebrew, and Lee (1990) has noted similar phenomena in Taiwanese children learning to read and write Chinese.

The work just discussed confirms that children, as they become literate, are creative constructors of their language or languages. Children engage in hypothesis creation and testing as they figure out how the written language works. They are in control of the processes as they use information from the environment (including the people around them) in their construction of meaning.

The social nature of children's construction of literacy

All of these findings emphasize the cognitive nature of literacy acquisition – that is, the child's active role in coming to understand and use written language. But literacy acquisition, like oral language acquisition, is also a profoundly social phenomenon. Children make sense of print in the environment because they encounter it as an integral part of interesting and important life activities in which they are engaged with others, such as having a hamburger or purchasing food (Smith, 1988). Storybook reading necessarily involves the interaction of a more fluent reader with a less fluent one. Although it may begin with one person reading to the other, it quickly evolves into joint, collaborative reading of and talking about stories (Baghban, 1984; Doake, 1985; Phillips & McNaughton,

1990; Snow & Goldfield, 1982). It is through a more proficient reader's demonstration of the literate behavior of reading, including the work of predicting or anticipating and inferencing, that beginning readers start to construct a text for themselves. And because more proficient readers respond to the apprentice reader's meaning-making by encouraging these constructions, children continue to experiment (Baghban, 1984; Smith, 1988; Weaver, 1988). Through interaction, children begin to understand the structures of narratives and the processes involved in constructing meaning (Heath, 1982). Adults respond to the child's intentions and influence the child's continuing to work at literacy and eventually using printed materials independently (Sulzby, 1985). Additionally, as children see adults read varied materials for varied purposes, they begin to construct a schema of purposes for reading.

Writing, too, is social as well as cognitive. Children come to understand the authentic purposes for which people use writing by watching those around them engage in writing. Not only do adults demonstrate as they write what writing is good for, they also encourage children to write for authentic purposes (Baghban, 1984; Smith, 1988), and they respond to children's attempts to construct texts by focusing on and attending to children's attempts to construct texts by focusing on and attending to children's intentions and meanings, rather than on the surface features or deviations from the use of the adult standard written system (Bissex, 1980). When adults, either in home or school settings, believe that children can write (in the sense of create meaning) before they use the standard written systems, their responses to children's work encourage children to continue trying to figure out how writing works and to write for a variety of purposes (Bissex, 1980; Calkins, 1986; Edelsky, 1986; Graves, 1983). A review of the research carried out with English as a second language learners reaches the same conclusion (Hudelson, 1989).

The social nature of learning has been brought home to me in the research currently in progress in a whole-language bilingual program, where I have come to appreciate how a literate adult is able to assist a child in accomplishing what the child is not able to accomplish on his or her own (Bayer, 1989; Vygotsky, 1978). For example, one of our case study children, Juan, used only vowels in his early writing even though he could identify some of the other letters of the Spanish alphabet and knew what sounds they represented. Although Juan could sometimes remember what he had written, it was impossible for anyone who had not been there to figure out his message (and often he could not remember what he had produced). This made it difficult for others (both teachers and children) to read and respond to his work. It also made it difficult for Juan to maintain story creation over several days because he had a hard time rereading what he had written.

Therefore, a strategy we adopted was to sit with Juan while he was writing, ask him what he was writing, and slowly pronounce the syllables in each word that he wanted to write, giving slight emphasis to the consonant sounds that were missing. This strategy allowed Juan to fill in at least some of the missing sounds so that his text became more readable to himself and to others.

While initially Juan required assistance to produce more than the vowel sounds in words, eventually he could produce readable text on his own. After he could produce text that included most of the sounds, an adult helped him understand spacing between words by underlining word segments in his texts. Eventually, Juan could do this on his own, and his texts became segmented more conventionally. Thus, working collaboratively with an adult helped Juan to create meanings that others could understand and appreciate.

I also have come to appreciate how children working together construct literacy. Our field notes record multiple instances of pairs, trios, and small groups of children sitting together and reading and rereading both familiar and unfamiliar stories, assisting each other in the construction of meaning. In writing, too, children, as well as teachers, assist each other in the creation of texts through varied means such as helping to figure out the spelling of a word, asking questions about and offering suggestions for a piece in progress, contributing illustrations, discussing an event that may later be turned into a story, or serving as a scribe as a report or learning log is prepared. Children play an important role in each other's literacy development whether in a first (Dyson, 1986, 1988, 1989) or a second language (Urzua, 1987). This is true even when children are playing (Daiute, 1990).

The reality of the social context for literacy development often leads to questions of whether culturally, linguistically, and socioeconomically varied home environments provide the demonstrations of and invitations to literacy documented among many middle-class families (Baghban, 1984; Heath, 1983; Taylor, 1983; see also Chapter 11). Evidence is accumulating that nonmiddle-class families *do* have a variety of reading materials in their homes and *do* engage in a range of literacy practices (Allexsaht-Snider, 1991; Delgado-Gaitan, 1990; Schiefflein and Cochran-Smith, 1984; Taylor and Dorsey-Gaines, 1988). Families do not necessarily have to engage in story reading to demonstrate literacy to children. Also expanding are traditional ideas that the "roots of literacy" (Goodman, 1980) are bound exclusively to written texts.

Working in non-mainstream communities where oral language is as highly valued as written language, educators are demonstrating that certain kinds of oral-language behaviors (such as narrating the events of a story; telling a story; sharing jokes, riddles, and gossip; teasing; constructing a story jointly; commenting about an event, story, or television or radio program; and questioning someone about an event or story)

utilize the same kinds of strategies or ways of thinking about or responding to text that schools expect and value when learners work with
written language. These strategies include sequencing, explaining, evaluating, elaborating and clarifying, arguing, persuading, responding, and
analyzing (Guerra, 1991; Pease-Alvarez, 1991; Vasquez, 1991). Therefore, they suggest expanding our definitions of what literate behaviors are
to include these kinds of uses of oral language.

In the collaborative work in which I am currently engaged, we are
finding a relationship between a strong background of oral storytelling (in
contrast to storybook reading) and the complexity and creativity of stories
that primary school children are writing in Spanish. We have discovered
that the children whose parents tell a lot of stories at home and who
encourage their children to participate in this kind of activity tend to be
the ones who will move beyond personal narratives to create fiction –
fantasy tales. This was the case with Juan, the child discussed earlier.
Oral storytelling was a family ritual engaged in as Juan's mother prepared
the family's dinner. During kindergarten, Juan demonstrated his sophistication with narratives as he created a lengthy story about his encounters
with *"Los Osos Malos"* ("The Bad Bears"). Juan narrated that the bears
chased him and even turned into ghosts in an attempt to capture him. He
finally escaped and resolved his dilemma. Juan's story was by far the
most complex of those produced by the kindergarten children. Juan's
work serves to demonstrate that prior experience with listening to and
telling stories in an oral tradition helps children understand the nature of
story. Children's own written stories reflect this understanding (Serna,
1991).

Strategies for second language literacy development

Given the cognitive and social nature of literacy acquisition, in both
native and second languages, what should educators (both grade-level
teachers with significant numbers of second language learners and formally designated second language teachers) do to promote learners' English literacy? To paraphrase Frank Smith (1988), a teacher's most critical
functions in facilitating children's literacy development are to demonstrate varied uses for reading and writing and to help children use reading
and writing themselves. In combining this general suggestion with the
broad goals for literacy set out earlier in the chapter, there seem to be
several instructional strategies teachers might make use of, choosing
those that fit the needs and interests of their students. What these strategies have in common is that they give second language learners the
opportunity to experiment with written language for multiple purposes;
they establish supportive environments where language use and experi-

mentation is encouraged, and they provide demonstrations of the functionality and power of written language. Some of these strategies are delineated in the discussions that follow.

Create a literate classroom environment

Set up a classroom environment that demonstrates the multiple functions of written language; in native language contexts, language arts educators term this a *print-rich environment* (see also Chapter 11). Include some or all of these: charts around the room connected to content area study and daily procedures such as attendance, lunch count and menus, calendar, classroom chores, and the words to favorite chants and songs; a classroom library containing books of varied genres and reading levels; written informational resources for science and social studies content work; written information about current events; a specially designated reading corner equipped with comfortable chairs or pillows; art projects titled and labeled with the artists' names; a writing center or area containing a variety of papers and writing implements; a place and organization for children's original writing in progress; a display of children's "published" works. In early childhood classrooms, centers such as housekeeping, store, restaurant, and so on could provide demonstrations of environmental print.

This kind of environment is important for demonstrating some of the purposes for literacy and inviting children to engage in literate behaviors. Special care may need to be taken both by the teacher and other children to make sure that second language learners understand and are involved in the literacy activities taking place in such a classroom.

Encourage collaborative learning

Develop a classroom that encourages children to learn with and from each other as well as the teacher. A collaborative classroom environment, one in which children see other children as resources, needs to be fostered. The classroom is to be viewed as a workshop where learners work together to ask questions, figure out ways to answer their questions, and use oral and written language collectively and independently as they are doing this. This kind of classroom certainly is not a silent place but one where talking is going on as children collaborate. Such a learning environment does not happen by itself. Nurturing this kind of environment takes time, effort, and patience. A sense of community must be developed so that children experience a sense of belonging and well-being in the classroom setting and a sense of responsibility for each other. Glover and Shepherd (1989) and Peterson (1992) consider ways in which a classroom community may be developed.

The kind of classroom where children can work independently of the teacher and interdependently with each other also means that the teacher will have more opportunity to move among children and work directly with individuals and small groups based on their specific needs and interests. The teacher still has a responsibility to teach, but the teaching is often more effective because it is geared to one child or a few children and not the entire class. The opportunity for individual attention and for small group interaction is of *special* importance to second language learners, in promoting both their understanding of and participation in learning activities and opportunities.

Utilize oral and written personal narratives

Involve learners (and teachers) in sharing their own personal stories. Narrative appears to be a fundamental process of the human mind, a basic way of making sense of the world (Gee, 1990; Paley, 1990; Polking-horne, 1990; Rosen, 1986). All of us have stories to tell, whether about something seemingly trivial that happened yesterday or an event of more significance, such as escaping one's war-torn country or the experience of life in a refugee camp. When individuals share their stories, they come to understand each other better and appreciate each other more, in terms of how they are alike and how they are different.

Sharing stories may be accomplished in different ways. One of the best documented of these is the creation of personal narratives through Writer's Workshop (Calkins, 1986). In Writer's Workshop, with the teacher's leadership and demonstration, children are able to (1) create stories based on events in their lives; (2) work over a period of time to draft stories; (3) in small and large group conferences read what they are writing for the purpose of eliciting other children's and adult's questions, comments, and suggestions; (4) make substantive changes in their pieces based on the comments of others and their own ideas; and (5) with the assistance of a teacher make editing changes to the final version of the narrative. In order for this to occur, the teacher works directly with individuals and small groups as well as circulating among the learners.

As learners generate topics and produce drafts of pieces, they use written language (and experiment with that language) to express their meanings. As they share work in progress and receive comments and assistance from peers and teachers, they take into account others' under-standings of their intentions. As they perfect final, published copies, they understand the need for getting to the standard form, to make the text readable for a wider audience. Second language learners have demon-strated that they are able to generate their own personal narratives and through sharing and conferencing both give and receive comments on their work in progress, comments which serve as the basis for revisions of their work (Samway, 1987; Urzua, 1987).

What appears to be different about second language learners (although there is also tremendous variation among native speakers) is the quality of the product (in terms of the learners' ability to express themselves in the second language), the amount and kind of revisions that learners make, and perhaps, early on, the level of participation in drafting and conferencing. It may take longer for these learners to feel comfortable talking about their work and the work of others. Also to be taken into consideration is the amount of editing, particularly of syntax, that should take place, given that these learners have only partial control over English. Some ESL teachers have concluded that they will encourage children's creation of personal narratives but focus on first draft fluency of expression and consider revision and editing later (Hudelson, 1989). At some point then, attention needs to be paid to form as well as to expression (Reyes, 1991).

Personal story sharing does not necessarily need to begin with written narratives. On the contrary, learners, particularly second language learners, may need the opportunity to hear stories shared orally before producing written stories. Sometimes teachers will demonstrate what they mean by a personal story by relating one about themselves. Then they have children pair off and share stories with each other. At other times, children will take turns telling stories from home before the class moves into writing down their stories. In these storytelling sessions, the listeners are expected to listen carefully (just as they would in Writer's Workshop) so that they can make comments afterwards on the teller's story.

Teachers may also demonstrate how to begin writing personal narratives by writing one of their own for the children to see and by asking the children to comment on it (Fournier, et al., 1991). Additionally, for some second language learners, teachers may choose to act as scribes by taking dictation as children narrate their stories (Rigg, 1989). Or teacher and child may participate in shared writing, where the child writes part of his or her story, and the teacher writes part when the child tires or becomes reluctant to continue (Serna, 1991).

Utilize dialogic writing

Provide the opportunity for learners to interact in writing with a more proficient user of English. Perhaps the easiest and the most direct way to do this is to use dialogue journals, with teachers and learners carrying on written conversations with each other. Since the focus is on personal communication, no overt correction of a learner's English is made (see Chapter 9). But learners do get to see and read standard written English in the form of the adult's responses to the child. This practice has been well documented with ESL learners of various ages and English language proficiency levels (Kreeft, 1984; Peyton, 1990; Peyton & Staton, 1993). It is also possible to have learner–learner pairings, instead of teacher–learner pairings, in second language contexts, with a more fluent user paired with a less fluent user of English (Flores, 1991; Peyton & Mackinson-Smyth, 1989) or an ESL learner with a native speaker.

Second language learners benefit from this activity in several ways. They engage in an authentic communication situation and need to make themselves understood. This provides an authentic reason for trying out the new language. They get a demonstration of standard written English, and they begin to see that one of the functions of written English is to establish and maintain interpersonal relationships – in other words, English can be used for personal reasons.

Utilize predictable books

This chapter supports the perspective that fluent, effective reading is a process in which a reader predicts his or her way through text, sampling the visual (graphophonic) display and using text content and the semantic and syntactic cuing systems to construct meaning (Goodman, 1967; Weaver, 1988). To develop fluent, effective readers, therefore, it is important to use teaching strategies that help learners view reading as a predicting process. Especially for beginning readers and for ESL readers whose English is less than fluent, predictable books (Heald-Taylor, 1987; Rhodes, 1981) may be utilized both as a strategy for helping to develop their abilities to predict their ways through texts and as a way of demonstrating the simultaneous utilization of the semantic, syntactic, and graphophonic systems of language (Goodman, Watson, & Burke, 1987). In our longitudinal research, we have discovered that fluent Spanish readers begin their venture into English reading by choosing to read for themselves predictable books that the teachers have previously shared with the class (Hudelson & Serna, 1991). Because of the familiarity and predictability of these texts, children are able to construct meaning from them so that their first forays into English reading are successful.

In addition to sharing predictable books and making them available to the children, teachers often use repeated readings of predictable books to help develop children's confidence in predicting. Working with teachers in New Zealand, Holdaway (1979) experimented with repeated readings of *Big Books,* which are highly predictable stories in enlarged text formats that enable children in a group to see text more easily in the context of a group. Holdaway stressed that with the repetitions, teachers could direct children's attention to particular features of the text. In addition to Holdaway, educators in the United States (Lynch, 1988; Strickland, 1988;

Strickland & Morrow, 1990) including those working with second language learners of varying ages (Nurss & Hough, 1985; Nurss, Hough, & Enright, 1986; Renault, 1981) have provided suggestions for repeated use of predictable books, whether in *Big Book* format or otherwise.

For example, children might be asked to use the illustrations to predict the contents of the text. After the first or second reading, a teacher may track part of the print of the story with a hand or pointer and encourage young children to read along as they see the words and hear the teacher pronounce them. As teachers reread a familiar story, they may stop at particularly predictable parts of the story and ask the learners to fill in the next word or phrase. In order to focus on meaning, it is important to encourage children to think of as many words as they can that would make sense in the context of the story. This kind of oral cloze may be followed by written cloze activities in which certain words or phrases are covered physically (or certain parts of a story may be written on a board or on chart paper with words and phrases deleted), and learners are asked to predict the missing words. Teachers may also cover up a word leaving only the initial letter or letters so that learners use graphophonic as well as syntactic and semantic cues to predict. It is also important to demonstrate to readers that when they don't know a word, they can read ahead and use the context that follows as well as the context that precedes the missing word or phrase. Finally, teachers may focus learners' attention on certain text features, such as repeated words, words that begin with a specific letter or cluster of letters, punctuation marks, capital letters, and so on.

Teachers and learners may also use predictable, familiar books for acting out stories and for creating their own books. Older children, working as tutors, may themselves become more effective readers as they read to younger students (Heath & Mangiola, 1991). What is crucial is that these activities are carried out with text that is familiar and predictable. What is also crucial is that the emphasis go from the whole down to the part rather than vice versa. Learning always begins with the experience of the whole story. Then, if the learners need specific instruction or focus on the parts, the teacher may use the text selectively to assist children in becoming independent, effective readers.

In addition to the utilization of predictable books, teachers working with second language learners who are beginning readers may also want to consider the selective use of alphabet books. A recent review of the research on children's knowledge of the alphabet suggests that, along with reading environmental print, participating in individual and group writing projects, and reading and spelling each others' names, children in primary classrooms learn the names of the letters by sharing alphabet books (McGee & Richgels, 1989). For second language learners especially, it needs to be stressed that the specific books chosen should be connected to something that the children are studying, for example, using animal alphabet books if the children are studying animals. Children should not use alphabet books on topics for which they have no experience, and they should not use alphabet books to drill on letters and sounds. In addition to reading published alphabet books, learners could create some of their own. Returning to the example of animals, a unit of study on animals could generate an alphabet book that would reflect the animals that the children had studied and what they had learned about them.

Read aloud to children daily

Demonstrate the power of written stories by reading literature aloud to children. If learners become aware of narrative structure and literary language through the experience of listening to (and later reading) literature, the activity of reading to children needs to be viewed as a curriculum basic rather than as a frill. Like native speakers of English, second language learners need to be read to, on a daily basis, by fluent models of English reading. They need to be read to from varied genres in order to hear and enjoy the richness and variety of the English language, begin to develop knowledge of the literary and story heritage of varied cultures, and begin to see literature as one way of coming to understand the world and the relationship of the individual to that world (Peterson & Eeds, 1990).

In thinking about the richness of literature that could be shared in extensive reading experiences, it seems appropriate to suggest that literature be chosen from multiple sources. One source would be quality children's literature by writers who are renowned for their ability to illuminate human experience and who use a variety of literary forms without specific regard for a cultural or ethnic group, for example, Natalie Babbitt and William Steig. Another source would be books that reflect multicultural perspectives, particularly the perspectives of the learners, but that also consider broader human themes. Thus, for example, with a group of Mexican-American learners from the Southwest I might use Byrd Baylor's *Coyote Cry* (1975), which tells the story of a sheepherder and his grandson. In this book, the grandfather teaches his grandson about the complexities of life through the coyote they encounter as they care for their sheep.

A third source would be literature that represents the specific traditions or stories of varied cultural groups, with an effort made to use some books that reflect the cultures of the children in the classroom. If, for example, there were significant numbers of children from the Caribbean, I would read some of the tales of the trickster figure Anansi the spider; with Native-American children I might use Paul Goble's renditions of

Plains Indians traditional tales; with Mexican-American children I might use Joe Hayes' *La Llorona* (1987). Choosing culturally familiar stories may be especially helpful to second language children because prior knowledge of characters and plots may make the stories potentially more comprehensible to the learners than unfamiliar stories. Still another source for read-aloud material is children's poetry, both humorous and otherwise, with its rhythm and rhyme.

A final source is reading material rich in content in areas of interest to children. A wide variety of well-written and illustrated informational books are available in school and public libraries. If children (both native speakers and second language learners) want to learn about something, they will work to construct meaning from a book being read to them.

In taking into account the special linguistic needs of second language learners, teachers need to be most concerned about choosing books from which learners will be able to construct some meaning, even if that meaning is not the same as the teacher's or other children's. Books that have especially clear illustrations and those that are predictable in one or more ways are especially beneficial for second language learners early in their English literacy development. In thinking about structuring read-aloud experiences, grouping children heterogeneously by language proficiency and encouraging responses to shared books may assist the learners to develop their English. Several authors have provided suggestions for stories and books to be read aloud (Trelease, 1989), as well as guidelines for the selection of books that reflect multicultural realities (Norton, 1990) and books to be read to learners at varying levels of English proficiency (Allen, 1989; Smallwood, 1990).

Organize for literature response

Plan opportunities for learners to respond to literature. It is not enough to share literature with children. Children need an opportunity to respond to what they have heard (and later what they read), to construct meaning, to relate a story to their own lives, to comment on emotions and ideas that a piece has evoked. This means that reading aloud to children must be followed by an opportunity to comment on the experience and to share those comments with other learners. This does *not* mean that it is necessary or even desirable to bombard learners with a variety of comprehension questions. Rather, learners should be given time to reflect on the literary experience they have had or to respond to a general question such as: ''What would you like to say about this book/chapter/poem?''

Another way of focusing on response to literature is through literature study, an activity that involves learners in intensive rather than extensive reading experiences (see Peterson & Eeds, 1990 for a thorough discussion of the framework for literature study and an explication of how literature study is accomplished). To carry out a literature study, learners working in groups choose a book that all the members want to read. Generally the teacher introduces several books to the class, and the class members choose a book that is appealing to them. With or without adult assistance, the members of the group read the selected book and come to literature study group prepared to talk about what they have read. The first session of the literature study provides an opportunity for learners to respond to the book personally as the teacher encourages responses by opening the discussion with a comment such as, "So, what did you think?" or, "What do you want to say about this book?" As the children talk, the teacher takes notes on their ideas and may offer some of his or her own as well. But the teacher does not ask a series of reading comprehension questions. Comprehension is assumed, so the emphasis is on the children's individual responses, on how they constructed meaning when they read this piece.

After the children have had a chance to share their responses, the teacher guides the group to choose a specific aspect of the book that they want to examine more closely. This may be done by reviewing some of the comments that the group members made. Or it may be done by asking the children to think about what they would like to reexamine. For example, if the children had read *Coyote Cry* (Baylor, 1975), they might have made comments about what the grandfather was like, or they might have talked about the fact that the place in the story was like the desert where they live. Children and teacher might decide to go back into the story to find places where the author made them envision the desert or places in the story where they learned about what the grandfather was like. The readers' task is to go back into the book (often this is accomplished by giving the learners Post-it notes to use when they find an example they want to discuss) and find examples of the aspect of the story that the group has decided to examine more closely. This provides an opportunity for children to reexamine their constructions of meaning by going back to the author's words; thus the children use the text to justify or reconsider their interpretations. Once again, the teacher, as a participant in the group, may contribute ideas and opinions, but the focus is not on one right opinion or interpretation. Rather, it is on the collaborative construction of meaning. Together, teacher and children decide how many sessions they will use to return to the text and investigate specific aspects of it.

Literature study recognizes that learners bring prior experiences with them to books that they read; these prior experiences will influence their constructions of meaning. Thus reading is a transaction between reader and text (Rosenblatt, 1988). But literature study also recognizes that learning is social and that readers can learn and grow in their interpretations of texts if they share their meanings and listen to the interpretations of others (Eeds & Peterson, 1991). Educators have demonstrated that second as well as first language learners can participate effectively in literature study (Bird & Alvarez, 1987; Fournier, et al., 1992; Samway, et al., 1991; Urzua, 1992)

Include opportunities for self-selected reading

Provide times for children to choose some of their own reading material and read it during school hours. In order to see themselves as readers and to view reading as something enjoyable, children need to be able to select some of their own reading material. In many classrooms, DEAR (Drop Everything and Read) or GRAB (Go Read a Book) time is a daily feature of instruction. The rule during DEAR or GRAB time (perhaps named more realistically than SSR – Silent, Sustained Reading – since in primary classrooms reading to oneself is not a silent activity) is that everyone reads something of any genre he or she has chosen to read. This activity may be accompanied by learners keeping a list of what they have read.

Include literacy development as a part of content study

Teachers should structure opportunities for learners to use oral and written language to learn about the world and to act in some way to transform it. A theme of several of the other chapters in this book is that language and content learning cannot be separated (see Chapter 7, for example). The most effective environment for language learning (including literacy learning) is one in which language is used to study content that is of interest and concern to them. Putting this generalization into practice has meant that educators have been struggling with teaching based on topics or themes, sometimes generated by the adults but often chosen by the learners themselves. Once a topic has been chosen, learners may brainstorm what they already know about the topic and subsequently generate questions that they want to investigate. They then use both oral and written language and work collaboratively to learn about the topic and answer their questions. This way of approaching content tends to make learners active and involved in their learning. The one element that I would add to this is a concern to have learners, in some of their content study, struggle with some of the issues of the day so that they are approaching content from a critical perspective and with the idea of what they can do to effect some changes in the world (Freeman & Freeman, 1991; Peterson, 1991; Walsh, 1990).

If, for example, students are studying Native Americans, a major issue is the past and the continuing injustices perpetrated on these people by the U.S. and Canadian governments and by citizens with racist and supremacist attitudes. When gathering materials for the study and when considering the kinds of questions to be asked, such issues need to be dealt with. Learners need to look at material critically and examine various perspectives in order to reach their own conclusions and act on these conclusions (Bigelow, 1989).

Another example would be environmental issues. In a fifth-grade class with a number of second language learners, the teacher wanted his students to become more aware of environmental issues affecting Arizona and beyond, and to consider steps that they and their classmates could take as responsible and active citizens. The teacher introduced the study by asking the students to brainstorm environmental issues that they had heard something about. After brainstorming, the learners decided that, in groups, they wanted to learn more about the following: air pollution, water use, destruction of the desert environment, and destruction of forests. Over a period of several weeks, the learners and teacher found materials about these topics, examined the materials, summarized the issues in writing, and formulated plans for what they might do to respond to each of the issues. Their informational reports, which included summaries of what they had learned and action plans, were shared with other classes in their school.

This stimulated the kindergarten classes to do a study of environmental pollution at the school building level. They chose an area of the school's playground and collected samples of what they found in the grass and dirt. They brought their collections into the class, categorized the items, and created a collage that was displayed in the school with a big sign explaining where the trash came from and exhorting students: Don't litter. Both of these groups of learners used oral and written language to investigate topics of interest. But more than that, both groups used literacy to act on the world.

One of the questions that may arise is whether second language learners will be able to handle the linguistic demands of this kind of work. The two classrooms studying environmental issues contained both native and non-native speakers of varying proficiencies. The teachers consciously grouped the children heterogeneously so that the more fluent users assisted those less fluent. But all the learners contributed to the final projects; all became involved in the content; all became more literate by engaging in purposeful reading and writing. In exclusively ESL classrooms, also, learners need to be challenged by meaningful content. Second language learners need to learn to be active, responsible citizens of the societies in which they live, as do native speakers. The school setting seems to be an appropriate place for this to happen.

Summary and conclusions

I conclude this chapter by returning to the request from a local educator and by noting that any discussion of second language literacy development be based on the "expert's" views of the nature of literacy and that person's interpretation of research and practice. This chapter reflects my own understandings and interpretations, which I summarize in the following way. I begin by noting that, for me, the core of literacy is the construction of meaning, either through the creation of one's own text or the interpretation of text written by others. I assert that the construction of meaning is central whether literacy is occurring in a first or a second language; in fact, I argue that it is absolutely imperative for teachers of second language learners to be concerned, above all, with meaning rather than form. I also note that research has demonstrated that the processes of reading and writing for children in a first and a second language are more alike than different. Both involve learners figuring out how written language works; both involve learners in interactions with others. For first and second language learners, learning occurs not only in formal school settings but also in homes and communities (see Chapter 4).

Given the similarities in first and second language literacy processes, the literacy practices discussed in this chapter reflect what is known today about children's language and literacy development. These practices, whether they be the utilization of dialogue journals, the creation of personal narratives, the focus on collaborative work in the study of important content, the practice of reading aloud from the wealth of children's literature, the utilization of predictable books, or the provision of opportunities for both independent reading and personal response to literature in group settings have several common characteristics:

1. They make learners active participants in their own learning.
2. They give learners opportunities to use oral and written language (both their own and others') for a variety of purposes.
3. They promote interaction with others as central to learning.
4. They involve learners in taking risks and being supported in their risk taking by adults and peers who respond to their efforts.
5. They necessitate the organization of learner-centered, language-rich environments that are both linguistically stimulating and intellectually challenging and rigorous places for children to spend their time.

The position I have taken is not a unique one. Organizations such as The International Reading Association, The National Council of Teachers of English, The Canadian Council of Teachers of English, The Association for Childhood Education International, and The National Association for the Education of Young Children have advocated the kinds of instructional strategies that appear in this chapter as being developmentally appropriate in terms of what is cognitively sensible for elementary school learners. One caveat for second language learners is the special need to be sensitive to their understanding of instruction and response to it, that is, to give special consideration to the sense that learners are making and to work hard to make sure that comprehension is there. Another caveat is to be sensitive to individual differences in rates of second language acquisition and to be reasonable in our expectations of learners' responses to instruction. A third caveat is to have faith that second language learners *will* learn, and therefore, to have high expectations for what can be accomplished. Second language learners have the same potential as native speakers, and they deserve the same high quality literacy opportunities.

References

Allen, V. (1989). Literature as a support to language acquisition. In P. Rigg & V. Allen (Eds.), *When they don't all speak English*. Urbana, IL: National Council of Teachers in English.

Allexsaht-Snider, M. (1991). Family literacy in a Spanish-speaking context: Joint construction of meaning. *The Quarterly Newsletter of the Laboratory of Comparative Human Cognition, 13*, 15–21.

Baghban, M. (1984). *Our daughter learns to read and write*. Newark, DE: International Reading Association.

Bayer, A. (1989). *Collaborative apprenticeship learning: Language and thinking across the curriculum, K–12*. Mountain View, CA: Mayfield Publishing Company.

Baylor, B. (1975). *Coyote Cry*. New York: Lothrop, Lee & Simon.

Bigelow, W. (1989). Discovering Columbus: Rereading the past. *Language Arts, 66*, 635–643.

Bird, L., & Alvarez, L. (1987). Beyond comprehension: The power of literature study for language minority students. *ESOL in Elementary Education Newsletter, 10*, 1–3.

Bissex, G. (1980). *GYNS at work: A child learns to write and read*. Cambridge, MA: Harvard University Press.

Bosma, B. (1987). *Fairy tales, fables, legends, and myths: Using folk literature in your classroom*. New York: Teachers College Press.

Calkins, L. (1986). *The art of teaching writing*. Portsmouth, NH: Heinemann.

Chomsky, C. (1971). Write first, read later. *Childhood Education. 47*, 296–301.

Clay, M. (1975). *What did I write?* Auckland: Heinemann Educational Books.

Clay, M. (1985). *The early detection of reading difficulties.* Portsmouth, NH: Heinemann.

Daiute, C. (1990). The role of play in writing development. *Research in the Teaching of English, 24,* 4–47.

Delgado-Gaitan, C. (1990). *Literacy for empowerment: The role of parents in children's education.* London: Falmer Press.

Doake, D. (1985). Reading-like behavior: Its role in learning to read. In A. Jagger & M. Trika Smith-Burke (Eds.), *Observing the language learner.* Newark, DE: International Reading Association.

Dobson, L. (1986). Emergent writers in a grade one classroom. Paper presented at the Fourth International Conference on the Teaching of English, Ottawa, Ontario.

Dyson, A. (1986). Transitions and tensions: Interrelationships between the drawing, talking and dictating of young children. *Research in the Teaching of English, 20,* 379–409.

Dyson, A. (1988). Negotiating among multiple worlds: The space/time dimensions of young children's composing. *Research in the Teaching of English, 22,* 355–390.

Dyson, A. (1989). *Multiple worlds of child writers: Friends learning to write.* New York: Teachers College Press.

Edelsky, C. (1986). *Writing in a bilingual program: Habia una vez.* Norwood, NJ: Ablex.

Eeds, M., & Peterson, R. (1991). Teacher as curator: Learning to talk about literature. *The Reading Teacher, 45,* 118–126.

Ferreiro, E. (1990). Literacy development: Psychogenesis. In Y. Goodman (Ed.), *How children construct literacy: Piagetian perspectives.* Newark, DE: International Reading Association.

Ferreiro, E., & Teberosky, A. (1982). *Literacy before schooling.* Exeter, NH: Heinemann.

Flores, B. (1991). The psychogenesis of literacy/biliteracy. Paper presented at the Title VII Summer Institute, Arizona State University, Tempe.

Fournier, J., Lansdowne, B., Pastenes, Z., Steen, P., & Hudelson, S. (1992). Learning with, about and from children: Life in a bilingual second grade. In C. Genishi (Ed.), *Ways of assessing children and curriculum: Stories of early childhood practice.* New York: Teachers College Press.

Freeman, Y., & Freeman, D. (1991). "Doing" social studies: Whole language lessons to promote social action. *Social Education, 55,* 29–33.

Freire, P. (1970). *Pedagogy of the Oppressed.* New York: Herder and Herder.

Gee, J. (1990). A linguistic approach to narrative. Paper presented at the Boston University Language Development Conference, Boston, MA.

Glover, M., & Shepherd, L. (1989). *Not on your own: The power of learning together.* New York: Scholastic.

Goodman, K. (1967). Reading is a psycholinguistic guessing game. *Journal of the Reading Specialist, 6,* 126–135.

Goodman, K., Goodman, Y., & Flores, B. (1979). *Reading in the bilingual classroom: Literacy and biliteracy.* Rosslyn, VA: National Clearinghouse for Bilingual Education.

Goodman, Y. (1980). The roots of literacy. In M. Douglass (Ed.), *Claremont Reading Conference 44th Yearbook.* Claremont, CA: Claremont Reading Conference.

Goodman, Y., & Altwerger, B. (1981). *Print awareness in pre-school children: A working paper.* Tucson, AZ: Program in Language and Literacy, College of Education, University of Arizona.

Goodman, Y., Watson, D., & Burke, C. (1987) *The reading miscue inventory.* New York: Richard C. Owen.

Graves, D. (1983). *Writing: Teachers and children at work.* Exeter, NH: Heinemann.

Guerra, J. (1991). The role of ethnography in the reconceptualization of literacy. *The Quarterly Newsletter of the Laboratory of Comparative Human Cognition, 13,* 3–8.

Harste, J., Woodward, V., & Burke, C. (1984). *Language stories and literacy lessons.* Portsmouth, NH: Heinemann.

Hayes, J. (1987). *La Llorona.* El Paso, TX: Cinco Puntos Press.

Heald-Taylor, G. (1987). Predictable literature selections and activities for language arts instruction. *The Reading Teacher, 40,* 6–12.

Heath, S. B. (1982). Protean shapes in literacy events: Ever shifting oral and literate traditions. In D. Tannen (Ed.), *Spoken and written language: Exploring orality and literacy,* pp. 91–117. Norwood, NJ: Ablex.

Heath, S. B. (1983). *Ways with words: Language, life and work in communities and classrooms.* Cambridge: Cambridge University Press.

Heath, S. B., & Hoffman, D. M. (1986). *Interactive reading and writing in elementary classrooms.* (Guidebook for *Inside Learners* [film]). Available from S. B. Heath, Stanford University, Stanford, CA.

Heath, S. B., & Mangiola, L. (1991). *Children of promise: Literate activity in linguistically and culturally diverse classrooms.* Washington, DC: National Education Association.

Holdaway, D. (1979). *The foundations of literacy.* Exeter, NH: Heinemann.

Hudelson, S. (1981–82). An introductory examination of children's invented spelling in Spanish. *National Association for Bilingual Education Journal, VI,* 53–68.

Hudelson, S. (1984). Kan yu ret an rayt en ingles: Children become literate in English as a second language. *TESOL Quarterly, 18,* 221–238.

Hudelson, S. (1989). *Write on: Children writing in ESL.* Englewood Cliffs, NJ: Prentice-Hall.

Hudelson, S. (1991). Developing Spanish writing in a bilingual first and second grade. Paper presented at the Annual TESOL Convention, New York.

Hudelson, S., & Serna, I. (in press). Mira, teacher – Escribi mi nombre en ingles: Beginning to become literate in a second language. Proceedings of The Whole Language Umbrella: Urbana, IL: National Council of Teachers of English.

Kreeft, J. (1984). *Dialogue writing: Analysis of student-teacher interactive writing in the learning of English as a second language.* Washington, DC: Center for Applied Linguistics (NIE-G-83-0030).

Landsmann, L. T. (1990). Literacy development and pedagogical implications: Evidence from the Hebrew system of writing. In Y. Goodman (Ed.), *How children construct literacy: Piagetian perspectives.* Newark, DE: International Reading Association.

Lee, Lian-Ju. (1990). *Developing control of reading and writing in Chinese.* Tucson, AZ: Program in Language and Literacy, Division of Language Reading and Culture, College of Education, University of Arizona.

Lynch, P. (1988). *Using predictable books and big books.* New York: Scholastic.

McGee, L., & Richgels, D. (1989). ''K is Kristen's'': Learning the alphabet from a child's perspective. *The Reading Teacher, 43,* 216–226.

Norton, D. (1990). Teaching multicultural literature in the reading curriculum. *The Reading Teacher, 44,* 28–40.

Nurss, J., & Hough, R. (1985). Story reading: Languages for limited English speakers. *ESOL in Elementary Education Newsletter, 8,* 1–2.

Nurss, J., Hough, R., & Enright, D. S. (1986). Story reading with limited English speaking children in the regular classroom. *The Reading Teacher, 39,* 510–515.

Paley, V. (1990). *The boy who would be a helicopter: The uses of storytelling in the classroom.* Cambridge, MA: Harvard University Press.

Pease-Alvarez, L. (1991). Oral contexts for literacy development in a Mexican immigrant community. *The Quarterly Newsletter of the Laboratory of Comparative Human Cognition, 13,* 9–13.

Peterson, R. (1992). *Life in a small place: Making a learning community.* Portsmouth, NH: Heinemann.

Peterson, R. (1991). Teaching how to read the world and change it. In C. Walsh (Ed.), *Literacy as praxis: Culture, language and pedagogy.* Norwood, NJ: Ablex.

Peterson, R., & Eeds, M. (1990). *Grand conversations: Literature groups in action.* Toronto, Ont: Scholastic TAB.

Peyton, J. (Ed.). (1990). *Students and teachers working together: Perspectives on journal writing.* Alexandria, VA: Teachers of English to Speakers of Other Languages.

Peyton, J., & Mackinson-Smyth, J. (1989). Writing and talking about writing: Computer networking with elementary students. In D. M. Johnson & D. H. Roeen (Eds.), *Richness in writing: Empowering minority students* (pp. 100–119). New York: Longman.

Peyton, J., & Staton, J. (Eds.). (1993). *Dialogue journals in the multilingual classroom: Building language fluency and writing skills through written interaction.* Norwood, NJ: Ablex.

Phillips, G., & McNaughton, S. (1990). The practice of storybook reading to preschoolers in mainstream New Zealand families. *Reading Research Quarterly 25*, 196–212.

Polkinghorne, D. (1990). Narrative and self-concept. Paper presented at the Boston University Language Development Conference, Boston, MA.

Read, C. (1975). *Children's categorization of speech sounds in English.* Urbana, IL: National Council of Teachers of English.

Renault, L. (1981). Theoretically based second language reading strategies. In C. W. Twyford, W. Diehl, & K. Feathers (Eds.), *Reading English as a second language: Moving from theory* (pp. 92–104). Monographs in Teaching and Learning, Bloomington, IN: School of Education, Indiana University.

Reyes, M. (1991). A process approach to literacy learning using dialogue journals and literature logs with second language learners. *Research in the Teaching of English, 25,* 291–313.

Rhodes, L. (1981). I can read: Predictable literature selections and activities for language arts instruction. *The Reading Teacher, 35:* 511–518.

Rigg, P. (1989). Language experience approach: Reading naturally. In V. Allen & P. Rigg (Eds.), *When they don't all speak English.* Urbana, IL: National Council of Teachers of English.

Rosen, H. (1986). The importance of story. *Language Arts, 63,* 226–237.

Rosenblatt, L. (1988). *Writing and reading: The transactional theory.* (Technical Report 13). Berkeley, CA: Center for the Study of Writing.

Samway, K. (1987). *The writing processes of non-native English speaking children in the elementary grades.* Unpublished doctoral dissertation, University of Rochester, Rochester, New York.

Samway, K., Shang, G., Cade, C., Gamil, M., Lubandina, M., & Phomma-chanh, K. (1991). Reading the skeleton, the heart and the brain of a book: Students' perspectives on literature study circles. *The Reading Teacher, 45,* 196–205.

Schiefflein, B., & Cochran-Smith, M. (1984). Learning to read culturally: Literacy before schooling. In H. Goelman, A. Oberg, & F. Smith (Eds.), *Awakening to literacy.* Exeter, NH: Heinemann.

Seawell, R. P. M. (1985). *A micro-ethnogrraphic study of a Spanish/English bilingual kindergarten in which literature and puppet play were used as a method of enhancing language growth.* Unpublished doctoral dissertation, University of Texas at Austin.

Serna, I. (1991). Case studies of children developing Spanish writing in a whole language bilingual kindergarten and first grade. Paper presented at the annual TESOL Convention, New York.

Serna, I., & Hudelson, S. (1993). Emergent Spanish literacy in a whole language bilingual program. In R. Donmoyer & R. Kos (Eds.), *At-risk students: Portraits, programs and practices.* Albany, NY: SUNY Press.

Smallwood, B. (1990). *The literature connection: A read-aloud guide for multicultural classrooms.* Reading, MA: Addison-Wesley.

Smith, F. (1988). *Joining the literacy club: Further essays into education.* Portsmouth, NH: Heinemann.

Snow, C., & Goldfield, A. (1982). Building stories: The emergence of information structures from conversations. In D. Tannen (Ed.), *Analyzing discourse: Text and talk.* Washington, DC: Georgetown University Press.

Strickland, D. (1988). Some tips for using big books. *The Reading Teacher, 41,* 966–968.

Strickland, D., & Morrow, L. (1990). Sharing big books. *The Reading Teacher, 43,* 342–344.

Sulzby, E. (1985). Children's emergent reading of favorite storybooks: A developmental study. *Reading Research Quarterly, 20,* 458–481.

Taylor, D. (1983). *Family literacy: Young children learning to read and write.* Exeter, NH: Heinemann.

Taylor, D., & Dorsey-Gaines, C. (1988). *Growing up literate: Learning from inner-city families.* Portsmouth, NH: Heinemann.

Teale, W., & Sulzby, E. (1986). Emergent literacy as a perspective for examining how young children become writers and readers. In W. Teale and E. Sulzby (Eds.), *Emergent literacy: Writing and reading.* Norwood, NJ: Ablex.

Temple, C., Nathan, R., & Burris, N. (1982). *The beginnings of writing.* Boston: Allyn & Bacon.

Trelease, J. (1989). *The new read-aloud handbook.* New York: Viking Penguin Press.

Urzua, C. (1987). "You stopped too soon": Second language children composing and revising. *TESOL Quarterly, 21,* 279–305.

Urzua, C. (1992). Faith in learners through literature studies. *Language Arts, 69,* 492–501.

Vasquez, O. (1991). Reading the world in a multicultural setting: A Mexicano perspective. *The Quarterly Newsletter of the Laboratory of Comparative Human Cognition, 13,* 13–15.

Vygotsky, L. (1978). *Mind in society.* Cambridge, MA: Harvard University Press.

Wallace, C. (1988). *Learning to read in a multicultural society: The social context of second language literacy.* Hertfordshire, England: Prentice-Hall International.

Walsh, C. (Ed.). (1990). *Literacy as praxis: Culture, language and pedagogy.* Norwood, NJ: Ablex.

Weaver, C. (1988). *Reading: Process and practice.* Portsmouth, NH: Heinemann.

Wells, G. (1990). Apprenticeship in literacy. In C. Walsh (Ed.), *Literacy as praxis: Culture, language and pedagogy.* Norwood, NJ: Ablex.

Additional readings

Bigelow, W., Miner, B., & Peterson, R. (Eds.). (1991). *Rethinking Columbus.* Milwaukee, WI: Rethinking Schools.
Bosma, B. (1987). *Fairy tales, fables, legends, and myths: Using folk literature in your classroom.* New York: Teachers College Press.
Freeman, Y., & Freeman, D. (1992). *Whole language for second language learners.* Portsmouth, NH: Heinemann.
Hayes, C., Bahruth, R., & Kessler, C. (1991). *Literacy con carino.* Portsmouth, NH: Heinemann.
Heald-Taylor, G. (1986). *Whole language strategies for ESL primary students.* Toronto: Ontario Institute for Studies in Education.
Rigg, P. (1991). Whole language in TESOL. *Tesol Quarterly, 25,* 521–542.

7 Teaching content through a second language

Mimi Met

The public media and educational literature have been replete recently with discussions of educational reforms, educational restructuring, and educational goals for the year 2000, goals that are the same for all our nation's schoolchildren. Yet for a substantial and growing segment of the school population, achieving the goals of schooling has an added challenge: How can they be attained when students have limited proficiency in English?

Many approaches to educating minority language students seem to be based on the assumption that proficiency in English is a prerequisite for academic learning, even though research seems to indicate that it may take as long as seven years for students to acquire a level of academic English proficiency comparable to native English-speaking peers (Collier, 1989; Cummins, 1981). Clearly, if minority language students are to achieve the goals of education, academic learning cannot be put on hold until students have acquired proficiency in English.

The results of foreign language immersion have shown that students can develop content knowledge at the same time as they develop language skills. In immersion, majority language students are educated in a new language. In total immersion programs, school activities – from mundane tasks such as collecting lunch money to cognitively demanding tasks such as learning how to read – are conducted in a foreign (second) language. Numerous studies of Canadian immersion programs have shown that English-speaking students schooled in French not only attain higher levels of proficiency in French than in any other school-based model of second language instruction but do so at no detriment to their native language, academic, or cognitive development (Genesee, 1987; Lambert and Tucker, 1972; Swain and Lapkin, 1985).

In the United States, schools are challenged to provide a quality education to students who are not yet proficient in English, and there are many teachers charged with developing these students' linguistic and academic proficiencies. Some teachers are English as a second language (ESL) teachers who see the children for part of the school day. Other teachers are grade-level teachers in whose rooms the students are "mainstreamed" for most of the day. And others are grade-level teachers whose students have been "exited" from ESL or bilingual programs but whose students continue to struggle with the linguistic demands of the academic curriculum. Yet other teachers of minority language students work in two-way immersion programs (also known as dual immersion, developmental bilingual, or two-way bilingual) or are bilingual education teachers whose students may have limited proficiency in English, and even perhaps their native language. These students must be provided with content instruction. The students of these teachers simply cannot wait to develop high levels of academic language proficiency before tackling the demands of the curriculum. A basic premise of this chapter is that *all* teachers who work with second language students – second language teachers, grade-level teachers, bilingual education or two-way immersion teachers – must enable their students to make academic progress *while* they are learning English. It is clear from the results of foreign language immersion that achieving such a goal is possible.

Foreign language immersion teachers must also develop the linguistic and academic competence of majority language students who are learning through a new language. Recently, increased attention has been given to identifying what immersion teachers do (or should do) to facilitate the codevelopment of second language proficiency and academic content learning (Lorenz & Met, 1988; Mojhanovich & Fish, 1988; Snow, 1987). This chapter will draw upon the roles and tasks of immersion teachers and apply them to second language teachers. First, we will see how planning for instruction is affected by consideration of students' limited proficiency in the language of instruction. Then, we will explore how, as in foreign language immersion, teachers may adjust classroom activities and the delivery of instruction when the demands of the curriculum exceed the linguistic skills of students. Third, the chapter will focus on how assessment of student progress may be done when students are educated in a non-native language. Finally, we will discuss the implications of redefining the roles of teachers who work with second language students as teachers of *content* as well as of *language,* and the implications of these roles for teachers' relationships with one another.

Planning for instruction

All good teachers must be good planners. Costa and Garmston (1985) have suggested that good teaching rests on good planning. They indicate that the planning phase of the teaching process requires high levels of thought and may be the most important element in successful teaching. According to Costa and Garmston, good teachers see each lesson in terms of long-range and short-term instructional goals. They think about the lesson from the viewpoint of the learner and consider how individual learning styles, preferences, and abilities will interact with the lesson to be delivered. They envision the lesson as it will unfold (almost as though viewing a video in their head). Effective teachers plan with precision, identifying what they and their students will be doing in each part of the lesson, anticipating areas that may cause difficulty, and ensuring that time and materials needed for the lesson will be available.

Teachers who educate students in a non-native language need to do all of the above. But their unique charge requires that they perform additional planning tasks as well. These include sequencing objectives, planning for language growth, identifying instructional activities that make content accessible, selecting instructional materials appropriate to students' needs, and planning for assessment.

Sequencing content objectives

Teachers responsible for developing the content skills may find it helpful to adjust the sequence of content objectives, as do foreign language immersion teachers. Immersion teachers develop long-range plans by considering the language demands of the academic objectives. Where the structure of the academic objectives permits, teachers may find it helpful to reorder the sequence of content objectives so that those requiring the most language skills are postponed until students have had an opportunity to increase their language proficiency. Some objectives can be taught primarily through hands-on or visual experiences. Others may be more difficult to demonstrate in the classroom, be more abstract, or require that students have a greater repertoire of oral or writing skills. For example, in a primary grade science unit on "Living Things Grow and Change," firsthand experiences allow students to develop concepts about the growth of plants, concepts which can be developed during a four-week time frame. In contrast, learning about the growth of people requires pictures and more discussion since students cannot experience the concepts directly in class in a reasonable amount of time. Similarly, the effects of adequate and inadequate nutrition on plant growth can be shown, whereas the effects on human growth must be talked about. By dealing with plant growth first, second language teachers, like immersion teachers, can build the language skills necessary for students to address the objectives related to human growth.

Planning content lessons that contain language objectives

Teachers need to view every content lesson as a language lesson. It is especially important for teachers to see every language lesson as an opportunity to enhance students' concept attainment. Snow, Met, and

Genesee (1989) have suggested a conceptual framework for identifying language objectives and have described how teachers in a variety of language teaching settings (ESL, bilingual, immersion, and FLES programs) fulfill their roles within this framework. The authors identify two kinds of language objectives: *content-obligatory* and *content-compatible* language objectives. Content-obligatory language is language so closely associated with specific content objectives that students cannot master the objectives without learning the language as well. For example, students cannot explain when to add and when to subtract without knowing the terms *add* and *subtract* and without some mechanism for expressing cause and effect relationships (e.g., "You add *because* . . ." "When you have . . . you add."). In contrast, content-compatible language can be easily taught through a content lesson, but the material could be taught and learned without knowledge of this vocabulary, grammar, or language functions. For example, sixth-grade students discussing the relative merits of different forms of government can enrich the quality of their arguments if they have a wide range of vocabulary at their disposal (e.g., liberty, despotic, tyrannical) but could learn the concepts of democracy, autocracy, and so on with more limited linguistic resources (e.g., free, unfair, can't do what you want, etc.).

Content-based second language learning can play an important role in providing students with the language of academics needed for successful content mastery. Working collaboratively with grade-level teachers, second language teachers can identify the content-obligatory language needed for subject matter mastery in the mainstream classroom. This language may then become the primary focus of second language lessons. Indeed, the teacher may teach the content lesson, incorporating the needed language skills and using activities that make the lesson and language comprehensible to students. Content-based classroom activities that use concrete experiences, manipulatives, and hands-on materials can facilitate the acquisition of content-obligatory language and may provide students with a valuable advance organizer for lessons on the same topic taught in the mainstream classroom. In bilingual or two-way immersion settings, teachers also need to identify content-obligatory language and plan conscientiously for the development of needed language skills in the course of content instruction.

Content-compatible language objectives are an important factor in students' continued language growth. They help teachers focus on how students' language skills can be stretched, refined, and expanded beyond their present level of attainment. Since students will always need to improve and refine their language skills (after all, even native speakers do), content-compatible language objectives are an important part of lesson planning. All teachers who teach students in a non-native language can find it helpful to build both content-obligatory and content-compatible language objectives into the planning of every content lesson.

Content-compatible objectives are drawn from three sources: (1) a second language scope and sequence that describes how students are expected to grow and develop in their second language skills; (2) the teacher's observation of student language skills and his or her analysis of their classroom needs; and (3) the anticipated linguistic demands of the content curriculum to be taught in future lessons. Many U.S. school districts define ESL objectives in a curriculum scope and sequence for ESL instruction. Traditionally these have been taught in isolation by ESL teachers. The teachers who may have seen their role as developing survival language skills or grammatical accuracy may find it more useful to see themselves as teachers of language through content (i.e., content-based ESL) and to conscientiously plan for teaching the language of the curriculum. By selecting content from the school's curriculum that is compatible with ESL objectives, teachers can use this content as a communicative and cognitively engaging means of developing language and also help to promote their students' mastery of content material. For example, a content-based ESL teacher might reinforce the mathematics curriculum and simultaneously develop the ESL curriculum objectives related to describing daily activities and routines. The teacher might have students determine the amount of time they spend on these daily activities and routines, convert the information into percentages (out of twenty-four hours), and display those data in a pie graph.

Another example of planning content-compatible language objectives derives from teacher observation of students' demonstrated language proficiency. The ESL, bilingual, or grade-level teacher may note that students consistently make errors of register when making requests of adults. The teacher notes that students frequently use commands ("Give me that!"), indirect declaratives ("I need that." "I want that."), or less polite forms of request ("Can I have that?"). Because the classroom provides few natural opportunities for students to develop skill in adjusting their speech register to their audience, the teacher plans an assignment that addresses both the social studies objective in *Explorers of the New World,* for example, and the language needs of students – students could role-play Christopher Columbus soliciting the support of the Spanish monarchs in order to give students opportunities to use language for making requests.

The third source of content-compatible language objectives is the teacher's *long-range* plans for content objectives and the sequence in which content objectives will be taught. For example, a first-grade teacher (grade-level, bilingual, two-way, or foreign language immersion) plans a science unit for December to teach the concept that some objects float and some objects sink. In theory, the teacher can use any objects to demonstrate the concept – a bar of soap, an eraser, a brick. But the teacher also knows that in January students will begin a social studies/ science unit on *Foods That Nourish the Body,* a unit for which the content-obligatory language will be vocabulary related to fruits and vegetables. Therefore, this teacher plans to use fruits and vegetables in December in the float/sink activities, making future content-obligatory language part of current content-compatible objectives. In a similar way, second language teachers can help to prepare their students for the language demands of content lessons to be taught in the mainstream classroom, by planning lessons that incorporate the anticipated language needs of the regular classroom.

Planning instructional activities

Once language and content objectives have been defined, teachers need to plan activities that are experiential, hands-on, cognitively engaging, and collaborative/cooperative. Planning for such activities is likely to be done by grade-level teachers (mainstream, bilingual, two-way, or foreign language immersion) and by content-based second language teachers.

Instructional activities and related materials must be both context-embedded and cognitively demanding. Cummins (1981) defines instructional tasks in terms of two intersecting continua. Context-reduced tasks are those that rely on few external supports for meaning (e.g., pictures, realia, manipulatives, or a meaningful context) (see also Chapter 1). In context-reduced tasks, meaning must be accessed primarily through language. At the other end of the continuum, context-embedded tasks use many supports for meaning to help make language, and thus the task, understandable. Listening to a lecture on an abstract topic is a context-reduced task; determining the weight of an object using a scale and metric weights is a context-embedded task.

Tasks may also be cognitively undemanding or demanding. Counting from one to one hundred is undemanding for most older children; finding the number that completes a pattern (e.g., 5, 9, 17, . . .?) is cognitively demanding. The challenge for teachers is to meet the cognitive demands of the curriculum by providing context-embedded instruction.

Students who are learning content in a new language have difficulty with cognitively demanding tasks in context-reduced situations. To allow students to acquire abstract concepts, teachers need to design instructional approaches that make the abstract concrete. By enabling students to match what they hear with what they see and experience, teachers can ensure that students have access to meaning. Experiential, hands-on activities make input comprehensible. In fact, it is precisely this process of matching experience with language that allows students to learn language from content instruction. The use of concrete materials, hands-on activities, visuals, and realia provide multiple access and a variety of multisensory approaches to learning. In sum, these experiences can make the abstractions of content learning, in Cummins' terms, context-embedded.

Cummins argues that the challenge of teaching students in a second language is to provide experiences that are both context-embedded *and* cognitively demanding. Too often, language instruction that is context-embedded is cognitively undemanding, simply a series of activities that are reduced, in the ultimate, to naming pictures. Content instruction by its very nature should be much more cognitively demanding. Teachers need to design activities that are accessible to students yet cognitively engaging. For example, rather than preteach vocabulary in isolation to describe what different objects are made of (wood, plastic, metal, etc.), one second-grade teacher used a lesson from a unit on *Conductors of Electricity* to demonstrate the meanings of these terms. As the teacher and students tested whether objects of wood, plastic, or metal in a battery's closed circuit would allow a bulb to light, students acquired both the language for describing matter and the concept that some materials do not conduct electricity.

Lastly, teachers must plan instructional experiences that provide for student-to-student communication. Students need frequent and sustained opportunities to produce language, opportunities best provided through collaborative group learning activities (Long and Porter, 1985; Swain, 1985). Such collaborative activities provide for critically needed practice in verbalizing content knowledge. In addition, in mainstream and two-way immersion classrooms, heterogenously structured pair and group activities also provide opportunities for students to use language for meaningful social interaction with peers.

Planning for instructional materials

One outgrowth of planning activities is the identification of materials needed for instruction. These will include manipulatives, visuals, and print and nonprint media. Although all teachers obviously have to think about the materials they will use during instruction, those who educate through a second language must add special criteria for selecting materials. Although there may be a large body of commercially produced materials available, these are rarely appropriate for students learning content in a language new to them. Most often, commercially available materials (developed for native speakers) demand a level of linguistic proficiency well beyond that of students, whereas materials that are at an appropriate linguistic level will often be inappropriate to students' cognitive maturity. Commercially produced materials targeted at native speakers are often culturally rich. This can be both an advantage and disadvantage. It is critically important for language learners to understand the culture of the language they are learning, but too often culturally rich materials provide an incomprehensible cultural context for learning (see also Chapter 2). For example, a mathematics word problem based on a visit to the state fair may confuse students who know the mathematical principles required for solving the problem but do not understand the setting, and thus the nature, of the problem.

Teachers must decide whether to adapt existing materials or develop their own. Some teachers are reluctant to develop their own materials, believing themselves less well-equipped to do so than professional authors and editors. While teacher-made materials have the distinct advantage of being designed to address the needs, abilities, and cultural background of students, they do require a considerable investment of teacher time and energy and often lack the color and artwork that is so appealing to younger learners. (A more detailed discussion of criteria for evaluating and selecting instructional materials may be found in Lorenz & Met, 1988.)

Integrating culture

Those who work with second language students (just like immersion teachers) will want to plan for the integration of culture. This may mean teaching students about the culture of the speakers of the language they are learning as well as that of the students themselves. Where possible, culture should be infused into other areas of the curriculum. Teachers who integrate the teaching of culture with the objectives of the school curriculum can more easily "find time" for one more set of objectives and enrich instruction because students' learning is integrated rather than fragmented. A French immersion teacher working on a grade four social studies objective, *geographic features of our region,* used this opportunity to compare and contrast the topography of the local area with that of a selected region in France. Another immersion teacher used a fifth-grade science lesson on climate as a springboard for understanding the implications of geography on climate in contrasting Spanish-speaking cities such as San Juan, Mexico City, Lima, and Buenos Aires.

Similarly, those who work with learners of English can and should ensure that planning for instruction includes attention to the sociocultural needs of students, to cultural information and attitudes that will help students function in a new culture, and reinforce positive attitudes to students' home culture (see Chapter 12).

Planning for assessment

Instructional planning requires teachers to think about how language and content objectives will be assessed (see Chapter 9). Instruction and assessment go hand-in-hand, and planning for assessment and planning for teaching should be done at the same time. When planning for teaching and planning for assessment are done in a coordinated manner, teachers are able to ensure that their objectives, their teaching, and assessment all fit together. If teachers know what they want students to be able to do, and if they know how they are going to find out if students can do it, then planning how students will be prepared to perform (that is, what teaching activities they will use to enable students to learn) also becomes clear. Particularly when content is taught through a language in which students have limited proficiency, decisions need to be made about how to assess content knowledge through language or independently of language. We will return to assessment later in this chapter.

In the classroom: teaching students in a second language

Enabling students to develop content knowledge and concepts when they are being educated in a language in which they have limited proficiency is not easy. Teachers must perform a variety of tasks and roles to ensure that students acquire the skills and knowledge in the school's curriculum at a level commensurate with those students who are learning it in their native language. To do this, teachers must be skilled in negotiating meaning; they must have well-developed skills in monitoring student performance; they must be expert in instructional decision making; they must serve as a role model for the use of language, cultural behaviors, and learning strategies; and they need to structure the environment to facilitate language learning. Each of these tasks is described in the following paragraphs.

Negotiation of meaning

Teachers who provide instruction in the student's second language must be continuously engaged in a negotiation of meaning process. In negotiating meaning, teachers and students endeavor to make themselves understood and to understand each other. It is a collaborative process of give and take in which each participant works to send and receive comprehensible messages (see, for example, Hawkins, 1988; Saville-Troike, 1987; Snow, 1989). Negotiation of meaning is critical in classrooms where students are learning content in a new language. If the meaning of what the teacher says is unclear, it will be difficult for students to acquire the skills and knowledge of the curriculum.

Although there are many aspects to this process, and some of these aspects often occur simultaneously, for the purposes of discussion here the role of the teacher will be discussed from three perspectives: (1) making language understandable to students; (2) helping students make their messages understood; and (3) stretching, expanding, and refining students' language repertoire. These roles are discussed in greater detail below.

MAKING LANGUAGE AND CONTENT ACCESSIBLE

When students' language proficiency is very limited, the teacher plays a major role in the negotiation of meaning process by using context-embedded instructional tasks and by interpreting students' responses (or lack of them) as an indicator of the effectiveness of his or her communication. Because comprehension is essential to the learning of content, the teacher must ensure that his or her (i.e., the teacher's) messages are being understood. In delivering content lessons, teachers accompany talk with many contextual clues. Most characteristically, such lessons rely heavily on concrete materials, hands-on experiences, manipulatives, and visuals. These help students match language with meaning.

Teachers of content (whether they be content-based second language teachers, mainstream teachers, or teachers in bilingual and two-way or foreign language immersion classrooms) can also help students with limited language proficiency acquire new concepts by linking new learning to background knowledge. For example, a social studies lesson on modes of transportation in the students' community can begin by having them classify miniature cars, trucks, planes, and so on according to whether they use them regularly, occasionally, or never; or students may classify these modes of transportation by the frequency with which they are used in their native country. A reading lesson on fables is easier for a fourth grader who is familiar with the structure of fables (e.g., a tale with a lesson at the end) than for one who is not.

Teachers also make language comprehensible by modifying their speech. They may speak more slowly, emphasizing key words or phrases. They may simplify their language, using more common vocabulary or simpler, high frequency grammatical structures. Redundancy provides additional supports for meaning. Teachers may restate, repeat, or paraphrase. Synonyms linking new vocabulary with known words facilitate both content and language learning, as does definition through exemplification. Similarly, antonyms provide counterexamples to meaning (e.g., "No, it's not cold; it's hot."). Body language, such as gestures and facial expressions, also help to link language to meaning.

HELPING STUDENTS COMMUNICATE

In the early stages of second language development, students have limited means of conveying their own messages in the new language. Teachers can play an important role in helping students get their meaning across, particularly in settings where students are taught by teachers who do not know the students' language. Just as teachers rely heavily on concrete materials, visuals, and body language, so too should students be encouraged to use these as enhancements for conveying meaning. Thus, students should have ready access within the classroom to visual and concrete materials. However, students should be encouraged to use *both* verbal and nonverbal means of communicating, or they may become overly reliant on nonverbal supports to their messages.

Teachers enable students to communicate verbally by making a "rich interpretation" of students' attempts to communicate (see, for example, Wells, 1986), and by maintaining open channels of communication. These are often accompanied by checks for understanding. When asked how Native Americans communicated across long distances, a fourth grader replied, "Smoke." The teacher interpreted his answer by responding, "Do you mean the Native Americans sent smoke signals to one another?" If there are students in the class with greater language proficiency, the teacher may ask them to expand on the first student's response ("Who can tell me more about what Juan has told us?") or ask a third student to paraphrase the response of the second ("Lupe, can you explain what Phan just said?"). These strategies encourage continued communication between teacher and students, allow teachers to check their own comprehension of students' messages, and check students' comprehension of content.

At this stage of linguistic development, when students are still quite limited in their abilities to understand and speak the new language, teachers may find it worthwhile to teach explicitly skills in conversational management. Students need to know how to say "I don't understand," or "Please repeat." Later, these skills can become more refined as students learn to rephrase these statements more politely ("Would you mind repeating that, please?").

EXPANDING AND REFINING STUDENTS' LANGUAGE

From the time students begin to produce language and as they continue to develop proficiency, teachers play an important third role. Gradually, as students become more skilled in their new language, teachers must help students expand their language skills and refine their existing ones. This is done both in the course of instruction, as teachers respond to students directly, or as they observe student-to-student communication. This, in turn, becomes observational data to be used in planning for students' language growth and in identifying content-compatible language objectives for future lessons.

Because continued growth in language proficiency depends upon extended opportunities for linguistic interaction, teachers need to provide for frequent collaborative learning activities both in the second language classroom among learners of English and in classrooms where students can interact with native speakers. These activities increase the frequency of opportunities for students to hear language used for meaningful communication and to test out their own growing language repertoire. Continued, frequent, and sustained interactions provide for both input and output. In mainstream and two-way immersion classrooms, communication between native and non-native students allows learners of English to hear ever-increasing examples of the language and how it is used. As they listen to others, students also come to recognize "That's how you say that!" Each time these students speak, they are testing hypotheses they have formed about how the language works. The nature of the responses they receive from teachers or classmates helps them ascertain the validity of their hypotheses.

While classmates thus provide an important vehicle for language practice, the teacher is equally important in refining student language. A sixth-grade student describing religious practices in Ancient Egypt indicated that the Egyptians would often "kill an animal for a god." The teacher replied, "Yes, it was a *sacrifice*." Teachers thus use content lessons as a means for stretching students' vocabulary, increasing their exposure to more sophisticated forms of academic discourse, and for explicitly developing language skills. These content lessons that embed language development were discussed earlier, in the section on planning when we examined the role of content-compatible language objectives.

The teacher as monitor

Teaching, it has been said, is like being inside a popcorn machine, with many things going on all at once. The teacher's task is to implement the lesson designed during the planning phase, yet monitor the lesson and students while teaching it. Monitoring is an integral part of the feedback cycle needed for effective formative evaluation. As teachers continuously monitor content mastery and language development, they observe and analyze students' verbal and nonverbal performance, checking for understanding of language and concepts. Often, it is difficult to ascertain whether students have difficulty with content because of their lack of language proficiency or despite it.

In a study of novice and veteran teachers, Berliner (cited in Brandt,

1986) found significant differences in their skills in monitoring multiple classroom events. When confronted with a bank of video monitors depicting several classroom settings and events, expert teachers were far more skilled in observing and reporting on their observations. Novice teachers, by contrast, were barely able to report accurately the events in one classroom. Teachers in mainstream, bilingual, or two-way immersion settings, in particular, need to be proficient in monitoring multiple classroom activities and events. These teachers have to contend with the range of ability levels characteristic of all classrooms and also with a significantly greater range of linguistic ability in the language of instruction. Because research supports the importance of providing students with extensive opportunities to use their growing language skills, second language teachers and other teachers who work with second language students need to provide for extensive pair and group work activities, and they, in turn, require greater monitoring skills on the part of the teacher (see Chapter 8). In addition, when learners of English are mainstreamed with native speakers of English, the teacher has more to monitor because of the distinct needs of ESL students in the class. Similarly, teachers in two-way programs face the greater challenges posed by the diversity of students' cognitive and linguistic proficiencies.

Skills in monitoring multiple classroom activities and events develop with time. A first and simple step in developing such skills is the awareness that such monitoring is not only desirable but an important element in managing learning in the classroom. A useful approach to monitoring student performance is to identify in advance indicators of on-task behavior, of successful content mastery, and of successful linguistic performance. Observations focused on such clearly identified indicators and use of record-keeping devices, such as checklists and anecdotal records, will promote effective monitoring of students and provide for sound instructional decision making (see Chapter 9).

Teachers' observations during the monitoring phase are a primary basis for instructional decisions. Teachers may use both informal and systematic observation of students. Students may be observed in cooperative groups or teacher-centered formats. Observations enable teachers to determine how well students are learning the curriculum objectives. A variety of information sources – anecdotal records, checklists, and data provided by student learning logs, for example – may provide teachers with the information needed to monitor the effectiveness of their instruction and make appropriate instructional decisions.

Instructional decision making

Jackson (1968) has noted that teachers may make as many as 1,300 nontrivial instructional decisions each day. *Effective instructional deci-*

*sion making requires a repertoire of instructional options, and the knowl-
edge base necessary for choosing wisely among the options.*

Providing instruction in a students' second language requires a greater
repertoire than that of teachers in monolingual settings. Teachers who
lack repertoire lack the flexibility to respond to learner's needs. Teachers
who know only one way to teach a skill or concept have no fallback
options if observations indicate that this one way is ineffective or inappropriate for a given individual or group of students. While all effective
teachers need a repertoire of instructional approaches, teachers in second
language settings need an expanded repertoire of strategies for making
abstract skills and concepts concrete. That is, not only must the teacher
have alternative approaches for teaching a given concept, the alternatives
must also address the special linguistic and cultural needs of students.
And the use of multiple approaches to making concepts understandable
often means that a variety of learning preferences are addressed (i.e., the
visual, the tactile, the kinesthetic, etc.).

Good decision making requires more than repertoire, more that is, than
an awareness of the many options available. It also requires that teachers
be able to select appropriately from this range of options. The ability to
choose within one's repertoire depends on a sound understanding of how
language and concepts are learned, and of how the characteristics of
learners and instructional settings interact. Good decision making is informed decision making.

For teachers who teach content in a language new to students, informed
decision making may depend upon an even deeper understanding of
students and how they learn than it does in a monolingual setting. The
teacher's knowledge of students' needs and abilities and of their linguistic
and cultural characteristics will help to determine which of the available
options is most appropriate at a given moment. For example, in a lesson
on the natural habitats of frogs, a minority language student states that
most frogs live in trees. The teacher's options include:

- accept the student's response without comment
- respond with positive reinforcement
- correct the student if the response is deemed incorrect
- probe to see if the student has misunderstood the lesson
- conclude that the student said *tree* because that is the only word for
  natural habitats the student knows, and therefore, the teacher decides to
  provide additional vocabulary options in her response
- conclude that the student has said tree because in Puerto Rico, where
  this student comes from, there is a common tree frog (*coqui*), and
  therefore, for this student, the answer is correct
- decide that further instruction using pictures and visual aids is needed

to ensure that students are aware that frogs have several natural habitats and that students have the verbal skills to discuss them

While teachers in monolingual classrooms may face similar decisions, teachers who work with second language learners will need to have a broader understanding of students' background and a broader range of repertoire in order to make appropriate instructional decisions.

The teacher as model

For students who are being educated in a second language, teachers are models of linguistically and culturally appropriate behaviors. The teacher models both the academic and social language students will need. As we have seen earlier, content lessons serve as a vehicle for teachers to model the language of the academic curriculum. Through these lessons students acquire both new knowledge and the means to talk about them. In addition, teachers have opportunities throughout the day to model social language. They greet students, discuss students' activities outside the school setting, describe their own activities, and conduct administrative routines that provide many opportunities for noninstructional interaction. Culturally appropriate behaviors (both linguistic and nonlinguistic) are also modelled through instructional and noninstructional interactions. Students may observe differences between the way teachers speak to one another, the principal, parents, and other adults in the school and the ways in which they speak with children. Students may also observe nonlinguistic features such as proximity, gestures, and other body language appropriate to their new language. These learnings, in the long run, contribute to the growing effectiveness of students' communication.

Like teachers of native speakers, second language teachers can also model learning. Such techniques as reciprocal questioning and think aloud protocols (Bereiter & Bird, 1985) modeled by teachers (and later used by students) have a dual function when students are learning content through a new language. In the first language classroom, these techniques help students to acquire useful strategies to improve and monitor their own learning. Teachers who model these techniques to students who are learning content in a new language are additionally providing these students with the language they need in order to be clear in thinking and talking about their content learning. Further, such strategies promote higher order cognitive processes. This is particularly important in second language classrooms where too often instruction can easily slip into mere rote recitation of facts, labelling, or naming activities.

Whether a second language, grade-level, bilingual, two-way immersion, or foreign language immersion teacher, it is helpful for teachers to be aware of and exploit opportunities to serve as models of language, learning, and culture.

Structuring the environment

Grade-level teachers can help students acquire content in a language new to them through a carefully structured environment. A daily schedule that follows predictable patterns can facilitate language comprehension in the early stages of language development. Students can surmise that the teacher is directing them to prepare for lunch if lunch predictably follows the end of the mathematics lesson each day. Similarly, other classroom routines (attendance, collection of lunch money, distribution of materials) can help students match language to experience. Environmental print can help students begin to recognize the relationship between the oral classroom vocabulary they know and associated print labels. Bulletin boards filled with an abundance of visual materials can support content objectives; print labels and text accompanying the visuals can also provide for increased content and language learning. Most importantly, learning centers filled with hands-on experiences and listening tasks can contribute to content learning and language growth.

A supportive, accepting learning environment benefits all students – regardless of their home language or culture. For students who may be anxious about trying to learn demanding content in a new language, a supportive environment is even more critical. Activities that are structured for success are likely to build the self-esteem needed for academic achievement. Frequent positive reinforcement helps uncertain learners know they are on the right track and encourage them to persevere. Wait time, which has been shown to increase the quality and quantity of student responses in native language classes (Rowe, 1978), is even more necessary in second language content classes. This is because limited-proficiency students must not only think about the right answer from the content perspective, but they also need time to formulate how they will communicate their response.

Assessing student progress

All teachers use assessment to measure how much students have learned; they use the results of assessment to evaluate the degree to which student learning meets their stated objective(s). When assessing students, teachers should be most concerned with finding out what students *have* learned, and they should allow students to *demonstrate* what they have learned. The emphasis should be on what students *do know and can do,* not on what they do not know and cannot do.

Assessment takes place both continuously and at the end of a unit of study. Teachers are continuously monitoring student performance informally during instruction. As was discussed earlier, such informal assessment provides important information for instructional decision making, enabling teachers to informally monitor the effectiveness of instruction in addressing the learning needs of students (see Chapter 9). Information about student achievement collected in such an informal manner is based on students' verbal and nonverbal feedback during the course of lessons. This kind of assessment information is extremely useful for modifying ongoing instruction to ensure that what is taught and how it is taught is effective in helping students learn concepts and language. More formal methods of assessment (such as tests) tell teachers how well individual students are progressing, whether they have attained unit objectives, and whether the teacher should advance to the next unit. Most commonly used forms of assessment are for these purposes.

Assessing concept mastery

Educating students in a second language presents unique problems in assessment. Teachers may have difficulty determining whether students fail to perform as expected because they have not mastered the concepts or because they simply lack the linguistic resources to demonstrate what they have learned. When students are extremely limited in their linguistic repertoire, it may be best to separate assessment of content mastery from language. What strategies can teachers of content use to ensure that students can demonstrate content mastery even when they are as yet unable to verbalize their knowledge and understanding?

Students may be asked to act out their knowledge. For example, students may take on the roles of the sun, moon, and earth and move in relation to one another to demonstrate their understanding of the concepts of revolution and rotation. Students may be given physical objects with which to demonstrate their understanding, as when students categorize plastic foods into the four basic food groups. Pictures can be part of paper/pencil tests, with students crossing out pictures that do not belong in a given group (e.g., Which of the following does not conduct electricity – a metal pin, a plastic ball, a piece of paper, or aluminum foil?). Or students may draw a picture to show what they know (e.g., foods the settlers of New England introduced to the Native Americans; foods the Native Americans introduced to the settlers).

Performance assessment is a way of measuring student achievement "by means of observation and professional judgment" (Stiggins, 1987, p. 33). It is "the process of gathering data by systematic observation for making decisions about an individual." (Berk, 1986, p. ix). Classroom-based performance assessment uses a variety of procedures and approaches for gathering information about student performance. Portfolios of student work (such as audiotapes and videotapes, writing samples, projects, posters, dioramas, and models), systematic observation of classroom performance, and conferences with individual students about their assignments and projects, are also effective ways to find out about student progress in relation to the objectives set for them. Because they are based on student performance, and not on some idealized, nonexistent average student or native speaker, they show what students actually *know and can do*. They can also be used to compare each student to his or her last performance and thereby give an indication of how individual students are progressing. Lastly, they are an appropriate way of ensuring that the delivery of content instruction is commensurate with the linguistic proficiency of the student at that point in time and in that content domain.

As students' language proficiency grows, and in particular their ability to read and write their new language, paper/pencil tests may be used for limited responses. For example, true/false items, multiple choice tests, fill-in-the-blank items (particularly when a word bank is provided) can provide opportunities for students to demonstrate their learning despite their limited expressive capabilities. These tasks may lead the way to even more linguistically demanding assessment tasks such as rewriting false statements as true ones or responding with simple sentences and short paragraphs.

Although decisions about appropriate content instruction for students with limited language proficiency should not be based primarily on language-based assessments, it is important that students eventually be able to demonstrate their knowledge both verbally and nonverbally because "language proficiency is important to nearly everything that takes place in education" (Oller, 1991). The more effectively one can express one's thoughts through language, the more clear and precise thinking becomes. Research on the process of writing, for example, has shown that the processes required to produce a good piece of writing require and produce higher levels of cognition (Olson, 1985; Tierney, Soter, O'Flahavan, & McGinley, 1989). Therefore, as students become increasingly proficient at expressing themselves (whether orally or in writing), it becomes increasingly appropriate for teachers to encourage students to demonstrate content learning through oral and written communication.

Assessing language proficiency

Perhaps the most neglected aspect of assessment is classroom-based assessment of students' language skills. While many teachers conscientiously assess how much content students have learned, assessment of language frequently is done only through standardized tests of English language proficiency for determining eligibility for special services.

However, second language teachers, along with grade-level, bilingual, and two-way immersion teachers, are both content and language teachers. They need to plan as conscientiously for language growth as they do for content and vice versa. To assiduously plan for language growth, ongoing assessment of students' proficiency is a must. Planning for language growth means the teacher must be continuously assessing where students are in relation to where they ought to be and using assessment data to identify areas where further development of language growth is needed. These data are one of the bases for identifying content-compatible language objectives. Language assessments are based on the objectives determined in the planning phase of instruction. These objectives will most likely include both content-obligatory and content-compatible language objectives. The planning phase should also include indicators of how teachers will know that students have achieved these language objectives.

Because language objectives are most appropriate when tied to the linguistic demands of content objectives, assessment of language skills may be made during the course of content instruction. Checklists that specify language functions, grammar, and vocabulary needed for content knowledge can be used for assessment of students during routine classroom activities. As students demonstrate (or fail to demonstrate) their ability to use the requisite language skills, teachers can keep records of students' language performance. Conferences with small groups of students or individual students that focus on content are also a good source of data on students' ability to understand and produce content-related language. Similarly, dialogue journals and learning logs provide teachers with information about students' ability to verbalize their content knowledge through print. It is extremely important that teachers have clearly defined objectives and criteria for students' linguistic performance in order for the data-gathering activities just described to be useful for assessing student progress and planning further instruction.

Classroom-based language assessments that are part of the instructional delivery system also help to identify content-obligatory language objectives for future lessons and units. Classroom-based language assessments help teachers know whether students have the language skills they will need for academic performance precisely because the assessment ties language to its purpose, which is content learning. Classroom-based language assessments are authentic in that they measure student proficiency in the real contexts in which language use occurs (learning of academic subject matter); they are integrative; and they assess the broad range of language skills needed in the classroom. Such assessment, in essence, has content validity.

From the day-to-day instructional perspective, the integration of language assessment with content assessment helps teachers – whether they are second language, grade-level, bilingual, two-way, or foreign language immersion teachers – engage in a constant formative/diagnostic feedback loop. Assessing students' background knowledge prior to introducing new concepts is important for all teachers. For those who teach content in a second language, assessing background knowledge also means knowing the range of the students' linguistic ability to handle the concepts. Teachers also need to know the language demands of their curriculum objectives, the extent to which students will be able to learn concepts and information from verbal input, and the extent to which special strategies, manipulatives, and concrete materials will be necessary for instructional delivery. Similarly, teachers need to know what supports must be provided to students for them to be able to demonstrate their knowledge and learning, especially when verbalization of what has been learned is not the best medium for getting and giving that information.

It is clear, then, that as instruction progresses, and as teachers observe the growth of students in the course of teaching and learning activities, a great deal of assessment data can be collected about the achievement of both content and language objectives. These data provide important information about individual students. In the aggregate, data from systematic observations, checklists, portfolios, and teacher-made tests provide information about the effectiveness of the instructional program.

Conclusion

Several implications emerge from the issues examined in this chapter. Perhaps the most salient is that it may be necessary for teachers who work with second language learners to redefine their roles vis-à-vis their students and vis-à-vis one another. If the purpose of schooling is to educate students, then *all* teachers must contribute to students' achievement of curriculum objectives. Language cannot stand apart from content learning; rather, language should be acquired through content learning just as content may be learned through language. Teachers may no longer be able to afford the luxury of a language curriculum separate from the demands of the larger school curriculum. Instead, the language of content may be the most appropriate second language curriculum. Survival language and grammar are important parts of the curriculum, but perhaps it is equally, if not more, important that second language teachers be defined as teachers of academic language.

Grade-level teachers, such as mainstream, bilingual, and two-way immersion teachers, will need to have a clearer responsibility for the language development of their students. This means ensuring that plans for every content lesson include language objectives as well. While content objectives may drive decisions about instructional activities and materials, teachers will also need to consider the academic language needed for successful mastery of current subject matter instruction (content-obligatory language), the anticipated language needs of students in future content lessons, and the language demands beyond the classroom (content-compatible language).

If teachers redefine their instructional responsibilities, they may also redefine their relationships with one another. Clearly, in schools where second language teachers work side-by-side with mainstream, bilingual, or two-way immersion teachers, there needs to be a coordinated approach to meeting the needs of students. Collaborative planning among teachers can ensure that the linguistic demands of content learning are addressed both in the second language and the content classroom. Similarly, collaborative planning can enable teachers to provide content-based lessons that support, reinforce, and coordinate with content lessons provided by other teachers.

Teachers have a significant leadership role to play. They may need to take the initiative in collaborative planning activities, in identifying the academic language skills students will need for success in content learning, and in planning content-based lessons that support those in other classrooms. They may also need to assist mainstream teachers to understand how theories of second language acquisition can inform content lesson planning and to understand how content lessons may be made more comprehensible to second language learners. Lastly, it may be necessary to restructure how students are grouped for instruction in pull-out programs (see Chapter 8). Rather than group students by language proficiency, it may be more useful to group them according to grade level (or rough approximations thereof). If second language teachers are to function as teachers of language through content and plan collaboratively with content teachers, then grade-appropriate content instruction will drive decisions about classroom activities. As such, it may be more feasible to group students with similar content (and language) needs than by overall language proficiency.

Second language teachers, bilingual teachers, grade-level teachers of minority language students, and foreign language immersion teachers all face the challenge of enabling students to learn content in a language new to them. This chapter has attempted to describe how teachers can enhance their effectiveness as teachers of language through content and of content through language, through the effective planning, delivery, and assessment of instruction. Despite differences in their roles, these teachers share a common goal: to develop students who demonstrate content knowledge, skills, and concepts at or above grade level expectations; students who are proficient in at least one language in addition to that spoken at home; and students who can function effectively and comfortably in another culture.

References

Bereiter, C., & Bird, M. (1985). Use of thinking aloud in identification and teaching of reading comprehension strategies. *Cognition and Instruction, 2,* 131–156.

Berk, R. A. (Ed.). (1986). *Performance assessment: Methods and applications.* Baltimore: The Johns Hopkins University Press.

Brandt, R. (1986). On the expert teacher: A conversation with David Berliner. *Educational Leadership, 44*(2), 4–9.

Collier, V. P. (1989). How long: A synthesis of research on academic achievement in second language. *TESOL Quarterly, 23*(3), 509–531.

Costa, A., & Garmston, R. (1985). Supervision for intelligent teaching. *Educational Leadership, 42*(5), 70–80.

Cummins, J. (1981). The role of primary language development in promoting educational success for language minority students. In *Schooling and language minority students: A theoretical framework.* Sacramento: California Department of Education.

Genesee, F. (1987). *Learning through two languages.* Rowley, MA: Newbury House.

Hawkins, B. (1988). *Scaffolded classroom interaction and its relation to second language acquisition.* Unpublished doctoral dissertation, University of California, Los Angeles.

Jackson, P. (1968). *Life in classrooms.* New York: Holt, Rinehart, and Winston.

Lambert, W. E., & Tucker, G. R. (1972). *Bilingual education of children: The St. Lambert experiment.* Rowley, MA: Newbury House.

Long, M. H., & Porter, A. (1985). *Group work, interlanguage talk, and second language acquisition. TESOL Quarterly, 19*(2), 207–227.

Lorenz, E. B., & Met, M. (1988). *What it means to be an immersion teacher.* Unpublished manuscript, Office of Instruction and Program Development, Montgomery County Public Schools, Rockville, MD.

Mojhanovich, S., & Fish, S. B. (1988). Training French immersion teachers for the primary grades: An experimental course at the University of Western Ontario." *Foreign Language Annals, 21* 4: 311–319.

Oller, J. (1991). Language testing research: Lessons applied to LEP students and programs. Paper presented at the Second National Research Symposium on Limited English Proficient (LEP) Student Issues, Washington, DC.

Olson, C. B. (1985). The thinking/writing connection. In Costa, A. (Ed.), *Developing minds: A resource book for teaching thinking.* Alexandria, VA: Association for Curriculum and Supervision Development.

Rowe, M. B. (1978). *Teaching science as continuous inquiry: A basic.* New York: McGraw-Hill.

Saville-Troike, M. (1987). Bilingual discourse: The negotiation of meaning without a common code. *Linguistics, 25,* 81–106.

Snow, M. A. (1989). *Negotiation of meaning in the immersion classroom.* Unpublished manuscript. Office of Instruction and Program Development, Montgomery County Public Schools, Rockville, MD.

Snow, M. (1987). *Immersion teacher handbook.* Los Angeles, CA: Center for Language Education and Research, University of California.

Snow, M. A., Met, M., & Genesee, F. (1989). A conceptual framework for the integration of language and content in second/foreign language programs. *TESOL Quarterly 23,* 2: 201–217.

Stiggins, R. J. (1987). Design and development of performance assessments. *Educational Measurement: Issues and Practice, 6,* 3: 33–42.

Swain, M. (1985). Communicative competence: Some roles of comprehensible input and comprehensible output in its development. In S. Gass & C. Madden (Eds.), *Input in second language acquisition.* Rowley, MA: Newbury House.

Swain, M., & Lapkin, S. (1985). *Evaluating bilingual education: A Canadian case study.* Clevedon, England: Multilingual Matters.

Tierney, R. J., Soter, A., O'Flahavan, J. F., & McGinley, W. (1989). The effects of reading and writing upon thinking critically. *Reading Research Quarterly, 19,* 2: 134–173.

Wells, G. (1986). *The meaning makers: Children learning language and using language to learn.* Portsmouth, NH: Heineman.

Additional readings

Berliner, D. (1981). Viewing the teacher as a manager of decisions. *Impact on Instructional Improvement, XVI*(Summer), 17–25.

California State Department of Education, Bilingual Education Office. (1984). *Studies on immersion education: A collection for United States educators.* Los Angeles, CA: California State University, Evaluation, Dissemination, and Assessment Center.

Cummins, J. (1981). Age on arrival and immigrant second language learning in Canada: A reassessment. *Applied Linguistics, II,* 2: 132–149.

Cummins, J. (1983). Language proficiency and academic achievement. In J. W. Oller (Ed.). *Current issues in language testing research.* Rowley, MA: Newbury House.

Cummins, J. (1984). *Bilingualism and special education: Issues in assessment and pedagogy.* Clevedon, England: Multilingual Matters.

Genesee, F. (1985). Second language learning through immersion: A review of U.S. programs. *Review of Educational Research, 55,* 4: 541–561.

Hakuta, K. (1984). *The causal relationship between the development of bilingualism, cognitive flexibility, and social-cognitive skills in hispanic elementary school children.* Rosslyn, VA: National Clearinghouse for Bilingual Education.

Harley, B., Hart, D., & Lapkin, S. (1986). The effects of early bilingual schooling on first language skills. *Applied Psycholinguistics, 7,* 295–322.

Lambert, W. E. (1984). An overview of issues in immersion education. In *Studies on immersion education: A collection for U.S. educators* (pp. 8–30). Sacramento: California State Department of Education.

Met, M. 1987. Twenty questions: The most commonly asked questions about immersion. *Foreign Language Annals, 20,* 4: 311–315.

Met, M. (1989a). Learning language through content: Learning content through language. In K. E. Muller (Ed.), *Languages in Elementary Schools.* New York: American Forum, 43–64.

Met, M. (1989b). Walking on water and other characteristics of effective elementary school foreign language teachers. *Foreign Language Annals, 22,* 2: 175–183.

Palincsar, A. S., & Brown, A. L. (1984). Reciprocal teaching of comprehension-fostering and comprehension-monitoring activities. *Cognition and Instruction, 1,* 2: 117–175.

Simich-Dudgeon, C., McCreedy, L., & Schleppegrell, M. (1988). *Helping limited English proficient children communicate in the classroom: A handbook for teachers.* Washington, DC: National Clearinghouse for Bilingual Education.

Skutnabb-Kangas, T., & Toukomaa, P. (1976). *Teaching migrant children's mother tongue and learning the language of the host country in the context of the socio-cultural situation of the migrant family.* Helsinki: The Finnish National Commission for UNESCO.

Stern, H. H., Swain, M., McLean, L. D., Friedman, R. J., Harley, B., and Lapkin, S. (1976). *Three approaches to teaching French.* Toronto: Ontario Institute for Studies in Education.

Swain, M., & Lapkin, S. (1991). Additive bilingualism and French immersion education: The roles of language proficiency and literacy. In A. G. Reynolds (Ed.), *Bilingualism, multiculturalism, and second language learning: The McGill conference in honour of Wallace E. Lambert.* Hillsdale, NJ: Erlbaum.

Wells, G. (1981). *Learning through interaction: The study of language development.* New York: Cambridge University Press.

8 Grouping strategies for second language learners

Donna M. Johnson

Major educational movements, such as whole language approaches (Goodman, Bird, & Goodman, 1991), cooperative learning (Kagan, 1986), and process approaches to writing (Atwell, 1987; Calkins, 1986; Graves, 1983), place a strong emphasis on the educational benefits to be derived from using well thought out pairing and grouping strategies. Much has been written about interaction strategies for education in general and for second language learners in particular. Within bilingual-education and second-language communicative pedagogy, small-group and pair work have also been promoted for some time (Celce-Murcia, 1991; Cummins, 1989; Enright, 1991; Enright & McCloskey, 1988) and have been the focus of a good deal of classroom research (Chaudron, 1988; Johnson, 1992; McGroarty & Faltis, 1991).

In this chapter I discuss ways of using grouping strategies in teaching second language students. The chapter is written for second language and bilingual teachers who are working or will work in a variety of instructional settings, as well as for other "regular" or "mainstream" teachers who have some second language students in their classes. I will use the term *grade-level teachers* to refer to the latter group, following Enright and McCloskey (1988: 31). Using the term *regular teachers* or mainstream teachers could imply that the roles of second language teachers are peripheral when, in fact, they are very central to the lives of second language children.

I first discuss implications of some recent theory and research for planning classroom interaction strategies. Based on this research, I suggest general principles to guide teachers as they plan grouping and interaction strategies. Then I provide a discussion of the major grouping structures addressing their uses, advantages, and disadvantages. Next, examples of activities through which teachers can apply these principles as they plan varied grouping strategies are offered. Finally, I conclude by

Appreciation is expressed to Fred Genesee, Ginger Snider, and Mara Thorson for helpful comments.

suggesting methods of assessing the effectiveness of various grouping strategies.

Principled creativity and flexibility

Principled and creative ways of organizing interaction are crucial in teaching second language students. Grouping is not simply a choice or a fun alternative to normal whole-class or individual activities. Nor are pair and small-group activities simply a passing fad. Rather, careful attention to grouping students is essential for supporting and promoting broad second language, literacy, and academic development in children. But, using effective grouping strategies does *not* mean giving a test, placing students in groups based on test results, and leaving them there indefinitely. Today's teachers have abandoned that static approach to grouping. Rather, they think continually about how the ways that they organize classroom activities provide opportunities for interaction that will support and encourage second language and academic development.

Interaction strategies should be both *principled* and *creative*. *Principles* are derived from what relevant theory, research, and experience tell us about how children learn; how language is understood, interpreted, and created in different situations; how language use varies across cultures and across situations; and how all of these processes relate to second language development. By drawing on a very large base of relevant theory, research, and practical experience, teachers can construct a set of operating principles to guide their actions in the classroom. These principles may be implicit and unstated. On the other hand, many teachers explicitly articulate and continually revise their own set of principles. For example, some grade-level teachers believe that spelling, phonics, and math are the easiest subjects to teach to second language students, and this belief, unfortunately, guides their priorities and practice (reported in Penfield, 1987). Some teachers believe and follow the general principle that providing multiple opportunities for meaningful oral and written interaction is the best way to promote second language and literacy development (Enright & McCloskey, 1988; Freeman & Freeman, 1989; Swain & Lapkin, 1989). Others also follow the principle that language and literacy development in the students' home language is a goal that is desirable and that also enhances overall academic and second language development (see Chapters 1 and 4). Whether such principles or beliefs are explicit or implicit, teachers tend to base their practice on them. This chapter offers three principles for teachers to consider in planning and organizing grouping.

Although ways of organizing instruction should be principled, they must also be *creative*. That is, they must be actively created in relation to continually changing classroom conditions. There are no foolproof recipes for organizing school experiences for second language learners. Every classroom, school, and community setting is somewhat different. In addition, classroom situations are continually changing as students come and go, as teachers adjust their approaches, as community conditions change, and as interactional dynamics shift. While teachers should link their practice to some guiding principles, they must also be highly flexible in adapting their plans to these changing conditions. They must be creative designers, continually watching, assessing, learning, rethinking, retooling, and improving their grouping strategies to provide the best possible learning experiences for all of their students. Both principled and creative flexibility, then, are basic to designing rich learning situations for students.

Principles for planning interaction

Before discussing specific grouping arrangements – such as pair work and small-group work – and how they are used, it is useful to look at grouping strategies from a broader perspective. In this section I propose three general principles that teachers can think about as they plan ways of organizing activities. These principles are: (1) Create opportunities to interact in a variety of participation structures; (2) Build from children's cultural and individual orientations toward classroom interaction; and (3) Create richness in oral and written performance by encouraging children to link language and content across situations. For each principle I discuss research that gives us insights about the ways that children approach language and literacy learning.

Varied participation structures

Arrange for a variety of ways of interacting   Teachers should structure activities so that students have opportunities to interact in a wide variety of participation structures. These include time alone to read, write, and think; pair work and small-group work with teachers and other students; and a variety of large-group arrangements.

Inflexible, limited approaches to grouping, whether in language classes, bilingual education classes, or in other grade-level classes, can seriously inhibit students' academic, linguistic, and even social development by limiting their opportunities. In many traditional classrooms, static grouping has been a common, accepted practice. Inflexible grouping has been documented in research on bilingual education programs as well. For example, in a national study of bilingual classrooms that I conducted a number of years ago with a team of researchers, we were interested in exploring the grouping practices teachers used. We were disappointed to discover that most teachers placed students into so-called ability groups (based solely on English language proficiency level) at the beginning of the school year and never changed these groups during the entire year (Horst et al., 1980). Fortunately, such rigid approaches have become much less common.

Why is it so important that second language students be given opportunities to interact in a variety of ways? Swain and Lapkin, drawing on their extensive research in second language acquisition in the context of immersion programs, suggest that to improve second language learning it is essential that teachers plan activities that give rise to a broad functional range of classroom discourse and that they allow students varied and extended opportunities for sustained second language use (1989). Using varied participation structures works toward meeting these goals (Edelsky, 1989).

In addition, the use of varied activities in varied participation structures has other benefits. It helps to encourage (1) different kinds of cognitive involvement on the students' part, (2) the use of students' home languages and cultural knowledge as cognitive resources, (3) the accommodation of cultural and individual differences and orientations, (4) the freedom to develop in unexpected ways, (5) and, finally, fun. Fun is not a trivial benefit of using a variety of participation structures because children learn through play and motivation. Motivation – whether task motivation, situational motivation, or global motivation – is a key to effective language and literacy development (Brown, 1987; Gardner, 1986).

Using varied and dynamic participation structures requires a *physical environment* that is flexible, enticing, and student-owned. Chairs nailed to the floor in rows, for example, should be rejected in favor of movable furniture.[1] The physical environment should not only facilitate many grouping arrangements but should be a rich and developing biliterate or multiliterate environment that reflects children's experiences and serves as a resource for further work. Edelsky (1991: 19) describes one teacher's approach to building up her classroom, an approach consistent with a whole-language, student-centered philosophy. When school begins, the classroom is relatively bare. As projects progress, the students begin "piling up" the room with their writing, art work, charts, and other student work. Gradually the room becomes a complex and dense jungle that not only displays the children's many capabilities but also records their shared history. Flexible arrangements and a rich multiliterate envi-

---

1 Enright and McCloskey, 1988, chap. 4, provide a useful discussion of specific
  ways to create a flexible physical environment in the classroom.

ronment go naturally with the use of a varied and dynamic participation structure.

Accommodating cultural differences in language socialization

Recognize and build from children's cultural and individual orientations toward social interaction and learning This principle is not something that teachers can learn to do in a few easy lessons. Rather, it represents a continual challenge and requires an open mind and an inquiring attitude (see Chapters 1 and 2). We still have a great deal to learn about how cultural experiences are related to classroom participation and to second language acquisition, but research is helpful in broadening our sociocultural perspectives.

A sociocultural perspective on language acquisition emphasizes the fact that language development and social growth go hand-in-hand. These two processes viewed together are called *language socialization.* That is, children are both socialized through language and are socialized to use language in culturally preferred ways (Ochs, 1988; Ochs & Schieffelin, 1984; Schieffelin, 1990; Schieffelin & Ochs, 1986). Language socialization practices from home and community can affect the ways that children interact in the classroom in their second language (Heath, 1983; Macias, 1987; Philips, 1983).

Willett (1987) conducted a very interesting ethnographically oriented study that shows how different ways of interacting that are brought from home can result in different paths to communicative competence in a second language. She studied two young children who had just arrived in the United States and were acquiring English in a preschool. The girls, both children of graduate students, were Jeni from Korea and Alisia from Brazil. Willett studied the girls as a participant observer in her own daughter's nursery school. She spent five months observing the children every day for thirty minutes and participated in classroom activities for about four hours each week for four months. She also gathered data through interviews with the girls' parents and teachers. Willett was interested in the girls' interaction patterns in the preschool, how the patterns might have be culturally shaped, and how they may have affected both the learning strategies that the children used and the English they learned.

She found that the two girls approached social participation, second language use, and language learning in very different ways that reflected their respective cultural values (see Chapter 5). Jeni began speaking English soon. She sought out interactions with adults and was able to nominate topics with them, elicit talk, and manipulate their speech. She tended to ignore her peers, however, and did not join their spontaneous activities. Jeni's pronunciation was poor, compared to Alisia's, and she made little use of formulaic phrases. On the other hand, she made rapid progress in semantic and syntactic development relying heavily on what Willett called a "one-word-at-a-time approach."

Alisia, unlike Jeni, was initially devastated to discover that she was not socially competent with her peers. She did not talk for about three months but was busy observing the interactional patterns of the children and joining in nonverbally. When she did begin to use English (starting with a highly appropriate "Please pass the bananas"), her pronunciation and intonation were nativelike, and she used a variety of formulaic chunks appropriately. She was not a risk taker with English but was careful to be sure that she knew a phrase well before using it. This strategy allowed her to interact effectively with peers.

Willett suggests that the girls' interaction styles at school reflected the respective values of their sociocultural environments at home. One of the major contrasts she drew was between the emphasis on peer sociability in the Brazilian family and on Confucian values and one-on-one learning interactions with adults in Korean culture. Specifically, she suggests that Jeni's superior syntactic development may have resulted from her adult interactions, whereas Alisia's appropriate use of formulaic routines and her excellent pronunciation may have resulted from her peer interactions.

Although it is important not to overgeneralize, this study illustrates that culturally shaped language socialization patterns from home can affect the ways that children interact in the classroom in their second language. It further illustrates that these different classroom interactions are a contributing factor in the alternative paths children take in learning aspects of the second language.

What, then, are the implications of this knowledge for planning interaction and grouping? One basic implication is that expanding their awareness of the kinds of interactions that are valued within different cultures can help teachers better understand their students. Teachers can assume that information about cultural groups will broaden their own expectations about what is common and what varies in language development (Heath, 1990). They can then expect that their students' attitudes and behaviors may conform to cultural patterns. At the same time, they can expect that individuals within a cultural group will differ to some extent. Moreover, it is important to realize that students are also culture creators who will invent new ways of interacting in new situations.

The more practical implication is that teachers can plan activities that will allow children to interact extensively in situations in which they are comfortable while also providing invitations and opportunities to participate in new ways. For example, more one-to-one interactions with a teacher might have helped promote Alisia's syntactic development, whereas carefully planned peer activities in which Jeni could successfully and comfortably participate might have promoted her ability to use formulaic phrases in social interaction. This does not mean that these girls would not develop in these areas on their own at their own pace; rather, it means that through planning the teacher can play a part in expanding children's experiences and the functional range of their language use.

A further implication is that strongly teacher-centered approaches to second language teaching that focus narrowly on limited aspects of language (such as a morphological and syntactic focus with restricted vocabulary and discourse, for example) can be very limiting for children like Alisia. On the other hand, approaches to promoting second language development that rely solely on unstructured peer interaction can be frustrating for children like Jeni who seek out and respond well to adult guidance (Wong Fillmore, 1990). By building on children's cultural and personal ways of interacting while at the same time providing new and expanded opportunities for successful interactions, teachers can help children expand their participatory and linguistic repertoires.

Textual and contextual richness in performance

Encourage students to link language and content across situations This principle deals with the relationships that teachers and students create across different activities. Teachers can plan classroom events in such a way that they encourage students to make meaningful connections across activities and situations. This principle promotes second language development by helping children expand meanings.

Teachers can encourage students to make connections through sequences of related activities. One way to do this is by using the *task-dependency principle* (Johnson & Morrow, 1981). This principle – widely used by both grade-level and second language teachers within thematic units – requires that tasks A and B be related so that B could not be completed without having done A first. For example, in Task A students (working individually or in pairs) might conduct an opinion poll about a current event. This activity is followed by Task B in which students (working in small groups) pool their information and construct a graph to display the information. Later, working individually or in pairs, they might write about their findings using their first language or their second language. The logical connection between these tasks is not only highly motivating but also provides for lots of repetition, recycling, and rehearsal of language that is not drill-like but natural, increasingly meaningful, and purposeful.

While individual teachers often use the task-dependency principle, two different teachers who teach the same students can collaborate to use this principle. For example, the opinion poll (Task A above) can be carried out under the guidance of the second language teacher, while the pooling of information (Task B above) can be done under the guidance of the grade-level teacher. Unfortunately, the task-dependency principle is less widely used across different teachers who work with same students, particularly when these teachers work in different locations. In fact, in a number of studies, researchers have observed and documented disjoint-edness and lack of continuity in the daily instruction of second language students. For example, in a study of the Migrant Program in California schools, it was found that individual and small-group instruction in a pull-out setting was associated with a disjointedness in the students' education. Through 86 observations combined with interviews, research-ers learned that grade-level teachers who chose to have the program aide pull the migrant students out of the regular classroom for supplemental instruction had very little knowledge about what students were doing in these pull-out sessions. On the other hand, teachers who chose to have migrant aides work with students inside the grade-level classroom made more effort to link the supplemental instruction to ongoing class activi-ties. In fact, in the schools that seemed to have the highest quality programs, there was close communication and coordination among all the teachers and aides who worked with the migrant students (Johnson, 1987).

There are various ways in which teachers can create continuity for students and make connections between activities planned by different teachers. For example, some teachers who teach in small-group pull-out settings ask students to explain to them what they learned in a previous social studies lesson given by a grade-level teacher (Hawkins, 1988). This can be done both through conversation and through writing. For example, during ESL class, students might write in content-response journals about the social studies content presented by their grade-level teacher. Also, many second language teachers coordinate closely with content-area teachers so that they can prepare students for upcoming lessons by introducing content-obligatory vocabulary or other language (Snow, Met, & Genesee, 1989).

We have said that the principle of encouraging children to link lan-guage and content across contexts helps promote conceptual and language development. In particular, this kind of emphasis helps them expand meanings. Another important advantage of encouraging children to make connections across activities is that it accommodates cultural and individ-ual differences in *text-context performance orientation*. This concept, which draws on and adapts work by Briggs (1988), requires some expla-nation.[2] I will first explain this notion and then suggest that classroom

---

2 Briggs (1988) studied the way that Spanish-speaking Mexicanos in New Mexico draw on folklore in their daily lives. He studied the verbal performance of six genres – historical discourse, proverbs, scriptural allusions, *chistes* (jokes), leg-ends and treasure tales, hymns and prayers – placing them along a text-context

tasks differ in text-context orientation and that individual students as well differ in their text-context orientation.

Many instances of written or oral production in the classroom can be viewed as a kind of performance given for a particular audience. Communicative competence in classroom language "performance" involves being able to draw appropriately on a variety of linguistic resources. For example, as children express themselves in speech and in writing, they draw on resources from both textual and contextual spheres. Adapting Briggs's notions to classroom language use, we can say that the *textual sphere* refers to authoritative texts and established genres of classroom discourse, such as stories, a teacher's lessons, and written texts. Children's language features that index (signal or make reference to) this sphere to an audience are termed *textual features*. For example, a child who copies an excerpt from a story is drawing on and indexing the textual sphere.

The *contextual sphere* refers to knowledge about life in the classroom, school, and community as well as aspects of the ongoing social interaction. Language features that index this sphere are *contextual features*. A child who writes a story that makes many reference to shared knowledge of ongoing classroom events and personal relationships, for example, is drawing on and indexing the contextual sphere. The ability to draw on and make reference to these textual and contextual spheres is an important aspect of communicative competence. Different school-related speaking and writing tasks require that children draw differentially on these spheres. For example, in writing personal dialogue journal entries, children may draw more heavily on the contextual sphere, while in writing literature-log entries, they may draw more heavily on the textual sphere.

In both cases, children's language use involves creative and dynamic interpretive processes as well as references to texts and contexts. That is, children continually reinterpret a host of prior texts through the eyes of the present. For example, a child may make an insightful connection between what she read in science (using English) today and what she did in math (using Spanish) yesterday, and may then write about this idea (using English) in her writing group, later discussing it with a peer (in Spanish) or a teacher (in English). When a piece of writing or an oral "performance" is embedded in a complex web of ongoing authentic activities, it exhibits textual and contextual richness. Such richness contri-

continuum (p. 223). He points out that communicative competence in performance involves "an intertextual process of reaching back into past performances, selecting a particular set of elements, and interpreting their meaning. It also entails a critical reading of the ongoing social interaction and perhaps other dimensions of modern society as well. As the two come together in performance, both are transformed" (Briggs, p. 357).

butes to second language development by helping students connect and expand meanings.

Not only do different speaking and writing tasks differ along the text-context continuum, but individual children differ in this way as well. Research has clearly shown us that child second language learners differ in their approaches to analyzing, using, and learning the second language (Hudelson, 1989; Saville-Troike, 1988; Wong Fillmore, 1990, 1992). Building on Briggs's notions, what I am suggesting is that children also differ in textual/contextual orientation. That is, they differ in the degree and ways in which they make use of textual and contextual resources when they "perform" (talk and write) in an additional language. Some children prefer to draw more extensively on authoritative texts, such as printed materials and the teacher's discourse, while other children find greater inspiration from ongoing, informal social interaction in the school or community. Jeni and Alisia differed in this regard because of cultural and personality differences. A different, more vivid example of a Japanese child, Akemi, will be provided. Teachers can take these ideas into account in designing activities. Using creative process approaches to writing within integrated, content- and theme-based classes encourages second language children to draw on many textual and contextual resources to express themselves. At the same time, encouraging children to make connections across activities carried out within different participation structures will promote second language and literacy development.

The principle of linking language and content across situations and contexts applies not only to academic activities; it also can be applied to linking the social and the academic. For example, understanding children's social purposes for writing can enrich classroom work. Dyson's (1987) ethnographic work in this area is relevant for ESL learners. She noticed in her observations of ethnically diverse classrooms that children construct an "underground writing curriculum" in addition to the teacher's agenda for writing. Children pass notes, copy stories, draw pictures, and write letters to one another. Dyson also documented that children "unintentionally" help each other learn by monitoring one another and talking about various features of writing. For example, they discuss spelling conventions, stylistic techniques, and even criteria for what makes good fiction. They do all of this, she points out, because they value writing as does the teacher, and they want to establish and maintain their group membership as well as their own individuality (Dyson, 1987).

Allowing children sufficient time to work in self-selected pairs and small groups will encourage these activities. In addition, teachers can recognize and incorporate these lively unofficial writing activities into their planning. For example, teachers can set up a message board or postal system within or across classrooms. Or students might write notes and letters to one another about books they are reading in ongoing literature logs.

To summarize, three principles are important in planning the kinds of participant structures that will promote second language and literacy development for students. First, it is essential to provide opportunities for active involvement in a variety of formats – from individual to pair to small-group to large-group sessions. Second, teachers can build on students' cultural orientations toward social interaction while, at the same time, encouraging them to participate in new ways. These broader ways of participating will expand the functional range of their language use. Third, teachers can encourage students to make multiple connections across learning contexts. Using these principles in planning activities should lead to enhanced second language development. We now turn to a discussion of specific grouping strategies.

Participation structures

Research on teaching has shown that lecture, whole-class discussion, recitation, and individual seatwork prevail as the favored methods in traditional classrooms (Gage, 1985). But teachers of second language students must depart from the prevailing methods of relying only on whole-class or individualized instruction. Rather, the use of a variety of participation structures is important so that children have varied opportunities for meaningful interaction as well as time to think and reflect. Second language, bilingual, and grade-level classrooms usually encompass a range of language proficiency levels. By using varied participation structures teachers also help ensure that students at different levels of proficiency can participate meaningfully. In this section we examine a number of participation structures, focusing on their uses and on their advantages and disadvantages.

Large-group instructional activities

The major advantage of large-group activities is that they allow children to build shared experiences that provide the contexts for making and sharing meanings in both academic and social spheres. For example, by taking a field trip, reading big books, watching a science demonstration, singing familiar songs, participating in cultural events, or seeing a historical film, students build up a wealth of rich experiences that they share with other students and teachers. These shared experiences then provide a common base of understanding and a foundation for writing, reading, and discussion related to the experiences. Large-group activities have another important and related social function. They help students feel that they are an important part of the group rather than isolated or stigmatized.

A primary disadvantage of whole-group activities that are teacher-centered is that some students may understand very little of what is going on. In the worst case, they may completely tune out, learning little or nothing (Miller, 1982). A further problem with large-group instruction is that teachers may make demands on students to perform verbally when they are not willing or able to do so. It is most important that students feel comfortable in the large-group setting, be motivated to attend to what is being said and done, and be able to participate successfully at their own level and in their own ways.

What can teachers do to ensure that students get as much as possible from large-group experiences? First, they can establish predictable events that help children to develop scripts and gradually learn the associated language (Saville-Troike, 1988; Wong Fillmore, 1985). Second, they can, as Enright and McCloskey (1988) put it, "think language" in everything they do. This includes consciously using oral discourse strategies – such as repeating, recycling, and rephrasing – that enhance students' comprehension. Even though teachers use these discourse strategies consciously, with different audiences in mind, they can use them in such a natural and meaningful way that monolingual English speakers barely notice while L2 students benefit from many additional chances to understand and learn.

Another way to help ensure that whole-group activities are meaningful is to provide planned opportunities for children to negotiate meaning with one another within the whole activity. For example, during a teacher-led social studies lesson, the teacher can stop often and ask students to "compare notes" with a partner. The teacher can pose questions such as "Why do you think that happened?" or "What do you think will happen next?," giving the partners a chance to compare interpretations using either a shared first language or English. Such student-student exchanges within a teacher-led lesson can be crucial in achieving better understanding of academic concepts (Lemke, 1985). These exchanges give students the flexibility to negotiate and build their own meanings, even within the teacher-led, large-group setting (also see Chapter 7 for a discussion of negotiation of meaning).

Enhanced individual work

In some traditional classrooms, individual work has primarily involved filling out worksheets, reading and answering questions, or doing exercises. Teachers often ask students to engage in these activities in silence and without the support of others. In today's classrooms, however, much individual work is focused on meaningful reading, thinking, and writing activities that are linked to language arts and content-area instruction. In addition, teachers make an effort to provide a supportive environment in which each child has access to many (textual and contextual) resources. This more recent notion of individualized work as a participation structure might be better captured by the term *enhanced individual work*. This term reflects teachers' efforts to create highly motivating activities in a resource-rich environment.

Writing activities provide good examples of enhanced individual activities. As children engage in transactional/informational, expressive/ personal, and poetic/literary writing along with their native English-speaking peers (Hudelson, 1989), they can draw on many resources. They can refer to printed materials, peers, and teachers. The notion of enhanced individual work also implies that students see a purpose for the individual work and see how it is related to prior and upcoming activities. For example, children may read and reflect individually in preparation for a group activity. Or children might engage in short, individual thinking sessions in which they list three ideas to bring back to a group task. This individual work is *enhanced* because not only do children have many resources at their disposal but they also see a social purpose for what they are doing individually.

Why is enhanced individual work important? First, children need a chance to process the second language at their own speed and in their own ways. Second language acquisition theory has placed a strong emphasis on the value of comprehensible input and meaning negotiation (Larsen-Freeman & Long, 1991). And, without a doubt, the communicative activities that these theories have supported represent a significant improvement over old, narrow language teaching methods. Yet cognitive activity that contributes to language learning does not occur only when listening to or reading comprehensible second language input or when engaging in negotiated interaction. Children are mentally active in many other ways that contribute to learning. They need time to let their minds work on what they are learning in their own unique ways. For some children, this involves mentally rehearsing an answer to a question. For others, it means repeating and playing or experimenting with forms (Saville-Troike, 1988).

An important advantage of enhanced individual work, then, is that children can work at their own pace. This gives them a sense of control over their own work. For example, they can read a book at their own speed, stopping to think about meaning or turning back to check on a picture or prior text. A further benefit of enhanced individual work is that it allows children the time they need to draw on linguistic resources. While writing a piece, children often need time to retrieve a word or expression they want to use from memory, from a prior text (their notes or a book), or from a teacher or classmate. Yet another advantage of individual work within an open, cooperative environment is that children help one another learn by monitoring one another, talking about features of writing, spelling, and style (Dyson, 1987). They need time to make their own choices about how they will go about this intentional or unintentional helping. Finally, and perhaps most important, enhanced individual work can help teachers accommodate and capitalize on children's individual learning strategies, styles, and strengths.

While it may be tempting for some teachers or administrators to isolate second language students, too much individual time, particularly in isolation from others, poses a real danger. Students need a great deal of comprehensible input (both oral and written) and meaningful communicative interaction to develop. Therefore, we should be careful to ensure that they are not isolated for long periods. For example, instruction for second language students should not be turned over to a computer so that students are isolated and subjected to poor computer-based ''curricula'' that cannot come close to providing rich learning experiences.

Rather, there must be a balance between large-group activities and quiet times to absorb, reflect, and read and write in a resource-rich environment. This can best be accomplished by planning a number of opportunities for enhanced individual work within and in between group activities. In this way, children will be preparing for or reflecting on social and academic uses of language in related activities.

Pair work

In addition to large-group activities and enhanced individual work, students also need many opportunities for communicative interaction (both spoken and written) in pairs and small groups that is fully meaningful to them and useful as linguistic input for learning (Wong Fillmore, 1985, 1992). Pair work can range from planned, highly structured activities to spontaneous, informal situations. Both are important. A useful way to think about pair work is to plan some structured activities but also to monitor what goes on in unstructured pairs and use this information in future planning.

One way to plan pair work is to structure the flow of information. For example, in an *information-gap task,* student A communicates some information to student B. Because this information is new to student B, a natural opportunity for authentic communication is created. For example, student A may read a short narrative or informative text and retell it to student B. Or student B may obtain information about the upcoming class party and share it with student A.

In a *two-way task,* new information flows in both directions. That is, student A communicates information that is new to student B, and student B shares information that is new to student A. For example, when each child conducts interviews with relatives and shares that information with a partner, there is a two-way exchange of information. One of the benefits of the two-way task is that students may engage in more negotiation of meaning than in a one-way task.[3] Most often, the partners then complete a task, such as writing a text, that draws on the contributions of both partners. For example, a pair may engage in a collaborative writing activity in which they draw on their journal entries about a recent field trip to a pumpkin farm. In this way, each contributes ideas that help shape their writing.

What are some considerations in forming pairs? It is important that members of pairs be compatible. In fact, students can form their own pairs for many activities. For other activities, teachers can set up the pairs to ensure that there is an appropriate balance of first and second (or third, etc.) language use throughout the day and over time. The building of new friendships with others is one of the most powerful motivators for language learning. Teachers can keep this in mind as they alternatively set up pairs and allow students to choose their own partners.

Many teachers pair second language students with monolingual, native speakers in very effective ways. The obvious advantage of this arrangement for second language development is that there is an authentic need on the part of the second language student to use the second language with such a partner. For students at a low level of language proficiency, a paired hands-on science or math activity helps them link meanings to the physical context. For students at higher levels of proficiency, this kind of pairing can be used in many activities, with partners actively contributing to the task in their own way, and second language students can learn the new language from their native-speaking partners.

Pairing a highly fluent bilingual with a second language student or pairing two students of different proficiency levels can also be effective for language and content learning. In this kind of pairing, some teachers worry that students will use only their common first language. One excellent way to address this issue is to allow students to use any language they choose during discussion of the activity [because research indicates that discussing concepts in the first language is associated with academic growth even when measured in English (Saville-Troike, 1984, 1991)], but to require that they jointly produce something in writing in English as an important part of the larger activity. Alternatively, students might produce both a first language version and an English version of their written piece. A concern about pairing two ESL students is that they will use English *interlanguage* with one another without refining their language abilities. A good strategy for addressing this concern is to plan

3 For discussions of research on task types with older learners, see Crookes and Chaudron, 1991, or Pica, 1992.

activities so that they are highly text-oriented (along the text-context continuum that has been discussed). These activities can include listening to tapes of books read aloud by native speakers (Wong Fillmore, 1992) or devising writing assignments in which children make much use of authentic, English texts.

Another issue to consider in planning pair work is the roles that students enact. Often second language students are assigned to subordinate roles or they choose, on their own, to assume subordinate roles. This is not necessarily bad because at times these students need to devote most of their energy to understanding what is going on. On the other hand, teachers might think about creating opportunities for second language students to assume leadership roles. The benefits can be not only linguistic and academic but social as well. First, children use different kinds of discourse as a leader (e.g., using "teacher talk," giving explanations and instructions, answering questions, using discourse markers to structure discourse) than they do as a follower (e.g., asking questions, agreeing, giving brief answers, etc.). Taking different roles broadens the functional range of their language use. Moreover, researchers have found that students display surprising competence when using language for peer-teaching tasks outside the teacher's direct control (August, 1988; Johnson, 1988; Steinberg & Cazden, 1979).

In all pair work, it is important that teachers monitor students, not so much that it stifles creativity, but enough to see that students are compatible and that they are communicating successfully and working productively with one another (specific suggestions for monitoring are provided below). Teachers can then adjust and form new pairs based on what they learn through observing (see Chapter 9).

Cooperative learning groups

Cooperative learning, the focus of a great deal of research in the 1970s, became a significant educational movement that continues in popularity (DeVillar, 1991; Enright, 1991; Kagan, 1986; McGroarty, 1989). Cooperative learning techniques and principles, such as positive interdependence and cooperative reward structures, are widely used in content classes, second language classes, and integrated classes. Research has shown that cooperative instructional arrangements can promote positive cross-cultural and race relations as well as enhanced content and language learning.

It is particularly important for grade-level classes with second language learners that a significant amount of class time be organized so that small, linguistically heterogeneous groups of students work cooperatively on meaningful tasks (Rigg & Allen, 1989). To some, cooperative learning may imply the implementation of a predetermined cooperative learning curriculum. For teachers working with second language students, however, it is most useful to define cooperative activities as students working together and using language to accomplish meaningful school tasks. There are two important cautions to consider regarding the first, more structured notion of cooperative learning. As teachers make use of some of the handbooks that are in wide circulation, they will need to integrate the suggestions these books offer with what they know about second language development and about recent developments in language arts and literacy instruction. For example, one recently published cooperative learning guidebook suggests activities for composing in which children produce a composition, then exchange papers and correct each others' errors. Clearly, error correction is not the first and only response a child should receive to a piece of writing. Current approaches to writing involve richer notions of response. One alternative is that students in a small cooperative group can respond to the content of one another's pieces by asking authentic questions that might lead to revision. Many children can be very successful in such a writing group (Urzua, 1987). Another common practice is for children to work carefully on correctness when a piece will be "published" or otherwise made available to a wider audience (Swain and Lapkin, 1989). Because many of the cooperative learning guidebooks are not written with second language children in mind, second language teachers and specialists must play a strong role in adapting commercial cooperative learning procedures to the needs of students. The best approach is to use these materials as just one resource along with many other resources and books.

A second caution to consider in using commercial cooperative learning materials is to avoid rigidity in structure and process. Strict adherence to a teacher's guide could lead to poor experiences for some students. Moreover, model cooperative learning programs that work well in one setting with one group of students may fail miserably with a very different group. Therefore, it is essential that teachers assess cooperative activities with their students in mind and have the flexibility to adjust assignments and task demands, rearrange groups, and do whatever is necessary to motivate students by making their interactions meaningful and successful without overwhelming them.

Teacher with small group

One of the most valuable participation structures for second language learning can be a teacher guiding a small group of students. In verbal interaction, a skillful and sensitive teacher can provide opportunities for each child to participate successfully in the second language at his or her own proficiency level. This is because the teacher can keep close track of each student, determine to what extent each is comprehending the second language, and then use a variety of strategies to make the language comprehensible (see Chapter 7). Such strategies could include repetition, rephrasing, using context, using the first language, and so on. Teachers can use these strategies, for example, in a discussion after a large-group activity such as seeing a film or after an enhanced-individual activity such as reading a self-selected book. Teacher talk, and peer talk as well, can work as useful linguistic input for acquisition in such a small group (Wong Fillmore, 1985). Over time, teachers can gradually encourage children to take on increasingly linguistically demanding roles within these events (Enright & McCloskey, 1988). The small group setting is ideal for a wide variety of other activities. For example, it is ideal for language experience writing and reading. By engaging children in dialogue about what they are reading and writing, the teacher can assess their understanding, provide challenges at the right level, and devise appropriate and motivating follow-up activities.

The teacher/small group setting can also be useful for mini-lessons on linguistic form. Kitagawa, for example, explains that instead of formal spelling, grammar, punctuation, and handwriting lessons in her multilingual grade-level classroom, she provides mini-lessons on conventions of usage through dictation exercises.

> I write or select the text to exhibit whatever aspects of language I want to present, and I try to make it something that has currency in our study or mutual experiences. It takes only about 60 minutes per week because the lessons are short and most of the study is homework; but it has proved to be the most efficient formal instruction device I have used, especially in a class of students of widely mixed language proficiencies. I can use the same materials but vary the expectations for those who find it more difficult. (Kitagawa, 1989: 80–81)

A teacher working with a small group can be one of the most valuable participation structures for learning English as an additional language, yet often the teacher who actually works with small groups is not highly proficient in English. Wong Fillmore has expressed concern about ESL children in classrooms in which nearly all the teachers, aides, and students are native speakers of Spanish, Chinese, and other languages and "interlanguage" users of English. In such cases, teachers can use highly text-oriented approaches. For example, they can read aloud to children from books and develop conversational and writing activities that are closely related to the texts (Wong Fillmore, 1992).

To conclude this section on participation structures, it is useful to point out that because teacher-centered, teacher-fronted classrooms are a traditional classroom structure around the world, children from some cultures may have had little or no experience with the varieties of pair work and group work widely used in U.S. and Canadian classrooms. In such cases, teachers need to initiate students explicitly and gradually into the procedures and into teacher's expectations for appropriate behavior. It can be very useful, for example, to post signs that explain guidelines and procedures to be followed (Enright & McCloskey, 1988). Students then have the opportunity both to hear this language and to see it.

Two examples of principles in practice

This section presents two specific activities that teachers can explore – multicultural literature and drama and dialogue journal writing – along with reports on their use and research results. Both of these activities involve the integration of conversation, reading, and writing. They can be used within second-language classrooms, bilingual education classrooms, integrated grade-level classrooms, or immersion programs. These activities also provide ways in which all teachers who are involved in a child's education can collaborate across settings to support children in their learning (Cazden, 1986; Johnson, 1987; Penfield, 1987).

Before discussing the two examples, we will briefly mention theme-based units. This approach, widely used by teachers, remains an excellent way to promote richly contextualized second language learning that is closely related to important academic content. Units often involve activities employing a variety of participation structures that can accommodate childrens' different cultural, individual, and textual/contextual styles as well as varied levels of English language proficiency. In addition, when teachers employ the task-dependency principle, for at least some of the activities, they encourage children to make multiple connections between language and content across settings. The following two examples of activities may or may not be part of thematic units.

Using multicultural literature and drama

Literature and drama can provide highly motivating ways to use and learn an additional language. The story of one kindergartner shows how this may happen. Yetta Goodman (1990) cites teacher-writer Vivian Paley's account of Akemi, a Japanese girl in Paley's class who was acquiring English as an additional language. Paley writes that Akemi was a girl who "knew the pleasure of easy communication (i.e., in Japanese, her native language) and was loath to flounder and stumble in a new language" (Paley, 1981: 121). As a result she was not comfortable with the other children. As Akemi's father explained to Paley, "Akemi does not permit herself mistakes" (p. 122). Like Willett's Jeni, who has been discussed, Akemi was determined to get it right. She made progress in

English at a rate that was disappointing to her teacher and parents until her interest was captured by drama and stories of magic.

The change in Akemi began when she became excited about acting in a play – a Japanese folktale about a woman who loses a rice dumpling. She enthusiastically learned the lines (in English) to take on this persona. Then she became entranced by stories of magic, and she would memorize lines from them, trying them out on her classmates. "I am the wishing bird," she would say and grant wishes with her wand. She gradually became a good storyteller (in English), telling stories to classmates and dictating stories to be acted out.

Entering the world of magic, then, seemed to be the key to using English for this child. Paley suggests that it was not only the chance to get it right that held the attraction for Akemi but also the certainty of outcome that was appealing to her: "The printed story . . . promises dependability. The soldier will always kill the witch; the lost child will invariably find his parents; everyone will live happily ever after" (1981: 122). Entering the world of magic and sharing stories with her classmates allowed this child to find voices that she wanted to use and make her own. Through these voices she expanded her second language competence and performed in ways that were consistent with both her cultural background and her personal goals.

What kinds of strategies did Paley employ? First, the teacher realized that, in order to use her second language, Akemi favored performance genres that were highly text-oriented. She encouraged her, therefore, to pursue this interest. The participation structures evident in Paley's account of Akemi's progress were varied and flexible: Paley read to the class (large-group sessions); children selected their own books with teacher guidance (enhanced individual work); Paley read to individual children at their request (teacher-student pair work); children interacted informally (enhanced individual or unstructured); children dictated stories to be acted out (small group); and children presented plays and told stories to other children (pair, small group, or large group). Using these activities within these participation structures allowed Akemi to find voices she was willing to use in her second language and provided the spark that accelerated second language acquisition for her.

Dialogue journals as flexible tools for interaction

The use of dialogue journals has been a major trend and a subject of considerable research in recent years. Teachers are using dialogue journals in a variety of ways: daily personal journals, literature response journals, content response journals, learning logs, and interactive written conversations among students, to name just a few (see Freeman & Freeman, 1989; Kitagawa, 1989; Peyton & Mackinson, 1989; Peyton &

Reed, 1990). Journal writing can be especially valuable for students because of its flexibility. That is, students of all ages, language backgrounds, literacy experiences, and language proficiency levels can benefit from interactive writing of many types. Journals are an important tool in integrative approaches to language learning because they involve reading and conversation related to the writing, and because students can use them to record their reflections about all aspects of their school life. Moreover, teachers can learn a great deal about their students (Andrade, 1991).

Journals can also provide one useful concrete record of students' written language development. Despite criticisms that too much emphasis on journal writing can discourage accuracy (Hoover, 1991; Reyes, 1991), this need not be the case. Journals can contribute to accuracy as well as fluency, especially when they are used as resources for other purposeful writing. When journal writing leads to more public or performance-oriented uses of language – writing newsletter articles, publishing books, performing skits and plays, sending authentic letters, and performing radio broadcasts – natural and motivating reasons for improved accuracy are intrinsic to the activity.

Perhaps the most common arrangement in journal writing is a two-way written conversation between teacher and student. An important question that teachers often ask is: How should I respond to journals? Peyton and Seyoum (1989) conducted a study to examine this question by working with a teacher, L. Reed, who was highly experienced and successful in using dialog journals with her second language students. The study focused on how this exemplary teacher's strategies promoted student participation in written dialogue.[4]

A common assumption is that asking students written questions to which they are expected to respond will elicit not only more writing but more complex writing from the students. Peyton and Seyoum found that

---

4 The researchers studied the interactions of twelve limited English-proficient students in Reed's sixth-grade class. Six of the students were Asians and six were Hispanics from El Salvador and Mexico. Peyton and Seyoum analyzed a sample of fifteen consecutive written interactions for each student to determine to what extent the teacher either initiated or responded to topics and to what extent she either requested replies or made personal contributions that did not solicit a response. They found that the teacher did not initiate topics in more than about one fourth of her journal entries. Rather, she tended to respond to the students' ongoing topics. She used this pattern for students at low and mid as well as high English proficiency levels. Moreover, she did not rely heavily on the common sense strategy of asking questions to solicit a reply. Analyses of the students' writing revealed that while teacher questions were successful in eliciting replies, students tended to write more when they were responding to a teacher entry that contained a question along with a personal contribution.

this was not true for this teacher and her students. Rather, the teacher made personal contributions in the majority of the entries, offering her own opinions and adding information about a topic. When she did ask questions, she often posed them in the context of her personal contribution (see also Kitagawa, 1989). Peyton and Seyoum concluded that "the success of the dialogue journal interaction lies precisely in the teacher's participation as an active partner in a meaningful, *shared* communication" (p. 330).

While journal writing is often a two-way interaction between teacher and student, or between two students, teachers can experiment with other grouping strategies that address their goals and the interests and needs of their students. For example, two Vietnamese students can pair up to exchange journal entries that focus on content with a pair of Spanish-speaking students. An additional benefit of this arrangement for second language and academic development is that it involves talking to negotiate the nature of the entry. While the written entries must be in the second language so that the other pair can understand, the discussion can be in the language students know best. Recall that research shows that discussing concepts in the first language is highly beneficial for academic progress and language development. This kind of arrangement, then, allows students to draw on all of their communicative resources and can help them in progressing toward the goals of advanced bilingualism and biliteracy.

Journal writing activities, and many other writing tasks as well, can be designed to meet the principles suggested in this chapter: using a variety of participation structures; building on children's cultural background and language and literacy socialization experiences; accommodating children's text-context orientations; promoting a broad functional range of language use and the use of extended discourse; and linking language and content across settings.

Conclusion: assessing the effects of grouping strategies on children

I conclude this chapter by discussing how teachers can assess the effectiveness of the grouping strategies they use. Continual, ongoing assessment of activities within varied participation structures is an essential part of good teaching (see also Chapter 9).

The teacher-research movement has shown that teachers can gain new and deeper insights into the effectiveness of varied interaction strategies by conducting their own small research projects (Cochran-Smith & Lytle, 1990; Miller, 1990). For some, teacher research involves simply observing and reflecting carefully on what happens in the classroom. For others, it involves more systematic approaches to investigating classroom processes. In either case, however, many language teachers, because of their linguistic and cultural knowledge, have unique perspectives that can lead to some very interesting projects and insights (Johnson & Chen, 1992). Following are several suggestions for exploring classroom interaction strategies. These methods of assessment are useful for teachers in training as well as experienced educators, both second language specialists and grade-level teachers. The projects offer interesting ways to assess both students and the teaching/learning environment.

Teachers' grouping principles Interview two experienced, excellent teachers to determine why and how they group students for various activities. Try to determine the teachers' underlying principles for grouping. What participation structures are used for which activities? How much choice do students have? What criteria do the teachers use for forming groups? What cultural issues are considered? In what ways do the grouping strategies promote language and literacy development in the children's second language? In the children's first languages?

The whole-day experience of students Observe a child throughout an entire school day, following her throughout all of her experiences. Record the nature of the child's participation, including both attentiveness/involvement and language use (both written and oral) in various settings. In what participation structures and activities does the child participate most productively? In what situations does she comprehend or produce extended discourse versus isolated sentences and one- or two-word utterances? What is the functional range of her language use (see Swain and Lapkin, 1989)? What adjustments would you suggest to enhance language-use opportunities? How do your observations and findings compare to those of your professional peers?

Applied ethnographic monitoring Pair up with another teacher who has complementary language abilities for this assessment procedure. Let us say that you know Spanish while your partner knows Chinese. Your partner will observe one of your own Chinese-speaking students in situations you would not normally have access to (such as first-language instruction, play with Chinese-speaking peers, pair work, leading a small group). You, in turn, will observe one of his Spanish-speaking students. How would you describe the child's personality, interests, and abilities? What is the nature of the child's extended discourse in his first language(s)? Record examples. How is the discourse related to the participation structure? Describe how these observations provide an ''expanded awareness'' of the child's abilities and overall language performance (Carrasco, 1981; Hymes, 1981; Johnson & Chen, 1992; Moll, 1989).

Underground curriculum   Explore the ''underground'' literacy curriculum of a class (Dyson's term, 1987). You might work in another's classroom or enlist the assistance of a student or two. What are some of the informal functions of reading and writing? What are the social networks involved in the underground writing? Which languages are used for which purposes? How could you use this information to devise ways to link class activities to student interests? What pairing or grouping strategies would you use?

Textual and contextual richness in writing   Examine an assigned piece of writing of one of your own students. What features in the writing index (make reference to) textual spheres? Contextual spheres? What aspects of the writing make reference to past or future texts and events? Can you trace these influences to work your student has done or will do in different participation structures, such as individual work, pair activities, group projects, or whole-class experiences? In what ways is this a textually and contextually rich piece of writing? What kinds of writing assignments might promote textual versus contextual richness? What kinds of writing assignments might best promote literacy development in the second language?

Each of these approaches to assessment can provide new insights into children's abilities as they are demonstrated in different contexts. Effective teachers need to know their students well so that they can design and organize activities in ways that will support language, literacy, and cognitive development. Much can be learned through ongoing observation of students' participation in varied contexts. Yet the ability of monolingual teachers to observe and assess their bilingual and multilingual students is limited. Consequently, collaboration among teachers with differing language abilities and cultural experiences will provide a much more complete picture of children's abilities and growth.

In a discussion of effective teaching, Ken Goodman (1991) suggests four roles for teachers: (1) kid-watchers, who observe their children at work and at play, watching for signs of growth, need, and potential, (2) mediators, who offer guidance, support, and resources for learning, (3) liberators, who help children take ownership of their own learning, and finally, (4) initiators, who rely on their professional knowledge and creativity to create exciting learning contexts for their students. Language teachers, bilingual education teachers, grade-level teachers, and teacher aides can best enact these roles by collaborating to use principled creativity and flexibility in planning the richest possible learning experiences for their students.

References

Andrade, R. (1991). Children's funds of knowledge: Getting to know students' social world. Paper presented at the Impact: Diversity in Action Conference, Tucson, AZ.

Atwell, N. (1987). *In the middle: Writing, reading, and learning with adolescents.* Portsmouth, NH: Heinemann.

August, D. L. (1988). Effects of peer tutoring on the second language acquisition of Mexican American children in elementary school. *TESOL Quarterly, 21,* 717–736.

Briggs, C. L. (1988). *Competence in performance: The creativity of tradition in Mexicano verbal art.* Philadelphia: University of Pennsylvania Press.

Brown, H. D. (1987). *Principles of language learning and teaching* (2d ed.). Englewood Cliffs, NJ: Prentice Hall.

Calkins, L. (1986). *The art of teaching writing.* Portsmouth, NH: Heinemann.

Carrasco, R. (1981). Expanded awareness of student performance: A case study in applied ethnographic monitoring in a bilingual classroom. In H. T. Trueba, G. P. Guthrie, K. H-P. Au (Eds.), *Culture and the bilingual classroom: Studies in classroom ethnography* (pp. 153–177). Rowley, MA: Newbury House.

Cazden, C. (1986). ESL teachers as language advocates for children. In P. Rigg & D. S. Enright (Eds.), *Children and ESL: Integrating perspectives* (pp. 7–21), Washington, DC: TESOL.

Celce-Murcia, M. (1991). *Teaching English as a second or foreign language.* New York: Newbury House.

Chaudron, C. (1988). *Second language classrooms: Research on teaching and learning.* New York: Cambridge University Press.

Cochran-Smith, M., & Lytle, S. L. (1990). Research on teaching and teacher research: The issues that divide. *Educational Researcher, 19* 2: 2–11.

Crookes, G., & Chaudron, C. (1991). Guidelines for classroom language teaching. In M. Celce-Murcia (Ed.), *Teaching English as a second or foreign language* (pp. 46–66). New York: Newbury House.

Cummins, J. (1989). The sanitized curriculum: Educational disempowerment in a nation at risk. In D. M. Johnson & D. H. Roen (Eds.), *Richness in writing* (pp. 19–38). White Plains, NY: Longman.

DeVillar, R. (1991). Cooperative principles, computers, and classroom language. In M. E. McGroarty & C. J. Faltis (Eds.), *Languages in school and society: Policy & pedagogy* (pp. 247–261). Berlin: Mouton de Gruyter.

Dyson, A. H. (1987). *Unintentional helping in the primary grades: Writing in the children's world.* (Tech. Rep. No. 8). Berkeley: University of California, Center for the Study of Writing.

Edelsky, C. (1989). Putting language variation to work for you. In P. Rigg

& V. G. Allen (Eds.), *When they don't all speak English: Integrating the ESL student into the regular classroom* (pp. 96–107). Urbana, IL: National Council of Teachers of English.

Edelsky, C. (1991). Great teachers: Chris Boyd. In K. Goodman, L. B. Bird, & Y. M. Goodman, (Eds.), *The whole language catalog* (p. 19). Santa Rosa, CA: American School Publishers.

Enright, D. S. (1991). Tapping the peer interaction resource. In M. E. McGroarty & C. J. Faltis (Eds.), *Languages in school and society: Policy & pedagogy* (pp. 209–232). Berlin: Mouton de Gruyter.

Enright, D. S., & McCloskey, M. (1988). *Integrating English.* Reading, MA: Addison-Wesley.

Freeman, Y. S., & Freeman, D. E. (1989). Whole language approaches to writing with secondary students of English as a second language. In D. M. Johnson & D. H. Roen, (Eds.), *Richness in writing: Empowering ESL students* (pp. 177–192). White Plains, NY: Longman.

Gage, N. L. (1985). *Hard gains in the soft sciences: The case of pedagogy.* Bloomington, IN: Phi Delta Kappa.

Gardner, R. (1986). *Social psychological aspects of second language learning.* London: Edward Arnold.

Goodman, K. S., Bird, L. B., & Goodman, Y. M. (1991). *The whole language catalog.* Santa Rosa, CA: American School Publishers.

Goodman, Y. (1990). Invited address for the ESL Assembly, National Council of Teachers of English, Atlanta, Georgia.

Graves, D. (1983). *Writing: Teachers and children at work.* Portsmouth, NH: Heinemann.

Hawkins, B. A. (1988). *Scaffolded classroom interaction and its relation to second language acquisition for language minority children.* Unpublished doctoral dissertation, University of California, Los Angeles.

Heath, S. B. (1983). *Ways with words.* Cambridge, England: Cambridge University Press.

Heath, S. B. (1990). In M. L. Rice & R. L. Schiefelbusch (Eds.), *The teachability of language.* Baltimore, MD: Paul H. Brookes.

Hoover, M. R. (1991). Using the ethnography of African-American communications in teaching composition to bidialectal students. In M. E. McGroarty & C. J. Faltis (Eds.), *Languages in school and society: Policy & pedagogy* (pp. 465–485). Berlin: Mouton de Gruyter.

Horst, D. P., Douglas, D. E., Friendly, L. D., Johnson, D. M., Luber, L. M., McKay, M., Nava, H. G., Piestrup, A. M., Roberts, A. O. H., & Valdez, A. (1980). *An evaluation of Project Information Packages as used for the diffusion of bilingual projects* (Vol. 1). Mountain View, CA: RMC Research Corporation (VR-460) (ERIC Document Reproduction Service No. ED 193 953).

Hudelson, S. (1989). A tale of two children: Individual differences in ESL children's writing. In D. M. Johnson & D. H. Roen (Eds.), *Richness in writing: Empowering ESL students* (pp. 84–99). White Plains, NY: Longman.

Hudelson, S. (1989). *Write on: Children writing in ESL.* Englewood Cliffs, NJ: Prentice Hall Regents.

Hymes, D. (1981). Ethnographic monitoring. In H. T. Trueba, G. P. Guthrie, & K. H. Au (Eds.), *Culture and the bilingual classroom: Studies in classroom ethnography* (pp. 56–68). Rowley, MA: Newbury House.

Johnson, D. M. (1987). The organization of instruction in migrant education: Assistance for children and youth at risk. *TESOL Quarterly, 21,* 437–459.

Johnson, D. M. (1988). ESL children as teachers: A social view of second language use. *Language Arts, 65,* 2: 154–163.

Johnson, D. M., (1992). *Approaches to research in second language learning.* White Plains, NY: Longman.

Johnson, D. M., & Chen, L. (1992). Researchers, teachers, and inquiry. In D. M. Johnson (Ed.), *Approaches to research in second language learning* (pp. 212–231). White Plains, NY: Longman.

Johnson, K., & Morrow, K. (Eds.) (1981). *Communication in the classroom.* London: Longman.

Kagan, S. (1986). Cooperative learning and sociocultural factors in schooling. In California State Department of Education (Ed.), *Beyond language: Social and cultural factors in schooling language minority students* (pp. 143–186). Los Angeles: California State University, Evaluation, Dissemination and Assessment Center.

Kitagawa, M. (1989). Letting ourselves be taught. In D. M. Johnson & D. H. Roen (Eds.), *Richness in writing* (pp. 70–83). White Plains, NY: Longman.

Larsen-Freeman, D., & Long, M. (1991). *An introduction to second language acquisition research.* London: Longman.

Lemke, J. (1985). *Using language in the classroom.* Victoria: Deakin University Press.

Macias, J. (1987). The hidden curriculum of Papago teachers: American Indian strategies for mitigating cultural discontinuity in early schooling. In G. Spindler & L. Spindler (Eds.), *Interpretive ethnography of education: At home and abroad* (pp. 363–380). Hillsdale, NJ: Lawrence Erlbaum.

McGroarty, M. (1989). The benefits of cooperative learning arrangements in second language instruction. *NABE Journal, 13,* 127–133.

McGroarty, M. E., & Faltis, C. J. (Eds.) (1991). *Languages in school and society: Policy & pedagogy.* Berlin: Mouton de Gruyter.

Miller, J. L. (1990). *Creating spaces and finding voices: Teachers collaborating for empowerment.* Albany, NY: State University of New York Press.

Miller, W. (1982). Language learning opportunities in bilingual and all-English classrooms. In L. Wong Fillmore (Ed.), *The language learner as an individual: Implications of research on individual differences for the ESL teacher.* University of California, Berkeley.

Moll, L. C. (1989). Teaching second language students: A Vygotskian perspective. In D. M. Johnson & D. H. Roen (Eds.), *Richness in writing: Empowering ESL students* (pp. 55–69). White Plains, NY: Longman.

Ochs, E. (1988). *Culture and language development: Language acquisition and language socialization in a Samoan village.* Cambridge, England: Cambridge University Press.

Ochs, E., & Schieffelin, G. G. (1984). Language acquisition and socialization: Three developmental stories and their implications. In R. Shweder & R. LeVine (Eds.), *Culture theory: Essays on mind, self, and emotion* (pp. 276–320). Cambridge, England: Cambridge University Press.

Paley, V. G. (1981). *Wally's stories.* Cambridge, MA: Harvard University Press.

Penfield, J. (1987). ESL: The regular classroom teacher's perspective. *TESOL Quarterly, 17,* 535–552.

Peyton, J. K., & Mackinson, J. (1989). Writing and talking about writing: Computer networking with elementary students. In D. M. Johnson & D. H. Roen (Eds.), *Richness in writing* (pp. 100–119). White Plains, NY: Longman.

Peyton, J. K., & Reed, L. (1990). *Dialogue journal writing with nonnative English speakers: A handbook for teachers.* Alexandria, VA: Teachers of English to Speakers of Other Languages.

Peyton, J. K., & Seyoum, M. (1989). The effect of teacher strategies on students' interactive writing: The case of dialogue journals. *Research in the Teaching of English, 23,* 310–334.

Philips, S. U. (1983). *The invisible culture.* White Plains, NY: Longman.

Pica, T. (1992). The textual outcomes of native-speaker–non-native-speaker negotiation: What do they reveal about second language learning? In C. Kramsch & S. McConnell-Ginet (Eds.), *Text and context: Cross-disciplinary perspectives on language study.* (pp. 198–237). Lexington, MA: D. C. Heath.

Reyes, M. L. (1991). A process approach to literacy using dialogue journals and literature logs with second language learners. *Research in the Teaching of English, 25,* 291–313.

Rigg, P., & Allen, V. (1989). *When they don't all speak English.* Urbana, IL: National Council of Teachers of English.

Saville-Troike, M. (1984). What really matters in second language learning for academic achievement. *TESOL Quarterly, 18,* 199–219.

Saville-Troike, M. (1988). Private speech: Evidence for second language learning strategies during the 'silent' period. *Journal of Child Language, 15,* 567–590.

Saville-Troike, M. (1991). *Teaching and testing for academic achievement: The role of language development.* Focus No. 4. Washington, DC: National Clearinghouse for Bilingual Education.

Schieffelin, B. B. (1990). *The give and take of everyday life.* Cambridge, England: Cambridge University Press.

Schieffelin, B. B., & Ochs, E. (1986). *Language socialization across cultures.* Cambridge, England: Cambridge University Press.

Snow, A., Met, M., & Genesee, F. (1989). A conceptual framework for the integration of language and content in second/foreign language instruction. *TESOL Quarterly, 23,* 201–216.

Steinberg, D., & Cazden, C. (1979). Children as teachers—of peers and ourselves. *Theory into Practice, 18,* 258–266.

Swain, M., & Lapkin, S. (1989). Canadian immersion and adult second language teaching: What's the connection? *Modern Language Journal, 73,* 150–159.

Urzua, C. (1987). "You stopped too soon": Second language children composing and revising. *TESOL Quarterly, 21,* 279–297.

Willett, J. (1987). Contrasting acculturation patterns of two non-English-speaking preschoolers. In H. T. Trueba (Ed.), *Success or failure?: Learning and the language minority student.* (pp. 69–84). New York: Newbury House/Harper & Row.

Wong Fillmore, L. (1985). When does teacher talk work as input? In S. M. Gass & C. Madden (Eds.), *Input in second language acquisition* (pp. 17–50). Rowley, MA: Newbury House.

Wong Fillmore, L. (1990). Teachability and second language acquisition. In M. L. Rice & R. L. Schiefelbusch (Eds.), *The teachability of language* (pp. 311–332). Baltimore: Paul H. Brookes.

Wong Fillmore, L. (1992). Learning a language from learners. In C. Kramsch & S. McConnell-Ginet (Eds.), *Text and context: Cross-disciplinary perspectives on language study* (pp. 46–66). Lexington, MA: D.C. Heath.

9 Classroom-based assessment

Fred Genesee and Else V. Hamayan

Assessment is an essential component of educational decision making. Some educational decisions concerning language minority students are made by testing experts, administrators, and speech and language specialists within a school district. The primary purpose of assessment in these cases is to make decisions about the initial placement of students into particular programs or about their reassignment to special remedial classes for individualized services (see Chapter 10). Other decisions and, in fact, the majority of decisions that affect the education of these students are the responsibility of teachers. In these cases, the primary purposes of assessment are to identify the specific needs of individual students, tailor instruction to meet these needs, monitor the effectiveness of instruction, understand student performance in class, and make decisions about advancement or promotion of individual students to the next level of instruction. In contrast to district-level assessment, classroom-based assessment is concerned with planning and monitoring instruction on an ongoing basis in order to optimize student learning.

This chapter is concerned with classroom-based assessment. It does not require specialized training in statistics, psychometrics, or research methods. The focus is on assessment of students learning a second language in contexts where that language is the primary language of education and of society at large. In other words, the focus is on students who need to learn a second language for academic purposes as well as for communication outside the school setting. It is addressed primarily to second language teachers. However, it is important that grade-level teachers who work with language minority students, regardless of the type of program the student is in (e.g., pull-out, bilingual, or immersion), also be knowledgeable about appropriate assessment techniques for second language students since they work extensively with these learners and share responsibility for their overall academic, cognitive, and social development in school. Aspects of assessment that may be relevant to grade-level teachers will be discussed where appropriate throughout this chapter.

Instruction for second language students

Instruction for children learning a second language and learning through that language in school has a number of important characteristics that should be taken into account when planning assessment. These learners need to develop proficiency in the second language at the same time that they expand and master conceptual knowledge and skills in academic domains. The guidelines that second language teachers have traditionally used for teaching language to these children have focused on language learning in isolation. However, it is becoming common practice for second language teachers to consult mainstream curriculum guidelines and, in particular, the content objectives of the core curriculum, in order to identify the language learning needs of their students. Snow, Met, and Genesee (1989) refer to these as content-obligatory language skills (see Chapter 7 for a more detailed discussion of this). In some cases, second language teachers are also assuming responsibility for teaching some of the content objectives. This makes sense since we know that children learn a second language more effectively when the language serves some useful and meaningful communicative purpose. Communication about schoolwork in mainstream classes is an important objective for language minority children, and the content of those classes thus provides a meaningful basis for teaching second language skills to these learners.

At the same time, grade-level teachers are increasingly being called upon to modify their instruction of content material by using second language teaching strategies to make content more accessible to language minority students and to promote acquisition of the language skills needed to master the prescribed content objectives. Rigid distinctions between language teaching and content teaching on the one hand and between second language and grade-level teachers on the other hand are impediments to effective overall education of language minority children.

Teaching the language skills needed for successful schooling is not the only responsibility of teachers working with second language students. Both second language and grade-level teachers are also expected to teach these students the communication skills and social behaviors they need in order to integrate with native-speaking children in the school and in the community at large. Snow, Met, and Genesee (1989) recommend "piggybacking" the teaching of these other language skills on the instruction of prescribed content in ways that are compatible with the content objectives. At the same time, language minority students will learn many of these skills from their native-speaker peers as they work and play together throughout the school day.

These features of schooling for language minority children have a number of important implications for classroom-based assessment. It means that second language teachers need to assess their students' ability to use the new language to communicate in a variety of authentic contexts, including the mainstream classroom and other nonschool settings – this is sometimes referred to as *performance assessment*. It means that grade-level teachers who share responsibility for the overall development of these students must be able to assess both their language development and their academic achievement. In particular, it is important that grade-level teachers be able to assess these students' content-obligatory language skills in order to devise effective strategies for teaching content that take into account the students' academic language skills at the same time as they extend students' acquisition of these skills.

The shift toward integration of language and content instruction in both second language and mainstream classrooms means that teachers working with second language students need methods of assessment that will allow them to distinguish between language and content learning. Incomplete second language acquisition may make it difficult at times for students to express what they know or what they have learned in the nonlanguage academic domains. Grade-level teachers, in particular, who are responsible for the general academic development of second language students, need a variety of assessment methods, some of which do not depend on language or require only basic language skills in order to make accurate assessments of their students' content learning, at least during the early stages of language acquisition (see Chapter 7). Likewise, second language teachers who aim to promote the development of their students' academic language skills by incorporating content from the curriculum in their teaching need a repertoire of alternative assessment strategies, some of which focus on language and some of which can distinguish between content mastery and language ability. And all teachers need ways of assessing these students' social language skills.

Finally, teachers working with second language students need to know how to use assessment to motivate second language learning. For children learning a second language, language learning is not an end in itself. Rather, it is a means to attaining academic success and social integration. The premise underlying content-based or integrated second language instruction is to respect this relationship and thereby to promote second language learning as a means to the larger goals of overall academic, social, and personal development. Assessment of the second language abilities of children should not focus on errors or areas of weakness in language in isolation. This can only serve to discourage the learners. It should always be clear to second language learners that assessment of their language skills can be a valuable tool for helping them attain their primary objectives of academic excellence and social integration.

Before discussing specific assessment procedures, let us consider classroom assessment in general.

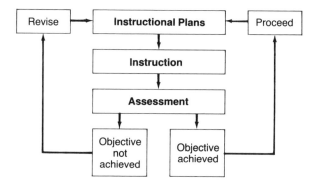

Figure 1   Classroom-based assessment.

Some general characteristics of classroom-based assessment

Classroom assessment is part of a feedback loop (Figure 1): Once placed into a particular program and classroom, students are often reassessed by both grade-level and second language teachers during the first week or so of school in order to determine their specific learning needs and to plan appropriate classroom instruction – this can be viewed as *placement* within the classroom. Having identified their students' needs, teachers then engage their students in learning activities that may have general or specific objectives and that are tailored to meet these particular needs and characteristics. The effects of these instructional activities on student learning are assessed in some way, and the results of the assessment are used to make decisions about the next round of instruction. If assessment indicates that the objectives have been achieved, the teacher moves on to the next unit of instruction, and the cycle begins again. If the results of assessment indicate that the objectives have not been achieved, decisions need to be made about how to modify further instruction so that it is more effective.

This description is idealized and simplified; teaching and learning seldom unfold in such a neat and systematic fashion. And, although our description depicts assessment in a step-by-step fashion, some of the steps are usually simultaneous in that initial assessment may not occur until learning activities have begun, and assessment and decision making usually occur as instruction is delivered. In fact, teachers continuously monitor and modify instruction in response to ongoing feedback from students.

In order to plan and tailor instruction so that it is appropriate for individual students or groups of students, it is necessary to understand the factors that influence student performance in class. This means going beyond assessing achievement. To illustrate this point, imagine a teacher who observes that many of her students' writing skills are not developing as she had planned and hoped for. As a result, she decides that changes in instruction are called for. However, the specific changes she makes will depend on her interpretation of why student performance is below expectation – the students may find the writing activities or materials uninteresting or irrelevant to what they need to know for their other classes; the students may find the writing activities or materials uninteresting or irrelevant to what they need to know for their other classes; the students may have been given insufficient time to master the skills she is aiming for; they may have used inappropriate or ineffective learning strategies; or they may lack the background knowledge or skills needed to get involved in the writing activities she has assigned. If the teacher thinks that it is because she simply spent insufficient time on the development of these skills, then she might extend the time devoted to this unit. If, however, she thinks it is because the students were unmotivated because the writing activities she used were irrelevant to the students' needs in their other classes, then she might review what writing is expected of them in their other classes and select alternative, more appropriate tasks.

The important point here is that decision making in the classroom is not only about achievement; it is also about those processes and factors that affect student achievement. Some of the factors that influence achievement can be found in the students' backgrounds – their prior educational experiences, their medical history, their family literacy and education, and so on. Consideration of the variety of linguistic, cultural, familial, and educational backgrounds students come from can be especially important when planning and evaluating the effectiveness of instruction for second language students. For example, some students may have already attained age-appropriate levels of literacy in their native language while others may not be literate at all. This is important to know because proficiency in the first language and especially experience with literacy in the first language can facilitate academic achievement and literacy development in a second language (Cummins, 1981). Often, language minority students have experienced trauma associated with poverty, war, or immigration prior to coming to school. They may have difficulty adjusting to school and may demonstrate lower levels of learning compared to students who have not had such experiences. Thus, these experiences need to be taken into account in order to understand the students and plan effective classroom experiences for them.

Information about important background factors can be obtained from

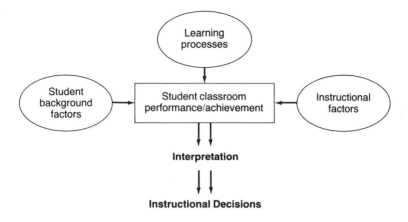

Figure 2   Assessment and decision making in the classroom.

students' school records, their medical reports, previous teachers, and parents. It generally entails consulting sources outside the classroom. Information about other factors that influence learning can be collected in the classroom itself – for example, information about the learning strategies students use to complete instructional tasks, their attitudes toward learning and school, their interest in specific instructional activities, and their study habits. Such information can be collected by observing students while they work, by talking with them about their work, by reading their journals, or by carefully examining their assignments and performance.

In this chapter, we will discuss some specific methods of assessment that can facilitate the collection of information about learning in the classroom. Because of space limitations, we will not discuss how to collect background information about students, but it is important to recognize that both classroom-based and background information along with information about achievement are part of assessment.

From this brief discussion, you can see that classroom-based assessment is part of a process that involves three components (Figure 2):

1. collecting information,
2. interpreting information, and
3. making decisions about instruction or students, or both.

Assessment, the focus of this chapter, is concerned with collecting information about (1) achievement or the outcomes of learning, (2) background factors that influence student performance in class, (3) learning processes in the classroom, and (4) instruction itself. In our framework then, assessment is more than achievement testing; it includes information about the whole child – past, present, and future – and about instruction.

Interpreting assessment information and making specific instructional decisions calls for a great deal of judgment. Teachers exercise their judgment every school day as they decide what is best for their students. The quality of teachers' decisions will depend on their beliefs, intuitions, and previous experience. In addition, and of particular importance for this chapter, the quality of teachers' decision making will depend in significant ways on the quality of assessment procedures that they use in the classroom. Thus, although assessment is not all there is to effective decision making (see Bertrand, 1991), it is an essential component of this process. Therefore, it is important that teachers develop a repertoire of effective assessment techniques for use in their classrooms.

Planning assessment

Effective assessment requires planning. Planning for assessment should be an integral part of planning each lesson or unit. It will also ideally be part of any general planning that takes place at the beginning of the school year. It is important to plan instruction and assessment together in order to ensure that instruction lends itself to assessment and that the results of assessment are useful for ongoing instructional planning. When thinking about a plan for assessment, the following questions are relevant:

1. Who will use the results of assessment and for what purpose?
2. What will I assess?
3. When will I assess?
4. How will I assess?
5. How will I record the results of my assessment?

Who will use the results of assessment and for what purpose?

The results of assessment can be used by different people for different purposes. Teachers are certainly the primary users of the results of class-room-based assessment. As we noted earlier, teachers use these results mainly to make decisions about ongoing instruction – about students' current learning needs, what instructional activities to use, when to move on to the next unit of instruction, when to provide remedial or additional instruction to individual students, and so on.

Students can also use the results of assessment to plan their own studying and learning (Lewkowicz & Moon, 1985; Oskarsson, 1978;

Tierney, Carter & Desai, 1991, Chapter 7). In fact, some students want feedback from their teachers in order to monitor their own progress. In addition, students can be trained to assess themselves – that is, to take a critical look at their own needs and development in order to decide where to devote their time and effort and how to proceed with learning. Self-assessment has the advantage that it is not limited to the classroom; it can extend to include communication needs and skills with native speakers in nonschool settings. Use of self-assessment will need to be tailored to correspond to the cognitive and metalinguistic maturity of the learners.

In the cases discussed so far, the results of assessment are used internally – by second language and grade-level teachers to plan ongoing instruction and by second language students to reflect on and plan their learning and study activities. The results of classroom assessment can also be used externally, that is, by people outside the classroom (Potts, 1985). More specifically, teachers are accountable to educational administrators, on the one hand, and to parents, on the other hand. While school authorities may carry out some of the assessment necessary for accountability, teachers themselves are often responsible for providing information for this purpose. Teachers also provide parents with feedback about their children – during routine parent-teacher meetings or at special meetings if certain students are having particular problems. Because language minority children are often regarded as ''special'' or even ''at risk,'' their progress is monitored carefully, and both their grade-level and second language teachers are frequently called upon to account for what they are doing in the classroom and how the students are progressing.

Deciding who will use the results of assessment and how they will be used is important because this may affect the method and frequency of assessment, the focus of assessment (i.e., achievement versus process), as well as how records of the results are kept. Assessment for accountability purposes (that is, for parents and school authorities) requires systematic and comprehensive assessment of all students that is related to clearly articulated and well understood learning outcomes. It also requires record keeping that is well organized, clear, and concise since the information is public and will be made accessible to others. In comparison, assessment for day-to-day instructional planning is largely an internal and therefore private matter. Thus, assessment procedures may be more informal and include background and process-oriented information as well as achievement results. Record keeping may be more anecdotal since others will not be shown these results. Assessment for internal purposes is generally more frequent in order to monitor the effectiveness of ongoing instruction as well as the effectiveness of complete units or lessons; such frequent assessment is probably not useful or interesting to outsiders.

What will I assess?

Clearly, an important focus of classroom-based assessment, whether it is for internal or external purposes, is student achievement – teachers need to determine what and how much students have learned in order to monitor the effectiveness of instruction, to plan ongoing instruction, and for accountability purposes. Assessment of language minority students' mastery of content objectives is of primary concern to grade-level teachers. However, in schools where second language teachers share responsibility for teaching content, they too will be concerned with assessing mastery of content. The district curriculum scope and sequence usually specifies the important content objectives and, therefore, those that should be assessed systematically. In general, it is important to assess mastery of these objectives in a representative way in order to have an accurate and thorough assessment of student learning. The same content objectives should be used to assess the achievement of all students – lower standards of achievement should not be established for language minority students.

Responsibility for assessing students' second language development should be shared by second language and grade-level teachers. In this regard, there may or may not be a prescribed scope and sequence to guide assessment. Even if one exists, it may be incomplete – it may lack the specific content-obligatory language skills that students need in order to benefit fully from instruction in their mainstream classes. Or, it may lack the social language skills that are important for students' integration with native-speaking children on the playground and in the community at large. Moreover, second language curriculum guidelines may need to be modified in unanticipated ways to reflect ongoing difficulties students have with the language used in the content areas or in social situations in school. Second language and grade-level teachers need to identify all of the language learning needs of their language minority students on an ongoing basis and use these to guide their assessment activities (see Chapter 7).

Assessment should not be limited to the second language. It is possible that some students, especially those who have attended school in their country of origin or those who are in bilingual programs where instruction is provided through the home language, have mastered academic concepts and skills in their first language. In these cases, academic assessment in the second language only can result in underestimates of academic achievement. Moreover, as Cloud (Chapter 10) points out, in order to understand students' second language development, it is useful to assess their skills, especially their literacy skills, in the first language. Thus, whenever human and material resources are available, assessment in and through the home language is advisable in order to ensure an accurate and complete assessment of students' academic and language development (see Chapters 7 and 10). Many of the assessment procedures described later can be adapted for use in other languages.

As noted earlier, assessment is not only about achievement. In order to understand student performance and to plan appropriate instructional activities, it is essential to know and understand the backgrounds of your students and the strategies and processes that mediate their classroom-based learning. Some examples of these kinds of information were given in the preceding section.

The specific distinctions that have been made here concerning assessment information are somewhat arbitrary. There may be other ways of thinking about this information that are more useful for individual teachers. The important point is that understanding your students and planning appropriate and effective instruction for them requires different kinds of information. And, as we will see shortly, different methods are required for carrying out comprehensive classroom-based assessment.

When will I assess?

Most teachers assess the effectiveness of their instruction informally on a continuous basis while they are teaching. Second language teachers especially need to assess students' language performance at all times, even when the explicit focus of attention is not on language – during mathematics lessons as well as during language lessons, and during formal instructional periods as well as during noninstructional periods (e.g., at recess and in the hallways). This is necessary in order to assess whether their students have acquired the language skills needed to keep up with content instruction and to socialize comfortably with native-speakers in the school.

Additional attention and time may be needed for systematic assessment, such as at the end of instructional units. This makes particular sense for grade-level teachers, who generally organize and deliver instruction in terms of units. Assessing student progress at the end of major units is useful for deciding whether the students are ready to proceed to the next unit and for planning the next unit. Assessment at the end of each unit of instruction can also provide useful information about how effective the unit was: Was it too difficult or easy? Was enough time allotted? Were the materials adequate and interesting? Did students have the necessary language and conceptual background skills?

It can also be useful to assess learning after several units, weeks, or months in order to determine how much students have retained from earlier instruction and whether they have consolidated or integrated skills, knowledge, or concepts taught over a longer period of time. Indeed, a developmentally sound curriculum will consist of integrated and overlapping objectives that aim for learning that is cumulative. Summative assessment at the end of the year may be required by the school district in order to assign grades for promotion purposes. Regardless of the specific grading procedures used in a district, it is important that all the information collected about students – qualitative as well as quantitative, and during as well as at the end of instructional units – be used to formulate student grades. Many of the assessment procedures suggested in this chapter, in fact, provide qualitative information about student performance.

Although it is a matter of some personal choice when to assess, the decision will also depend to some extent on how the results of assessment are to be used and who will use them, as discussed in the preceding sections. Assessment at the end of each unit of instruction is probably useful for both internal and external purposes; in other words, it is of interest to teachers for planning instruction, to students for organizing their own learning, to school authorities for accountability, and to parents interested in their children's progress. Assessment after each lesson is most useful for internal purposes – for teachers as they plan day-to-day instruction and for students as they plan their studying and learning activities; it is probably not very useful for external purposes since it provides more detail than is usually necessary. Summative assessment at the end of the year is not particularly useful to teachers because it fails to capture important changes in student learning as they occur throughout the year and because it cannot be used to impact on current student learning; it may, however, be required by local educational authorities.

Let us now consider some alternative methods of assessment.

How will I assess?

There are many different methods of assessment. We will discuss four in this chapter: observation, conferences, interactive journals, and tests. We do not intend that all of these methods be used at all times. Some teachers may decide to use one or two as primary sources of information, supplemented by information from other procedures. Of course, it is also a question of which method or combination of methods is the most appropriate for a particular purpose at any particular time. In fact, not all are useful for collecting all kinds of information. For example, tests can be useful for collecting information about student achievement under certain restricted conditions, but they are not particularly useful for collecting information about students' attitudes, motivation, interests, and learning strategies. Systematic observation, conferences, and journals can be more useful for collecting these types of information. The latter methods can also be used to collect information about learning outcomes – a conference can reveal a lot about oral language skills, and journals can reveal a lot about writing skills. Finally, some of these alternative methods of assessment – observation and conferences – can be used for instructional purposes, therefore allowing teachers to make efficient use of their time: Teachers can assess as they teach.

We will now briefly discuss each of these methods. Our discussion will highlight the systematic use of each method, but it is important to point out that observation, journals, and conferences are especially useful because they can reveal unexpected or unplanned aspects of teaching and learning in the classroom. Teachers should always be ready to see those unexpected but significant events in their classes that can give them insights about themselves and their students. Individual teachers will appreciate this feature of these alternative methods of assessment as they begin to use them systematically.

Alternative methods of assessment

Observation

Observation is basic to assessment. In fact, all methods of assessment, including conferences, interactive journals, and tests, can be thought of as specialized methods for eliciting behavior to be observed under specific conditions. Observation is a useful method of performance assessment. It can be used to assess students' language use during routine school activities that are not intentionally evaluative, for example, during small group instruction, at recess or lunch, in the hallways or playground, and so on. Therefore, it is particularly useful for teachers who need to assess the communicative skills of their students at all times throughout the school day. Observation is also useful for assessing planned language-based activities (e.g., role plays and oral reading; see Watson & Henson, 1991) and non-language-based activities (e.g., students' demonstration of grouping principles in a math lesson). A major advantage of observation over other methods of assessment is that it can be done unobtrusively, without interfering with what is being observed.

Most second language and grade-level teachers observe their students on an ongoing basis for evidence of successful learning and to gain insights about how and why students are learning and performing the way they are. Indeed, teachers plan their instruction from day to day and from moment to moment based on their informal observations of how well their students are doing. Thus, observation is not new for teachers. However, the challenge for teachers is to organize classroom observations in an efficient and effective way at the same time that they are actively engaged in classroom management and instruction. This requires planning. Without a plan, observations may be fragmented and disorganized and, therefore, less effective. Effective use of observational information also requires systematic record keeping. If records of observations are not kept systematically, much valuable information can be forgotten or recalled inaccurately.

What follows is a simple set of guidelines for planning classroom observations.

First, *identify what you want to observe.* Some examples include a student's communication skills with other students during small group classroom activities, a student's understanding of planetary movement using a mechanical model of the solar system, a student's ability to explain the water cycle orally or to describe it appropriately in written language, or how a student goes about solving math problems.

Second, *identify how you want to observe.* This entails several choices:

a) *Whether to observe individual students or groups of students?* On the one hand, observing individual students can provide useful diagnostic information about particular students who are experiencing difficulty or students who have just joined the class. On the other hand, observing individual students can be time consuming, and some students may be uncomfortable being singled out for observation by the teacher. Observing groups of students takes less time and can give you a general sense of overall learning within each group.

b) *Whether to observe activities planned for assessment (e.g., role plays) or routine lessons and activities?* Observing planned activities usually means assessing a specific and limited set of objectives. It also means that you can control to some extent what the students do and, therefore, what you can observe. Observing routine activities lends itself to observing spontaneous and unexpected events, behaviors, and interaction patterns.

c) *Whether to observe students in an activity that requires language or one that is largely nonverbal (e.g., dioramas, demonstrations)?* In the early grades and for beginning students who may have limited language skills, you may want to use demonstration-type activities that require little language to assess how well students are learning content, whereas in the higher grades, and for students whose language learning has advanced, you may want to use activities that call for more language.

d) *Whether to observe on one specific occasion or on more than one occasion?* In general, it is preferable to make repeated observations in order to ensure the reliability of your judgments. It is particularly important for teachers to observe students using language on different occasions and under different circumstances in order to determine the range of language skills they have and to assess how much students can generalize language skills taught in the second language class to content classes and social situations.

Third, and finally, *choose and devise a method of recording your observations*. It is important to devise an efficient and systematic method of recording your observations; otherwise, they risk being forgotten or distorted over time. More will be said about this later.

Conferences

Conferences generally take the form of a conversation or discussion between the teacher and one or more than one student about school work. In some cases, the conference is about work or tasks that the student performs in the presence of the teacher – for example, the student reads a short story aloud and recounts what he or she has read (Goodman, Watson & Burke, 1987; Reardon, 1991), or the student solves mathematical or conceptual problems while the teacher observes. Alternatively, teachers have conferences with students about work they have completed or are working on in learning centers or at their desks, such as a writing assignment for the class newspaper or a model for a science project. In any case, the teacher directs questions to the student about the processes and strategies he or she is using to perform the task – for example, in a reading conference, the teacher might ask the child which words were difficult, why they were difficult to read, and what strategies he or she used in order to figure out their meaning. The heavy reliance on verbal interaction during conferences makes it difficult for students with limited proficiency in English to participate fully and meaningfully in them; alternative assessment procedures are needed in these cases.

It is their focus on *process* that makes conferences distinct from other methods of assessment and, therefore, distinctively useful. They are especially useful for teachers who are unfamiliar with the diversity of learning strategies and performance styles that students from different cultural and linguistic backgrounds bring to the tasks that confront them in school. It may be difficult to gain these insights otherwise since language minority students are sometimes "invisible", at least in the beginning, because they are reluctant to participate actively and publicly in whole-class or small-group activities that include native speakers. Moreover, routine classroom activities usually reveal little about learning strategies; rather, they tend to focus on the products of learning – what students know or can do.

Conferences can also be an occasion to ask students about their reactions to instruction – including, for example, their understanding of the purpose of classroom activities and assignments, their satisfactions and/

or frustrations with their own learning, and their understanding of the goals of instruction. Some or all of this information can be useful in explaining a student's performance in class and planning instruction to better meet his or her needs. In addition, the interaction between student and teacher during such exchanges provides second language learners with opportunities to use language in ways that go beyond the simple question-answer formats that characterize many classrooms.

Conferences with second language students about their other subjects (e.g., math or science classes) can give teachers a close look at their students' content-obligatory language skills – asking a fifth-grade student to describe the method and results of an experiment on osmosis carried out in the science class, for example, can reveal a lot about the student's language proficiency in that content domain without the teacher having to observe the student in the class. Such information can be used to tailor the language-learning objectives in second language classes to be more sensitive to the specific language needs of students in their content classes.

In addition to their role in assessment, conferences can be an extremely useful instructional tool. Their use in the development of writing has been well established (Calkins, 1983). Process-oriented questions during writing conferences allow teachers to understand children's development in writing and, at the same time, to nurture that development. From the point of view of oral language instruction, conferences allow teachers to model appropriate content-obligatory language that is tailored to the needs of individual students and that can be useful to students in their content classes. The line between assessment and instruction becomes very fine – conferences help teachers gain insights about student learning and, simultaneously, the assessment procedure itself promotes learning.

It is advisable to plan conferences in advance. Think about what you want to assess and what tasks you want to use. Generally, it is a good idea to use the same tasks or same kinds of tasks you use in teaching. It can be useful when planning individual conferences to devise an interview protocol that specifies the questions and sequence of questions to be asked of each student (see Reardon, 1991, p. 79, for an example of questions during a literature interview). This will help ensure that you tap the specific knowledge, concepts, and skills that you want to assess. It also ensures uniformity so that you can form general impressions of all your students in addition to forming impressions of each student individually. If the questions are chosen carefully, you can elicit content-obligatory language skills. Planning questions ahead of time does not prevent you from asking unplanned questions.

Conferences may be awkward and perhaps not very useful at first if students are not sure what to expect or what is acceptable and if they are not experienced at introspecting about their own learning. They may require modelling and coaching in order to become comfortable and effective with the process. While this is probably true for all students, it can be especially true of language minority students who may not be used to teachers seeking their opinions or feelings about what is going on in class and how they are doing.

Student journals

For student journals to be useful in assessment and instruction, they should be used interactively – they should be shared with teachers who in turn should respond in writing to their students. In these cases, they are often referred to as *dialogue* or *interactive journals*. To ensure that journal writing does not become like other writing assignments, such as essays or reports, it is important that no limits be put on what students write about. And to ensure spontaneity in journal writing, it is important to avoid direct evaluative feedback to students about their writing skills in their journals. Comments that teachers might make regarding the linguistic forms used by students should focus on communication and should be supportive and only indirectly evaluative. For example, a teacher may say, "I am not sure what you mean by this; can you say it in another way?" or provide a "corrected" paraphrase of the students' entry and ask if this is what he or she means. Some educators recommend that no evaluative feedback of any type be given in response to students' journals entries. However, this is a matter of personal choice and will depend, in part, on what the students themselves want. In fact, some second language learners, especially older ones, may explicitly seek feedback about the form of their language in their journals.

When used in these ways, dialogue journals have some of the same advantageous characteristics as conferences – they are personal, individualized, private, and instructional. Like conferences, interactive journals can be used to collect different kinds of assessment information: about writing itself, about learning, and about students' reactions to school in general or to instruction in specific subject areas. At the same time, they have some distinctive features that are useful for assessing second language learners.

Most obviously, journals can be used to assess students' writing skills and the strategies they use when writing. They are particularly useful for this purpose if they are done routinely so that they provide a continuous record of writing development. They can reveal much about writing strategies if the students' entries are spontaneous and free flowing, including any or all corrections and editing. Students should be encouraged to use whatever means of expression they have in order to say what they want, even pictures, and they should not feel that their language has to be correct or perfect. If they feel they lack certain means of written expression, they should be encouraged to ask for help. Evidence in students' journals of recurrent or specific difficulties can be used to plan writing activities or lessons of a more formal nature at another time.

Of course, dialogue journals are an opportunity for students to provide feedback about their learning experiences: Are they able to keep up in their math class? Did they understand the teacher's language? Did they enjoy working more by themselves or with other students? and so on. It may be helpful and, indeed, necessary to give specific guidelines to let students know that it is alright to comment on such classroom matters and to express their feelings about what teachers are doing in class. It is important that teachers not judge or comment critically on such feedback if students' journal entries about classroom life are to be spontaneous and candid.

A special use of student journals is the *learning log,* in which students describe what they have learned during the day or in a specific class (e.g., math), what difficulties they had, what they enjoyed learning, and so on. Students can have separate logs for specific subjects – a science log or a math log, for example. In addition to providing information about students' learning experiences, learning logs can also indicate to teachers whether students are making connections within subject areas and, where appropriate, between subject areas. Learning logs can be especially beneficial for second language teachers who want to stay in touch with what their students are doing in the content areas but cannot know firsthand. They can reveal where students need additional language or subject matter assistance. Students themselves can use learning logs to monitor their own progress toward achieving the objectives in specific content areas and to identify areas of difficulty in attaining specific objectives.

Because of their personal, student-centred nature, interactive journals have the added advantage that they allow students opportunities to express themselves in writing in personal ways and at length through the second language. As noted in the case of conferences, language minority students may feel reluctant to express themselves in such ways during regular classroom activities for linguistic or cultural reasons. This, in turn, allows teachers opportunities to assess their students' ability to use the second language to express themselves personally in writing without the academic demands that usually apply during other classroom activities.

It is advisable to set aside regular times for students to write in their journals. Teachers should collect, read, and respond to students' journals in a regular and timely fashion. As with conferences, students will probably need some guidance and encouragement when beginning to use journals in order to become familiar with the general procedure and with the expectations of specific teachers.

Tests

Tests and testing have recently come under considerable criticism. Much of this criticism, although not all, comes from a basic misunderstanding of the purposes of testing. It is commonly thought that the purpose of tests is to assess what students know. While this is partially true, it is not the whole story. A primary purpose, if not *the* primary purpose of classroom testing, should be to assess how effective instruction has been. Knowing what students have learned from instruction as indicated by their test performance, as well as from the results of other assessment procedures, is an important aspect of assessment. Moreover, some school districts require the use of tests, either teacher-made or standardized, and it is therefore important that teachers working with language minority students feel comfortable and competent using tests (see Mattes & Omark, 1984, Appendix C, for possible criteria and a form for evaluating standardized and other types of tests).

It is generally not advisable to use test results alone to make educational decisions, especially decisions that impact on individual students (e.g., promotion) since students may do poorly on a test or on tests in general for reasons that have nothing to do with what they actually know. For example, they may have been tired the day of the test, they may have misunderstood the test question, or the test itself may have been misleading or inadequate for some reason. Language minority students might do poorly on tests in general for linguistic reasons or because of lack of experience taking tests. Therefore, test results, especially those of second language students, should always be backed up by other sources of information before making decisions.

Unlike the other methods of assessment we have discussed, tests do not allow for much individualization because they consist of one or more standard tasks that all students are expected to respond to in more or less the same way. While this can be undesirable at times, at other times, when you want systematic, uniform feedback about students, it can be an advantage. Testing is also most useful when you know fairly specifically what you want to assess and you have fairly specific criteria for assessing learning. This follows from the fact that it is difficult to select appropriate test tasks and to assess performance on tests if you are not sure what you are looking for and if you have poorly defined expectations about what students should have learned. Other methods of assessment we have discussed are more useful for exploratory purposes.

In order for performance on a test to be a valid indicator of what students have learned, test tasks should be selected carefully to match the objectives that were taught. The skills, concepts, and knowledge demanded by the test tasks should correspond to the skills, concepts, and knowledge described by the learning objective. It is important that the test tasks be an adequate sample of what has been taught as well. In other words, all major objectives should be assessed and more important objectives should be given more importance than less important objectives. If the skills, concepts, and knowledge included in a test are indeed representative of the objectives that were taught, then it is reasonable to interpret high test scores to mean that those students have probably learned most of the important objectives and vice versa for low test scores.

There are many different types of test tasks. Different tasks provide different kinds of information about instruction and learning (see Carlson, 1985, for some creative types of test item formats). Closed-ended or multiple-choice tasks are useful for assessing comprehension skills but not production skills. Open-ended test items, such as short essays, can be used to assess production skills, including organization, creativity, and grammar skills. Selecting the most appropriate test tasks is a matter of sound judgment based on a good understanding of your objectives and what specific kinds of tasks can and cannot tell you about learning. Selecting test tasks is also a matter of practicality. Some tasks, such as open-ended formats, are easy to devise but time-consuming to grade, while others, such as multiple-choice formats, are difficult to devise but easy to grade. It is important to think carefully about what specific test formats reveal about student learning and performance and whether they are appropriate for assessing the language skills and/or content-area knowledge and skills you are interested in (see list of additional readings for further examples of test formats).

When selecting content-area test tasks, second language teachers need to consider how much and what kinds of language skills are called for in order to complete the test successfully (see Chapter 7). On the one hand, if the purpose of assessment is to determine mastery of content independent of language skills, then it is appropriate to choose tasks that require relatively little language or to use the students' home language, in order not to handicap students with limited language proficiency. On the other hand, if the purpose of assessment is to ascertain both what content has been learned and which content-obligatory language skills students have mastered, then tasks that integrate language and content are appropriate.

In summary, tests are most useful when:

- you want systematic and uniform feedback about student learning and the effectiveness of instruction
- there is a clearly defined set of learning objectives to be assessed
- there are clearly defined criteria for assessing learning
- the test is a good representation of learning objectives
- you have other pertinent information about learning to base decisions on

Record keeping

Good record keeping is essential for effective assessment (see Church, 1991; Porter, 1986; Tierney, Carter, & Desai, 1991; Chapter 8). Good record keeping will help you:

- keep track of important information about student learning and the effectiveness of instruction
- form sound impressions of student achievement and progress
- accurately identify persistent difficulties and problems of individual students
- report individual student progress to other educational professionals and parents
- assign formal grades to students, if required to do so
- monitor, evaluate, and redesign instructional plans

Like assessment, record keeping is an ongoing process that takes time – it should take place not only after each unit, but every day, after specific lessons, and even during lessons. Effective assessment requires a combination of methods, some for daily recording and some for periodic recording, some that focus on students and some that focus on instruction, and some that are narrative and some that are checklists. In this section, we will consider student portfolios, narrative records, and checklists.

Student portfolios

A useful way to monitor and record student progress is to collect samples of student work throughout the year in individual files, boxes, or portfolios (Freeman & Freeman, 1991; Tierney, Carter, & Desai, 1991). The work samples can be originals (such as writing samples, drawings, and work sheets) or copies (such as photocopies of paper-and-pencil work, photographs of science and history projects, and audio recordings). Portfolios can contain samples of any of the student's school work or, alternatively, they can contain samples of work from a specific domain, such as in a writing portfolio or a science portfolio. Specialized portfolios are particularly useful for assessing progress in specific academic domains.

Students either by themselves or in collaboration with the teacher can be asked to select their best or favorite work to include in their portfolios. Each work sample should be dated and include a brief description of the work. Teachers and older students may want to include additional comments about each sample so that subsequent progress can be assessed more easily against comments made about earlier samples. This gives second language learners the added opportunity to use the target language in authentic academic contexts to comment on their own learning. By actively participating in the assessment process in this way, students take pride in their school work and learn to take responsibility for their own academic progress. Moreover, portfolios are a noncompetitive way in which individual students can "put their best foot forward" and are therefore particularly useful for students from different cultural backgrounds.

Student portfolios are especially valuable as records of student progress over the school year. They can be consulted by teachers, parents, and students themselves to review where progress has been made. More specifically, teachers can consult them whenever decisions are to be made about specific students, for example, for referral, grading, and advancement. Portfolios can be particularly important for second language learners because they can see the real linguistic progress they have made since the beginning of the school year. It is easy to take language development for granted if there is no concrete documentation of how much progress has been made. Sharing student portfolios with parents also gives them concrete evidence, which they might not otherwise have, of their own children's achievements in language and the content areas throughout the year.

Narrative records

Teachers need ways of recording spontaneous, unexpected, or unique observations throughout the day, for example, about activities that worked particularly well or poorly, the accomplishments of individual students, or student behaviors that suggest that they are having difficulty with certain skills or concepts. Narrative or anecdotal records are useful for this purpose (Kitagawa, 1989: 108; Morrissey, 1989). Narrative records can also be used in conjunction with the other assessment procedures we have discussed – for noting observations during conferences with individual students, while marking tests, or while reading students' journals, for example.

Narrative records can be made on file cards, adhesive labels, or clipboards with notepaper left in strategic locations around the classroom so that you can record your observations quickly and easily no matter where you are or what you are doing. Alternatively, they can be recorded in a book or journal kept especially for this purpose – a teacher's journal. It is important to date each entry and describe briefly the context in which the observation was made. It is also useful to organize your comments according to student name or instructional unit in order to facilitate retrieval of information about specific students, units of instruction, or lessons at a later time.

As noted at the outset, second language teachers need to monitor all aspects of their students' language development, and they need to do this at all times during the school day. Narrative records can be particularly useful for this purpose because they are relatively open-ended and, therefore, lend themselves to recording all aspects of language use. In addition, they are an unobtrusive way of recording observations about students' language use during activities, such as play or spontaneous discussions among themselves, that the teacher has no control over and, indeed, may not even be part of.

They can be especially useful for new, inexperienced teachers who have not yet developed systematic or precise ways of observing their students. Once teachers develop more precise criteria for assessment, other methods of record keeping, such as checklists, can be used. Narrative records are useful for all teachers, however, for keeping track of those events and reactions that make each group of students unique and somewhat unpredictable. Over time, narrative records can sharpen and focus teachers' attention to what is happening around them so that important events are not overlooked.

Checklists

Unlike anecdotal records, checklists consist of lists of predesignated categories for recording observations about teaching and learning. In some checklists, teachers check off those categories that they have observed or not observed; in other cases, teachers rate each category on simple rating scales; and in yet other cases, teachers record anecdotal observations in response to each category. Checklists can also be used by students for self-assessment purposes. Table 1 includes some examples of checklists appropriate for assessing different kinds of language skills. In any case, checklists are useful when teachers have precise and well-articulated criteria for observing and assessing student performance or instructional activities. Numerous checklists appear in published form (see Genishi & Haas Dyson, 1987; and Sabers-Dalrymple, 1989, pp. 116–120, for some examples), but the best checklists are those devised by teachers themselves to meet their particular instructional needs and objectives. Be prepared to revise your initial attempts at checklists until they satisfy your particular goals and needs.

Checklists can be devised to focus on specific kinds of language skills – for example, reading (e.g., Goodman & Burke, 1980) or writing (Morrissey, 1989), or they can focus on students' general behavior in school (sociability, attentiveness, talkativeness, etc.) or their general communication skills (e.g., in class, in the school yard, or during small group work). Special checklists can be devised for use in conjunction with the other assessment procedures we have discussed here – to record

Table 1. *Examples of checklists*

I. Teacher checklists

A. Observation of Language Usage by ESL Students

Situation/ language use	Only English	Mostly English	Equal Mixture	Mostly L1	Only L1
Informal with peers (bus, play-ground, cafeteria)					
Informal with adults (hallway, gym, office)					

....

B. Checklist for Evaluating Use of Written Conventions (Genishi & Dyson, 1987)

Name	Begins sentence with capital	Ends sentence with period	Ends question with "?"	Uses commas in list	Uses apostrophes
Juan					
Kim					
Olga					

....

C. Reading Checklist: Early to Beginning Stages (from Church in B. Harp, 1991)

Codes: **M** = most of the time   **S** = some of the time   **N** = never

	Month			
	1	2	3	4
Displays interest in books				
Chooses to spend time with books				
Displays sense of story				
Recognizes some words				
Focuses on deriving meaning from text				

....

D. Indicators of Attitudes and Social Behavior: Developing to Independent Stages (from Church in B. Harp, 1991)

Code: **M** = most of the time   **S** = sometimes   **N** = never

	Date of Entry			
	1	2	3	4
Cooperates with others				
Learns from watching others				
Is willing to be challenged				
Displays sensitivity and respect for others				

Table 1. (*cont.*)

II. Student checklists

A. Student Writing Process Checklist

Directions: Please indicate the extent to which you agree or disagree with each of the following statements. Respond to each statement by circling one of the following: **1** = strongly agree, **2** = agree, **3** = undecided, **4** = disagree, **5** = strongly disagree.

	SA	A	U	D	SD
When I wrote this paper, I knew how to get the ideas.	1	2	3	4	5
When I wrote this paper, I wasn't sure how to organize it.	1	2	3	4	5
It was easy for me to get started writing.	1	2	3	4	5

....

B. Student Evaluation Sheet for Writing to Convince (from Reardon in B. Harp, 1991)

Directions: This evaluation sheet has been devised by students in collaboration with their teachers and is to be completed by the author (Auth), their writing partner (Part), and the teacher (Teac). Only selected examples of the types of items included in this sheet are presented.

	Auth	Part	Teac
What I want the reader to do is clear.			
There are logical reasons given.			
Capital letters are used where needed.			
I considered the comments and questions of my response group.			

....

C. Student Self-Assessment Form (Speaking) (adapted from Oskarsson, 1978)

Directions: Imagine that you meet an English-speaking person who knows nothing about you. Indicate your ability to use English to do the following things.

	Yes	No
I can tell him or her when and where I was born.		
I can describe my home to him or her.		
I can tell him or her how I feel at the moment.		
I can tell him or her what I like to do in my free time.		

observations during student conferences or while reading students' journals. It can be useful sometimes to allow for repeated entries so that you can monitor changes in student performance over time.

Checklists can be a particularly useful form of record keeping when every student is asked to do the same thing, such as explain a science project to their classmates, or report to the class information they have collected about local plants and animals, or when they are engaged in the same kinds of activities repeatedly, such as journal writing or reading conferences. It can be useful when observing second language students' content learning to include categories in checklists that refer to nonverbal demonstrations of knowledge. Assessment information that is recorded in this way is comprehensive and concise. It is useful for both internal and external evaluation purposes – it can be shared easily with parents or other educational professionals to document individual student performance.

Checklists can be devised to meet the special assessment needs of teachers of language minority students. For example, checklists can be devised to assess students' use of English outside the classroom – in the school yard or in the lunchroom. Of course, checklists can be devised to monitor students' acquisition and use of the second language in the classroom as well, both specialized language that is associated with particular content areas and language that is required for general classroom functioning and socializing.

Conclusions

To be effective, assessment should be an integral part of instructional planning. Indeed, a number of the assessment activities described here can also serve instructional purposes – student conferences, interactive journals, and even open-ended test tasks, such as essays, oral presentations, or demonstrations. If assessment is planned along with instruction, then time will be made available for it, activities that compliment instruction can be selected, and instructional activities sensitive to the results of assessment can also be planned.

Effective assessment should also be an ongoing part of classroom activities and, in the case of students who are developing proficiency in a second language, of school life in general. Therefore, it is essential to plan assessment activities that can be used efficiently and comfortably throughout the school day, both in class and outside the classroom. Tests are clearly limited to classroom use whereas observation can take place at any time anywhere in the school. Effective assessment entails the collection of overlapping information about teaching and learning. Decisions about instruction and especially about students should always be based on converging but different sources of information. This will ensure sound, reliable decision making. This is particularly important for second language teachers who must conduct a comprehensive assessment of their students' language development at the same time as they distinguish students' language development from their progress in the content areas. A comprehensive assessment also includes information about (1) students' background, (2) classroom-based learning processes, and (3) proficiency in the students' first language as well as the second language.

Effective assessment must be practical. We have described a number of different methods of assessment and record keeping and suggested ways of using them. It is not intended that all the methods described here be used at all times for all purposes. Nor is it intended that these methods be used in exactly the way they have been suggested here. Adaptations will be called for if they are to be effective in particular classrooms. Each teacher must decide which methods best meet his or her needs and how to use them effectively. It is possible that each method of assessment and each method of record keeping described here could be useful as part of an overall evaluation plan. It is a question of when to use which method, for what purpose, and how. To be effective, each teacher needs an assessment plan consisting of a combination of methods to correspond to his or her unique classroom circumstances.

References

Bertrand, J. (1991). Assessment and evaluation. In B. Harp (Ed.), *Assessment and evaluation in whole language programs* (pp. 35–50). Norwood, MA: Christopher-Gordon.

Calkins, L. (1983). *Lessons from a child*. Portsmouth, NH: Heinemann.

Carlson, S. (1985). *Creative classroom testing*. Princeton, NJ: Educational Testing Service.

Church, J. (1991). Record keeping in whole language classrooms. In B. Harp (Ed.), *Assessment and evaluation in whole language programs* (pp. 177–200). Norwood, MA: Christopher-Gordon.

Cummins, J. (1981). The role of primary language development in promoting educational success for language minority students. In *Schooling and language minority students: A theoretical framework* (pp. 1–50). Los Angeles, CA: Evaluation, Dissemination and Assessment Center.

Freeman, Y., & Freeman, D. (1991). Portfolio assessment: An exciting view of what bilingual children can do. *BEOutreach, 1,* 6–7.

Genishi, C., & Haas Dyson, A. (1987). *Language assessment in the early years*. Norwood, NJ: Ablex.

Goodman, Y., & Burke, C. (1980). *Reading strategies: Focus on comprehension*. New York: Richard C. Owen.

Goodman, Y. M., Watson, D. J., & Burke, L. B. (1987). *Reading miscue inventory alternative procedures*. New York: Richard C. Owen.

Kitagawa, M. M. (1989). Guide, son of the shoemaker. In K. S. Goodman, Y. M. Goodman, & W. J. Hood (Eds.), *The whole language evaluation book* (pp. 101–110). Portsmouth, NH: Heinemann.

Lewkowicz, J., & Moon, J. (1985). Evaluation: A way of involving the learner. In J. C. Alderson (Ed.), *Evaluation* (pp. 45–80). Oxford: Pergamon Press.

Mattes, L. J., & Omark, D. R. (1984). *Speech and language assessment for the bilingual handicapped.* San Diego: College Hill Press.

Morrissey, M. (1989). When "shut up" is a sign of growth. In K. S. Goodman, Y. M. Goodman, & W. J. Hood (Eds.), *The whole language evaluation book* (pp. 85–97). Portsmouth, NH: Heinemann Educational Books.

Oskarsson, M. (1978). *Approaches to self-assessment in foreign language learning.* Oxford: Pergamon Press.

Porter, W. R. (1986). Towards more effective record keeping. In A. Cohen & L. Cohen (Eds.), *Primary education: A source book for teachers* (pp. 272–284). London: Harper & Row.

Potts, P. J. (1985). The role of evaluation in a communicative curriculum, and some consequences for materials design. In J. C. Alderson (Ed.), *Evaluation* (pp. 19–44). Oxford: Pergamon Press.

Reardon, S. J. (1991). A collage of assessment and evaluation in primary grade classrooms. In B. Harp (Ed.), *Assessment and evaluation in whole language programs* (pp. 87–108). Norwood, MA: Christopher-Gordon.

Sabers-Dalrymple, K. (1989). "Well, what about his skills?" Evaluation of whole language in the middle school. In K. S. Goodman, Y. M. Goodman, & W. J. Hood (Eds.), *The whole language evaluation book* (pp. 111–130). Portsmouth, NH: Heinemann Educational Books.

Snow, M. A., Met, M., & Genesee, F. (1989). A conceptual framework for the integration of language and content in second/foreign language instruction. *TESOL Quarterly, 23,* 201–217.

Tierney, R. J., Carter, M. A., & Desai, L. E. (1991). *Portfolio assessment in the reading-writing classroom.* Norwood, NJ: Christopher-Gordon.

Watson, D., & Henson, J. (1991). Reading evaluation – Miscue analysis. In B. Harp (Ed.), *Assessment and evaluation in whole language programs* (pp. 51–72). Norwood, MA: Christopher-Gordon.

Additional readings

Airasian, P. W. (1991). *Classroom assessment.* New York: McGraw-Hill.

Goodman, K. S., Goodman, Y. M., & Hood, W. J. (Eds.), *The whole language evaluation book.* Portsmouth, NH: Heinemann.

Harris, D. P. (1969). *Testing English as a second language.* New York: McGraw-Hill.

Heaton, J. B. (1979). *Writing English language tests.* London: Longman.

Hamayan, E. V., & Damico, J. S. (1991). *Limiting bias in the assessment of bilingual students.* Austin, TX: Pro-ed.

Hughes, A. (1985). *Testing for language teachers.* Cambridge, England: Cambridge University Press.

Jacobs, H. L., Zinkgraf, S. A., Wormuth, D. R., Hartfiel, V. F., & Hughey, J. B. (1981). *Testing ESL composition: A practical approach.* Rowley, MA: Newbury House.

Madsen, H. S. (1983). *Techniques in testing.* Oxford: Oxford University Press.

Omaggio, A. C. (1983). *Proficiency-oriented classroom testing.* Washington: Center for Applied Linguistics.

Underhill, N. (1987). *Testing spoken language: A handbook of oral testing techniques.* Cambridge, England: Cambridge University Press.

Valette, R. M. (1977). *Modern language testing.* New York: Harcourt, Brace, Jovanovich.

SECTION IV:
ADDITIONAL CHALLENGES

The chapters in Section IV continue to examine issues of relevance to the classroom. Here, the focus is on the needs of language minority students who face additional challenges in school. Cloud (Chapter 10) focuses on students with intrinsic impairments or disabilities, Hamayan (Chapter 11) considers students with low-literacy backgrounds, and Coelho (Chapter 12) discusses the social needs of immigrant and refugee children whose lives have been seriously traumatized in various ways. Each author in this section first asks ''What is the nature of these students' particular needs that calls for special attention?'' and then ''How can teachers and other educational professionals restructure the classroom and, in some cases, the whole school environment so that the social and personal needs of these students are better accommodated and their learning facilitated?'' As in the preceding section, the authors seek to respond to the practical needs of second language and grade-level teachers working with language minority students while at the same time recognizing the diversity of teacher needs and goals by presenting general frameworks for thinking about and planning instruction for these special kinds of students.

10 *Special education needs of second language students*

Nancy Cloud

Introduction

João arrived from Portugal with his family two years ago. His mother reports that he had trouble learning in Portugal. He likes to be with peers, but his behavior is socially unacceptable. He acts out all the time and isn't making much academic progress. After much repetition and reinforcement of specific vocabulary words, for example, he has hardly any retention. I asked the school nurse to examine him in case he had a vision or hearing problem, but she found that his hearing and vision are excellent. I considered referring him to special education, but it's such a hard decision to make. I guess I'll wait till the end of the next marking period to decide what to do.

In the past few years it seems that so many children I come in contact with have had traumatic experiences – Southeast Asian children in my class experience tearful flashbacks of family members being swept away while crossing a river on foot; others are traumatized by war experiences in Central America where they witnessed mutilations, murders, and bombings, and are withdrawn, periodically ''space out,'' and are often fearful. One thirteen-year-old boy was extremely disruptive, causing the class to focus on him constantly. It seemed he was extremely angry and holding most of it inside. Later I found out that both of his parents were killed in front of him. Then he had to come to this country to live with his aunt, uncle, and cousins, whom he had never met. How can I expect students like these to be successful learners when they're hurting so much? At times, I don't feel I have the training or resources to cope with these children. Where can I turn?

Migdalia is a sensorially impaired first grader. She has vision problems and she is almost deaf in one ear. Because she just arrived from the Dominican Republic and doesn't speak a word of English, she's been placed in a bilingual class with ESL support. Neither her bilingual teacher nor I have ever had experience working with second language learners like Migdalia. Because we have no training in this area, we're beginning to believe she'd be better off with a special educator who is trained to work with such children. It's an agonizing situation, however, because it seems neither setting is totally prepared to meet her needs.

Nelson, a sixth-grade boy, originally from Taiwan, is a below-average student and has difficulty learning. He's easily distracted and often instigates misbehavior in others. Yet, I enjoy having him in class, for when he finally understands an idea, I can see the pleasure in his face. In his mainstream class, Nelson has a difficult time grasping concepts, and his teacher is feeling frustrated and has come to me to see if we should refer him to special education. I just wish I felt secure that referral was the right thing to do for Nelson.

Second language teachers are increasingly confronted by children such as the real-life cases described in these vignettes. Some children's problems are emotional, others' behavioral and still others have problems that may signal an underlying neurological, sensorial, or cognitive barrier to learning. In other cases, we know that it is probably a life circumstance (e.g., war, educational disruption, or poor educational programming) that prevents these children from learning. All of these varied cases cause second language teachers to consider referral to special education, where trained specialists are available to intervene and enhance children's performance if disabilities are present. But do all of these youngsters belong in special education?

According to Carrasquillo (1990), language minority students with disabilities are "those students whose impairment adversely affects their ability to benefit from a regular educational program (including ESL and bilingual programs) and who require special education and related services. Such students may be categorized as deaf or hard of hearing, speech impaired, learning disabled, mentally retarded, orthopedically impaired, other health impaired, autistic, emotionally disturbed, visually impaired, or multiply handicapped" (p. 12). These are the students special education programs are designed to serve.

Students who do not possess an intrinsic impairment or disability but are undereducated or "miseducated" cannot be considered *special education* students. For example, some students have been out of school for a period of years due to political unrest or instability in their country of origin and so their schooling has been disrupted. Because they have not been in school, they are seriously behind their peers in all academic areas. Other students have received minimal or poorly conceived support services (e.g., second language or native language instruction) in their current school environment. For these students, lack of progress can be explained by poor or inadequate current instruction. In other words, external conditions rather than a condition *within* the learner are disabling the youngster. In comparison, special education is for those students who have a documented disability or handicapping condition that they bring to the learning situation and that seriously impedes their achievement despite the fact that they are offered an adequate and continuous educational program. The locus of the "problem," our perception of the student's abilities, and the nature of our intervention will differ in each case. In one case the problem lies outside of the student and in the other case it lies within. Effective intervention should be clearly directed at the source of the problem.

Not only are second language teachers asked to make decisions about which of their students to refer to special education, but also when and on what basis referrals of culturally and linguistically different students should be made. This chapter is written to assist second language teachers and other interested professionals work through some of the thorny issues involved in making educational decisions about the kinds of children represented in the vignettes above, children with whom all of us will surely come into contact over the course of our teaching careers.

A major premise of this chapter is that serving such children requires the combined skills and efforts of all instructional service providers: grade-level teachers, bilingual/second language teachers, and special educators. By working together with other teachers and including, where appropriate, auxiliary personnel (psychologists, social workers, speech and language clinicians, and health providers), and school administrators, we can provide coherent educational programs that fully serve such youngsters. The use of collaborative problem solving at the local level to respond to children's special educational needs is the centerpiece of current best practices. A collaborative approach to service delivery will be further explored in a later section of this chapter.

A framework for understanding disabilities in language minority students

Because of teachers' educational role with second language learners, it's fruitful to consider the issue of potential disabilities through the window of language acquisition. Since this is an area we know well, it will make it easier to understand the ways in which a variety of disabilities can impact on learning. In addition, it is the arena in which we can observe language minority children to identify possible disabilities.

A theorist who has conceptualized the language acquisition process in a way that will allow us to consider these issues is Bernard Spolsky (1989). The framework he has articulated allows us to identify and analyze major clusters of factors involved in second language acquisition and the effect potential disabilities in each area might exert on learning. While allowing us to tease out distinct clusters of factors for separate

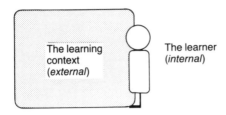

Figure 1   Conditions that affect second language learning.

consideration, the model also captures the dynamic and interactive nature of these factors and their effects on second language acquisition. Spolsky's model is particularly useful because it helps us evaluate the ways in which internal conditions of the learner interact with external conditions surrounding the learner to affect language learning.

For Spolsky, there are two major clusters of conditions that affect second language learning (Figure 1). The first cluster is *external* to the learner and is related to the social context in which language learning takes place; the second is *internal* and is related to the learner as he or she is engaged in the language learning process. As has been previously suggested, this internal/external dichotomy can help us to separate students with disabilities from those who experience failure because they are placed in debilitating educational contexts.

With regard to the external conditions, we know that the social context in which language is learned affects learners' attitudes, expectations, motivation, and access to the target language (Ellis, 1986; Krashen, 1982; Spolsky, 1989). Some external conditions affecting language learning include: (1) the sociopolitical context (e.g., immigration/migration patterns), (2) the sociolinguistic context (e.g., type of language community), and (3) the sociocultural context (e.g., family, neighborhood, and school characteristics). This cluster of conditions can help explain, for example, how refugee status might negatively affect language learning due to the lack of educational opportunities afforded children in war-torn nations, how language minority status might negatively affect language learning due to the marginality and discrimination often experienced by language minority children, or how the challenge of urban schooling conditions might negatively affect the quality and extent of language learning opportunities provided to these children.

The second cluster of conditions that affect language acquisition is *internal,* that is, related to conditions within the learner (e.g., what the learner brings to the task of learning a second language). Some internal conditions are the learner's age and gender, the learner's sensorial, neurological, and psychological status, as well as his or her cognitive and linguistic capabilities. These internal conditions can enhance or detract from language learning. There are temporary conditions present in learners that affect language learning, such as fatigue, distraction, and preoccupation. There are also more stable conditions that affect language learning, such as hearing loss, cognitive limitations, or emotional disturbance. The latter are precisely those we seek to identify when we believe children have special education needs.

According to Spolsky, it is the *interplay* between the language learner and the opportunities provided for language learning that determines *language learning outcomes*. From our perspective in this chapter, it is this interplay that must be analyzed in all its complexity in order to understand a child's failure to learn a target language. When we attempt to determine why learning outcomes have not been achieved at school, we must evaluate the learning environment (teacher expertise, curriculum, and amount and nature of instruction provided) as much as we evaluate characteristics of the student, since either aspect or both could explain the lack of achievement. This type of assessment is known in special education as *ecological assessment* (Heron & Heward, 1982) because all aspects of the "ecosystem" are considered as possible sources of explanation of learning failure and as potential avenues for intervention to reinstitute effective learning. Current best practices advocate such assessment in order to prevent erroneous referrals to special education and to respond fully to any occurrence of low student achievement (Cloud, Landurand & Wu, 1989; Cummins, 1989; Ortiz & Garcia, 1990; Willig, 1986). Although there is a clear need to examine the educational program in which the child is having difficulty at the same time and with the same intensity that we look for within-child characteristics that could explain the lack of progress, Cummins (1989) asserts that a tremendous imbalance has occurred in this regard, such that all too often the child is seen as deficient or defective while the programmatic features go unquestioned. He states:

Historically, in many Western countries, psychological assessment has served to legitimize the educational disabling of minority students by locating the academic "problem" within the students themselves. This had the effect of screening from critical scrutiny the subtractive nature of the school program, the exclusionary orientation of teachers toward minority communities, and transmission models of teaching that suppress students' experience and inhibit them from active participation in learning. (p. 116)

In order to respond to this criticism, we must carefully account for all of the factors or conditions that impact on language learning – those related

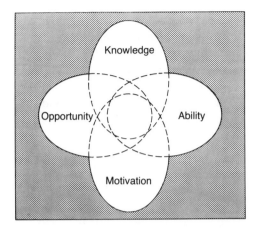

Figure 2   Major clusters of factors involved in language learning.

to the teacher, the curriculum, the school context, and the learner. In the next section, we will look in more detail at Spolsky's model, one that helps us to consider the major factors that impact on language learning.

In the sections that follow, each of the four aspects that Spolsky believes are integral to second language learning (Figure 2) will be discussed in greater detail, making it possible to consider the effect potential disabilities could have on that area and hence on a learner's performance. The interplay between external conditions of the learning context and internal conditions in the learner is clearly evidenced throughout the discussion that follows.

Spolsky believes that in order to understand the language-learning process we must first carefully specify the nature of the language-learning outcomes we seek. *Knowing a language* means different things to different people. For some it means possessing *linguistic knowledge* (phonology, morphology, lexicon, and syntax). For others it means having functional *abilities in general skill areas* (listening, speaking, reading, and writing). Still others concentrate on the communicative functions or *pragmatic abilities* of learners (ability to coax, request, inform, etc.). Each of these represents a different aspect of what it means to know a language. When we claim that children are "not learning English," what is it specifically that we mean? This is the first question second language teachers must ask. Once this is done, teachers can then analyze each of the major areas that influence learning outcomes, the first of which is current or present knowledge of the learner.

PRESENT KNOWLEDGE

Assessing a learner's present level of knowledge in the first language is essential because research has shown that concepts and skills acquired in the first language transfer to or are accessible through the second language (Cummins, 1981, 1984). It is interesting to note that spontaneous transfer from the native to the second language occurs in a variety of student populations (e.g., normal, learning disabled, and mentally retarded) (Bruck, 1982; Greenlee, 1981). For example, if a student learns to identify colors in the first language and is informally exposed to a second language, the color words are quick to appear in the second language. The greater the first language abilities and the more linguistic knowledge available to support the development of the second language, the more rapid and complete the acquisition. Life experience and background knowledge also support the development of the second language by giving the learner more to draw upon during the acquisition process. By knowing a student's present level of knowledge and skills, we can make predictions about the relative ease or difficulty that student would have in acquiring a second language. If a learner's present knowledge of the native language and his or her life experiences and background knowledge are limited, this will weaken the development of the second language. Comprehensive native language assessments and the collection of information about the student's educational and life histories will be required in order to answer questions about this area (see Hamayan & Damico, 1991; Mattes & Omark, 1984).

ABILITY

A second cluster of factors involved in second language acquisition relates to the constitutional characteristics of the learner that are involved in receiving, processing, storing, retrieving, and expressing language: cognitive abilities, sensory abilities, and neurological and health status. Limitations or barriers in any of these areas can affect the student's ability to learn and use language. For example, if a child is mentally retarded, this will reduce the amount of language that can be received, processed, stored, retrieved, and expressed. If a child has a sensory impairment (vision or hearing), input will not be well received and language acquisition will be affected. If a child is medically fragile, he or she will not be available for learning because of health conditions that interfere with the learning process. In each area – cognitive, neurological, sensorial, and general health – there is a threshold level of functioning that must exist in the learner in order for language to be acquired. Culturally and linguistically sensitive psychological assessments and comprehensive medical assessments will be required to answer questions that arise in this area (see Hamayan & Damico, 1991).

MOTIVATION

This area encompasses factors related to the psychological readiness, the emotional and motivational status, and the attitudes of the learner toward the target language and its speakers. Research has shown that negative affect can impede the reception of otherwise comprehensible input: Because the learner is not motivated, he or she rejects the language and its speakers or is distracted for emotional reasons (Brown, 1987; Gardner & Lambert, 1972; Krashen, 1982). Some special education categories such as emotional disturbance and behavioral disorders are directly related to psychological, emotional, or behavioral characteristics that impede a student's learning process. In identifying minority language students as emotionally disturbed or behaviorally disordered, we must take into account the cultural frame of reference of the assessment procedures utilized and of the assessment personnel drawing conclusions from the data. Clinical personnel must ensure that the procedures they are using are culturally fair, since considerable cultural variation occurs in these aspects of functioning (see Barona & Santos de Barona, 1987; Fradd, Barona, & Santos de Barona, 1989).

OPPORTUNITY

Opportunities for language learning are determined *formally* through laws and provisions (state and federal regulations and district guidelines) and *informally* by the role assigned each language in the family and community, the sociolinguistic situation in the city and state in which the student resides, and the conditions of schooling. The amount of exposure, the roles the language serves in the environment, and the general perception of the value of the language all affect the amount and the types of opportunities provided to learners over time. A child's opportunities for learning must be evaluated in order to interpret current levels of performance meaningfully. For example, if a child has had extensive opportunities for learning and high quality instruction but his or her language performance is low, then this would point to causal factors in the learner. In comparison, if opportunities for learning have been limited, then this would point to causal factors outside of the learner.

PUTTING THINGS TOGETHER

If we consider Spolsky's framework in its entirety, we see that a variety of internal and external factors, classified into four major clusters that he labels knowledge, ability, motivation, and opportunity, must be considered when attempting to understand a learner's performance. It is also important to remember that these four major areas interact in important ways. Elements in the ability cluster interact with elements in the motivational cluster, and so forth. For example, a student with learning disabilities may experience low self-concept due to below-grade-level performance in reading or writing, which in turn may create additional barriers to learning. Therefore, it is likely that multiple factors are contributing to a lack of achievement and that all must be identified and addressed in order to enhance learning.

Spolsky's framework reminds us that language learning is a complex, interactive process. It also provides us with a framework for answering two important questions: Why isn't learning occurring? and What kind of intervention is called for to enhance the learning process? The next two sections of the chapter will address these two questions. The first concerns the identification and assessment of second language learners with disabilities. It presents guidelines for appropriate and sensitive diagnosis of disabilities in culturally and linguistically diverse learners. The second presents guidelines for planning responsive intervention programs for such youngsters that take into account the all-important interplay between individual learner factors and educational context factors. These sections are designed to operationalize and extend Spolsky's framework to actual educational decision making.

Diagnosing disabilities in students

This section will present recommended procedures for the assessment of second language learners with potential disabilities. It will begin with a discussion of prereferral procedures that can help prevent the erroneous referral of language minority youngsters to special education and will describe common practices that have been linked with erroneous referrals of language minorities to special education. Next, it will suggest more reliable practices for assessing second language learners for potential disabilities as well as indicators of disability that have been advanced by assessment specialists. Finally, it will review the advantages of an ecological assessment approach, both at the prereferral and actual multidisciplinary-team-assessment phases.

Prereferral

PURPOSE

"An effective prereferral process can help distinguish achievement difficulties associated with a lack of accommodation of individual differences in regular classrooms from problems that stem from a handicapping condition'' (Ortiz & Garcia, 1988). In the prereferral process, the child's performance is examined in the context of current educational arrangements, and alternative instructional methods are tried within the child's existing placement (Willig, 1986). It is a proactive process that attempts to enhance the learning of children who are currently not achieving by altering the current external learning conditions. It seeks to avoid labeling the child as "deficient" and, wherever possible, referring the youngsters to stigmatizing or restrictive educational settings. Prereferral is intended to respond to external factors prior to suspecting internal conditions within the learner that would prompt a referral to special education. Where it is documented that children are being systematically provided with inferior instructional programs, referral is a totally inappropriate response to children's documented low performance since such low performance can be explained by the quality of instruction provided and since it is the quality of the instruction provided that requires intervention. Cummins (1984) refers to miseducated or undereducated children as suffering from "pedagogically induced" learning disabilities, and Hargis (1982) refers to such youngsters as "curriculum casualties." A quality prereferral process can prevent these tragic outcomes from occurring in our schools by properly locating the source of the educational failure. It helps us to initiate justifiable referrals to special education, where in-depth, culturally and linguistically sensitive testing can be conducted.

COMPONENTS

For prereferral to be effective it must take account of internal and external conditions, with input gathered from a variety of sources, including teachers, parents, administrators, and students. It is ecological in nature in that it analyzes the learner's performance *in context* and considers student, teacher, curricular, and instructional variables that impinge on the teaching-learning process. Student-related factors, such as sensory functioning, health and nutritional status, language performance, socio-cultural and experiential background characteristics, learning style, patterns of participation, cognitive functioning, academic achievement, and socioemotional adjustment are assessed (Ambert & Dew, 1982; Ortiz & Garcia, 1988). However, the student is observed using a "systems approach," meaning that consideration is given to the context in which learning takes place. Therefore, teacher, curricular, and instructional variables are also examined since these characteristics can affect student performance (Ambert & Dew, 1982; Ortiz & Garcia, 1988). The following teacher factors should be looked at: qualifications, experience and language facility, interaction patterns and personality, teaching style (e.g., type of instructional and behavioral management strategies favored), attitudes (e.g., expectations for student success or perceptions of students' abilities), gender, socioeconomic status, and ethnicity. Curricular factors must also be examined. These include: curriculum relevance, organization, clarity, and visual presentation, curricular "fit" with the learner, and continuity of exposure to the existing curriculum. In addition, instructional factors must be assessed, including the patterns of instructional delivery, the language of instruction, and the adequacy of instructional programs offered in a school, to name a few (Ambert & Dew, 1982; Ortiz & Garcia, 1988).

DATA COLLECTION METHODS

In order to collect these different types of information, a variety of procedures are needed. Simich-Dudgeon (1986) advocates observation in the classroom setting on several occasions (see Chapter 9). She concludes that observation of the student in selected teaching situations is essential to the design of responsive instructional programs since the child's performance is only interpretable in context, during interaction with particular teachers and peers in particular instructional settings. She recommends that the information collected during classroom observations be combined with information from school records, such as the child's educational history (e.g., nature and extent of second language instruction previously provided), from interviews with parents and teachers, and from language proficiency test results in order to formulate an effective preservice intervention plan. Effective prereferral processes are designed to prevent erroneous referrals of second language learners to special education. The next section will discuss two of the major sources of erroneous referrals of these students.

Preventing erroneous referrals

Researchers have pointed out some difficulties in identifying second language students for referral using procedures designed for mainstream, monolingual youngsters. They point out that if behaviors that are included on problem behavior checklists for native speakers were applied to normally developing second language learners, they would result in misidentification of these learners as disabled. Willig (1986) states: "Many child characteristics that are considered to be symptomatic of a learning disability in monolingual children are so closely related to language that, when applied to children trying to function in an unfamiliar language, they simply describe aspects of the second language learning situation." For example, in the area of language development, such checklists often include behaviors such as "speaks infrequently," "refuses to answer questions," or "has poor comprehension." While these items may signal potential problems for native speakers, in many cases they can lead to misjudgement of second language learners (Ortiz & Maldonado-Colón, 1986). Indeed, Figueroa, Fradd, and Correa (1989), in a summary of the findings of two research institutes that studied the special education offered to Hispanic children with mild disabilities, concluded it is precisely these types of behaviors (e.g., poor comprehension, limited vocabulary, grammar and syntax errors, and problems with English articulation) that trigger erroneous referrals. Therefore, a first step in removing existing barriers to correctly identifying students with special needs is the development of identification procedures that account for the second language status and/or cultural characteristics of language minority children (Fitzgerald & Miramontes, 1987; Willig, 1986).

Cummins (1980) warns of a further problem that can create erroneous referrals to special education. Educators often attribute wide-ranging or general proficiency to second language students once they have mastered certain interpersonal communication skills (see Chapter 1). However, face-to-face, interpersonal oral communication skills are only one aspect of English proficiency required for school success. Students must also manage academic English – the language of the teacher, textbooks, and tests. This second type of language proficiency is both academically demanding and decontextualized, meaning that the cognitively demanding message is held in the verbal or written language, and there is no contextual support (actions or visuals) to convey the meaning as there is in face-to-face communication. Thus, for example, when a child is reading a social studies textbook or taking an achievement test, if the child cannot derive the meaning from the written language, his or her performance will be impaired. Cummins warns that if teachers consider students who adequately handle interpersonal communication in English as being fully proficient in English, they may erroneously believe that any difficulties noted in academically demanding situations are due to learning problems rather than the learner's second language status and need to develop this second type of proficiency. In all too many cases, second language programs contribute to this problem by focusing on the development of oral language and not fully developing second language learners' reading and writing skills to the level required to be competent in academic settings. Thus, in order to prevent later school failure, second language development programs must seek to establish both interpersonal communication skills and cognitive/academic language proficiency (Cummins, 1984).

Thus, we have seen that the first step in diagnosing disabilities in language minority children is the implementation of an effective prereferral process, one that uses fair criteria and is implemented by knowledgeable educational personnel. Through this process, we will carefully consider other potential sources of learning failure prior to suspecting the existence of a disability in the learner.

Using an ecological assessment approach within special education

An ecological approach to assessment is recommended not only at the prereferral stage but also for the more formal assessment that is conducted once students are referred to special education. In order to ensure accurate identification of language minority children with special education needs, we must obtain clear results from a thorough assessment that fully evaluates the learner in the learning context (Wallace & Larsen, 1978). An ecological assessment takes into account school and classroom learning climate, physical aspects of the learning environment (lighting, seating, or noise level), interpersonal interactions between the teacher and the student and among students, the effectiveness of the curriculum and instruction provided, and home factors that may be having an effect on student performance (Heron & Heward, 1982). At the same time, it seeks to identify conditions that learners bring to the learning situation which detract from their achievement. In ecological assessment, a variety of data collection procedures are employed, including review of records, interviews, tests (both formal and informal), observations, and work samples. Here assessment personnel gather information from a variety of sources, including students, teachers, parents, and assessment specialists. Although such a procedure is time-consuming, it is well worth the time invested because it ensures that students have been accurately evaluated and provides guidance for the development of effective intervention plans.

A thorough ecological assessment describes a student's instructional needs. It documents the learner's language characteristics, cultural characteristics, and disability characteristics. Such information is essential if programs are to be responsive to each student's unique learning characteristics. For procedures for conducting a comprehensive assessment, the reader is referred to Hamayan and Damico (1991) listed in the reference section provided at the end of this chapter. One aspect that a comprehensive assessment should successfully resolve is that of distinguishing language and cultural difference from disability. The next two sections will consider methods and criteria for making such essential determinations.

Distinguishing difference from disability

A particular challenge for educators serving language minority students is that of distinguishing language differences from language disorders.

There are several positions currently advanced as to how to conduct a fair and comprehensive assessment of language that accomplishes this objective. Ortiz and Garcia (1990) recommend that norm-referenced language assessment instruments be supplemented by other procedures that describe both spontaneous conversation and cognitive/academic language skills. They further recommend that assessments be current and describe both receptive and expressive skills in the first and second languages. Damico (1991), on the other hand, advocates a total abandonment of the traditional norm-referenced, discrete-point approach in favor of a more descriptive communicative-assessment approach. In advocating a paradigm shift in the way we assess the communicative behavior of second language learners, he recommends using a descriptive approach to screen for language disorders, as he has documented that this results in a more accurate identification of children with "true" disabilities. He defines a descriptive approach as one that relies on pragmatic assessment methodology and provides a detailed and authentic description of the student's communicative performance as observed in a naturalistic setting. He contrasts such an assessment with the more common "discrete-point" methodology, in which the components of language are analyzed separately, and then the results of the analysis are used to draw conclusions about communication abilities as a whole. He criticizes the norm-referenced, discrete-point approach as fragmented, focusing heavily on the structural aspects of language, containing inherent and unavoidable bias, and underestimating performance because it is administered under standardized conditions. He concludes that pragmatic and naturalistic descriptions enable a more valid, reliable assessment that is effective for describing communication problems, for differentiating between language and cultural differences versus language impairment, and for planning coherent and effective intervention programs to respond to identified needs.

Because of all of the problems inherent in the use of norm-referenced language tests with language minority children, the alternative approach advocated by Damico deserves our serious consideration. However, in order for this paradigm to gain more widespread use, it will be necessary to advocate for changes in special education regulations since such regulations often require normative data in order to prove the existence of a disability and to qualify students for special funding.

Crosslingual assessment of disability

Beyond the question of assessment approach, we must also consider the language in which children are assessed as this also contributes to our ability to accurately identify language minority children with disabilities. A number of researchers have documented the advantages of assessing youngsters in their primary language when diagnosing potential disabilities (Ambert, 1986; Juarez, 1983; Mattes & Omark, 1984; Miramontes, 1987). Ambert (1986) warns that these children are at risk of misidentification when they are assessed in a language they have not mastered, or when they are observed in an instructional program where their performance is judged only against the performance of native speakers of the language. She suggests that we can more reliably identify language disorders or delays in contrast to incomplete acquisition of language if persons fluent in the child's primary language and regional variety evaluate the student's competence, considering both the structural and pragmatic aspects of language.

A commonly cited indicator of "true" disability in second language learners is that the disability expresses itself across languages. This is because true disabilities are usually unrelated to or independent of a particular language or cultural minority status. Irrespective of the specific type of assessment advocated (discrete-point versus naturalistic), various language assessment specialists advocate using the criterion of cross-lingual evidence of disability to confidently label second language learners as exceptional. For example, Juarez (1983), a bilingual speech and language specialist, asserts that a bilingual language-disordered child will not have a language disorder in one language that does not occur in the other, because common cognitive, neurological, and linguistic processes contribute to the production of surface features in both languages. Therefore, in order to differentiate between a language disorder and limited acquisition in a second language, she recommends that the ability to express intentions and to convey meaning between the speaker and listener in a variety of contexts be assessed both in the native and second languages. She recommends more traditional procedures for conducting such an assessment. While advocating a paradigm shift away from discrete-point assessment and toward more naturalistic assessment procedures, Damico (1991) also observes that communication disorders are often expressed cross-lingually in second language learners. Because of this, he believes that a critical question for examiners to ask is whether or not the student exhibits the same types of problematic behaviors in the first language as in the second.

Miramontes (1987) also found that assessment of children's reading skills in the native language improved the accuracy of the identification of a learning disability. The results of her study suggest that a process-oriented assessment procedure, conducted across languages, provides important insights about the reading strategies used by language minority students. She further found that the information gathered during assessment was useful not only for identification of students with learning disabilities but also for the development of successful intervention programs. Thus, assessment in the child's native and second languages enhances our ability to validly identify children with special learning needs. However, native-language assessment should not be conducted without carefully considering a variety of factors that impact on the design, delivery, and interpretation of such assessment.

Willig (1986) argues that educators should identify language minority students with disabilities by testing them in their strongest or dominant language (not necessarily the native language). She uses Mattes and Omark's (1984) definition of a child's dominant language: the one that is more developed, is preferred when the two languages are equally appropriate, and intrudes on the phonological, syntactic, lexical, or semantic system of the other. Willig asserts "If there is no disability in the child's dominant language, there can be no disability [in the second language]." She further recommends that language proficiency be assessed in both languages using different types of tests so that patterns of results can be examined. Such an assessment would include both informal (e.g., a study of language samples) and formal (e.g., the use of language proficiency tests) procedures. Citing Cummins (1984), she cautions that due to the degree of language loss in the native language or failure to develop academic language abilities in the native language, testing of academic language proficiency should *not* be conducted in the native language after two years of monolingual education in the second language. Thus, according to Willig, first language assessment is warranted as long as it is the primary language of the child, and as long as the development of that language has occurred to the extent necessary for academic testing to be supported in that language. Since language is dynamic and because there are so many profiles of language use and proficiency that could emerge among the various populations of language minority children, she advocates sensitive language assessment on a case-by-case basis as a prerequisite for the decisions that must be made concerning the appropriate education of these students.

In this section, we have discussed precautions that need to be taken to improve the accuracy of the assessment process for culturally and linguistically diverse learners. Beginning in the prereferral stage, a comprehensive, ecological assessment would focus on all aspects of the teaching-learning process that affect children's performance. It is suggested that culturally and linguistically fair procedures be employed, that the full range of a child's language proficiency be assessed, that cross-lingual assessment be employed to more validly identify children with special needs, and that multiple procedures (qualitative and psychometric, as well as formal and informal) and vantage points be used to enhance our understanding of children's educational needs in order to ensure the effectiveness of the intervention programs we design. The next section of this chapter considers program planning for culturally and linguistically diverse exceptional learners that is based on this type of assessment.

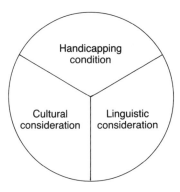

Figure 3   Cross-cultural special education (Ratleff, 1989).

A framework for planning effective instruction for language minority students with disabilities

Throughout this chapter we have used Spolsky's concept of two major clusters of conditions that affect learning – one internal to the learner, that is, what the learner brings to the learning context, and the second more external – what is provided to the learner in his or her learning environment. In planning effective instruction for language minority students with disabilities, we will start with the learner, focusing on what he or she brings to the learning context. In this section, we will discuss what it means to respond to the "whole child" when the child is culturally and linguistically diverse and has identified disabilities. From here we will move to consider the instructional environment and discuss ways in which teachers can manage three major components of the instructional environment – teaching methods, behavior management, and environmental arrangements – for the learner's benefit.

According to Ratleff (1989), there are three primary characteristics – handicapping condition, language, and culture – that define the learning needs of language minority students with disabilities and therefore influence program planning (Figure 3). While a learner's disability is a primary determinant of programming, the linguistic and cultural characteristics of that learner must also be considered. Indeed, they serve to differentiate the instructional planning for culturally diverse exceptional children from that for language majority children. In planning instruction for language minority students with special needs, it is important to remember that disability characteristics are not more important than language characteristics and that language characteristics are not more important than cultural characteristics, and vice versa: *They share equal importance.* In responding to the *whole child,* all aspects must be integrated simultaneously in programming efforts. For example, in planning a child's reading program, it would be important to take into account both the student's oral language base and his or her culturally determined knowledge base in order to ensure comprehension while at the same time planning to circumvent any disabilities that would affect reading performance. In responding to the whole child, we reject the common misconception that language minority students' disabilities are somehow related to their language or cultural difference since this is rarely the case. Instead, we will want to see language and culture as vital characteristics of the child that, when accounted for, strengthen the teaching-learning process. Now let's look at each characteristic in more detail so that we can effectively respond to each one in our intervention efforts.

A basic principle of all effective special education, which certainly also applies to language minority students with special needs, is that instructional programming must respond to students' *disability characteristics.* Therefore, the nature of the disability (cognitive, neurological, emotional, or sensorial) and the extent of the disability (mild, moderate, or severe) must be taken into account in programming efforts in order for instruction to be effective. For example, if a learner is sensorially impaired (e.g., visually or hearing impaired), the teacher might use large print materials and amplification as well as whole-body instruction to communicate the meanings of the target language. If cognitive ability is low, the teacher might select only high-frequency, high-utility language for instruction and increase the learner's opportunities to use that language in highly motivating and rewarding ways.

Instructional programming for disabled second language learners must also respond to a number of *language characteristics* of the student and of his or her primary caregiver(s). First, the primary and second language status of learners must be considered in all program planning efforts. Where children are more proficient in their first language, services should be delivered in that language since it would be the most powerful medium for intervention. At the same time the second language would continue to be developed, and eventually a transition to delivery of services in that language could be accomplished. In comparison, for children whose primary language is now their second language, intervention should be planned accordingly.

Second, the language use pattern of parents/caregivers must be considered in all program planning efforts. Parents should be encouraged to interact with their child in their dominant language, because in doing so, they are modeling language that is more complex and complete and therefore expresses content that is more cognitively challenging, all of which benefits the child (Cummins, 1976). It is neither beneficial nor desirable to encourage the premature use of a second language by parents whose proficiency is so limited that it would reduce both the quantity and quality of interactions in the home (Feuerstein, 1980). Even in cases where the child has the requisite proficiency for intervention in the second language, parents should be encouraged to interact with their child in their more proficient language. In these cases, parents can provide opportunities for their youngster to further develop his or her second language in a variety of ways, such as enrolling the child in school-based activities or clubs, encouraging out-of-school friendships with youngsters proficient in the second language, or watching educational television programs in that language. Rather than simplistically matching the language in which support is offered at school with the language spoken at home, believing that this is the critical variable, we can coordinate our efforts across learning environments according to the overarching goals of intervention (e.g., helping children to follow directions or develop more precise vocabulary). If home and school can work together on important educational goals, each from a position of strength, we will maximize the growth of individual children in their two languages and in their two primary educational settings.

Appropriate educational services for language minority students with disabilities will also respond to children's *cultural characteristics*. The cultural characteristics of the learner are important because the background knowledge and schemas children have acquired, the norms and values that guide their behavior and help them to interpret the behavior of others, and their preferred learning style are largely culturally determined. Culture is not a superficial aspect of instruction. Cultural characteristics affect performance at many levels. For example, reading comprehension depends on the knowledge bases children bring to the text they are processing. If the text taps into children's culturally determined knowledge base, comprehension increases; if it relates to content outside of children's experience, comprehension is reduced. Ethnic self-identity and self-concept are other characteristics of the child determined by cultural context that can affect the teaching-learning process in significant ways. If the child feels marginalized in school and if assimilationist values predominate, communicating that the child's cultural group and language are not valued and are to be replaced, this can impact negatively on school performance. If neglected, such culturally determined characteristics can impede school performance. But if incorporated into instructional plans, they can become strong supportive elements in meeting the special needs of second language students with disabilities (Collier, 1983; Ortiz & Garcia, 1990).

Creating responsive learning environments

In this section we will consider the learning environment from the vantage point of teaching a second language. As suggested by Spolsky's discussion of the major clusters of factors involved in second language learning, educators have four major responsibilities in teaching language minority students with disabilities: (1) to advance learners' knowledge of the second language, (2) to manage or circumvent the conditions in the learner that might prevent acquisition from taking place, (3) to create positive attitudes and expectations in learners about their second language learning, and (4) to ensure the provision of adequate learning opportunities, both formal and informal. In order to accomplish this, teachers need to manage the following components of the learning environment for the learner's benefit: *teaching methods, behavior management,* and *environmental arrangements.* The more factors teachers are able to manage, the greater the benefits for the learner.

Teaching Methods   A variety of teaching strategies are recommended for language minority students with disabilities (see Carrasquillo & Bonilla, 1990; Cloud, 1990; Wilkinson, 1989) – multisensory methods (e.g., Total Physical Response, Asher, 1982); cognitive strategies training [e.g., Cognitive Academic Language Learning Approach (CALLA); Chamot & O'Malley, 1987; Learning Strategies in ESL, Oxford, 1990], therapeutic language methods (e.g., Counseling/Learning, Curran, 1976), work-related language training (e.g., functional/vocational ESL, Friedenberg & Bradley, 1984); peer tutoring/cooperative learning (Gaies, 1985); and whole language approaches (Hamayan & Pfleger, 1987). These particular strategies have been recommended because they enhance learning and retention, and because they focus on meaningful communication. The selection of a specific strategy calls for careful analysis of learner characteristics (Cloud, 1990, pp. 116–120). For example, the level of a student's impairment would directly affect selection. When teaching reading to severely retarded limited-English-proficient youngsters, Duran (1985) suggests a functional approach. She feels that the reading needs of these students should be determined by observing daily activities, with consideration for the words that must be read at home, at school, and in the community, and with consideration of the language(s) in which reading is required (native or second). She advocates the teaching of functional reading through meaningful activities, using dual language instruction where possible.

While various methods have been proposed, we are beginning to accumulate information that would suggest that a holistic, reciprocal-interaction paradigm of instruction is superior to a discrete-skills, transmission-oriented paradigm of instruction for language minority students with special education needs (Cummins, 1984; Flores, Rueda, & Porter, 1986; Ortiz & Garcia, 1990; Willig, 1986). The direct transmission model is one in which teachers transmit individual elements of the learning task in discrete steps through direct instruction. Learning is "broken down" into consumable segments that are directly taught to the learners. However, the fragmentation of instruction in this way may actually make the learning of complex skills more difficult, because the child does not see how the pieces fit together. Moreover, such instruction is often disembedded and has little relevance or meaning for the learner (see Chapter 2). This type of instruction is also generally characterized by rote learning, where many of the activities required of learners consist of sterile drill-and-practice exercises that actually reduce a learner's motivation to perform. Hence motivation to learn in these situations is largely extrinsic, provided by the teacher; little or no intrinsic motivation is engendered.

In comparison, in the holistic, reciprocal-interaction model, learning is facilitated through an interactive process whereby an "expert" assists a "novice" to complete a whole and meaningful learning task. The learner attempts a complex task and eventually is able to perform the task in all its complexity through a series of guided "approximations." In the early stages the "expert" facilitates the learner's performance by sharing successful strategies and modeling the desired behaviors. However, the "expert" gradually withdraws his or her support as the "novice" becomes more capable of performing the task independently. Here, teachers are urged to view learning as a developmental process whereby over time, through reciprocal interaction with more capable peers and adults, learners successively approximate the behavior of proficient speakers of the second language. In this paradigm, learning tasks have an immediate and useful purpose, and because of this, the student is intrinsically motivated to learn (Cummins, 1984). Several specific examples of the holistic, reciprocal-interaction model, as advocated for second language learners with disabilities, will be described briefly now.

The first example is specific to the teaching of reading; the second is a more general framework for the instruction of mildly handicapped youngsters; and the third relates to the teaching of writing. Each will be briefly described in the text that follows, and the major principles advocated by each author or group of authors will be outlined in an accompanying table. Following the holistic, reciprocal-interaction paradigm and building on the cognitive theories of Vygotsky (1978) and the psycholinguistic theories of Goodman (1967) and others, Flores, Rueda, and Porter (1986) speak of the need to provide "assisted interactions" to second language students with special needs when developing their literacy skills. They advocate a conceptualization of literacy instruction as a "social, functionally embedded activity" and provide instructional guidelines to teachers working with this population. (See Table 1.) Their model stresses that

Table 1. *Guiding assumption for literacy instruction for bilingual special education students*

1. Language and literacy (either in L1 or in L2) are best learned when presented in authentic situations reflecting real needs, purposes and functions (Halliday, 1973).
2. Language and literacy represent transactive processes (Rosenblatt, 1978) that focus on the construction of meaning (Goodman, 1967).
3. Control of the form (i.e., the mechanics) is best learned in the context of its authentic use (function, purpose, need).
4. The teacher promotes the development of language and literacy by deliberately creating a social context in which they form a central part of the activity.
5. Social interaction between "novices" and "experts" in the "zone of proximal development" is the primary mechanism which drives the process of learning (Vygotsky, 1978).

Source: Flores, Rueda, & Porter (1986, p. 149)

instruction be meaningful and purposeful, and it emphasizes the interactive nature of learning.

A second instructional framework for effectively teaching language minority students with mild disabilities is explored by Ruiz (1989). This approach can be characterized as holistic and dialogical; its main principles are summarized in Table 2. In presenting each instructional principle, Ruiz carefully outlines the research basis for the principle. Of particular importance, she reminds us that the situational features of the language learning environments that teachers construct can affect the verbal and academic performance of children in significant ways, and that students display both competence and incompetence depending on the way that the classroom environment and the actual learning events are organized. Thus, by creating "optimal learning environments" we can optimize children's verbal and academic performance. In addition to the features previously elaborated by Flores, Rueda, and Porter (1986), this model stresses parental involvement and instruction that is responsive to children's backgrounds.

In a similar vein, Colley (1990) has formulated a cognitive framework for planning for the development of written communication skills in exceptional students from culturally and linguistically diverse backgrounds. She views the development of written communication skills as dependent upon three major components: (1) cognitive processing, (2) cultural/learning experiences, and (3) language abilities in the native and second language of the students. Based on her conceptualization, she outlines six considerations for the teaching of writing to second language

Table 2. *Instructional principles for optimal learning environments for language minority students with mild disabilities*

1. Take into account students' sociocultural backgrounds and their effect on oral language, reading and writing, and second language learning.
2. Take into account students' possible learning handicaps and their effects on oral language, reading and writing, and second language learning.
3. Follow developmental processes in literacy acquisition.
4. Locate curriculum in a meaningful context where the communicative purpose is clear and authentic.
5. Connect curriculum with the students' personal experiences.
6. Incorporate children's literature into reading, writing, and second language lessons.
7. Involve parents as active partners in the instruction of their children.
8. Give students experience with whole texts in reading, writing, and second language lessons.
9. Incorporate collaborative learning whenever possible.

Source: Ruiz (1989, p. 134)

learners; these are summarized in Table 3. Distinctive features of this framework are its stress on teaching students active learning strategies and the use of all curriculum areas as opportunities for learning to write.

These instructional frameworks show us that there is considerable consensus concerning the principles that should guide second language instruction for language minority students with disabilities. These authors stress the importance of making instruction culturally and linguistically congruent, of fostering social conditions that support learning, of making instruction meaningful and purposeful as well as developmentally appropriate, and, of course, of taking students' disability characteristics into account.

BEHAVIOR MANAGEMENT

While these authors have carefully examined the underlying theoretical considerations that lead to effective teaching activities, they do not focus much attention on the area of behavior management. Behavior management is an important aspect of instruction to consider because some language minority students' major disability is emotional or behavioral. In such cases, it is important to manage the student's emotional status and behavior so that learning can take place. Behavior management can be accomplished by

- teaching self-management strategies to students
- implementing reinforcement programs

Table 3. *Major consideration in the development of writing in exceptional language minority students*

1. Use the proficient language of the students as the basis for the development of written communication skills through a holistic, pragmatic orientation.
2. Base the transfer of written communication skills into the second language on sound second language acquisition principles and execute after mastery of such skills in the native language.
3. Offer opportunities across the curriculum to use written communication as a vehicle to enhance cognitive and language skills.
4. Teach students cognitive monitoring strategies which correspond to the context of the writing situation that will aid them when monitoring their own written communication.
5. Use the cultural/experiential background of exceptional students as the foundation for written communication in order to incorporate existing schema, reflect personal meaning, and capitalize on the purpose of the communicative act.
6. Account for the learning characteristics of students. Use cultural values and school experiences to modify instruction in the classroom and provide positive outcomes for all students.

Source: Colley (1990, p. 165)

- carefully planning when and where instruction will take place and how students will interact with one another
- preteaching the social skills that are required in the language learning situation
- creating options for students who have difficulty working in groups
- using therapeutic second language teaching methods as needed, such as counseling/learning (Curran, 1976)
- ensuring that needed medication is given on schedule

For further reading on the topic of behavior management, the reader is referred to Knitzer, Steinberg, and Fleisch (1990), Peterson and Ishi-Jordan (in press), and Rizzo and Zabel (1988).

ENVIRONMENTAL ARRANGEMENTS

Finally, in order for second language instruction to be meaningful for students with disabilities, the teacher will utilize all types of *environmental arrangements* to enhance learning. These include student grouping strategies (see Chapter 8), classroom design, and the use of special equipment or forms of prosthesis (e.g., large print, braille, closed-caption videos, amplification, computers with voice synthesizers, communication boards, and barrier-free environments to maximize linguistic interactions). For example, large print and bold typeface can assist learners with visual impairments in processing text in their first and second languages. Students with hearing loss can benefit from closed-caption videos that augment the verbal message with print. Computer-based prosthetic equipment is available to assist learners with physical disabilities in performing actions they would otherwise be unable to do (Behrmann, 1984). By carefully planning room and student grouping arrangements, we can maximize students' interactions to enhance language learning. Dunn (1982) has outlined a system for assessing children's learning styles that actively considers normal environmental variables (e.g., light and temperature, sound, and room design). Second language teachers will want to explore all of these environmental options to maximize learning for their students.

As one would expect, there is a multiplicative value in considering teaching methods, behavior management, and environmental arrangements simultaneously. These are the elements that together will create a powerful learning environment for each exceptional language minority student.

Effective program delivery for language minority students with disabilities

The delivery of effective programs to language minority students with disabilities extends beyond the boundaries of the individual classroom. In this section, we will explore some larger programmatic issues in delivering appropriate intervention to these students.

Flexible service delivery

Special education students are served in a wide variety of settings: (1) regular education settings (consulting teacher models), (2) pull-out programs (resource rooms, speech and language services, and physical therapy), (3) full-day special programs, (4) special schools, (5) homes and hospitals, and (6) residency programs or institutions (Cloud, 1990). Culturally and linguistically appropriate instruction must be available in all of these varied educational settings. Although a bilingual approach to special education has been advocated as the most efficient way of providing for all of the potential needs of exceptional language minority students (Ambert & Dew, 1982; Baca & Cervantes, 1989; Carrasquillo, 1990), a bilingual approach to special education is not always possible. A bilingual approach to special education is one where a bilingual professional, trained in special education, uses the first and second language to deliver intervention. Here, a single professional is equipped to provide first and second language instruction as required while accounting for the disability characteristics of the youngster. In some cases, the students to be served may represent one homogeneous group of language minority students (e.g., Hispanic learning-disabled students) and, therefore, the use of the first and second language in special education intervention in a bilingual classroom may be a feasible way to serve the youngsters. However, in other cases, language minority children from a number of ethnolinguistic groups may be identified as needing special services (e.g., speech and language impaired students from various language backgrounds) or a single language minority child (e.g., an Urdu-speaking multiply handi-capped child) may require a special program. In these latter cases, deliv-ering services in the first language may not be feasible for practical reasons (Simich-Dudgeon, 1986). Therefore, districts must explore all program models that have potential for serving language minority stu-dents with disabilities and flexibly deliver a variety of programs that best meet each student's needs. In most districts, flexible service delivery is the key to ensuring that all culturally and linguistically diverse students receive appropriate programs that respond to their particular learning needs.

In all cases, in order to facilitate the attainment of the goals and objectives for a particular language minority student with disabilities, primary service providers need to possess the combined expertise from bilingual, second language, and special education. In order to integrate knowledge from these fields to deliver an effective program, various instructional arrangements are possible: The use of a special educator trained in bilingual or second language teaching, team teaching with a bilingual or second language teacher and a special educator, or the use of a monolingual special educator and a bilingual paraprofessional (Ambert & Dew, 1982). Simich-Dudgeon (1986) calls for this type of collabora-tion among all professionals serving language minority students with special needs. She argues that a cooperative, collaborative framework is indispensable for the development of an appropriate educational program for these students because their needs go beyond the expertise of individ-ual professionals. In order to implement such a model, she believes, cross-training is necessary, meaning that each professional involved must learn about the other's field in order to access necessary information and techniques. This type of professional collaboration will be described further in the next section.

Collaborative problem solving

Because of dramatic increases in the number of children identified as mildly handicapped, there is currently a movement within special education to find alternative forms of problem solving and educational intervention that represent alternatives to referral to special education (Chalfont, Pysh, & Moultrie, 1979; Graden, 1989; Hudson, 1989; Idol, Paolucci-Whitcomb, & Newin, 1987; Pugach & Johnson, 1989; Zins, Curtis, Graden, & Ponti, 1988). Collaborative models are being advanced as promising alternatives. Pugach and Johnson (1989) have outlined some of the problems with conventional referral that have spurred recent interest in using teacher-to-teacher collaboration as an alternative. They view conventional referral as part of a hierarchical, bureaucratic, and centralized problem-solving process in which a problem is presented publicly, data are accumulated to verify the problem's existence, and then problem "ownership" is transferred to a specialist for appropriate solutions. This process is seen as disempowering grade-level teachers because while the teacher "owns" the problem, he or she does not "own" the solution. In comparison, in collaborative consultation approaches, bilingual, second language, grade-level, and special educators work as a team to formulate an educational response to a student's identified needs – all without referring the youngster elsewhere. Such collaboration reduces the isolation that characterizes the work of many grade-level teachers, provides ready assistance to teachers, encourages retaining the responsibility for learning failure within schools, and redirects the time and energy of instructional personnel toward solving problems rather than extensively documenting them in the process of referral.

In the introduction to this chapter, four vignettes were presented. Each of these cases could be solved through a collaborative approach. For example, in the case of Migdalia, the sensorially impaired first grader who recently arrived from the Dominican Republic, the bilingual teacher, second language teacher, special educator, nurse, and parents might work together to establish a systematic response to all of her identified needs. First, the nurse could initiate comprehensive hearing and vision screening to establish the extent of Migdalia's sensory impairments. Migdalia might be provided with amplification in the bilingual and second language classrooms and at home. Her bilingual and second language teachers might be assisted by the special educator to create large print learning materials using a primary-school typewriter, or they might create enlarged print using a computer. Corrective lenses could also be used if helpful for her problems. The teachers and parents might observe lessons in special education classrooms designed for sensorially impaired youngsters to see how lessons are presented. They might receive training and support from vision and hearing specialists. All of this knowledge would be incorporated into Migdalia's bilingual and second language classrooms so that instruction is meaningful for Migdalia, given her disabilities. The home and school efforts would be actively coordinated. In a collaborative approach, some team members are direct service providers, while others serve in a support capacity, giving guidance and training to the primary providers. In this way, the student receives the most cohesive and responsive program in the least restrictive environment.

Collaboration has also been advocated to combat the existing fragmentation of programs and services in schools (Johnson, Pugach, & Devlin, 1990). These authors conclude that given the current growth in the diversity of the student population, if present trends continue, the use of separate programs to serve students with diverse needs must be called into question, as schools will have fewer and fewer students in regular classes and more and more in special class settings.

Of course, collaboration can be hampered by a number of factors. Collaboration requires time and administrative support. Jurisdictional or program boundary issues can impede the process, since those collaborating often belong to separate departments or organizational structures (special education, regular education, bilingual/second language education). Sometimes this kind of problem solving is prevented because teams have limited representation from classroom teachers or because expert involvement curtails teacher participation in the problem-solving process (Phillips & McCullough, 1990). Collegial collaboration is meant to be a mutual and reciprocal helping relationship among coequals (Chalfont, Pysh, & Moultrie, 1979). To the extent that direct service providers are able to establish such a relationship, they will be able to create the required climate for this type of professional problem solving to occur. According to Phillips and McCullough (1990) and Pugach and Johnson (1988), intervention acceptability, intervention effectiveness, and teacher empowerment are the hallmarks of a successful collaborative effort.

Involving language minority families

Service providers must view each student as part of a larger family system that both affects and is affected by the educational intervention provided to the student (Cloud, 1991). Parents should participate to the degree they desire in planning their children's intervention programs. Service providers should explain the various programming options to parents and ask which they think will be of most benefit to their youngsters. In each case, school personnel should explain ways in which the family can support the learning goals that are collaboratively established.

Bernheimer, Gallimore, and Weisner (1991) remind us that a family's interpretation and response to their child's intervention plan is indelibly influenced by their perceptions, beliefs, and values. Culturally specific and family-specific knowledge is required by professionals so that they can offer recommendations that fit a family's values and beliefs regarding an appropriate education for their handicapped child. Some families will see their role as providing for their child's physical needs and m↳ development and the school's role as providing for their child's educa-tion. In cases such as these, families may be confused as to why these boundaries are being crossed, why they are being asked to guide their child's education, and why educational goals are being formulated that have to do with their child's physical needs or moral/ethical development. When we formulate an intervention plan, we must construct intervention goals that are congruent with high-priority family goals, otherwise, the interventions themselves may place additional stress on families or be displaced by goals that are more urgent to the family (Bernheimer, Gallimore, & Weisner, 1991). What matters is what is real to the family – the family's social construction of their circumstances, of their child's needs, and of the most appropriate means of achieving their goals for their child (Seligman & Darling, 1989). We must not lose sight of the dynamics at work that will allow these two major educational systems, home and school, to collaborate effectively to foster the greatest growth for individual children.

Conclusion

This chapter has focused on the identification and instruction of language minority students with special needs. In doing so, both theoretical and practical issues have been explored including the impact of potential disabilities on the second language acquisition process, ways of distin-guishing within-learner characteristics from external sources of learning failure, and effective teaching approaches and strategies for working with this group. Naturalistic forms of assessment, flexible service delivery arrangements, and active collaboration among educational professionals in the child's school and the child's primary caregivers have been recom-mended to the reader as mechanisms for responding to this special popu-lation of youngsters. Whether or not we are able to correctly identify and serve exceptional language minority students will be determined largely by our understanding of the issues involved, the quality of the services we design to meet their needs, and the continued development of our own professional skills.

References

Ambert, A., & Dew, N. (1982). *Special education for exceptional bilingual students: A handbook for educators.* Milwaukee, WI: Midwest National Origin Desegregation Assistance Center.

Ambert, A. N. (1986). Identifying language disorders in Spanish-speakers. *Journal of Reading, Writing, and Learning Disabilities International, 2,* 1: 21–41.

Asher, J. J. (1982). *Learning another language through actions: The complete teachers guidebook.* Los Gatos, CA: Sky Oaks Productions.

Baca, L. M., & Cervantes, H. T. (1989). *The bilingual special education interface* (2nd ed.). Columbus, OH: Merrill Publishing Company.

Barona, A., & Santos de Barona, M. (1987). A model for the assessment of limited English proficient students referred for special education services. In S. H. Fradd & W. J. Tikunoff (Eds.), *Bilingual education and bilingual special education: A guide for administrators* (pp. 183–209). Boston: College-Hill.

Behrmann, M. (1984). *Handbook of microcomputers in special education.* San Diego: College Hill Press.

Bernheimer, L. P., Gallimore, R., & Weisner, T. S. (1991). Ecocultural theory as a context for the individual family service plan: Abridged version. Reston, VA: ERIC Clearinghouse on Handicapped and Gifted Children (*ERIC Excerpt 17*).

Brown, H. D. (1987). *Principles of language learning and teaching* (2nd ed.). Englewood Cliffs, NJ: Prentice-Hall, Inc.

Bruck, M. (1982). Language disabled children: Performance in an additive bilingual education program. *Applied Psycholinguistics, 3,* 45–60.

Carrasquillo, A. L. (1990). Bilingual special education: The important connection. In A. L. Carrasquillo & R. E. Baecher (Eds.), *Teaching the bilingual special education student* (pp. 4–24). Norwood, NJ: Ablex Publishing Corporation.

Carrasquillo, A. L., & Bonilla, M. A. R. (1990). Teaching a second language to limited English proficient learning disabled students. In A. L. Carrasquillo and R. E. Baecher (Eds.), *Teaching the bilingual special education student* (pp. 67–89). Norwood, NJ: Ablex Publishing Corporation.

Chalfont, J. C., Pysh, M. V. D., & Moultrie, R. (1979). Teacher assistance teams: A model for within-building problem solving. *Learning Disability Quarterly, 2,* 85–96.

Chamot, A. U., & O'Malley, M. O. (1987). The cognitive academic language learning approach: A bridge to the mainstream. *TESOL Quarterly, 21,* 2: 227–249.

Cloud, N. (1990). Planning and implementing an English as a second language program. In A. L. Carrasquillo & R. E. Baecher (Eds.), *Teaching the bilingual special education student* (pp. 106–131). Norwood, NJ: Ablex Publishing Corporation.

Cloud, N. (1991). Mediated learning experience and cultural diversity. Hempstead, NY: Hofstra University, Counseling, Research, Special Education and Rehabilitation Department (ECSE Newsletter 2).

Cloud, N., Landurand, P. M., & Wu, S. T. (1989). *Multisystem: Systematic instructional planning for exceptional bilingual students.* Reston, VA:

The Council for Exceptional Children. (Originally published by the Institute for Urban and Minority Education, Teachers College, Columbia University, New York, NY.)

Colley, D. A. (1990). Written communication for exceptional students from culturally and linguistically diverse backgrounds. In A. L. Carrasquillo & R. E. Baecher (Eds.), *Teaching the bilingual special education student* (pp. 148–168). Norwood, NJ: Ablex Publishing Corporation.

Collier, C. (1983). *Acculturation and implications for culturally and linguistically different exceptional children.* Paper presented at a Symposium on Research in Bilingual Education, Vail, CO. (ERIC Document Reproduction Service Center No. ED 271 953).

Cummins, J. (1976). The influence of bilingualism on cognitive growth: A synthesis of research findings and explanatory hypotheses. *Working Papers on Bilingualism, 9,* 1–43.

Cummins, J. (1980). The entry and exit fallacy in bilingual education. *NABE Journal, 4,* 25–60.

Cummins, J. (1981). The role of primary language development in promoting education success for language minority students. In Office of Bilingual Bicultural Education, California State Department of Education (Eds.), *Schooling and language minority students: A theoretical framework* (pp. 3–49). Los Angeles, CA: Evaluation, Dissemination, and Assessment Center, California State University.

Cummins, J. (1984). *Bilingualism and special education: Issues in assessment and pedagogy.* San Diego: College-Hill Press.

Cummins, J. (1989). A theoretical framework for bilingual special education. *Exceptional Children, 56,* 2: 111–119.

Curran, C. (1976). *Counseling-learning in second languages.* Dubuque, IA: Counseling Learning Publications.

Damico, J. S. (1991). Descriptive assessment of communicative ability in limited English proficient students. In E. V. Hamayan & J. S. Damico (Eds.), *Limiting bias in the assessment of bilingual students* (pp. 158–217). Austin, TX: Pro-ed.

Dunn, R. (1982). The sum and substance of learning styles. *Early Years, 12,* 5: 30, 31, 80–82.

Duran, E. (1985). Teaching functional reading in context to severely retarded and severely retarded autistic adolescents of limited English proficiency. *Adolescence, 20,* 78: 433–440.

Ellis, R. (1986). *Understanding second language acquisition.* Oxford: Oxford University Press.

Feuerstein, R. (1980). *Instrumental enrichment: An intervention program for cognitive modifiability.* Baltimore, MD: University Park Press.

Figueroa, R. A., Fradd, S. H., & Correa, V. I. (1989). Bilingual special education and this special issue. *Exceptional Children, 56,* 2: 174–178.

Fitzgerald, J., & Miramontes, O. (1987). Language assessment barriers in perspective. *Academic Therapy, 23,* 2: 135–141.

Flores, B., Rueda, R., and Porter, B. (1986). Examining assumptions and instructional practices related to the acquisition of literacy with bilingual special education students. *Reading, Writing and Learning Disabilities, 2,* 2: 147–59.

Fradd, S. H., Barona, A., & Santos de Barona, M. (1989). Implementing change and monitoring progress. In S. H. Fradd & M. J. Weismantel, (Eds.), *Meeting the needs of culturally and linguistically different students: A handbook for educators.* Boston: College-Hill.

Friedenberg, J. E., & Bradley, C. H. (1984). *The vocational ESL handbook.* Rowley, MA: Newbury House.

Gaies, S. J. (1985). *Peer involvement in language learning.* Washington, DC: Center for Applied Linguistics.

Gardner, R., & Lambert, W. (1972). *Attitudes and motivation in second-language learning.* Rowley, MA: Newbury House.

Goodman, K. S. (1967). Reading: A psycholinguistic guessing game. *Journal of the Reading Specialist, 4,* 126–135.

Graden, J. L. (1989). Redefining "prereferral" intervention as intervention assistance: Collaboration between general and special education. *Exceptional Children, 56,* 3: 227–231.

Greenlee, M. (1981). Specifying the needs of a "bilingual" developmentally disabled population: Issues and case studies. *NABE Journal, VI,* 1: 55–76.

Halliday, M. A. K. (1973). *Explorations in the functions of language.* London: Edward Arnold.

Hamayan, E., & Pfleger, M. (1987). *Developing literacy in English as a second language: Guidelines for teachers of young children from non-literate backgrounds.* Wheaton, MD: National Clearinghouse for Bilingual Education.

Hamayan, E. V., & Damico, J. S. (Eds.) (1991). *Limiting bias in the assessment of bilingual students.* Austin, TX: Pro-ed.

Hargis, C. H. (1982). *Teaching reading to handicapped children.* Denver: Love Publications.

Heron, T. E., & Heward, W. L. (1982). Ecological assessment: Implications for teachers of learning disabled students. *Learning Disability Quarterly, 5,* 117–125.

Hudson, P. J. (1989). Instructional collaboration: Creating the learning environment. In S. H. Fradd & M. J. Weismantel (Eds.), *Meeting the needs of culturally and linguistically different students: A handbook for educators* (pp. 106–129). Boston: College-Hill Press.

Idol, L., Paolucci-Whitcomb, P., & Newin, A. (1987). *Collaborative consultation.* Austin, TX: Pro-ed.

Johnson, D. W., Johnson, R. T., Holubec, E. J., & Roy, P. (1988). *Circles of learning: Cooperation in the classroom.* Alexandria, VA: Association for Supervision and Curriculum Development.

Johnson, L. J., Pugach, M. C., & Devlin, S. (1990). Challenges of the next decade: Professional collaboration. *Teaching Exceptional Children, 22,* 2: 9–11.

Juarez, M. (1983). Assessment and treatment of minority-language handicapped children: The role of the monolingual speech-language patholo-
gist. *Topics in Language Disorders, 3*, 57–66.

Knitzer, J., Steinberg, Z., & Fleisch, B. (1990). *At the schoolhouse door:
An examination of programs and policies for children with behavioral
and emotional problems.* New York: Bank Street College of Education.

Krashen, S. D. (1982). Bilingual education and second language acquisition
theory. In Office of Bilingual Bicultural Education, California State
Department of Education (Eds.), *Schooling and language minority students: A theoretical framework* (pp. 51–79). Los Angeles, CA: Evaluation, Dissemination, and Assessment Center, California State University.

Mattes, L., & Omark, D. (1984). *Speech and language assessment for the
bilingual handicapped.* San Diego, CA: College-Hill Press.

Miramontes, O. (1987). Oral reading miscues of Hispanic students: Implications for assessment of learning disabilities. *Journal of Learning Disabilities, 20,* 10: 627–632.

Ortiz, A. A., & Garcia, S. B. (1988). A prereferral process for preventing
inappropriate referrals of Hispanic students to special education. In A.
A. Ortiz & B. A. Ramirez, *Schools and the culturally diverse exceptional student: Promising practices and future directions* (pp. 6–18).
Reston, VA: Council for Exceptional Children.

Ortiz, A. A., & Garcia, S. B. (1990). Using language assessment data for
language and instructional planning for exceptional bilingual students.
In A. L. Carrasquillo & R. E. Baecher (Eds.), *Teaching the bilingual
special education student* (pp. 25–47). Norwood, NJ: Ablex Publishing
Corporation.

Ortiz, A. A., & Maldonado-Colón, E. (1986). Recognizing learning disabilities in bilingual children: How to lessen inappropriate referrals of language minority students to special education. *Journal of Reading, Writing, and Learning Disabilities International, 2,* 1: 43–56.

Oxford, R. L. (1990). *Language learning strategies: What every teacher
should know.* New York: Newbury House Publishers.

Peterson, R. L., & Ishi-Jordan, S. (Eds.), (in press). *Multicultural issues
in the education of behaviorally-disordered youth.* Cambridge, MA:
Brookline Books.

Phillips, V., & McCullough, L. (1990). Consultation-based programming:
Instituting the collaborative ethic in schools. *Exceptional Children, 56,*
4: 291–304.

Pugach, M. C., & Johnson, L. J. (1989). Prereferral interventions: Progress,
problems, and challenges. *Exceptional Children, 56,* 3: 217–226.

Ratleff, J. E. (1989). *Instructional strategies for crosscultural students with
special education needs.* Sacramento, CA: Program, Curriculum, and
Training Unit, Special Education Division, California State Department
of Education. (Available from Resources in Special Education, 900 J.
Street, Sacramento, CA 95814-2703).

Rizzo, J. R., & Zabel, R. H. (1988). *Educating children and adolescents with behavioral disorders: An integrative approach.* Boston: Allyn and Bacon.

Rosenblatt, L. (1978). *The reader, the text, and the poem.* Carbondale, IL: Illinois University Press.

Ruiz, N. T. (1989). An optimal learning environment for Rosemary. *Exceptional Children, 56,* 2: 130–144.

Seligman, M., & Darling, R. (1989). *Ordinary families, special children.* New York: Guilford Press.

Simich-Dudgeon, C. (1986). A multidisciplinary model to educate minority students with handicapping conditions. *Journal of Reading, Writing and Learning Disabilities, 2,* 2: 111–122.

Spolsky, B. (1989). *Conditions for Second Language Learning.* New York: Oxford University Press.

Vygotsky, L. S. (1978). *Mind in society: The development of higher psychological processes.* Cambridge: Harvard University Press.

Wallace, J., & Larsen, S. C. (1978). *Educational assessment of learning problems: Testing for teaching.* Boston: Allyn and Bacon.

Wilkinson, C. Y. (1989). AIM for the BESt: update: An Innovative Approaches Research Project. *The Bilingual Special Education Perspective, IX,* 6–7.

Willig, A. C. (1986). Special education and the culturally and linguistically different child: An overview of issues and challenges. *Reading, Writing, and Learning Disabilities, 2,* 2: 161–173.

Zins, J. E., Curtis, M. J., Graden, J. L., & Ponti, C. R. (1988). *Helping students succeed in the regular classroom: A guide for developing intervention assistance programs.* San Francisco: Jossey-Bass.

Additional readings

Disabilities and second language learners

Cummins, J. (1984). *Bilingualism and special education: Issues in assessment and pedagogy.* San Diego: College-Hill Press.

Willig, A. C., & Greenberg, H. F. (1986). *Bilingualism and learning disabilities: Policy and practice for teachers and administrators.* New York: American Library Publishing Co., Inc.

Assessment of second language learners with special needs

Hamayan, E. V., & Damico, J. S. (Eds.) (1991). *Limiting bias in the assessment of bilingual students.* Austin, TX: Pro-ed.

Mattes, L., & Omark, D. (1984). *Speech and language assessment for the bilingual handicapped.* San Diego, CA: College-Hill Press.

Collaborating with families

Carrasquillo, A. L., & Baecher, R. E. (Eds.) (1990). *Teaching the bilingual special education student*. Norwood, NJ: Ablex Publishing Corporation.

Sample curriculum materials

Fairfax County Schools. (1986). *Teaching directions using a controlled prepositional vocabulary. Supplementary lessons for use with limited English proficient (LEP) students enrolled in ESL or special education classes. Grades K-3*. Fairfax, VA: Fairfax County Schools (ERIC Document Reproduction Service Center No. ED 279 157).
Seagan, F. (1991). *Project PORVENIR curriculum units*. New York: Board of Education of the City of New York, Division of Bilingual Education (131 Livingston St., Brooklyn, NY).

Comprehensive

Baca, L. M., & Cervantes, H. T. (1989). *The bilingual special education interface* (2nd ed.). Columbus, OH: Merrill Publishing Company.
Fradd, S. H., & Weismantel, M. J. (1989). *Meeting the needs of culturally and linguistically different students: A handbook for educators*. Boston: College-Hill Press.

11 Language development of low-literacy students

Else V. Hamayan

The focus of this chapter is on language minority children who enter school with little exposure to literacy. Such children enter school at all grade levels and, in many cases, have little or no proficiency in reading or writing their native language, let alone a second language. Some may come from rural communities where schooling – and consequently literacy – do not play a primary role in a child's life. Some may have had their schooling interrupted, and some arrive with no schooling at all, having spent their lives in refugee camps. Still others may have had only sporadic exposure to school because of war or continual migration. The parents of children from rural communities are not likely to be literate themselves; parents of refugee children may or may not be literate, depending on their own background in the home country. From the point of view of reading and writing, the common element among these children is that literacy has played a minimal role in their lives.

The development of literacy, incorporating all aspects of reading and writing, is likely to follow similar general patterns in all children, irrespective of whether they come from a literate background or one that is poor in literacy (see Chapter 6). Nevertheless, characteristics of children from low-literacy backgrounds will lead them to approach the acts of reading and writing in ways slightly different from other children. Consequently, how they are introduced to literacy in a classroom setting may need to be different from that for children with age-appropriate levels of literacy in their native language (Clay, 1975; Ferreiro, 1986; Sulzby, 1985). For ESL children learning to become literate in an English-speaking country, literacy is an important link not only between the child's home and school, but also between the child's home and the larger society. If the parents are not literate themselves, the child may in fact play the role of the reader and writer for the entire family. Instead of reading (or being read to) from storybooks, the child is given employment forms, notices from the landlord, and notes from school to read. This process may result in conceptualizations of literacy that are unique to these children, and it may even result in significant changes in the basic dynamics of the family. Thus, the development of literacy skills is a crucial aspect of these children's personal development as well as their social development. Therefore, it is a responsibility that requires teachers' serious attention.

This chapter begins with a description of specific characteristics that make this population of second language learners unique in their approach to reading and writing. It proceeds with a discussion of the failure of exclusively structural approaches to teaching literacy with this population; it then discusses the need to incorporate formal structural aspects of language as part of a meaning-based functional approach to literacy instruction, and it considers the conditions necessary for creating an environment that is most conducive to the development of literacy among low-literacy students. Interwoven with the discussion are descriptions of classrooms and instructional strategies that show how these conditions can be realized.

Although the focus of this chapter is on ways of helping children become literate in a second language, the strategies discussed could apply to the development of native language literacy skills as well. The instructional programs described here lacked the resources to develop students' literacy skills in their first language or in a second language on the basis of their first language skills. Nevertheless, the advantages of building second language literacy skills on the basis of first language skills, and literacy in particular, warrants serious attention where such resources are available (see Chapter 6).

This chapter is obviously written from the perspective of a literate person and, thus, is likely to be tainted by the assumptions that literate individuals make about literacy or the lack of it. Since very little research has been carried out with second language learners from low-literacy backgrounds, much of the following discussion is based on my interpretations of research with literate children, as well as on my own experience with children from low-literacy backgrounds.

My first contact with such children was in two ESL programs for Southeast Asian refugee children in the Philippines. As a result of my experience with these children, I acquired a new outlook on the emergence of literacy, and I have attempted to make that process as efficient and effective as possible for them, experimenting and discovering ways of learning and teaching as the children progressed. Both programs, PREP (Preparing Refugees for Elementary Programs) and PASS (Preparing for American Secondary Schools), are located in the Philippine Refugee Processing Center in Bataan. The PREP program was designed for children between 6 and 11 years of age, and the PASS program was designed for 11- to 17-year-olds. The goal of the programs is for students to develop proficiency in English as a second language and at the same time (1) acquire knowledge and language in the academic content areas (specifically, math and science), (2) become acquainted with features of

North American life that are relevant to children their age, and (3) become familiar with the system and structure of school. Because of funding limitations, it was not possible to include native language support in the program in any formal way; however, the teachers used the students' native language to some extent informally as a basis for instruction. In addition, aspects of the children's native culture were included in the curriculum and into classroom activities as much as possible.[1]

Characteristics of low-literacy second language students

The students who are the focus of this chapter came to school with lower levels of literacy than would be expected of children in their age group simply because of a prior lack of experience with printed materials. I am concerned in this chapter with the possibility that lack of literacy experiences is a significant issue for students who come to school beyond the normal entry level of 5 or 6 years of age. Younger children coming from low-literacy backgrounds who begin school at the normal age of entry have an advantage over older children because the younger children are at an earlier stage of cognitive development; hence, they may be more receptive to new ways of interacting with their environment. They are not likely to have formed set ways of dealing with their surroundings and circumstances, and they may be open to replacing their nonliteracy-based systems with those appropriate for the effective development of literacy. In addition, the classroom environment usually created for younger children is likely to lead to the natural emergence of literacy, whereas the classroom environment usually created for older children tends to treat language abstractly and assumes a literate base for children's interaction with the world (see Chapter 5).

I will not address the needs of younger children, namely kindergarteners and first-graders, who come from low-literacy environments prior to entering school. See Chapter 6 for a discussion of literacy in general. Neither will I address the needs of children with lower-than-expected levels of literacy resulting from some basic language learning disability. Although the performance and behaviors of these two types of learners are very similar, different treatment must be provided to learners who are nonliterate in their native language and learners who suffer some kind of perceptual or cognitive disability. Therefore, it is important to distinguish between these learners, which makes essential the need for an informal

1 Detailed descriptions of these and other refugee training programs can be obtained from the Center for Applied Linguistics, Refugee Service Center, Washington, DC.

approach to assessment that includes a comprehensive description of the child's background (see Chapter 10).

This chapter does not address native language development, nor ways in which second language literacy can be developed by first promoting native language literacy. However, the absence of these issues should by no means be interpreted as a reflection on the insignificance of the learners' native languages in building second language skills.

Where do they come from?

Children who have lower-than-expected levels of literacy in both their native language and a second language because of past experiences are likely to come from one of the following environments: isolated rural communities with one-room schools, refugee camps, war-torn countries, and families with persistent migration patterns. In many cases, these children have not attended school at all, and their access to printed materials has been limited. The paucity of printed matter can best be illustrated by the following informal inventory I took at a Southeast Asian refugee camp.

Starting at a point farthest away from the refugees' living quarters, that is to say, in their neighborhood, the following types of environmental print could be observed: The doorways of the neighborhood organization offices, clinic, library, and classrooms are labeled in English; the neighborhood bulletin board carries messages and announcements in both English and the various native languages represented in that neighborhood; the main streets as well as the pathways dividing blocks of housing units are not shown by signs, but doorways designating the refugees' housing units are marked with letters and numbers; the neighborhood market, an extremely colorful environment, has a few signs. The stores and stalls do not need to be named since it is quite evident by the flagrant display of goods exactly what is available without the help of a printed label. However, the goods in the stores carry typical labels, mostly in English. The temples and churches are also labeled in both English and the native language, and they display various religious sayings in the native language. Beyond this, the streets and buildings are rather void of print.

In the refugees' homes, each of which consists of a lofted room and a small kitchen area, ESL books of various levels of English proficiency are scattered around. In addition, the adults, who are themselves ESL students, bring home their worksheets and homework and paste them up as decorative wallpaper. Thus, the children are surrounded by ESL dialogues, pattern drills, and fill-in-the-blank exercises, and, as will become apparent in a later section of this chapter, take advantage of this more-or-less random print to the best of their ability. Since books in the refugees' native languages are not readily accessible, children do not have much experience handling books themselves or even seeing books in use by adults or older siblings. Letters are written, received, and read, but quite infrequently.

Thus, the paucity of environmental print in these children's daily lives is evident in both its quantity and quality. It is also evident in the extent to which the children or their family members participate in literacy acts. This type of environment presents quite a contrast to most urban and suburban communities in which children are bombarded with environmental print from all directions.

Familiarity with the different forms of literacy

Because of these and other differences, children from low-literacy backgrounds often approach literacy in distinctive ways. One is in their initial early awareness of literacy. Children who come from literate backgrounds are likely to be familiar with the different forms of literacy. For example, they are likely to be aware of newspaper reading versus storybook reading, of writing a letter versus writing checks to pay bills. They are also likely to be familiar with the structure of different forms of literacy, such as story grammars (Heath, 1982; Yaden, Smolkin, & Conlon, 1989). In contrast, second language children from low-literacy backgrounds often do not understand some of the most basic rules governing literacy, nor do they have an awareness of the basic characteristics of print and printed materials. An example from a nonliterate 11-year-old Cambodian student illustrates this point.

Lathikhone was hunched over an illustration he was drawing. We had just finished reading *Hatupatu and the Birdwoman,* and some pages of the version that the class was "writing" remained unillustrated, that is to say, with writing at the bottom of the page and enough room on top set aside for a drawing. We were going to bind the pages and produce an illustrated class edition of the book. Students working in pairs or individually were illustrating the blank pages as they read them, and Lathikhone insisted that he also do a drawing. I had had enough verbal and nonverbal indicators of comprehension from earlier small-group and individual activities to know that he comprehended the passage. Thus, there was no reason to doubt that he understood the entire story or the specific part of the story that was on the page he was illustrating. He was thrilled to get the assignment.

He set about intently copying a drawing from another children's book that he had fetched from the bookshelf. This may have been adequate were it not for the fact that the picture he was copying was from a story about Eskimos and the story he was supposed to illustrate took place in the jungle! I realized that he had little or no sense of storybooks and the function of illustrations in storybooks. For Lathikhone, a blank space anywhere on a page was an invitation to fill it with a drawing – any drawing, even one that had nothing to do with the text on the page. I had assumed that an 11-year-old child, even one with very little exposure to literacy, would have a clear notion of the role that illustrations or pictures play in storybooks. This awareness, which emerges naturally in children from literate backgrounds, usually on the lap of a parent or older sibling, was obviously not present in this 11-year-old child.

This situation presented an interesting dilemma to me: Should I teach this concept explicitly and directly, or should I let it emerge naturally, assuming that through adequate exposure to storybooks, Lathikhone would acquire it eventually? Because of this child's age, reasoning ability, and comfort level in my class, and because of the pressure to finish the task, I opted for explicit teaching – I pointed out to Lathikhone that illustrations in storybooks correspond to the particular part of the story that appears on the same page. Since Lathikhone did not have the vocabulary to talk about language and literacy in English, this mini-lesson took place through a "buddy-interpreter." Lathikhone's illustrations in subsequent projects showed a grasp of this concept, and so, my decision to take the explicit approach appeared to be successful. This is by no means the only or the best approach in all situations; rather, the approach used was appropriate for this particular child at that particular moment.

Familiarity with the functions of literacy

Another way in which children from low-literacy backgrounds can differ from children from literate backgrounds is in their understanding of the functions of literacy. Most children from literate backgrounds, who have seen literacy serve important and diverse functions in their daily lives, have no difficulty beginning to use written language for communicating with others or self-expression (Dyson, 1984; Ferreiro and Teberosky, 1982). Children from low-literacy backgrounds, on the other hand, may need to be eased into trusting the functionality of writing before they actually start using it for purposes of communication. The process by which my 13-year-old nonliterate students got started on dialogue journals illustrates their hesitation.

I explained the purpose of keeping dialogue journals to my students in their native language to ensure that they understood what was expected – I was to write to them and they were to respond and write to me. We were to keep up this dialogue as long as they were interested in doing so. The few students who decided to start this activity were quite excited.

They proudly handed me their notebooks the following day, and as I leafed through them casually, I was pleasantly surprised to see not only a few sentences but pages and pages of writing! However, a closer look at the entries later revealed a disappointing surprise – for the most part, the entries consisted of noncommunicative, nonfunctional language. One student's entry included the national anthem of the United States; another included pattern drills and dialogues that are typical of ESL textbooks! (See Figure 1 for example.) The children had obviously copied this "language" from their parents' worksheets, which were probably pasted on the wall, very close to the table where the children did their homework.

It appeared that for these children, writing, perhaps especially to a teacher, did not automatically represent a means to an end; writing did not elicit communicative use of language. Rather, one wrote for the sake of practicing writing. This conceptualization of writing in nonfunctional ways may have been exacerbated by the absence of a formal native language component in the curriculum. If the children had been invited to begin writing in their native language, I suspect that their writing would have been more functional in nature, given that they would be using a language that had a significantly more communicative role for them in their daily lives.

This situation also presented an interesting dilemma: whether or not to point out the learners' misunderstandings of the purpose of dialogue writing. Research suggests that the effectiveness of dialogue journals lies in the indirect way in which feedback is given to the writer, that is, without focusing the learner's attention on form or structure (Peyton, 1988; Staton, 1988). Trusting the learner's ability to acquire the notion that all writing ultimately serves a communicative function, I responded to the children's entries simply by answering only those portions that I believed to be communicative, and I ignored everything else. The strategy seemed to work; the second entry from Hien, whose first entries can be seen in Figure 1, was authentic communication. Although it contained far less language and far more errors than her first entries, her second entries (see Figure 2) were much more valuable as a catalyst for real language development.

In some ways, these low-literacy students' conceptualizations of written language are similar to those of monolingual English-speaking children who are placed in low-level reading groups because of ability tracking. A survey of third- and fourth-graders by Bondy (1985) found that children in high-level reading groups saw reading as a source of pleasure and a way of obtaining new information, whereas children in low-level reading groups saw reading as a chore and a meaningless activity. All too often, children who are identified as "poor readers" are given worksheet activities that represent a contrived form of literacy,

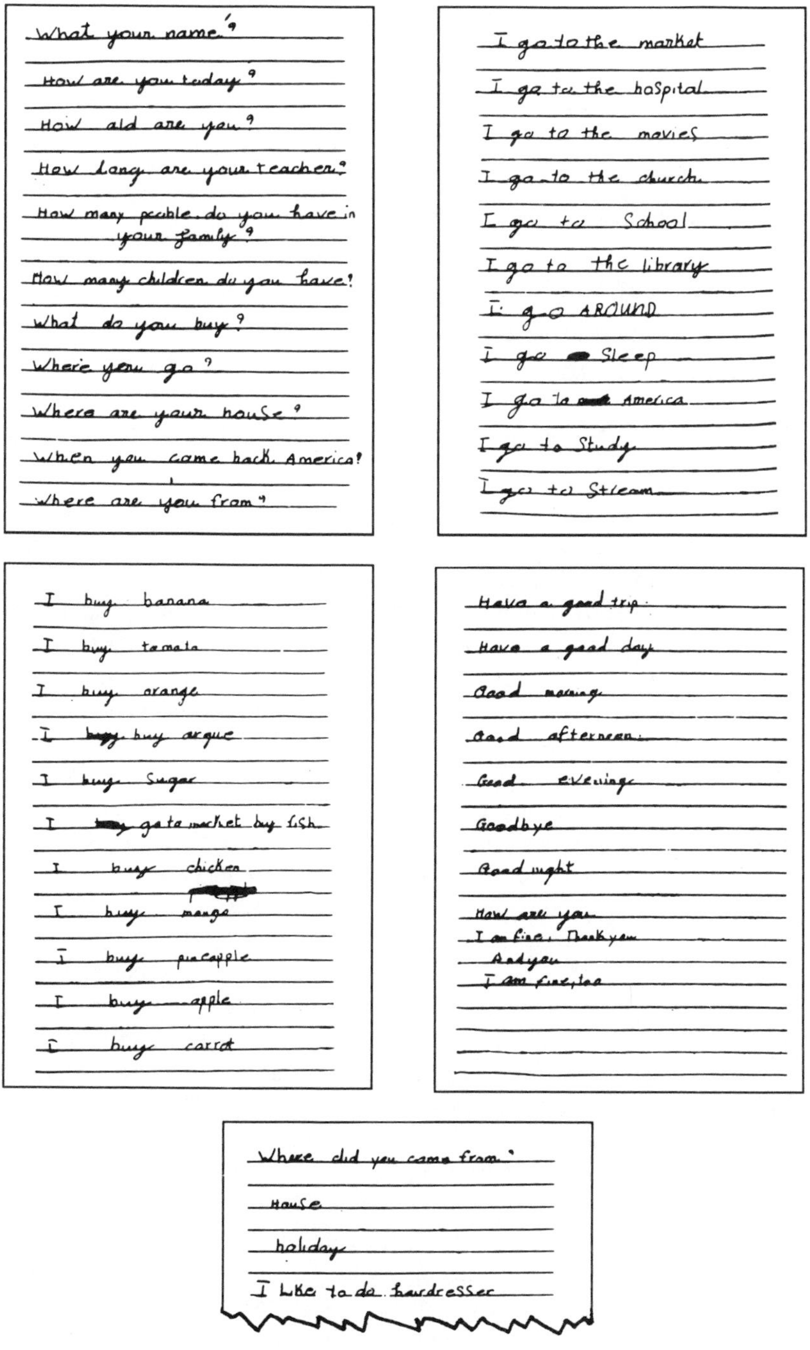

What your name?

How are you today?

How old are you?

How long are your teacher?

How many people do you have in your family?

How many children do you have?

What do you buy?

Where you go?

Where are your house?

When you come back America?

Where are you from?

I go to the market

I go to the hospital

I go to the movies

I go to the church

I go to School

I go to the library

I go AROUND

I go Sleep

I go to America

I go to Study

I go to Stream

I buy banana

I buy tomato

I buy orange

I buy buy argue

I buy Sugar

I go to market buy fish

I buy chicken

I buy mango

I buy pineapple

I buy apple

I buy carrot

Have a good trip

Have a good day

Good morning

Good afternoon

Good evening

Goodbye

Good night

How are you.
I am fine. Thank you
And you
I am fine, too

Where did you come from?

House

holiday

I Like to do hairdresser

Figure 1   Hien's first dialogue journal entry.

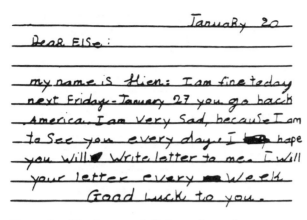

Figure 2   Hien's second dialogue journal entry.

whereas children who are labeled "good readers" are given interesting reading activities, such as reading storybooks.

To sum up, children from low-literacy backgrounds enter school with an approach to and a conceptualization of literacy that may be quite different from that of literate or preliterate children. First, children from low-literacy backgrounds may not have a clear understanding of the various functions, purposes, or uses of written language. For these children, literacy is closely associated solely, or primarily, with schooling, and their notions about literacy activities are likely to be colored by their notions about school activities, hence, their willingness to engage in meaningless writing exercises rather than the more natural acceptance of literacy as a tool for communication and self-expression.

Second, children from low-literacy backgrounds have little familiarity with diverse types of literacy and literacy activities. Having had little exposure to storybooks, they may not be familiar with either the actual physical form of storybooks or the rhetorical form of stories. This lack of familiarity with forms and types of literacies may make it less likely for children from low-literacy backgrounds to form appropriate hypotheses about written language and the rules that govern its use. Children who are literate in their native language can transfer their experience with literacy to a second language, and they can formulate hypotheses about the way written language works (Hudelson, 1987). Children who lack experience with any type of literacy in the preschool years have little to guide them in figuring out how writing and reading work.

Finally, children from low-literacy backgrounds may feel little control over the meaning that is represented by the written word. In this aspect, their process of literacy development may be quite different from that of literate children. Children from literate environments who are learning a second language move from a global understanding of the written language to a more specific and refined understanding, based on the meaning that is given to the written word (Hudelson, 1987). The task of making meaning out of written material is made doubly difficult for low-literacy second language children who not only have little oral proficiency on which to build meaning but who also have few tools to control the meaning of written language.

Integrating structural and holistic approaches

Because of the special characteristics of children from low-literacy backgrounds, careful planning must be given to the creation of a classroom environment that will be most conducive to the emergence of literacy. In this regard, there has been a debate among researchers and educators in general about the best approach to teach reading and writing. The choice of instructional approaches has been polarized between a focus on form versus a focus on function. The form-based approach is best exemplified by the phonics method, in which children are taught symbol–sound correspondences, combinations of symbols, and the rules governing their use (Adams, 1990). Phonics-based instruction begins with the small units of language – such as phonemes – and then proceeds to bigger chunks – such as sentences and paragraphs. Great attention is paid to accuracy of the form of language. The functional communicative approach is exemplified by the whole language method, in which children are encouraged to interact with whole texts and meaning is used as the basis for decoding written language (Newman, 1985). Children read whole stories and are encouraged to write for communication and self-expression rather than for perfection of the surface forms of language.

In many cases, a single approach has been adopted, making it seem as though there is a best approach, but in fact the highly complex process of language learning in general and of literacy in particular necessitates multifaceted instructional approaches. I believe that a well-planned combination of holistic meaningful instruction with a systematic focus on the formal aspects of the structure of language may well be the most effective for most second language students, but particularly for those who come from low-literacy backgrounds.

Since many language learning materials used to develop literacy are heavily biased toward form and structure, I will begin my discussion with the shortcomings of exclusively structural approaches. Then, I will argue for the need to teach formal aspects of language in the context of meaningful whole texts. The principles and arguments put forth apply to the development of beginning literacy skills in any language, including the children's first language.

288 *Else V. Hamayan*

Shortcomings of structural approaches

Exclusive use of structural approaches to teaching reading and writing, which are for the most part phonics- and grammar-based, fails to meet the needs of second language students with low-literacy backgrounds (Cambourne, 1987). First, structural approaches do not satisfy the learners' need to acquire an understanding of the functional aspects of literacy. Second, because of this lack of focus on function, literacy is forced to emerge in an unnatural way and in an artificial form. Third, a focus on the form and structures of language without a functional context makes learning abstract and therefore meaningless and difficult. Finally, literacy is reduced to a boring chore.

In formal structural approaches to teaching reading and writing, low-literacy children's basic need for functional literacy and their need to learn the functions of literacy are not satisfied. Older nonliterate children who suddenly find themselves in a literate environment have pressing needs to develop functional facility with nonacademic environmental print (e.g., labels in the supermarket), school-related environmental print (e.g., signs identifying different classrooms), and written language in academic content areas. Since literacy is a social act that occurs in a social setting, it is important to teach reading and writing skills that are most functional for learners and that fit their specific social needs. An exclusively structural approach may force a set of materials and activities on the student that are totally lacking communicative functions or that require students to read and write language that diverges widely from their immediate social needs.

Moreover, language learning in general and the development of literacy in particular are processes that are culturally and contextually embedded (Heath, 1983). Since the students in question come from cultural contexts that are quite different from those represented in most published materials, especially ESL reading texts, the students end up reading and writing language that is very different from their own language, both in form and content. When children are given instructional materials that are not directly related to their past experiences or to their current daily lives, reading and writing become irrelevant and the motivation to become literate diminishes (Edelsky, 1986). Because student-generated texts that reflect learners' own cultural experiences are not an integral part of structural approaches, the use of supplemental materials that are based on the students' own experiences and their cultural backgrounds becomes essential.

The second reason that exclusively structural approaches in the classroom fail second language children from low-literacy backgrounds is that literacy is not allowed to emerge in natural developmental stages (see Chapter 6). In such classrooms, students' production, in both reading and writing, is controlled in order to reduce the likelihood of errors. Perfection is often required long before the child is ready to be close to perfect. This requirement prevents the gradual and natural emergence of reading and writing (Calkins, 1983; Cambourne, 1987) and is likely to lead to an artificial type of literacy. The establishment of artificial nonfunctional literacy is exemplified by the willingness of Hien and my other students to spend time at home "writing" sentences that made little or no sense to them. Since these students do not have much exposure to environmental literacy outside of the school, it is essential that the approach to reading and writing development in school be as rich and authentic as possible in order to allow literacy to develop naturally.

A third reason why exclusively structural approaches are inappropriate for low-literacy students is that they tend to focus on sounds and words in isolation. Because isolated sounds and words do not carry much meaning, activities that focus on these aspects of written language are relatively meaningless; thus, learners are less likely to understand them or to make them part of their language system than activities derived from connected prose (Goodman, 1986; Smith, 1989). The definition of *literacy* that I find useful is based on the notion that the construction of meaning is central to reading and writing (Hudelson, 1986). It follows, therefore, that burdening the learner with meaningless tidbits of language only makes the search for meaning more difficult.

Another reason why learning to read by focusing on the smallest units of language, namely sounds and symbols (letters), is difficult for ESL students stems from the nature of written English. The sound–symbol correspondence rate is remarkably low in English. Many symbols (letters) represent more than one sound, and many sounds are represented by more than one symbol (letter), making it very difficult to generalize phonic rules. Thus, if a child learns that the letter *c* corresponds to the sound [k], that knowledge is not likely to be of great use in deciphering a great many words containing the letter *c*. Further, focusing on the form of language without reference to its meaning or functional relevance forces the learner to take an abstract view of language, which is developmentally difficult for children from low-literacy backgrounds. Language is something one does rather than something one talks about. Yet, at other times, it is this very lack of an abstract view of language that makes it essential for the teacher to focus on the structures and rules of written language in order to build metalinguistic awareness that may not emerge naturally. I will return to this later.

The last reason why exclusively structural approaches fail to meet the needs of developing second language readers and writers, and perhaps the most important one, is that they reduce reading and writing to tedious chores. Analyzing written language, practicing its rules, and manipulating its minute forms turn children away from literacy because such activities lack an inherently attractive incentive. They are devoid of the joy of reading and writing. Most children from literate backgrounds may experience such joy outside of the classroom (although to what extent is certainly debatable); however, children from low-literacy backgrounds are not likely to have interesting stories read to them or to have significant people in their lives who are overjoyed about a writing sample they have produced. These shortcomings may be even more pronounced in the case of second language children from low-literacy backgrounds who are not receiving instructional support in the native language because their only exposure to literacy is in the classroom and in a language that is removed from their personal lives. This means that it is all the more important for teachers to create learning environments in school that are meaningful and stimulating.

Teaching the form and structures of language

Although an exclusive use of structural approaches falls short of the needs of children from low-literacy backgrounds, explicit attention to the rules and the structures of written language can help learners become literate and develop higher-order thinking skills and learning strategies. Because of a lack of experience with school and with school-type activities, some children may in fact need to be taught not just the formal aspects of written language but also strategies they can use to complete tasks that are typical of any classroom setting. Thus, rather than simply ignoring the structural aspects of written language, effective ways of getting children with low-literacy backgrounds to understand and master the form and structure of written language must be explored.

One of the reasons for teaching the formal aspects of language is that learners can and do make use of such knowledge for decoding and comprehending (Adams, 1990). It is not uncommon to see children going up to a familiar word that is pasted on a classroom wall in order to seek out a letter or letters that they need in order to write other words that contain the same sounds. For example, Kham-Aen, a 12-year-old Cambodian child, would often go up to the wall displaying a picture of Hatupatu, the hero about whom we were reading. Being thoroughly familiar with the name of the character, he would copy the letter *t* from the word *Hatupatu* written underneath the picture. He would then take that letter back to his table and use it as a guide to help him write *table*.

Explicit teaching of reading or learning strategies has been shown to be helpful for literate learners of a second language (see, for example, Carrell, Pharis, & Liberto, 1989). Although little is known about the effectiveness of explicit strategy training for nonliterate children, I have found that showing second language children some simple learning and literacy strategies helped them save time and made their work with written language much more efficient. As the following example demonstrates, when children were explicitly taught a learning strategy to help them complete a simple school activity – in this case, filling in the blanks in a cloze passage – they were able to make use of that strategy on other occasions.

Four students were working together completing a cloze passage with ten blanks. A word bank had been provided, and each time the students reached a blank, they started checking each word in the word bank until they arrived at the one they, or one of them, thought appropriate. Since they did not put a check mark next to the words that they had already used, the process was taking an unnecessarily long time. In pointing out this strategy of eliminating what had already been used, the task was made much more efficient, and the children were able to use the strategy in subsequent activities. Perhaps the direct approach worked because these children were at least 11 years of age. Of course, it is possible that the children would have arrived at that strategy by themselves. It is not clear, however, that letting the children discover the strategy by themselves would have been more effective than simply explaining or showing them the use of the strategy explicitly.

Another type of explicit formal instruction that benefits low-literacy children relates to the different literary forms that are used in academic settings – for example, science reports, essays, short-answer questions, and narratives. Since many low-literacy children lack prior school experiences, they are likely to be unfamiliar with many of these forms of literacy. Explicitly teaching them the characteristics, qualities, and functions of each can help shape their writing or the way they approach different texts.

One of the activities we did in class was a comparison of different books. Groups of students compared and contrasted an illustrated storybook, a science text, a children's book, and a collection of nursery rhymes. Through the activity, students discovered and were told about the characteristics of the different types of text. Had they been more proficient writers, an effective follow-up activity might have been to have the students produce samples of the different types of text revolving around a topic they had just finished studying.

As will be evident in the following sections, a focus on the forms of written language should always be embedded in meaningful, whole language activities. This is equally true for the development of literacy skills in a first language. It may be especially important for children who are developing literacy skills belatedly, whether or not this is done through the first or a second language, since they may not yet have acquired functional conceptualizations of literacy activities.

Instructional strategies for literacy development

To make it possible for children from low-literacy backgrounds to become proficient and enthusiastic readers and writers, special consideration needs to be given to the instructional environment. What follows are suggestions for things to do that allow for a holistic introduction to literacy in either a second language or in the child's first language. Once a meaningful context has been established, ways to help children master the constituent linguistic skills that make up reading and writing are suggested. Finally, strategies and activities that can help students attain reading and writing competency in academic content areas are suggested.

Creating a literacy-rich environment

First, classrooms should be saturated with meaningful environmental print. Children in such an environment will get used to seeing labels, announcements, names, and signs with as many contextual clues as possible indicating their meaning. As a general rule of thumb, every object in the classroom should be labeled. Because the words representing the various objects surrounding the child (e.g., table, door) are meaningful, the child will begin to associate the visual symbols with their meaningful oral forms and will eventually begin to make symbol–sound associations (Calkins, 1983; Dyson, 1984). With help from the teacher, the students themselves can supply all of the classroom environmental labels. This not only saves the teacher a tremendous amount of busy work, but it provides students with practice writing, albeit in a very limited and controlled way. Even more important, it gives students a sense of pride to see labels in their own handwriting put up on the walls, desks, shelves, and even on the teacher! This is also a very easy and effective way of incorporating the children's native language(s) into their beginning literacy experiences. Labels can be bilingual or trilingual, preferably with each language being distinguished by a different color. For example, English labels could be green, Vietnamese labels blue, and Cambodian labels pink.

To encourage children in the PASS program (mentioned earlier) to experiment with writing and to provide everyone in the classroom with easily available writing material, the tables at which the children were seated were covered with butcher paper. When it was time to make labels, the teacher would simply write the word on the butcher paper for the students to use as a model. In this way, the tabletop became the students' notebooks where rough drafts and other writing activities could take place. The butcher paper that covered the tables also became a valuable record of the students' work and the teacher's written interactions with the students.

Doing meaning-based activities

Second, the activities designed to develop children's reading and writing must be based on the construction of meaning. As noted earlier, children can learn to read and write much more easily if activities are based on what they already understand rather than what they do not understand. It is especially important for second language students from cultural backgrounds that are very different from that of the school to start reading and writing about "the known" before they move into "the unknown." This means starting students with concrete familiar topics and tasks and gradually moving into more abstract unfamiliar topics. This also means that the primary focus of instruction should be on meaning, or the content of language, rather than on the form of language, or language for its own sake. Thus, classroom literacy activities can revolve around specific content of interest to learners and should create a real communicative environment that will engage the learner.

One of the ways in which literacy activities may become more meaningful to students is by basing literacy activities on the children's oral language. This can be accomplished by doing extensive prereading activities to prepare students for specific reading passages or specific writing tasks (McGee & Richgels, 1990). By making a close connection between children's oral language and what they read and write, it becomes easier for children who have not had extensive exposure to print to see that print can be a representation of speech.

Making a close connection between speech and literacy not only ensures that children understand what they read and write, but it also ensures the relevance of the literacy material to the children's daily lives. Instruction would thus take into account the whole child and build on his or her skills and abilities (Goodman, 1986). Using student-generated materials also confirms and reaffirms to children their own worth and the value of their cultural and personal experiences.

To help make literacy activities more meaningful and to ensure that they are based on students' oral language, reading and writing tasks in the PREP and PASS programs were almost always preceded by extensive preparatory activities using the language experience approach (LEA) (Allen & Allen, 1982). In a LEA activity, the whole class participates in an experience, such as making pancakes or constructing a bird's nest. As the activity is being conducted, oral language is generated, reinforcing key vocabulary items. When the activity is finished, the teacher elicits an oral story about the activity from the students. The oral story is then written down either by the teacher or by groups of students.

A language experience activity can also be used as a prereading activity, as the following example shows. We chose to read the last segment of *Hatupatu and the Birdwoman* in a shared reading format with a big book. In this particular segment, the evil birdwoman is chasing Hatupatu through the jungle. As the birdwoman jumps over boiling mud and bubbling water, steam gets in her eyes, and she falls and meets a gruesome death. To prepare students for the unfamiliar words they would encounter in the passage, such as *boiling, bubbling, mud,* and *steam,* we conducted a simple LEA activity in class: We boiled water, observed it bubbling, made mud, watched it boil, and took turns feeling steam get in our eyes. By the time we finished writing about this simple experience, the students were thoroughly familiar not only with the meanings of the key words that would appear in the book, but also with their written forms and the different ways in which they could be used. This simple prereading activity made the reading of the text meaningful, comprehensible, real, interesting, and related to the oral language that the students had, to some extent, generated.

Allowing literacy to emerge naturally

Third, literacy must be allowed to emerge in natural developmental stages. More specifically, children need to go through a silent period in reading – when they start to read, they may do so simply by mouthing words while the teacher is reading aloud. Similarly, children must be allowed to start writing in the most rudimentary fashion available to them and gradually refine their writing in approximation to an acceptable form. Teacher expectations may have to be tempered to conform to the learners' current abilities. Every word or utterance in a second language is a step forward and should be seen for what it accomplishes rather than for what it fails to do. Everything the learner says should be encouraged, even if it is fraught with errors. Errors are a natural and necessary part of the development of language. Rather than simply trying to eradicate them, teachers need to make use of errors as a valuable source of information. Errors are indicators of the strategies that a learner is using in the process of language acquisition; they can help the teacher figure out what rules a particular child is using in his or her attempts at constructing meaning in the second language.

Dialogue journals, by their nature, encourage the emergence of language in a natural developmental way. In dialogue journals, the teacher acknowledges, condones, and reaffirms everything the child produces while providing a correct model for the child to see. Sometimes children with very low second language proficiency may produce so little writing that it may be difficult to provide them with many good responses. Chau Vong, a 12-year-old Vietnamese boy of Chinese descent, could write only one thing: his name in English and in Chinese characters, and that was what he wrote as his first entry in his dialogue journal notebook. That wasn't much to go on, but nonetheless the only way to look at his attempt was as a success rather than a failure. The teacher responded with the following entry: "Dear Chau Vong, How wonderful that you write your name in Chinese and English! Who taught you how to write Chinese?" With the help of a fellow student, Chau deciphered the response and also with the help of his friend, he wrote: "Dear Miss Gallinero, granmather chinese," and added his signature in Chinese. This response was clearly a step forward!

When the child is rewarded for his or her attempts at literacy, no matter how meager the result may be the fourth characteristic of environments that are conducive to developing literacy in a second language emerges.

Lowering the anxiety in second language literacy development

The fourth characteristic of effective literacy environments should be that they are free of anxiety. For children who have little or no prior experience with reading and writing, venturing into literacy in a formal classroom setting can be threatening. Children can be made to feel at ease if they know that their attempts at reading and writing are seen as successes rather than failures. Thus, when children realize that writing a few words in their journals is going to be rewarded, they are likely to feel comfortable writing and will write more.

Children can also be made to feel at ease if the classroom is a familiar and predictable place rather than one where they are visitors in a foreign land. Using the children's culture, no matter how much it diverges from the mainstream culture, as a basis for creating literacy activities can help make the classroom a more familiar place for the child. Establishing routines around literacy activities also helps make the classroom a more familiar place for children. Expanding this principle one step further takes us to the fifth characteristic of effective second-language environments for students from low-literacy backgrounds.

Motivating children to read and write

The fifth characteristic of activities that lead children into literacy is that they should be motivating: A child who enjoys reading and writing is motivated to read and write; the child will engage in literacy more frequently, and by doing so, the child will become a better reader and writer (Cambourne, 1987; Graves, 1991). It is especially important for children from low-literacy backgrounds to find classroom literacy activities motivating because these children have not experienced literacy at home as a rewarding and enjoyable activity (e.g., by seeing a parent relaxing by reading). If anything, these children may have only seen their parents frustrated over written material that they had to deal with. These children have probably also not experienced literacy through "story time," an immensely enjoyable activity shared with a parent.

The following example demonstrates, again through the use of dialogue journals, how authentic decoding of written language is motivationally driven. When dialogue journal notebooks are returned to individual students, there is usually a flurry of activity in the classroom. The teacher's responses invariably contain language that is just beyond (or sometimes significantly beyond) the students' ability to read. Rather than give up, which is bound to happen with reading material that the children have no interest in, students who have received their notebook back from the teacher rush to a buddy in class and, with that buddy's help, try to figure out what the message says. Perhaps it is a situation, such as the one previously described, where the learner is extremely motivated to decipher a brief written message, that qualifies as the teachable moment for the instruction of decoding and word attack skills in a formal and explicit way. Instruction that focuses explicitly on the form and structure of language needs to be part of the environment that surrounds these children, but it has to take place at the right time and in the appropriate context. The next section addresses that need.

Integrating structural and functional aspects of literacy

Once a meaningful context has been established, children's attention can be directed to focus on specific structures and forms of written language. Any activity used to engage the child in reading and writing, such as a language experience activity, shared reading, or individual creative writing, can serve as a launching pad for follow-up activities that focus on specific formal aspects of language. Thus, rather than using words or sentences from the reading text, such as a basal reader (for which students may not have a strong oral base), the same language that was generated through a hands-on activity can serve as the material for decoding or phonics exercises.

To teach the beginning consonant blend *cl*, I chose all the words beginning with *cl* that my students had already come into contact with and, I hoped, understood. The words came from a story we had just finished reading (clouds), from labels in the classroom (closet and closed), and from the students' own dialogue journals. I had to turn to all three of these sources of written language to find words beginning with *cl* because, unlike basal texts, naturally occurring authentic language does not control the occurrence of certain sounds, letters, or combinations of letters.

By starting with a holistic and functional literacy activity, such as a language experience activity, children were able to manipulate written text that was familiar to them and presumably, which they were motivated to read and write. The use of words that the students had generated, either in the form of classroom labels or dialogue journal entries, had the great advantage that it legitimized and validated the learners' attempts at English. The use of classroom-generated language, however, does not eliminate the usefulness of formal reading textbooks.

Formal reading textbooks, such as basals, can be useful for integrating the formal and functional aspects of literacy because the sequence, content, and strategies for teaching formal and structural aspects of written language are usually clearly delineated. These textbooks can serve as a guide to decisions about what to teach, when to teach it, and how to teach it. Nevertheless, the actual material used for explicit instruction need not come from the reading textbook or the basal. Instead, learners, teachers, and classroom activities can quite easily generate the material that is needed.

Integrating content area instruction with literacy

Literacy activities can also be extended into academic content areas. By integrating literacy instruction with the acquisition of knowledge in academic content areas, teachers can help students apply the language that they are just beginning to learn to other contexts, namely the academic subject areas that they will encounter in mainstream classrooms. For example, when we finished reading *Hatupatu and the Birdwoman*, the students were studying weather in the social studies class. It was logical to take the story, which was set in the jungle, and create a unit on geography and weather conditions based on the events in the book. Thus, rather than studying about weather conditions in the abstract, the students discovered certain things about Hatupatu's environment and formulated hypotheses as to where the story took place. They were able to apply their developing literacy skills to strengthening newly acquired concepts in social studies and vice versa.

This type of integration of content and second language instruction is crucial for students with low-literacy abilities because it is very difficult for them to handle information about new concepts through a language in which they are not literate as well as not orally proficient (Crandall, Spanos, Christian, Simich-Dudgeon, & Willetts, 1988). Instruction in mainstream content area classrooms typically tends to be more abstract and less experience-based and poses a burden for children (see Chapter 7). Integrating content instruction with literacy provides children with continuity in their school day and enriches their exposure to diverse forms of the written language.

Conclusions

Children from low-literacy backgrounds face tremendous hurdles in school. They have special needs that distinguish them from second language learners with more literate backgrounds. Low-literacy children may not have a clear understanding of the forms and the functions of literacy, and because of this, they may not be as ready as more literate children to construct meaning from written language.

The challenges that face teachers of low-literacy second language children are also enormous. Because of the complexity of literacy development and the special characteristics of low-literacy children, various instructional approaches that provide meaningful and functional literacy activities while teaching the specific forms and structures of written language need to be part of the classroom environment. Teachers should feel free to apply these principles and use these practices in teaching in the second language or in the child's native language. The following classroom characteristics make for an environment that allows for literacy to emerge in a natural and efficient way:

1. The classroom must be rich with meaningful environmental print.
2. The construction of meaning must be the basis of all literacy activities.
3. New literacy skills should be allowed to emerge naturally and in a low-anxiety environment.
4. Literacy activities in the classroom must be motivating to children.
5. Instruction about linguistic forms and structures should be embedded in meaningful functional language activities.
6. Literacy instruction should be integrated with instruction of academic content.

Creating such an environment is not an easy task, given the many constraints under which teachers have to work. However, a classroom environment, as described in this chapter, can be a truly enjoyable place where both teachers and students learn together.

References

Adams, M. J. (1990). *Beginning to read: Thinking and learning about print.* Cambridge, MA: MIT Press.

Allen, R. V., & Allen, C. (1982). *Language experience activities (2nd ed.).* Boston: Houghton Mifflin.

Bondy, E. (1985). *Children's definitions of reading products of an inter-*

active process. Paper presented at the annual meeting of the American Educational Research Association, Chicago, IL.

Calkins, L. (1983). *Lessons from a child*. Portsmouth, NH: Heinemann.

Cambourne, B. (1987). Language, learning, and literacy. In A. Butler and J. Turbill (Eds.), *Toward a reading-writing classroom*. Portsmouth, NH: Heinemann.

Carrell, P. L., Pharis, L., & Liberto, J. C. (1989). Metacognitive strategy training for ESL reading. *TESOL Quarterly, 23,* 4: 647–678.

Clay, M. M. (1975). *What did I write?* Auckland: Heinemann.

Crandall, J., Spanos, G., Christian, D., Simich-Dudgeon, C., & Willetts, K. (1988). *Combined language and content instruction for language minority students*. Wheaton, MD: National Clearinghouse for Bilingual Education.

Dyson, A. H. (1984). Emerging alphabetic literacy in school contexts: Toward defining the gap between school curriculum and school mind. *Written Communication, 1,* 5–55.

Edelsky, C. (1986). *Writing in a bilingual program: Habia una vez*. Norwood, NJ: Ablex.

Ferreiro, E. (1986). The interplay between information and assimilation in beginning literacy. In W. H. Teale & E. Sulzby (Eds.), *Emergent literacy: Writing and reading*. Norwood, NJ: Ablex.

Ferreiro, E., & Teberosky, A. (1982). *Literacy before schooling*. Exeter, NH: Heinemann.

Goodman, K. (1986). *What's whole in whole language?* Portsmouth, NH: Heinemann.

Graves, D. (1991). *Build a literate classroom*. Portsmouth, NH: Heinemann.

Heath, S. B. (1983). *Ways with words*. Cambridge, England: Cambridge University Press.

Heath, S. B. (1982). Questioning at home and at school: A comparative study. In G. Spindler (Ed.), *Doing the ethnography of schooling: Educational anthropology in action*. New York: Holt, Rinehart, and Winston.

Hudelson, S. (1986). ESL children's writing: What we've learned, what we're learning. In P. Rigg & D. S. Enright (Eds.), *Children and ESL: Integrating perspectives*. Washington, DC: Teachers of English to Speakers of Other Languages.

Hudelson, S. (1987). The role of native language literacy in the education of language minority children. *Language Arts, 64,* 827–841.

McGee, L. M., & Richgels, D. J. (1990). Learning from text using reading and writing. In T. Shanahan (Ed.), *Reading and writing together: New perspectives for the classroom*. Norwood, MA: Christopher-Gordon.

Newman, J. (1985). Insights from recent reading and writing research and their implications for developing whole language curriculum (pp 7–36). In J. Newman (Ed.), *Whole language: Theory in use*. Portsmouth, NH: Heinemann.

Peyton, J. K. (1988). Mutual conversations: Written dialogue as a basis for building student-teacher rapport. In M. Farr (Ed.), *Interactive writing in dialogue journals: Practitioner, linguistic, social, and cognitive views.* Norwood, NJ: Ablex.

Smith, F. (1989) *Understanding reading* (4th ed.). Hillsdale, NJ: Lawrence Erlbaum Associates.

Staton, J. (1988). Dialogue journals in the classroom context. In M. Farr (Ed.), *Interactive writing in dialogue journals: Practitioner, linguistic, social, and cognitive views.* Norwood, NJ: Ablex.

Sulzby, E. (1985). Children's emergent reading of favorite storybooks: A developmental study. *Reading Research Quarterly, 20,* 468–487.

Yaden, D. B., Smolkin, L. B., & Conlon, A. (1989). Preschoolers' questions about pictures, print conventions, and story text during reading aloud at home. *Reading Research Quarterly, 24,* 188–214.

Additional readings

Hamayan, E., & Pfleger, M. (1987). *Developing literacy in English as a second language: Guidelines for teachers of young children from non-literate backgrounds.* Silver Springs, MD: National Clearinghouse for Bilingual Education.

Rigg, P., & Enright, D. S. (Eds.), (1985). *Children and ESL: Integrating perspectives.* Washington, DC: Teachers of English to Speakers of Other Languages.

Videos

International Catholic Migration Commission & the U.S. Department of State, Bureau for Refugee Programs (Producer). (1990). *Opening the word: Narrative activities for ESL students.*

Media Group & the U.S. Department of State Bureau for Refugee Programs (Producer). (1988). *Sing a song together: The story of PREP.*

12 Social integration of immigrant and refugee children

Elizabeth Coelho

Background: the impact of immigration

This chapter is concerned with the immigrant experience and its effects on the social integration and academic success of immigrant children and the children of immigrants. The chapter describes some strategies and initiatives to support immigrant children and families and promote effective integration.

Immigration is a major life experience. It is one that most teachers in North America and other English speaking countries have not had, and they may not always be aware of the effects of this experience on the children in their classrooms. The first part of this chapter is concerned with the process of immigration, with the effects of the experience on immigrant families, and with the impact of the experience on the children's integration into the academic and social life of the school.

Immigration trends

The flow of immigrants to developed countries is increasing rapidly (see Chapter 2). For example, in Canada, the number of immigrants more than doubled between 1986 and 1990. In 1990 new higher targets were announced in a five-year plan. The target between 1992 and 1995 is 250,000, an increase of 30,000 over the number of immigrants who arrived in 1991.

Increases in immigration may not be welcomed by many members of the host society who are several generations removed from the immigrant experience. Some may regard immigration as a benefit to the immigrant only – an altruistic gesture of goodwill towards those unfortunate enough to have been born as citizens of less developed societies, a humanitarian rescue of the victims of war and persecution, or a privilege to be jealously guarded and grudgingly dispensed. Popular attitudes are influenced or expressed in the media through the use of such terms as *flood, wave,* or *influx,* implying that the host society is in danger of being overwhelmed by newcomers. In fact, although immigration has increased over the last five years, the new levels are not the highest intake levels in Canada's history. Between 1910 and 1913, Canada gained more than 1.3 million new residents.

Teachers who work in multilingual, multiracial, and multicultural classrooms need accurate and up-to-date information about immigration – its rationale, its procedures, and its effects on host and immigrant populations – to establish a context for their work not only with immigrant and minority children and parents but with the children and parents of the host society as well.

Why do immigrants come?

Immigrants leave their homelands to emigrate to North America, Australia, and the United Kingdom for a wide variety of reasons, which are often categorized as the "pull factors", the reasons that host countries recruit new residents, and the "push factors", the reasons that immigrants feel a need to leave their homelands or present country of residence.

"PULL FACTORS"

Apart from the aboriginal peoples, people came to North America or Australasia because, at some point in a country's history, it was expedient to import people who would settle and farm the land, defend borders, build railroads, or develop a mining industry. In earlier colonial times this was achieved by deporting convicted criminals or destitute persons from the metropolitan country, by implementing programs of indentured labour, and by the forced immigration of millions of enslaved Africans to North America. Volunteer immigrants from Europe were attracted by offers of free land to homesteaders.

Contemporary immigration policies still reflect the needs of the host country. Canada, for example, like many industrialized societies, has an aging population. More than 10 percent of Canada's population is over 65, and this proportion is increasing. As a result, Canada has an urgent need to replace and expand the workforce in order to support the social services that this population will require, as well as to revitalize and expand the economy. Today, immigration helps Canada, Australia, and the United States to develop resource and manufacturing industries and fill labour-market gaps, most recently in service jobs such as child care and hospital care that "older" residents no longer are inclined to do. In Canada, for example, there is a strong focus on labour-market demands; potential immigrants must score a certain number of points allocated for such factors as age, level of education, knowledge of English or French, training and job experience, and the current demand for the occupation in Canada.

There is also an emphasis on importing capital and entrepreneurial skills through the recruitment of "business immigrants". An example of the benefit to the host country is the billions of dollars that have flowed into Canada from Hong Kong in the last three years. This is translated into the creation of new jobs and the bolstering of consumer demand. Thus, immigrants represent an important resource to the host country, a workforce whose education and training education were provided in the country of origin. Middle-class and professional immigrants are attracted to North America and Australia by the opportunity to take up similar positions in developed countries for much greater material reward and many do so. Many students educated abroad also apply for permanent resident status when their studies are completed. This creates a "brain-drain" from the home country, which has invested its scarce educational resources in the training of this group. Their loss is the host country's gain.

Unfortunately, the real benefits of immigration are not well known to most citizens of the host country. In times of economic depression or recession, immigrants become a target of considerable ill will as they are commonly (and erroneously) believed to "take people's jobs", "cause pressure in the housing market", and "be a drain on the social services". Teachers who work in multiracial schools have to make sure that they share positive values about immigration and immigrants, not only with the children of immigrants and the children who represent the "host" community but also with parents and colleagues.

"PUSH FACTORS"

Historically, immigrants have left their homelands to escape religious or political persecution, to flee from poverty and famine, or to seek land ownership or increased economic opportunity. Today, the same factors apply in somewhat different contexts. Whereas until the middle of this century the immigrants were predominantly from European countries, in the last three or four decades the source countries of immigration have become predominantly Asian, African, Caribbean, or Latin American. This is a result of the changes to immigration policy in the 1960s, in both Canada and the United States, eliminating quotas based on country of origin. Also, few of the conditions that prompted major waves of emigration (for example, the Irish Potato Famine) are present in Europe today and most Western Europeans have a standard of living equivalent to what they would have in North America or Australia.

Most immigrants today come from developing or war-torn countries (often both). They are fleeing political and economic oppression in Africa, Asia, and Latin America. Many have fled to neighbouring countries where they apply for refugee status. They are processed according to the criteria established by the United Nations High Commission on Refugees. Claimants are required to prove that they are in danger of persecution or loss of life, on the basis of religion, politics, or ethnic origin if they return to their homeland, and that it is not possible for them to stay where they are – for example, in refugee camps. Host countries have yearly targets for refugees and apply their own screening procedures in the selection of the most suitable candidates. Factors such as "personal suitability" (in the opinion of the immigration official) or "political suitability" are considered in the screening. There are millions of refugees worldwide, and host countries can be extremely selective in choosing from this labour pool.

The immigrant experience

Immigration is a period of very great stress. Some individuals and some families are able to adjust more easily to their changed circumstances than others. The Report of the Canadian Task Force on Mental Health Issues Affecting Immigrants and Refugees (1988) concludes that the stress of moving from one country to another does not, by itself, threaten individual well-being or mental health; however, mental health is threatened when a number of other "risk factors" are added to those of immigration and resettlement. Some of the factors that determine how much stress a family or an individual may have to cope with will now be examined.

CHOICE

It is much easier to adjust to a new situation if it is a situation of one's own choosing. Refugees have little or no choice; most would not have chosen to leave but for catastrophic events or extreme hardship in the home country, and most who leave have little or no choice about which country will offer them asylum.

Entrepreneurial and independent immigrants choose to make this change in their lives and generally feel positive about the new opportunities they hope to find. However, it is extremely rare for dependent children to have any involvement in the decision, and in some cultures the adult women have no say either. Lack of choice and feelings of powerlessness may have very negative effects on the eventual adjustment of immigrants to their new life.

PREPARATION AND SUPPORT

Those who choose to leave their countries and emigrate to another have time to prepare themselves financially and emotionally. They often have relatives in the host country to help ease the transition and are usually quite well informed about the new country. If they are joining an already established community, resources and orientation services will be available to them. Some immigrants have little opportunity to prepare themselves for their new country. Refugee families, in particular, lack the resources to prepare themselves for the transition to a new country.

FAMILY SEPARATION

It is quite common for immigrant families to arrive in stages. Often, one parent will arrive first and send for spouse and children once established in a job and a place to live. This may be a matter of months, or of years.

Family reunification after years of separation is often extremely difficult for parents and children alike. If a family arrives as a unit, all members experience adjustment at the same time. There is a commonality of experience to help bind the unit together. However, if parents and children are adjusting to each other as to strangers whom they barely remember, there is an additional stress, one that many immigrant families never fully overcome.

Even when families arrive as a unit, the loss of extended family can have far-reaching effects. At a time of acute stress, family support systems are no longer available. Immigrant children and parents may be very reluctant to confide in teachers or guidance counsellors the problems they may be having at home or at school, particularly if they perceive the cultural gap between the teacher or counsellor and themselves to be so wide that there is little possibility of mutual comprehension. These feelings of isolation make many immigrant children feel very helpless.

PROFICIENCY IN ENGLISH

Children who have had some exposure to English in their own countries, or whose language is related to English through Germanic or Latin roots, are likely to feel fairly confident about learning English. However, increasingly large numbers of immigrants are arriving from very different language backgrounds, where the script may not use the Roman alphabet; these students may be more intimidated by the prospect of learning English. Students in Toronto describe their feelings about themselves as learners of English (Porter, 1991):

I went to elementary school in a special class which was for students from other countries to learn English. But all the other students were better than I in English, and I was the only one who spoke no English. This made me nervous and lonely. Fortunately, there were some Chinese students in the class. I did not know what to do when the other students spoke to me because I did not understand them. I was forced to use signs with my hands to communicate with people, just as if I were deaf and dumb. I hated the students who spoke to me. When the teacher wanted to speak to me, he had to get the other students to translate. Sometimes there was a joke, and I had to laugh with the others even though I did not know what the joke was, because I was afraid of being laughed at. I hated myself for being in such a situation, and I wondered when I would be able to understand what the people were talking about!

Gary Que (China)

PREVIOUS EDUCATIONAL EXPERIENCE

Children who have been to school in their own countries, whose education has been uninterrupted, and who were experiencing at least average success, are likely to make a smoother transition to school in the new country. The new school system may be very different from the previous one, but the experience is still recognizable as schooling.

However, some immigrants are coming from countries where educational opportunities are extremely limited or where education has been totally disrupted for a number of years by war and civil turmoil (see Chapter 11). Children with little or no educational experience, who may not yet have learned to read and write in their own language or who have not yet developed some notion about schooling, books, and study, are likely to have a difficult time understanding what is required of them and may be very afraid of the whole school environment. They may be almost paralyzed by culture shock.

ENVIRONMENTAL FACTORS

Most immigrants to English-speaking countries settle in the large cities. For many, this is their first experience of life in a large urban centre and their first experience of apartment life. This kind of transition represents a major lifestyle change. Many immigrants have difficulty in adjusting to their new environment. They may be anxious about activities that other residents do as a matter of course, such as using public transit. Parents may worry about the safety of their children on the way to and from school or about the safety of the elevator in the apartment building. Apartment living isolates families from each other in a way that living in a house in a neighbourhood does not. Moreover, apartment life requires each family to spend much more time together in very close quarters, and if relationships are strained, this can become another source of stress.

Adjusting to a different climate can also be physically stressful. The first winter may be very difficult for immigrant families from warmer countries. Weather forecasts of temperature and wind-chill factors mean little to those who have not experienced them, even if they understand the language in which they are broadcast. Wearing so many clothes feels awkward and bulky, and the cost of buying different clothes for different seasons creates financial difficulty as well.

CULTURAL ISOLATION

Many immigrant families have very limited opportunities for social interaction with the mainstream culture. Many adults work in "ghettoized" occupations, such as textile work or contract cleaning, where the workforce is predominantly immigrant and often predominantly from one language group. Children at school often socialize within their own cultural group; the older they are the more evident this is (Kagan, 1986). It is especially difficult for newcomers to integrate socially when they don't speak English, don't know the schoolyard games, don't know the rituals and symbols of the peer culture, and may even prefer not to be noticed at all for the first few months. Immigrants rarely receive invitations into the homes of their coworkers or classmates unless they are of the same cultural and social class background. This is not because the host community is cold or unfriendly but because the social structure of the workplace or classroom provides insufficient opportunities for different groups to get to know each other and recognize commonalities.

Current practices in organizing ESL support and instruction in the second language may impede social and racial integration. For example, in some jurisdictions, language minority children are placed in special second language or bilingual programs for all or most of the day. The fewer opportunities the children have for interaction with their native-speaking peers, the more socially isolated they are likely to be. Unless the school and classroom program is structured in such a way as to promote positive intercultural interaction, minority children have little opportunity to find out first-hand about the majority and other minority cultures. Similarly, children of the majority culture have little opportunity to develop nonstereotypical views of minorities.

MINORITY STATUS

For most immigrants, resettling in a new country involves coming to terms with their new minority status. In their own countries they were likely to be able to identify with the majority population, and children were presented with authority figures (teachers, the judiciary, the medical profession, politicians, and other public figures) with whom they could identify as role models. In their new environment they may be presented with few positive images of people like themselves and be in contact with few people of their own background who are in positions of respect and authority in the mainstream society. This can have a very negative impact on self-esteem and damage a child's motivation to learn.

Some children may begin to question their own identity (Porter, 1991):

Of course, I am not Canadian. But it seems I am no longer Chinese either. Then, who am I? Who will I be? I feel so confused.

Xuan Cen (China)

Others try to assume a new identity in order to fit in with their peers at school:

It was four years ago when I suddenly became a different person. I don't mean that I physically changed or anything, but my personality changed because I had been known as Khan and then I became Chris. When I came to school, I wanted the teacher to call me Chris because it was easy for them.

Chris Truong (Vietnam)

Some ESL children are given English names by their teachers; others take English names for themselves in order to save themselves and/or their teachers embarrassment. In both cases this may represent a denial or rejection of the child's identity.

LOSS OF STATUS

Many skilled and professional immigrants, recruited for their labour-market skills, are unable to find employment in their fields in the new country. This may be because adequate language training is not available, or because the individual needs updating and retraining in the field (for example, in the use of computers), or because many employers do, routinely, discriminate against immigrant applicants (Henry & Ginzberg, 1985). Many well-qualified immigrants find themselves forced to take low-paying service or manufacturing occupations where lack of proficiency in the second language is not a problem – and where they will find little opportunity to improve it. For many these jobs become a dead end rather than a transition to the kind of employment they expected. Many working adults are emotionally exhausted from the frustration of being trapped in occupations for which they are overqualified and that do not provide the stimulus, challenge, or satisfaction they hoped for.

Children may begin to view their parents as diminished; they may also feel responsible for what has happened to their parents, who are willing to sacrifice themselves for the sake of their children's opportunities in the new land:

We arrived at the airport where my father, who had come to Canada three years previously, greeted us. Unfortunately, my first impression of Canada was not a pleasing one because of my father, who looked weaker and older than he should have. It seemed to me that hard labouring work had taken away the strength, confidence, and dignity which he used to have when he was a colonel in Korea. Well, it might have been our fault because he had been working so hard to bring us to Canada, but that was the way I felt then.

Steve Lee (Korea)

POVERTY

Poverty is a major cause of academic failure for children of all racial and cultural backgrounds, including those of the white majority culture in North America. Poverty does not make people stupid, but it does make it extremely difficult for families to provide the kind of environment and support that helps children to become successful at school (Hess, 1989).

Large numbers of immigrant and minority children live in poverty. According to Lincoln and Higgins (1991), this places them "at greater risk of failing, dropping out of school, and growing up unprepared for the kind of work they will be expected to do in our turn-of-the-century economy". This kind of waste of human potential not only represents cultural, racial, and economic inequity but also forecasts economic catastrophe and social disaster.

PARENTAL INVOLVEMENT

In English-speaking school systems, the active involvement of parents in their children's education is widely recognized to be a major factor in academic success. For several reasons, the parents of immigrants may not become effectively involved in their children's education. One reason is that many immigrants find themselves doing more than one job or doing shift work. Because of this, they have little time available to interact with their children and help with schoolwork or attend school events. Another reason for the low involvement of many immigrant parents is that many feel handicapped by their lack of fluency in English or their lack of knowledge about the educational system.

Also, in many countries, the involvement of parents in their children's schooling is neither expected nor desired. The role of the parent in many countries is to send the children to school, provide the books and uniforms, and exhort the children to success. The teacher and the school are entrusted with the rest. This is why, when teachers call immigrant parents about a concern over their child, the teachers are sometimes surprised and somewhat indignant when the parents seem to hand the problem back to the teacher. On the other hand, some immigrant parents wonder what kind of "soft" system the schools are running if the teachers can't take care of the children without advice from the parents.

THE CULTURE OF THE SCHOOL

Student-teacher relations in North American schools are very different from student-teacher relations in many other parts of the world. Many immigrant children and parents are accustomed to schools where all the children wear uniforms and the teachers follow a dress code; where the students stand when the teacher enters the classroom and whenever they are called on to answer a question; where teachers are addressed respectfully by name or title; where students seldom ask questions or initiate discussion but wait to be called on. These and other symbols of "respect" are highly ritualized and visible.

In contrast, immigrant and minority children in English-speaking countries find an almost total lack of the symbols of respect that they recognize. Many are extremely uncomfortable with a classroom culture that allows students to leave their seats, work in groups, initiate discussion with the teacher, and joke with their peers or the teacher. They are unable to discern the "invisible discipline" that informs the other children how far the informality can go and often conclude that there is no discipline or classroom structure at all. Some withdraw from interaction in an unpredictable, incomprehensible environment. Others become boisterous and playful, testing the limits of this new and strange classroom environment.

Another source of difficulty is the miscommunication that occurs when cultural miscues in language and nonverbal behaviour communicate messages that were not intended. Examples of such cultural miscues include cultural differences about how far apart speakers should stand; when and with whom it is appropriate to make eye contact; how loudly one should speak; how tone may change or add meaning; or how direct requests, warnings, advice, or refusals should be. Such miscues are the cause of much frustration in cross-cultural communication.

Different cultures develop and value different learning styles. In North American schools, for example, the emphasis in recent years has been on student-centered learning, inquiry and discovery approaches to new skills and information, and dynamic teaching and learning approaches such as "active learning", "cooperative learning", "collaborative learning", and so on (see Chapter 8). Immigrant children, accustomed to teacher-centered classrooms with a transmission approach to education, may be reluctant to participate in classroom interaction and may feel lost and uncomfortable without the structure to which they are accustomed.

The content of the curriculum is usually based on the values and experiences of the middle and upper classes of the majority culture (see Chapter 1). As a result, the immigrant experience is seldom a topic of inquiry or discussion, except in the second language classroom. Immigrant and minority children find it difficult to relate to a curriculum that concerns itself with concepts with which they are unfamiliar – for example, the emphasis on the needs, wishes, successes, and hopes of the individual rather than the family. Children of the majority culture, validated by a curriculum that represents, affirms, and celebrates only their own cultural background and experience, develop an exaggerated sense of the importance of their own group and are not helped to an understanding of the experiences of their classmates.

The images and events that are celebrated in the school give strong messages about the relevance or importance of the different racial and cultural groups in the school. These messages are communicated by the absence or equitable inclusion of people of different backgrounds in the visual material posted in the halls and the classrooms, and in the material in the library. The presence or absence of material in languages other than English also give children and parents a clue about who is expected to participate in the life of the school. Holidays and festivals that are celebrated or ignored tell them who is important in the school and in the society.

SHIFTS OF POWER IN THE FAMILY

In some immigrant families, a power shift occurs between the genders and between the generations after arrival in the new country. Few families in North America now exist on one income, and many immigrant families have to make the adjustment to both parents' going out to work. Traditional male/female roles begin to break down; women have less time to give to domestic responsibilities and in the workplace become exposed to different sets of societal values about gender roles, the rights of women and children, and so on. These values are often in conflict with those of the traditional culture and entail for many males a loss of power and status within the family and the community. This loss of status may result in anger and frustration, and occasionally this anger may be acted out in family violence.

Another power shift occurs between parents and children. The children often acquire English more quickly than their parents and may be required to act as family negotiators and go-betweens. Teenage children may also have part-time jobs after school and on weekends. New responsibilities cause children to claim rights, privileges, and independence at an age that would be unthinkable in the home country. This can be another source of conflict as the family adjusts to new roles and relationships.

CULTURAL CONFLICT BETWEEN HOME AND SCHOOL

Children are exposed at school to many values that are in conflict with those of the home. It is relatively easy for immigrant children to change extrinsic cultural traits such as style of clothing; but the intrinsic values of a culture are more deeply ingrained and much more integral to the individual's identity. These intrinsic values are challenged daily by exposure to a new set of cultural values. For instance, respect for elders may be less evident among native-English-speaking children than in immigrant families. Individual choice and self-determination is another cultural value that is often in conflict with the emphasis many other cultures place on duty towards the family and the community. Older children are in contact with a teenage lifestyle that is very different from the life of adolescents in their own cultures. Courses such as "Sex Education", "Sociology", "Family Studies", and "Personal Life Management" emphasize personal choice and autonomy and relate to a lifestyle that is promoted in music videos and other media.

Some parents react with fear and suspicion when they feel that their children are being attracted to aspects of the new culture that the parents find disturbing. They may attempt to control exposure by refusing to allow their children to participate in certain activities such as field trips or coeducational sports.

It is very difficult, and the source of much personal confusion, for immigrant children to navigate between both cultures. If they attempt to integrate into the school culture, they may have feelings of disloyalty and dishonour towards their parents and community; if they choose to adhere wholly to their parents' values, they remain isolated on the fringes of the new community and unable to participate in all that school has to offer.

As the children acquire English, they may become less proficient in the language of the home. According to Yao (1985), "When English becomes a child's primary conversational language, parents have difficulty communicating with them in their native tongue . . . subsequently, poor communication between parents and their children leads to learning and behavioural problems in schools".

THE REFUGEE EXPERIENCE

In addition to the stresses that most immigrants face, even those immigrating under optimum conditions, those who arrive as refugees have lived through traumatic experiences of war and flight. Many have seen family members murdered or do not know the whereabouts of some of them. Most have experienced some kind of family separation. By the time they arrive in their new country, some have spent many years in refugee camps, often in appalling conditions, waiting for official recognition of their status as bona fide refugees and then waiting for one or another of the refugee sponsoring countries to accept them. This wait is a period of extreme stress, and adults and children alike often become anxious and depressed. Previously good family relations may be worn down during this time by squalor, noise, and despair; some adults retreat into silence and therefore are not providing the linguistic interaction their children need in order to develop proficiency in the first language.

Mental health experts have described typical phases in the refugee's adjustment to life in the new country (Canadian Task Force on Mental Health Issues Affecting Migrants and Refugees, 1988). Initially there may be a phase of great elation and relief at having escaped from persecution or death at home and intolerable conditions in transit. However, it is not unusual for individuals to begin feeling very guilty about their own deliverance when so many of their relatives and friends did not escape or even survive. For some, there is a stage of realization that their escape represents long-term exile, perhaps forever. This can be a period of great depression.

Many young children of refugee families exhibit various symptoms of posttraumatic stress disorder: depression, withdrawal, hyperactivity, aggression, fearful behaviour, and reactions of intense anxiety to situations that recall some traumatic event (e.g., the sound of a car backfiring, the sight of an armed police officer, or a helicopter flying overhead). The artwork of many refugee children reveals some of their anxieties and preoccupation through their depiction of war and violence: planes, falling bombs, soldiers, and so on.

How to promote academic and social integration

In this section, suggestions are made for meeting language minority children's needs by viewing the school and the classroom as a social support system, and the teacher as a mediator and advocate on behalf of immigrant and minority students.

Reception and orientation

All schools should establish some procedures for the reception and orientation of newcomers whether they are arriving from a neighbouring city or from halfway around the world. The first impression that the new arrival receives is very important; from this first day the child will form expectations about the school and how well he or she will fit into it. If the school seems less than welcoming or if routines seem to be disarranged and personnel put out by the arrival of a newcomer, the child and

Figure 1   A sample welcome sign. *(Courtesy of the North York Board of Education)*

parents may be intimidated from the very beginning, and future efforts to involve parents may be futile.

The following procedures will help to ensure a smooth transition for the child and the classroom teacher and reassure parents about what is to happen to their children:

- Create welcome signs, like that in Figure 1, in the languages of the community and display them prominently.
- Make sure that school support staff, often the first contact with the new family, are trained to receive new students in a welcoming manner and know what routines to follow.
- Designate a person or team responsible for reception. In a small school, this may consist of the principal and the second language teacher. As soon as a new family arrives, this individual or a member of the team is called down to the main office and welcomes the family to sit in a comfortable private space – perhaps a conference room or the principal's office.
- Use an interpreter. This should be a professional employed by the school district, someone with competence in both languages and a good understanding of the school system. It is not a good idea to use another

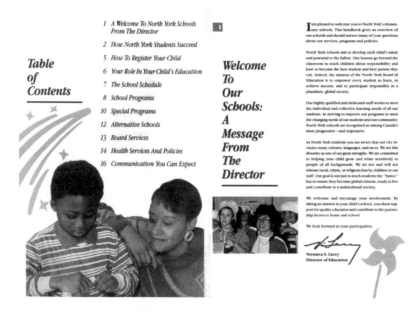

Figure 2   A sample welcome booklet. *(Courtesy of the North York Board of Education)*

student to interpret what may include some confidential or sensitive information.

- Allow plenty of time for the interview. It takes more than twice as long to communicate through an interpreter; not only must the words be translated, but whole concepts must be explained (e.g., What is a brown-bag lunch?).

- Provide basic information about the length and structure of the school day, what the child needs to bring to school, and holidays. Do not overload the family with new information during this first encounter; establish a relationship so that orientation can continue during the weeks and months ahead.

- Give parents a ''Welcome Booklet'' (Figure 2) in their language, giving basic information about the school program, the structure of the school day and the school year, special activities and events, and the role parents are encouraged to take. Include a page where you can provide personalized information – the name of the child's classroom teacher and second language teacher, the principal's name, the school phone number, and what to do if the child is absent.

- Provide the child with a basic ''starter kit'' of materials: pencils, coloured markers, a ruler, an eraser, a notebook, a picture dictionary.

- Place the child with his or her age peers. Newcomers will not acquire the second language more quickly by being placed with younger students, and the resultant loss of self-esteem may cause them to withdraw and learn less.
- Introduce the grade-level teacher and the second language teacher.
- Introduce a "student ambassador" from the child's new class (see page 317):
- It might be advisable to place the new child in the second language classroom for a significant portion of each day, for the first few days, in order for the teacher to make some assessment of the child's linguistic and educational needs.
- Provide information about heritage language programs and indicate support for these. Encourage parents to use the first language at home to support the child's language development; explain that this development will support the acquisition of English.
- Provide information about community language programs for adults.
- Escort the family on a brief school tour, including a visit to the child's classroom and the second language room.
- Set aside funds to assist refugee families and others who would have difficulty providing school supplies and clothing, such as gym shorts. Use this fund to subsidize field trips.
- Organize a clothing exchange. Families send clothing (especially winter clothing and boots) to the school. To save children potential embarrassment, exchange the clothing with another school so that the original owners of the clothes don't recognize them on the new owner. Organize a small "clothing store" so that the clothing looks attractive. Grade-level teachers can bring individual students to the store to choose appropriate items.

In the classroom

CREATING A WELCOMING AND SUPPORTIVE LEARNING ENVIRONMENT

New students will adjust to classroom routines and expectations more positively if the class and the teacher already have some routines for welcoming the newcomer and integrating him or her into the class from the beginning. Some of the following suggestions are for the first days; others are intended to make the classroom program an inviting, inclusive, culturally sensitive learning environment for all children, newly arrived and otherwise.

- Introduce newcomers as children who speak _____ and are also learning to speak English. Avoid speaking about the child as someone

Student Ambassadors

In elementary schools, every class should have "classroom ambassadors" (one boy, one girl). It is advisable to avoid the word "buddy" because this implies that the students must become friends; this is not realistic. The ambassadors' tasks should be specific and finite; if friendship results, that is an additional benefit, but it is not the purpose of the program.

The role of ambassador could rotate every few weeks, so that many students have an opportunity to take this leadership role. These students should reflect the ethnic and racial make-up of the school, and some of them should be of the same linguistic or cultural background as the incoming students. Most newcomers will be more comfortable with someone of their own gender. It is especially encouraging to newcomers if they meet others from their own background who have already successfully navigated the adjustment period and are comfortable in the school; however, it is not always necessary to assign an ambassador of the same background.

Ambassadors should receive special recognition: a button to identify their role, a letter home to parents (in the appropriate language) praising their child's helpfulness, addition of the child's name to a list on display in a prominent place, a classroom visit and handshake by the principal, and so on.

Classroom and school ambassadors will need some initial training in cross-cultural communication and a specific list of duties for which they are accountable. The list of duties might include the following, adapted to suit classroom and school routines:

- Sit beside the newcomer for one week to help him or her follow classroom routines.
- Show the newcomer where the washrooms are; point out the words or symbols for *boys* and *girls;* explain how to ask for permission to leave class and go the washroom.
- Take the new student on a tour of the school; make sure he or she knows how to find the office, the lunchroom, the gym, the health room, and other places in the school.
- Make sure the student knows who the principal is and knows the names of the principal, the grade-level teacher, and the school secretary.
- Invite the newcomer to join you at recess and lunch for the first few days.
- If you were the newcomer, what would you like someone in the class to do for or with you?

who "doesn't speak English"; nobody likes being described in terms of what he or she cannot (yet) do.
- Learn how to pronounce the new student's name. A useful strategy at the beginning of the year, or at any time that classroom groupings change, is to provide a structured activity to help students introduce themselves to each other.

What's Your Name?

- Group children so that several linguistic and cultural backgrounds are represented in each group. Groups of four are the most useful because they can easily become sets of pairs for some activities. Larger groups are generally too large to promote optimum interaction.
- Within the groups of four, students divide into pairs to interview each other. Provide some interview questions such as the following, adapted as appropriate for the age of the students:

What is your name?
How do you spell it?
Where were you born?
What language(s) do you speak?

- Encourage children to think of other questions to ask about their partners.
- After children have obtained some information, have them introduce their partners to the other members of their group of four.
- At the end of a specified period, children are accountable for knowing the names and something about the backgrounds of everyone in their own group. Call on children at random to introduce their group members to the class: *This is _____. He/she was born in _____.*
He/she speaks _____.

(Note: The structure of these questions and answers will reinforce the first phrases that the newcomer will be exposed to in the second language program)

- If the student speaks no English yet, seat him or her beside someone who speaks the native language for the first week or two.
- Have an up-to-date political world map permanently displayed in the classroom. For each child, make a small name tag (or have the children make their own) and pin it on their country of origin. Add newcomers to the map as they arrive.
- Take a photograph of every child in the class. Depending on the age of the children, write for them or have them write a sentence or two about themselves. Keep this as a permanent display. Children may add to the

information about themselves at any time. Add newcomers as they arrive. Include yourself in the display.

- Create a "Welcome Box" for the classroom. This should be filled with items for newcomers to work on for short periods of time with a peer tutor (let students take turns doing this). Include the following in the box: magazines and catalogues, scissors, markers, drawing and writing paper, coloured blocks and other math manipulables, a teaching clock, pictures and real objects to identify and place in categories, labels for classroom furniture and equipment, and for younger children, toys and models of all kinds. Try to include pictures and models of items that may be familiar to the newcomer: animals, plants, food, clothing, and so on that are part of the former environment. Make sure that people in the pictures are multiracial.

- Make note of important announcements and make sure that someone translates and explains them to newcomers. For instance, make sure that your language minority students know when there is to be a public holiday or professional activity day. It is very unnerving for newcomers to arrive to a closed school, and the unsuspecting parents may be at work, with no one else at home to receive the children.

- Communicate positive attitudes towards linguistic and cultural diversity. The second language students are not "having language difficulties"; they are linguistically very enriched, and bilingualism is an intellectual asset.

CURRICULUM CONTENT

This section suggests ways of modifying curriculum content to include the experiences, perspectives, and values of all the children in a multiracial, multicultural classroom (see also Chapter 7).

- To assist students in relating to their new classroom program, take into account the students' previous educational experiences (see Chapter 11). Start with materials, content, and methodology with which the students are familiar, and move gradually into mainstream content and materials and more student-centred approaches to teaching and learning. You may have to modify content in order to introduce concepts that newcomers are unfamiliar with. Examine reading materials: Do they make assumptions about the background and experiences of the readers that do not hold true for some or many of the children in the class? The reader who is not familiar with the kinds of scenes and experiences described and depicted is not able to utilize some essential cognitive strategies in reading: predicting what is coming next, making inferences about the meanings of new words, and so on.

- Evaluate the content used in the skills development aspects of the curriculum and use content relating to the cultures represented in the classroom.

- Provide bilingual instruction for students whose limited educational background would make it difficult for them to relate to the classroom program even if they were fluent in the language of instruction. Children who have missed years of schooling have not had opportunities to develop concepts that might be taken for granted in children who have been in school full time.
- Children in a culturally diverse classroom should be presented with a wide variety of such tales from many cultures, including their own, and discover some commonalities among cultures. Encourage a multicultural perspective on universal human values and practices. Topics such as "Birthdays", "Elders", "Coming of Age", "Getting Married", and so on provide opportunities for children to share and understand cultural diversity in a way that emphasizes the underlying commonality of human experience and expression.
- The curriculum has to relate to the real life experiences of the students if they are to make sense of it. Make sure to choose material that shows people of all racial backgrounds and both genders acting as problem solvers.

CURRICULUM DELIVERY

This section suggests some ways to adapt or diversify classroom strategies to suit the learning styles of all the children in the class and make material more comprehensible to the language learners.

- Modify classroom language. A useful basic principle in working with students who are still in the process of acquiring full proficiency in the language of instruction is to pay attention to the balance between language and content. If the content is new, simplify the language in order to assist students to comprehend. When the content is understood, then the students can be introduced to new terminology and more complex language structures that are of high frequency in that particular context (see Chapter 7 for more detail).
- Use cooperative learning techniques to promote interaction (see Chapter 8). Cooperative learning techniques provide an effective way for students to be involved in oral interaction in the target language with a peer group smaller and less judgmental than the whole class. Cooperative learning also helps you to provide in-class support systems by providing opportunities for students to work together and take on responsibility for each other. Other benefits of cooperative learning include positive race relations, higher self-esteem, more on-task behaviour, and enhanced academic achievement, especially for minority students (Slavin, 1990).

- Use peer tutors. A classroom or cross-grade tutoring program can be established to assist new students in adjusting to school and classroom routines. Teachers can assign specific responsibilities and provide recognition for students who undertake them. For example, a student can be assigned to work together with the second language student on oral interpretation of a graph or chart. If the second language student can verbalize the significant data and conclusions at the end of a specified period, both students should receive recognition.
- Be aware of different learning styles. Newly arrived students from other areas of the world are often bewildered by our more student-centred approach to learning. They may be very insecure in a class where the teacher does not direct and monitor every step of the learning process. Introduce new ways of learning in a very structured way. For instance, the group or individual project is a learning experience few immigrant students or parents are familiar with, and some parents may require guidance in order to help their children with projects. Their children will need assistance with choosing a topic, finding the resource material, learning how to paraphrase rather than copy or memorize verbatim from the text, and how to organize and present the material. The parents will also need some information on what a project entails and what their expected role is.

ASSESSMENT

It is important to be as accurate as possible when assessing the progress of second language learners. A fundamental premise you should work with is that the students always know more than they can show you in the second language (see Chapter 9 also). Here are some ideas to consider:

- Recognize that most newcomers need a ''silent period'' of observation in order to adjust to classroom routines. Also, many children require a period in which they can absorb language without being required to produce it. They may appear to be very passive at first, but they are absorbing a lot of information and language that they cannot yet display.
- Recognize that most standardized tests assume a long-term involvement with the majority culture and its schools. There are no culture-free, unbiased standardized tests that can be applied fairly to all populations. The alternative, when assessing the educational background and experiences of language minority children, is to bias the tests in favour of the children's cultural backgrounds by using tasks and materials with which the children are familiar.
- If you use tests, provide practice tests that students do in groups. The next day, they take the individual test that is the same or almost the

same as the practice test. (In math, for example, the problems are the same except that the number values are changed.)

- The language minority child's proficiency in reading English is not necessarily the child's level of reading proficiency; many of these children are proficient readers in languages other than English (see Chapter 11).
- When written tests are used, remember that second language students need more time to process ideas in two languages. Avoid multiple-choice questions that involve a lot of reading or depend on comprehension of fine differences in vocabulary. Alternatively, matching tasks (including matching captions to visual representations of information), cloze passages, sentence completion, true-false or yes-no questions are useful. Avoid "trick" questions where one word may mislead language minority students.
- Use a variety of assessment procedures. Perhaps the students can take an oral test, perhaps through an interpreter, or they can show what they know using visual and concrete representations (see Chapter 9).
- Use observation of students' behaviour and involvement in classroom activities: coming to class on time, coming prepared, keeping notebooks up-to-date, keeping a vocabulary notebook, helping with group presentations by providing visual or concrete material, and so on. You will have more opportunities to do this if you have implemented cooperative learning activities that allow you to circulate from group to group.
- In general, assess the children's performance on tasks they have already had a chance to practise and improve.
- Make sure your assessment relates directly to your learning objectives.
- Always be alert to unexpected or spontaneous indicators from your new students that they are making progress or having difficulty with specific tasks or skills. Make a note of these and consider what to do about them.

THE SCHOOL ENVIRONMENT

- Promote the hiring of teaching and nonteaching personnel who speak the languages of the school community. These individuals can perform many unofficial and important functions: provision of role models for children, provision of linguistic and cultural interpretation to parents and children, and provision of first-hand information to other staff about the cultural backgrounds of different groups of children in the school.
- Celebrate the major holidays of all the cultural groups in the school whether these are public holidays or not. Stress commonalities; for instance, Hanukkah, Christmas, Diwali, and other holidays can be

explored and celebrated as "Festivals of Light". Children can take part in official announcements on those days.

* Make important announcements in the major languages of the school. Multilingual announcements not only ensure that all the children in the school understand what is going on; they also communicate that all languages are important as means of communication and confer status on the children making the announcements.
* Select multiracial and multicultural library and classroom materials to reflect many types of family structure, different socioeconomic status, and different cultural values. Include classroom and library materials in the languages of the school. Parents may be able to help find and evaluate these.
* In general, ensure that the images presented to the students in hallway displays and throughout the school equitably represent positively the presence and the experience of all the groups in the school.

School/community relations

The interaction between home and school is of great significance in the adjustment of language minority children to the new school environment. Adjustment should be seen as a two-way process; it involves not only the adaptation of the individual to the environment but also the restructuring of the environment to accept and integrate the individual (see Chapter 4).

A school that is responsive to a multilingual, multiracial, multicultural community will implement some of the following routines and strategies:

* Establish a second language program for adult learners in school and encourage parents to attend. The content of the program may include, in addition to general orientation and survival information and skills, information about the school program in which the children are involved. The teacher of this class can organize classroom visits so that parents can see first-hand what their children are doing.

  It is to the children's as well as the parents' advantage if they are able to access services (such as education) in the second language. Parents who continue to rely on interpreters are less likely to initiate or respond to interaction with the school or other institutions.
* Establish and promote heritage language programs in the school. These are usually offered after school, at lunchtime, or on weekends. In some jurisdictions, such as the Toronto Board of Education, these are integrated into the school day, thus endowing these programs with the status of the mainstream academic program of the school. According to a discussion paper prepared by the Canadian Teachers' Federation (1989), "Self-esteem is a crucial issue for all children, but it is especially important for minority children whose cultural identity is

changing. At its best, a heritage language program can confirm identity, self-respect, increase support from the home and capitalize on the first-language skills of immigrant and refugee children''.

- Inform parents of the value of continuing to use the first language rather than a poor model of the second language at home. Cummins (1981) describes several studies that indicate the importance of the first language as a tool for the development of concepts that can be transferred into the second.

  If parents read or tell stories to their children in the first language, the children will continue to acquire a variety of rhetorical forms and genres of the written language as well as in the language of day-to-day interaction. The richer their experience with the first language, the more easily they will acquire the second. Children who already read and write the first language should continue to do so as this will facilitate their reading and writing in their second language.

- Set up a home reading program using books in the second language, books in the community languages, and bilingual books. Parents may need support in finding a role that is effective and realistic given their own educational background and the amount of time they have. Studies have shown that parents who do not speak the second language, or even who are not literate in the home language, can still play a vital role in supporting their children's development of literacy. In fact, a parent-child reading program can make more difference than any amount of ''remedial'' reading instruction (Tizard, Schofield, & Hewison, 1982).

  Establishing a home reading program requires some training of parents. Some jurisdictions have developed multilingual video and print resources to help teachers help parents respond effectively to their children's literacy development (Davies, Logan, Paige, & Williams, 1990).

- Promote effective communication with parents. Many schools hold meetings with specific groups of parents, using interpreters to communicate with the parents in their native languages. Some schools hold meetings in the community, in apartment recreation rooms, or community centres. It is useful to organize meetings to discuss specific topics such as ''Parenting in a New Culture''. Invite representatives of community groups to act as resource persons for such meetings.

- Hold meetings at times convenient to parents. It may be necessary to repeat meetings at different times so that parents have more flexibility in attending. Personal telephone calls in the home language, usually in the evenings, are the most effective way of communicating with parents and inviting them to meetings. Remember that parents may assume that the child is in some kind of trouble unless the purpose of the telephone call or the meeting is very clearly explained.

- Improve communication in parent-teacher interviews by asking the parent what was understood by a certain piece of information, oral or written. Asking people to summarize what was said ensures that the message received is the one that was intended, especially in situations where the professional sometimes uses jargon that is mystifying to the layperson or where the speakers use different varieties of English. Teachers can also paraphrase what they are hearing from the parents to make sure that they have understood what was said.

- Ensure that there is a two-way flow of information and advice between parents and teachers. Parents must see that there is some follow-up if they are to become involved in the life of the school. The school must be seen to pay attention to parental concerns and requests and be prepared to negotiate some compromise. Too often, parent-teacher meetings become a once-only effort to inform the parents of the expectations of the school.

- Evaluate the ways that the school routinely communicates with parents in writing: school handbooks, report cards, newsletters, information about field trips, and so on. How much prior knowledge of the school system do they assume? Are they translated into the major languages of the school? Is the information in report cards and other documents accurate, clear, and useful?

- Make sure that expectations about the completion of homework, arriving on time, being prepared for class, and so on are explicit and clear to both parents and children. The consequences for failure to meet these expectations should be meaningful, explicit, and fairly but rigorously applied. Schools may have to change some of their notions of what constitutes appropriate discipline, in order to meet some of the expectations of many immigrant and working class families in the community.

- Promote community use of the school for cultural events, organizational meetings, and religious observance.

Conclusion

Immigrant and other language minority children come from many different backgrounds and bring with them a great variety of experience. They face a period of adjustment on entry to school systems where a new language is spoken; for some, this period is very stressful. During this period they need the support of their teachers and the acceptance of their peers. The school program itself is also required to change in order to reflect the presence of all the children in positive ways. Major initiatives in curriculum development, staff development, and community outreach have to be implemented in order to create an appropriate learning environment and home-school relationship.

References

Canadian Task Force on Mental Health Issues Affecting Migrants and Refugees. (1988). *After the door has opened*. Ottawa: Multiculturalism and Citizenship Canada.

Canadian Teachers' Federation. (1989). Responding to the needs of immigrant and refugee children. Discussion paper prepared by the Ad Hoc Committee on the Needs of Immigrant and Refugee Children. Ottawa: CTF.

Cummins, J. (1981). *Bilingualism and minority-language children*. Toronto, Ontario: OISE Press.

Davies, L., Logan, M., Paige, C., & Williams, J. (1990). *Book Time*. North York, Ontario: North York Board of Education.

Henry, F., & Ginzberg, E. (1985). *Who gets the work? A test of racial discrimination in employment*. Toronto: Social Planning Council of Metropolitan Toronto.

Hess, M. (1989). *Children, schools and poverty*. Report for the Canadian Teachers' Federation Ad Hoc Committee on Children and Poverty.

Kagan, S. (1986). Cooperative learning and sociocultural factors in schooling. In *Beyond language: Social and cultural factors in schooling language minority students*. Los Angeles, CA: Evaluation, Dissemination, and Assessment Center, California State University.

Lincoln, C. A., & Higgins, N. M. (1991). Making schools work for all children. *Principal*.

Porter, J. (1991). *New Canadian voices*. Toronto, Ontario: Wall and Emerson.

Slavin, R. (1991). *Cooperative learning: Theory, research, and practice*. Englewood Cliffs, NJ: Prentice Hall.

Tizard, J., Schofield, W. N., & Hewison, J. (1982). Collaboration between teachers and parents in assisting children's reading. *British Journal of Educational Psychology, 52*, 1–15.

Yao, E. L. (1985). Adjustment needs of Asian immigrant children. *Elementary School Guidance and Counselling, 19*, 3.

Additional readings

Clarke, J., Wideman, R., & Eadie S. (1990). *Together we learn: Cooperative small group learning*. Scarborough, Ontario: Prentice Hall.

Coelho, E. (1992). Cooperative learning: Foundation for a communicative curriculum and Jigsaw: Integrating language and content. In C. Kessler (Ed.), *Cooperative language learning*. Englewood Cliffs, NJ: Prentice Hall.

Cook, B., & Olah, M. A. (1990). *Celebrations*. North York, Ontario: North York Board of Education.

Cook, M. (1987). *Talk it over (encounters of the problem solving kind)* Balboa Island: Marcy Cook Math.

Derman-Sparks, L., & A. B. C. Task Force. (1989). *Anti-bias curriculum: tools for empowering young children.* Washington, DC: National Association for the Education of Young Children.

Erickson, T., (1989). *Get it together: Math problems for groups.* Berkeley, CA: Regents of the University of California.

Family Pastimes. *Catalogue of Co-operative Games.* R.R. 4, Perth, Ontario, Canada K7H 3C6.

Gibbs, J. B. (1987). *Tribes: A process for social development and cooperative learning.* Santa Rosa, CA: Center Source Publications.

Johnson, D., & Johnson, R. (1991). *Learning together and alone* (3rd ed.) Needhan Heights, MA.: Allyn and Bacon.

Law, B., & Eckes, M. (1991). *The more than just surviving! handbook: ESL for every classroom teacher.* Winnipeg: Peguis Publishers.

Metropolitan Toronto School Board. (1990). *Great beginnings: English as a second language in junior division classrooms.* Willowdale, Ontario: Metropolitan Toronto School Board.

Orlick, T. (1978). *The cooperative sports and games book.* New York: Pantheon Books.

Parry, C. (1987). *Let's celebrate!* Toronto: Kids Can Press.

Rigg, P., & Allen, V. D. (Eds.) *When they don't all speak English: Integrating the ESL student into the regular classroom.* Urbana, Illinois: National Council of Teachers of English.

Schniedewind, N., & Davidson, E. (1983). *Open minds to equity: A sourcebook of learning activities to promote race, sex, class and age equity.* Englewood Cliffs, NJ: Prentice-Hall.

Slavin, R. E. (1990). *Cooperative learning: Theory, research, and practice.* Englewood Cliffs, NJ: Prentice Hall.

Stenmark, J. K., Thompson, V., & Cossey, R. (1986). *Family math.* Berkeley, CA: Regents of the University of California.

CONCLUSION

In "Putting It All Together," Handscombe provides a synthesis for the reader. But Handscombe's contribution is more than a synthesis of the other chapters – building on the ideas of the others, she provides an integrative framework that analyzes and expands, in some cases, the contributions of the other authors. She provides a useful checklist of sorts that can assist the reader to use the material contained in this book to take stock of their own schools and classrooms and act on the perspectives and recommendations presented throughout the book.

13 *Putting it all together*

Jean Handscombe

Where does all this leave those of you who are teachers, principals, or program directors as you work at planning a new program for young second language learners or reviewing an existing one? What should you be aiming to create, reinforce, or change? And what about those of you who are teacher educators preparing the next generation of teachers for our schools or helping the present one adjust to a changing student population? What advice might you extract from what is contained in this book?

The purpose of this chapter is to provide a framework within which all educators whose work involves young language minority learners can think about what needs to be done in planning and reviewing programs and preparing and supporting teachers. This framework is built largely from the ideas contained in the preceding chapters and is organized around the following five questions:

1. What tasks do young language minority learners face in school?
2. What resources do these youngsters bring to these tasks?
3. What understandings and skills are required by the professionals employed to help language minority learners accomplish these tasks?
4. What roles can families and communities play in educating language minority children?
5. What are the advantages of engaging the whole school environment in educating young language minority learners?

The answers to these questions given by the authors in this volume show considerable consistency across chapters. The consistency compels attention because the authors, given their different academic and profes-

This chapter owes much to Mary McGroarty for the excellent model she provided in *Beyond Language* (1986) on how to write an action-oriented summary of an entire volume's contents, to D. Scott Enright for his crystal clear articulation of what is essential in educating ESL children, to all the other authors in the book for their vivid examples and insightful analyses, and to Fred Genesee for his meticulous, yet respectful, editing.

sional interests, might just as well have been a group of the proverbial blind men let loose on different parts of an unidentified phenomenon. The differences among them are not trivial: The educational jurisdictions in which they have worked span several countries; they are employed in capacities as different as that of teacher, researcher, teacher educator, program director, teacher consultant or a combination of these roles; the age of the children whom they are writing about ranges from preschool to young adolescent; the potential barriers to learning which each describes invite differentiated responses to each identified problem. Yet, in spite of all this diversity of perspective, they demonstrate essential agreement on the major issues. Not only did they all identify the elephant, they also came up with substantially the same recommendations for its care and nurturance!

What they have in common, of course, is access to, and familiarity with, a body of theory about how young children learn, and learn through, a second language, and also how that learning can be facilitated, or blocked, by factors within the learner or within the setting in which the learning is taking place. References to the published work of researchers such as Collier, Ellis, Giroux, Hakuta, Heath, Krashen, Moll, Ogbu, Tizard, Vygotsky, Wells, and Wong Fillmore figure prominently across chapters. Each author in the present volume has made a unique contribution by providing his or her interpretation of this body of theory and in some cases an original contribution to it. They also share a respect for actual classroom interaction as the best source of evidence to validate theoretical models of children's learning in school. To use Cloud's phrase (Chapter 10), "the current best practice" which each seeks to present is thoroughly grounded in theory which in turn has been subjected to the harsh light of classroom reality. Taking a look at each of the five questions, then, what answers can the authors' collective wisdom provide?

What tasks do young language minority learners face in school?

A major theme of this book is that, although the acquisition of second language skills is important for young learners who lack such skills on entry into school, second language acquisition is not the most important task they face. Their academic achievement and their social integration are far more important. Second language learning, therefore, needs to be recast as a means to greater ends (Chapters 1, 2, 5, 6, 7, and 9). This shift of focus to outcomes which reach beyond language competency has broad-ranging implications. Let us consider in turn the overarching goals of academic achievement and social integration.

Academic achievement

When attending school in their new community, it is clear that language minority children share the prospect of undertaking probably most of the rest of their academic and vocational education through the medium of a new language. Wherever this is so, the level of proficiency which they must attain is far higher than that of learners who have more limited uses for their additional languages. More limited goals might be appropriate for language students who want to be able to use their new language skills to understand sports or opera scores, read magazine articles or find their way around the streets and through the menus of the country in which that language is used. Young language minority students, however, eventually need to be able to accomplish in their new language far more than all of the above put together. They need to develop nothing less than native-like proficiency across a broad range of domains and in both spoken and written modes. Such learning takes time; estimates range from five to nine years before second language learners have caught up with their peers (Chapter 2; Collier, 1989; Wong Fillmore, 1983). The crucial point is, given the time it takes to learn English, "if minority language students are to achieve the goals of education, academics cannot be put on hold until students have acquired proficiency in English" (Chapter 7). Since it is impossible anyway to teach language devoid of purpose or content, and since academic success is such an important goal for all children, it makes good sense to use the topics and tasks of the "regular" curriculum as the "driver", not just the "carrier" of the language curriculum (Chapters 2 and 7). As young language minority learners take on the challenge of academic work, they are faced with a number of important subtasks.

FROM KNOWN TO NEW

These children need to learn the linguistic forms that will enable them to express concepts in their second language which they already know in their first. Then they need to move beyond the known using their developing proficiency in the second language to grapple with new concepts (Chapters 1, 7, and 9).

BEYOND THE HERE AND NOW

In addition to consolidating familiar concepts and learning new ones, these children need to develop context-dependent language which is closely tied to the individual's here and now or recent past experiences. Then gradually they need to move towards understanding and using context-reduced language which is more abstract and operates without the benefit of immediate contextual support. Becoming a proficient user of context-reduced language is eventually essential for achieving high levels of academic success (see Chapter 2). Johnson (Chapter 8) expands this notion by drawing attention to the complementary spheres which young children are able to draw on when learning – the *contextual sphere,* which relates to their knowledge about life in the classroom, the school or their wider community, and the *textual sphere,* which refers to established genres of classroom discourse such as teachers' lessons, stories and written material created in, or brought into, the classroom. Different school tasks require children to draw differentially on these spheres. Neither is sufficient alone, but together – for example, "when a piece of writing or an oral 'performance' is embedded in a complex web of ongoing authentic activities" – they can contribute significantly to a child's cognitive and linguistic development.

NOT JUST THE FACTS

These children need to confront cognitively challenging content which reaches beyond the memorization of facts to the exercise of higher-order thinking skills such as analysis and evaluation. This curriculum content needs to be pitched at least at the same level as that designed for their already fluent native-speaker peers, or they will soon fall behind those peers in both academic achievement and intellectual development (Chapters 7 and 9). Wong Fillmore and Meyer (1992) warn against the tendency of schools to "dilute" program offerings to students who are still developing proficiency in English as a second language by reducing the range of content courses or reducing the breadth or depth to which these courses are taught.

When content courses are pruned from the LEP (Limited English Proficient) students' curriculum, too often what remains is an instructional program that teaches English as a second language and little else. The danger here, as with any skills instruction, is that instruction becomes an attempt to teach students how to speak, read and write in English in a learning situation in which there is little of substance worth talking about. In observations in many schools serving language minority students, we have found it a common instructional coping strategy to delay challenging LEP students with much content until they have been taught basic English, on the grounds that English is the requisite skill they must have before they can learn anything else. In some cases the students' schedules are reduced to several courses of English as a second language, supplemented only by 'non-academic' courses that are less linguistically demanding (i.e., physical education, woodwork, or arts and crafts). In other cases, especially in elementary classrooms, LEP children may be physically present in the classroom when content instruction occurs but set apart to work in separate groupings or on individual tasks or seatwork focused on ESL. The problem with such arrangements is that the students receive little more than formal language instruction; the other courses or activities add little intellectual substance to their programs of studies. (p. 648–649)

TOWARDS A CRITICAL LITERACY

These children need to develop high levels of literacy which will assist them in learning about and interpreting the world, in Hudelson's words (Chapter 6), ". . . to explain, analyze, argue about, and act upon the world." Cummins (Chapter 2) concurs in this view of the type of literacy needed: Literacy should allow everyone to demonstrate "the power to use language for our own purposes as well as those that the institutions of our society require of us." This combination of developing a critical awareness of how language is used, achieving personal literacy goals, and meeting societal expectations regarding the use of literacy skills in education, work and civic duties is a far cry from the skills required to read a set of directions or write a formula letter!

The language which language minority children need to accomplish these tasks will be learned most efficiently, not as a precursor to, but simultaneously with, their engagement in academic work (Chapters 7 and 9).

Social integration

In describing the task of social integration second, there is no intention to diminish its importance. In fact, children who do not experience at least a minimal sense of comfort around the second language speakers in their environment, as well as some desire to interact with them, are unlikely to make any headway with either academic learning or social integration. Tabors and Snow's vignette (Chapter 5) about the little girl who learned no English in her first year of preschool provides striking evidence of a child who decided that the social and cognitive effort in learning how to communicate with this whole other world of people was simply not justified. Again, as young language minority learners undertake the task of becoming integrated into the social setting of the school they are faced with a number of important subtasks.

BUILDING AN IDENTITY

These children need to build an identity which resists assimilative forces bent on eradicating any vestiges of cultural and linguistic distinctiveness they may display vis-à-vis the dominant culture. McKeon (Chapter 1) points out clearly how cultural messages about an individual's value to society, or lack of value, can be influential in creating either a positive or negative self-concept. Even those whose identity is enhanced rather than damaged by the process will need to think about what causes the wider society to appreciate them and not others. As the literature on racial stereotyping in young children so chillingly demonstrates, children are never too young to learn stereotyping attitudes and behaviours (Milner, 1983; Williams & Morland, 1976). Fortunately, they are also never too young to be asked to reflect on these and other issues of social justice (Chapter 2). As Pease-Alvarez and Vasquez point out in their contribution (Chapter 4), language minority children come to school with distinctive identities and ways of interpreting the social world that have been shaped in important ways by their particular linguistic and cultural experiences. These identities are essential to their sense of well-being and have a profound effect on the way they negotiate new social situations.

DEVELOPING INTERCULTURAL UNDERSTANDING

A strong sense of self, firmly rooted in family and community, along with an emerging ability to recognise and act upon unfairness in all its forms, is a solid foundation on which to begin the task of developing intercultural understanding (Chapters 1, 2, 4, and 7). This task is, of course, one which is shared by all participants in a classroom community whether they are learning a new language or already fluent speakers of that language.

LEARNING HOW TO "DO SCHOOL"

This task involves learning how to interact verbally and nonverbally with both adults and peers. An adult-generated list of skills required to accomplish this task would probably include items such as learning when and how to take a turn, what response to make to invitations to participate, how to negotiate roles or how to offer assistance. A child-generated list, on the other hand, might include rather more items like learning when and how to stop other children from interfering with their activity, how to complain to the teacher if their efforts to achieve the latter fail, how to justify their behaviour if challenged by a child or an adult, when to divert a teacher from dealing with an issue that might prove embarrassing – for example, why they were not paying attention or had not finished their work – how to persuade a teacher to deviate from an unpopular routine and, in extreme cases, how to terminate a teacher's conversation. Teachers need not worry, however, if they have not included the items in the child-generated list in their lesson plans; children usually attend to such imperatives without adult prompting.

Again, the language which they need to accomplish these tasks will be learned most efficiently not as a precursor to, but simultaneously with, their attempts to become a member of the classroom community (Chapters 2 and 9).

What resources do these youngsters bring to these tasks?

Life experiences

This book provides ample evidence that, even at the preschool stage, these young learners are anything but blank slates. They bring with them a dizzying array of life experiences which, along with their differing cultural and linguistic backgrounds, make them anything but a homogeneous group.

SOURCES OF DIFFERENCE

These children may have been born in the country where they are now attending school into a family which uses a minority language as its primary means of intrafamily communication; alternatively, they may have emigrated from another country and have already begun their schooling there. Their families may occupy any position on the socioeconomic scale. For some of them, their adopted country may have opened up all kinds of economic and educational opportunities which had been denied them previously, whereas others may be experiencing a more restricted lifestyle than they have been used to. The children may have been to high- or low-quality schools and their education may have been continuous or sporadic. Their previous life experiences may have left them traumatized and perhaps even physically damaged, or they may be in good physical and mental health. They may be used to rural or urban environments. They may be able to continue their connection with their previous country through visits or be unable to return "home" because of political or economic realities. They may be involved with a large, already settled community of their compatriots in their new environment, or they may be isolated from others who speak their language and share their cultural values and practices. They may be here as an intact, multi-generational family or as a small splinter from a much larger family grouping. Such differences are important for educators to know about and take into account when interacting with the children and their families and when planning programs to help them adjust to their new environment (Handscombe, 1989).

BENEATH THE DIFFERENCES

Fortunately there are also some universals which can provide a sense of continuity and a measure of consistency when everything else they are experiencing seems so alien. These universals include experiences of being part of a family, however constituted or dispersed at present; experiences of living arrangements, where the child sleeps, eats, and gathers with other family members; experiences of clothing, reflecting climate and often cultural tradition, as in what children wear as "best clothes" for special occasions; experiences of illness, of their own or family members; experiences of work, what work the adults in their community do or how else they provide the necessities of life and what contribution, if any, the children make to that endeavour; experiences of play, games with siblings, friends and adults, engaging in art activities, being entertained by performers, alive or broadcast – jugglers, clowns, storytellers or cartoon characters – or providing entertainment for others through music, dance or drama; experiences of travel, from going shopping or on vacation to undertaking a long trip to emigrate to a new country; experiences either at first hand or through their parents' stories of what it is like to be an immigrant or refugee; and last, but by no means least, experiences of building an identity, of which their name is an important symbol. Integration into the new school setting is more likely to take place when teachers tap into these universal experiences (Chapters 4 and 12).

Learning experiences

EARLY ACCOMPLISHMENTS

These children have been using their skills as learners to make sense of these life experiences since they were babies, and it is these same skills which will help them with the tasks they face as they enter their new school setting. Within a matrix of social interaction, they have used their minds and senses to actively construct their knowledge of the world and establish predictable patterns from the events taking place around them (Chapters 2 and 6; Gardner, 1991). Similarly, they have learned their first language by identifying regularities in the speech which surrounds them, using several of their senses to connect language form to what is being referred to (Chapter 1). By the time they reach school age, they have had considerable practice in solving these kinds of cognitive and linguistic problems and have been faced with a great deal of information to process. As McKeon and Pease-Alvarez and Vasquez illustrate (Chapters 1 and 4), the learning skills they bring to school may be culturally shaped. Teachers whose experience has been mostly with children from the dominant, middle-class, Anglo culture may be unfamiliar with learning skills developed in other cultural environments. Language minority children children, therefore, may need some time to adjust their skills to fit the culture of the school. At the same time, the teachers may need to rethink their concept of what makes for effective learning strategies and communication styles to accommodate and validate culturally diverse experiences (Corson, 1992a; Heath, 1983; Ochs & Schieffelin, 1984). Not all children, however, are able to call on a full range of well-developed learning skills. As Cloud (Chapter 10) reminds us, some children are affected by temporary conditions, such as fatigue, distraction and preoccupation, which can interfere with their learning. Some are affected by more stable, perhaps even permanent, conditions such as hearing or sight loss, cognitive limitations due to neurological damage or serious emotional disturbance. These children will need special support and encouragement to help them develop ways of accessing, processing and shaping information which others do with apparent effortlessness.

TRANSFER ACROSS LANGUAGES

It is now generally recognised that many of the concepts and skills which children have learned in their first language transfer readily to their second. Many children have been raised in a cultural milieu in which conversational skills are highly prized and story telling is a favourite pasttime, especially as a means of intergenerational communication. Others come from print-rich environments where the adults in their community demonstrate daily their reliance on the written word as a means of accessing and manipulating information and as a source of intellectual and emotional satisfaction. Children only need to learn these kinds of skills once. If they listen to a respected adult take pains to find the right word or phrase in Spanish to express a particular idea, then they have learned that such care and precision is possible in any language. If they understand that different Farsi-speaking individuals, looking at the same written Farsi on a page, can produce oral versions which sound alike, then they know that the same can be done in any language.

McKeon, Cummins, Goodz, Pease-Alvarez and Vasquez, Tabors and Snow and Hudelson (Chapters 1, 2, 3, 4, 5, and 6) all illustrate clearly how children exploit their ability to transfer skills from their first language to their second. In fact, teachers take children's ability to apply what they know in their first language to the task of learning their second so much for granted that it is only when children have no possibility of making such a transfer that they really notice what a significant foundation the first language can provide. Thus, Hamayan (Chapter 11), in considering the case of children who come from communities where written language is used infrequently, describes how these children are faced with the triple task of learning what reading and writing are all about, learning how to read and write and learning how to do so in a second language.

In view of this crucial relationship between the first and second languages, it is indeed surprising that children's first languages are perhaps the most undervalued of all the resources which young language minority learners bring with them into school. Perhaps we need to be reminded that a pedagogical rationale, no matter how well supported logically and empirically, cannot withstand the political forces which are always present in situations characterized by uneven power relationships. As Corson (1992b) indicates, though there is compelling evidence that would support the establishment of schooling in multilingual and multicultural settings in which all children, even the native speakers of the dominant language, could be educated in more than one language, examples of such programs are few and far between.

Schooling experiences

ADDITIVE OR SUBTRACTIVE BILINGUALISM

The value of children's first languages, however, is not simply in the ease with which concepts and skills can be transferred into a second language. All too many bilingual programs see the native language as no more than a piece of scaffolding to be discarded when the real building – the second language – is firmly erected. In such programs, children usually enter school largely monolingual in their first language and leave school still largely monolingual, but now in their second language. Lambert (1980) refers to this situation as *subtractive bilingualism.* Unfortunately, it is not only the first language which is taken away. Subtractive bilingualism can have damaging social and cognitive repercussions; both social integration and academic achievement can be negatively affected. Lambert contrasts this state of affairs with *additive bilingualism,* which makes far better use of these children's first language resources. In the latter case, the aim is to enable them to function in each language community and cope with the literacy demands which each language community expects of its educated users by the time they are ready to graduate from high school.

MORE LITERACY

Though the majority of their first language development, including much of their awareness of print and its uses, will have taken place within the family and immediate community, previous schooling may also have extended young second language learners' skills in language use, particularly in its written forms. Children who have prior schooling experiences will also have learned a great deal about how to "read" the educational environment and manipulate it to their ends. These more social aspects of literate behaviour include how to find a place within a group, how to attract a teacher's attention or hide from it, how to work out what is expected in school and what the sanctions are for noncompliance, and how to weigh one's options! Young children, especially when faced with long hours of school tasks which do not fully occupy their minds, have an antipathy towards boredom and an almost irrepressible need to have some fun. Both factors result in their creation of an ''underground'' curriculum, to borrow Johnson's term (Chapter 8), which most teachers recognize as a useful, if sometimes annoying, adjunct to the formal work of the day. Children with previous schooling, though they may not know the particulars of how their new school or classroom operates this subterranean program, do know that they should be on the lookout for this phenomenon.

LEARNING PREFERENCES

As Johnson (Chapter 7) further reminds us, children develop both cultural and individual orientations towards the more conventional and public forms of classroom interaction. Children who have learned to value advice and attention from the teacher will probably not appreciate always having their requests for teacher assistance diverted back to the peer group. Conversely, children who feel more relaxed and engaged when watching and listening to peer group interaction would probably prefer not to be pressured into premature interaction with the teacher one-on-one. Both groups of children possess a technique which, at least at this initial stage when they are feeling most vulnerable and insecure, acts as a much-needed security blanket. Teachers would be well advised not to insist that the blanket be left outside the classroom door.

What understandings and skills are required of the professionals employed to help the children accomplish these tasks?

The ''professionals'' referred to in this section may be principals, program directors, teacher educators or program evaluators. Most of the individuals who come into regular contact with language minority children, however, are teachers. They are the people who make hundreds of decisions daily that influence the education of these children. Consequently, the question of what knowledge, skills, and attitudes are needed to inform those decisions is considered largely from their point of view. These teachers may be assigned to work exclusively with language minority students either in a separate area of the school or within the mainstream classroom. Alternatively, they may be grade level teachers who have watched the population of their classes become more linguistically and culturally diverse with each passing year. Many of the notions in this section of the summary reflect ideas expressed more fully in this volume (see Chapters 1, 7, 8, 9, 10, 11, and 12).

What do they need to know?

Johnson's succinct summary (Chapter 8) of the knowledge base which teachers require includes ". . . how children learn; how language is understood, interpreted and created in different situations; how language use varies across cultures and across situations; and how all of these processes relate to second language development." Teachers also need to know how children's learning styles are affected by their previous educational experiences and by any physical, emotional or neurological barriers to learning which they may have. Students' emotional readiness to learn the new language is another important consideration. This readiness varies according to the stages in adjustment which students go through, a developmental process with which teachers need to be familiar. The motivation to become a member of the new speech community is also related to the value which the host society places on students' various backgrounds (Chapter 1). Teachers need to know of the existence of this cultural "pecking order" and know how to counteract the effects of the wider society's negative reactions to certain groups. Teachers need to recognize the significance of the experiences which students have had prior to joining their new school as well as the continuing contribution to their learning made by events in their present lives outside of school.

What skills do they need to have?

Teachers need to be able to plan and deliver a program and assess that program's impact on the individual students in their classes. Given the diversity of starting points of the learners, it would probably be more accurate to think of "program" in the plural. At the same time, teachers are usually faced with learners in groups, not individually, so what is required is a total program within which different students will be learning different things simultaneously. Though it might seem as if "planning", "delivering" and "assessing" are three distinct, sequential activities, in fact they are interrelated in a complex way (Chapter 9). Thus, teachers might begin the day with a specific plan in mind which is quickly aborted as superior "teachable moments" present themselves. Assessment, too, is often, and increasingly, an integral part of a learning activity as, for example, when teachers use student writing portfolios as the source of samples to monitor student progress in moving from initial idea to final written product. Recognizing, therefore, the individual nature of the learning going on within the group as well as the overlapping nature of the three activities, we can summarize major subskills which teachers are called on to use as follows:

- Discuss with learners and their parents possible learning goals and how those goals might be reached.
- Articulate and record the agreed-upon goals and the means to be used to reach them.
- Collaborate with learners and colleagues to design and implement a program that will:
  - build on students' previous experiences and preferred learning strategies.
  - extend those experiences, especially in areas related to academic achievement and social integration, and broaden their repertoire of learning strategies.
  - use a variety of techniques and resources to promote the comprehension of unfamiliar concepts and/or new language forms and their use.
  - provide opportunities for many different kinds of interaction, for example, between children and materials, child and adult, child and child, child and children, second language learner and another second language learner, fluent native-speaker and second language learner.
  - include units or sequences of tasks dependent on each other which embed concepts and language in authentic and increasingly meaningful contexts.
  - adjust input according to how cognitively demanding the topic is likely to be for individual children and in ways that exploit their learning strengths and compensate for any weaknesses.
- Be an excellent role model demonstrating how to learn, solve problems, take risks, be creative, use language well and interact positively with others.
- Support students in their learning and advocate on their behalf whenever their rights are threatened by individuals or by entrenched societal power relations.
- Monitor student progress and program effectiveness in moving towards the agreed upon goals.

What attitudes should underpin their actions?

Teachers who work with language minority students need to see cultural and linguistic diversity not as a liability but as a resource, and to recognize that cultural and linguistic variation does not mean cultural and linguistic deficit and unequivocally does not imply social or intellectual inferiority (Chapter 5). They need to be convinced that all children are capable of learning and to recognize that teachers, too, can continue to learn from their students throughout their teaching career. They need to expect the unexpected; to accept calmly the fact that students will choose unique routes to reach their destinations, certainly different in some cases from the path teachers might select; and to delight in the creative solutions which many children will come up with to solve problems important to them. Teachers must be prepared to share responsibility for educating these children with members of the children's families and communities, acknowledging the primacy of the family in shaping the youngsters' emerging values.

What should teachers do to continue to learn?

Just as young second language learners exhibit preferences for one way of approaching learning tasks over another, so do teachers when undertaking their own professional development. For some, a conversation with a group of students or a colleague or the opportunity to see what is happening live in the next classroom – or through videotape in their own – are the activities which most stimulate reflection and encourage experimentation. For others, attending courses, workshops or seminars or reading accounts of exemplary practice or research studies provide the basis for rethinking and redesigning. It is the latter set of activities most teachers would regard as "serious professional development". There is increasing evidence, however, that the former should be valued more by teachers and administrators alike (Chapters 1 and 8; Fullan, 1991; Kutz, 1992; McDonald, 1986; Newman, 1990). Looking carefully at what happens in classrooms, conducting needs analyses, facilitating group and individual input and feedback sessions as well as opening one's daily planner, one's door, and one's mind to colleagues – all provide a rich source of new information. An added bonus is that quite a lot of this information can be gathered in the course of the normal work week.

What roles can families and communities play in educating language minority children?

The movement of immigrants and refugees into the major English-speaking countries of the world has obliged all the receiving countries' educational systems to make some provision for children of diverse linguistic and cultural backgrounds. As they have done so, these countries have noticed, often reluctantly, that already residing within their borders were many other linguistic and cultural minorities whose children were entitled to an education equal in quality to that provided for the children of the

Anglo majority. The question of what constitutes "equal in quality" has received a variety of answers over the years (Chapters 2 and 9).

Churchill (1986) provides a useful categorization of the responses of school systems to this challenge and identifies their underlying assumptions about what language minority students need in order to be successful in school. As he points out, most of the responses to date assume that language minority children are lacking something; it might be that they lack the language of the majority culture or the skills and knowledge base required to live successfully within the majority culture. Their premature loss of first-language skills has also been seen as inhibiting transition to the learning of the majority language due to cognitive and affective deprivation. In each of these cases, the "norm" is the majority language and culture. Even if the minority group's first language is seen as worthy of support, that support is in the service of learning the second, or dominant, language.

A very different approach is to view minority children as having languages and cultures which not only provide an excellent platform on which to build a second language and culture, but also merit respect in their own right. As the minority child becomes increasingly bilingual and bicultural through contact with the institutions of the majority community, so too can the members of the majority group be enriched by the linguistic and cultural knowledge and skills which they acquire from contact with the minorities with whom they coexist.

The authors in this book share this latter view. They do so partly because they are acutely aware of the dangers described by Coelho (Chapter 12) and Wong Fillmore: "When parents lose the means of socializing and influencing their children" (quoted in Chapter 4). They will not be party to those who seek to drive a linguistic and cultural wedge between child and family. But they also appreciate what both minority and majority group members stand to gain if minority group experience is accepted as a valid basis for education. Instead of trying to make students' homes and communities more like school, they agree that it is time to restructure the school environment to recognize and capitalize on the resources that are part of students' everyday lives outside of school. The role that children's families and communities play in contributing to the educational experience of their, and other, children is clearly of great significance (see Chapters 1, 3, 6, and 11).

Families

If minority children's languages and cultures are to be valued and shared within schools, it follows that the families which impart to the children those languages and cultures must also be valued. Moreover, families must be encouraged to participate in the ongoing education of their children, and that of their children's peers, whether the peers come from the same or different linguistic and cultural backgrounds. Family participation can take many forms:

- Families can be requested to continue to use their primary language in communicating with each other, with all parties recognising that it is through this modelling of a well-developed, complete language system that family members will be able to expose children to the most cognitively challenging content (Chapters 4 and 10).
- Families can support their children's initial attempts at creating meaning through reading and writing even before the children are able to use standard written forms (Chapters 6 and 11).
- School events and activities can be vehicles for genuine two-way communication. During events such as registration, child pick-up and drop-off, classroom visits, "open houses", phone calls and interviews, as well as through written notes, report cards, and samples of childrens' work, teachers can seek out families' views, responses and reactions. They can use these opportunities to learn more about how different families support the linguistic, cognitive and social development of their children (Chapter 12). This kind of approach contrasts sharply with the all too common view of teacher-parent interaction as an opportunity to tell parents how the school operates and what the parents need to do to support the school's efforts.
- Family members can be asked to share their knowledge and skills as part of the instructional program, making presentations to and answering questions from the whole class, or helping with small groups and individuals (Chapter 4).
- Regardless of the language spoken in the home or the level of education of the parents, all families can be encouraged to participate with their children in a variety of homework – or "homefun" – assignments to be completed at home and then brought back to school for sharing (Enright and McCloskey, 1988).

Relations between home and school

School districts which have highly diverse populations in terms of cultural, racial, linguistic, socioeconomic, political and religious backgrounds rarely have a staff complement which reflects this diversity. This being the case, some tensions are likely to surface which in turn will form a barrier to easy communication. If each side has conflicting, deeply held beliefs and values about what constitutes good child-rearing practices and quality education for young children, and if teachers and parents also view each other as rivals engaged in a power struggle over who knows what is best for a specific child, then a distrustful relationship is almost certain to develop.

Sara Lawrence Lightfoot's brilliant analysis of these kinds of relationships is tellingly entitled *Worlds Apart* (1978). Yet Lightfoot's message to educators and parents is not all one of despair. She advises teachers and parents to anticipate and tolerate a certain level of tension resulting from their differing perspectives and value systems. She insists that these differences should be discussed, making explicit what is causing the anxiety and distrust. She also urges that areas of responsibility and competence of both parties be clarified, and agreement sought on those aspects of the child's educational development which will most benefit from close collaboration between them.

Even in those circumstances where teachers and parents have reached substantial agreement on the goals for the child, problems can arise when teachers make suggestions as to how parents can assist, without considering carefully enough the family's socioeconomic situation or its culturally preferred ways of interacting (Chapter 10). Activities which demand a lot of time when parents are working long hours or cost money which the family either does not have or would choose to spend on something else are unlikely to be well received. So too are those which run counter to parents' beliefs about how children learn and how children should behave with their parents. When suggestions are rejected, the teacher may feel let down and the parents may feel either guilty about their noncompliance or affronted by the teacher's ignorance of their situation or insensitivity towards it.

As teachers become more familiar with the lives of their students and their families, they will make fewer of these errors and will be able to tailor their suggestions to better fit in with those lives. In the process, they will come across evidence which may dispel some commonly held myths regarding issues such as how much language minority parents care about the education of their children, how frequently they engage in literate activities, what "funds of knowledge" they use "to survive, to get ahead or to thrive" (to use Moll's apt words as quoted in Chapter 4). And as teachers come to know more families from the same or similar cultural background, they will also come to appreciate the variation that exists within the group (Commins, 1992).

Communities

Beyond the individual family is the wider community which the school serves. Sometimes this community is fairly homogeneous but more often it comprises a number of segments whose members may congregate according to which gender, class, linguistic, ethnic or racial group they belong to, or where they work or how they spend their leisure time. An important function of the school is to extend children's understanding of what this wider community is like and to demonstrate the ways in which the community is similar to, or different from, society at large.

Teachers who work within diverse communities of this kind can often find themselves playing the role of information broker; they perform a useful service in providing details of resources within the community which minority children and their parents, especially those who have recently arrived in the country, are unlikely to know about but are very likely to benefit from (Chapter 4). But what about the situations, also explored in Chapter 4, in which teachers are information seekers, not providers? When teachers search out individuals from the community who have useful skills and knowledge to share with the children, they may indeed select the parent of a particular child. When the individual is introduced, however, it should be both as a parent and as a member of the community. And when schools organize systematic explorations of the local community, children and teachers can look beyond the specifics of individual families to find the patterns of cultural organization which characterize that community. In other words, it is important for teachers and parents to recognise when they are interacting as an individual teacher with an individual parent and when they are interacting as a representative of the school system with a representative of the community or a segment thereof.

This point becomes particularly crucial when considering school governance. If minority children are to be viewed as equal participants in the schooling endeavour, then any advisor or decision-making body established to assist with school governance must represent their interests. No people are better qualified to do so than members of the language minority community itself. Ensuring that parent/teacher councils or boards of trustees do indeed contain representatives of these families is no easy task. Minority community members may be reluctant to become involved in such political action or may be too preoccupied with making a living. They may feel shut out by the group which is already firmly entrenched in positions of power or superfluous, especially when the rhetoric employed by those in power is laden with reassurances as to the importance of special provision for minorities. If they do attend an initial meeting, they may feel uncomfortable about the way the meeting was conducted or inadequate because they could not express their views fluently. Specific steps need to be taken to encourage minority community members to run for office, to help with campaigns of minority candidates, and to provide translation services where necessary during the conduct of meetings and in the preparation and dissemination of written materials. When these challenges are met and minority parents really begin to participate in the governance of schools, then perhaps the adjective "minority" will begin to lose its "second-class" overtones.

What are the advantages of engaging the whole school environment in educating young language minority learners?

As McKeon, Tabors and Snow, Hudelson, Met, and Coelho all point out (Chapters 1, 5, 6, 7, and 12), the numbers of children from different cultural and linguistic groups entering schools in which English is the primary medium of instruction is large and growing annually. In some jurisdictions, so-called "minority" children already constitute the numeric majority. It will not be long before the same situation will exist in many other schools, especially in urban centres. Attempts to deal with such a substantial percentage of the student body by adding "special" programs on top of "regular" ones will quickly result in school systems competing within themselves for resources such as people, materials, time and even space. Logistics alone point to the need to consider these children as an integral part of the school rather than marginal to it.

There are reasons in addition to administrative convenience which suggest that it is advisable to rethink "add-on" programs for minorities. As was outlined earlier in this chapter, the academic, social and linguistic tasks which these children face will not be accomplished in a matter of months. Therefore, to be effective, the programs to help them accomplish these tasks must be developmental in nature and long term, not "quick fix" remedies. There may be occasions when it would seem considerate to separate a group of minority students for instruction. Examples include times when children who have missed a lot of schooling are offered upgrading using the medium of their native language or when newcomers who feel intimidated by the mainstream classroom are offered the relative comfort of a small group of other recent arrivals and the encouragement of a second language teacher. It is also arguable that the need to separate for these purposes is simply a reflection of the inadequacy of the mainstream classroom. Why should upgrading using the first language not be delivered within the mainstream classroom? Who is causing the newcomers to feel so uncomfortable that they need the refuge of a small group and a sympathetic instructor? Any plan to separate language minority children from others must consider what is being relinquished in the process. If what is gained outweighs what is lost, then separate provision may, occasionally, be justified. In all cases, the gains relating to children's learning should weigh heavier than ease of scheduling or a teacher's preference not to work with certain students.

What the mainstream classroom can offer minority students

What second language students do not need is the exclusive company of other children who know the same, or even less, than they do about the new school setting, the unfamiliar curriculum, and the strange language. Nor do they need a fragmented day in which they move from instructor to instructor for different segments of work with the likelihood of coordination of that instruction diminishing with the addition of each segment. Participation in mainstream classrooms can offer minority students an integrated learning environment consisting of a peer group with varied levels of concept development and language skills and from different linguistic and cultural backgrounds. In effective mainstream classrooms, all students are socialized to accept responsibility for their own and each other's learning, their safety in the school setting, and their feeling of belonging to the class group. The teachers of these classes are knowledgeable in the content of the curriculum and skilled at planning and conducting learning activities that provide both a shared experience for the class as a whole and learning opportunities for individual students, regardless of their present level of functioning or linguistic and cultural background. Undoubtedly there are separate programs for minority students which provide much higher quality educational experiences in terms of academic, social and linguistic development than do those mainstream classrooms which fall far short of this "ideal". What is important to stress, however, is that it is very difficult to duplicate the teaching of curriculum content at the appropriate conceptual level and to provide the helpful peer modeling and interaction opportunities within a program designed exclusively for minority students (Chapter 8). Modifying a mainstream classroom to meet the additional challenges posed by the presence of a more heterogeneous population is a more straightforward task.

What language minority students can offer the mainstream classroom

Language majority students and their teachers stand to gain from the presence of language minority students. Both students and teachers have firsthand opportunities to communicate with children and their parents who speak other languages and who either have learned, or are in the process of learning, a second language. As every language teacher knows, helping someone else learn how to communicate in a new language inevitably increases the helper's awareness of language forms and functions. In other words, in those classes with second language learners, the already fluent students and teachers have the possibility of extending their understanding of how their language works in ways which will make them more critical consumers and users of that language. The already developed, or developing, bilingualism of language minority children and their parents also contains an important message which is rarely lost on those who are monolingual, namely that people who can switch from language to language communicate with a wider range of people than those who are restricted to a single language. For monolingual youngsters, the fact that they see children of their own age exhibiting this skill can be a powerful motivator in terms of their own learning of another language.

Curricular objectives related to global education and intercultural understanding come alive in a setting in which diversity of experience and interpretation is a fact of everyday life. Teachers can anchor complex concepts, such as global interdependence, in examples of experience from the classroom and the surrounding community rather than presenting the issue as something remote, exotic, and unconnected with any of the children's lives. Coelho (Chapter 12) provides the following clear statement of the "bottom line" in this regard: "Unless the school and classroom program is structured in such a way as to promote positive intercultural interaction, minority children have little opportunity to find out first hand about mainstream and other minority cultures; similarly, children of the mainstream culture have little opportunity to develop nonstereotypical views of minorities."

In classes with cultural and linguistic diversity, there is also likely to be a rich mix of individual learning styles as Tabors and Snow (Chapter 5) illustrate from a preschool perspective. Teachers will find that learning preferences often cross cultural lines and that the shy majority student may well thrive on some of the activities which were set up to encourage participation by a group of newcomers. Techniques designed with second language learners in mind, such as greater use of visuals for presentation of ideas, will often be advantageous to majority children for whom aural learning is difficult or who need visual reinforcement to build up a background schema with which to approach written texts. The presence of language minority children with obvious learning needs can help teachers recognise that there may be majority group children with similar needs.

Perhaps the major advantage of having language minority students in mainstream classrooms is the possibility for collaborative teaching among instructional staff who were previously employed in providing separate instruction. Such collaboration can take many forms, such as planning together who will do what, when and with whom so that the task of programming for a heterogeneous class is more manageable but at the same time coordinated; experimenting with different groupings to provide a broader range of teacher and student input and output opportunities; watching and listening to each other interact with class members with a view to extending each other's repertoire of teaching skills; and sharing information about individual children which each has gathered in the course of everyday interaction, to provide a richer and more reliable assessment of student progress.

A "whole school" approach

Extrapolating from McKeon, Cummins, Johnson, Genesee and Hamayan, Cloud, and Coelho (Chapters 1, 2, 8, 9, 10, and 12), the following are some of the characteristics which we would expect to find in a school which has opted for a ''whole school'' approach to the education of language minority children.

- Hiring decisions and performance appraisal of staff includes an assessment of competence in working with language minority students. Promotion becomes contingent on the demonstration of such competence. Individuals who are bilingual and bicultural occupy positions at all levels of responsibility within the school.
- The entire school staff (not just the second language or bilingual education staff) accepts the challenge of working with a diverse student population and is committed to building on that diversity, not minimizing it.
- Staff members routinely practise assessment procedures which allow them to accurately and adequately assess all children's previous educational accomplishments in light of opportunities to learn and identify appropriate short- and long-term goals to build on those experiences.
- Curricular objectives for all grades include developing knowledge about other cultures, skills in cooperation and negotiation within and across cultures, and an attitude of tolerance in the face of difference.
- Languages, in both their oral and written forms, are seen as powerful tools for learning about the world, shaping a personal response to it and communicating with others. Additionally, the development of high-level bilingual skills is seen as a desirable educational outcome for *all* children.
- The curriculum is delivered through themes, often interdisciplinary, employing instructional strategies effective for both minority and majority students. Care is taken to avoid bias in favour of any single group in the selection of instructional strategies and learning materials.
- Instructional groupings are determined by their efficacy in promoting high levels of academic achievement, respectful and harmonious social relationships, and proficiency across a wide range of language functions, both receptively and productively. In those instances where minority children are grouped for instruction specific to their needs, attention is paid to ensuring coordination of this instruction with all other parts of the day.

- Team planning, including the sharing of information about children among team members, is accorded a high priority when organising the school's timetable and allocating professional development funds.

Conclusion

Twenty years ago, it was not uncommon to find language minority youngsters seated around a small table in the school health room, practising dialogues from a textbook designed for their parents; typical topics included how to open a bank account and how to conduct oneself in a job interview – not exactly an 8-year-old's prime concerns! Or they would be working with a teacher who had been trained in foreign language teaching which, in the 1960s and 1970s, was still heavily influenced by audiolingualism, with its set order of presentation of structures from "simple" to "more complex" and its aim of error-free mastery of one segment of the target language before moving on to the next.

Gradually, materials relating to children's needs and interests have taken the place of adult hand-me-downs and audiolingual techniques, which may have been defensible in a setting where the teacher and the textbook were the only sources of the target language, but which have come to be regarded as less than adequate in settings where second language learners find themselves for the rest of the day in the company of adults and peers who are operating almost exclusively in the target language. With all kinds of linguistic demands being placed on their fledgling language skills, as Ellis (1984) points out, "I don't know" becomes a much more crucial phrase to learn than "I know".

The imperatives of helping young language minority students integrate socially and succeed in school is another factor which has led to an expanded view of what is involved in educating these children. The children themselves have contributed to this changing conception by demonstrating how they can use their already developed learning skills in new settings. Their parents, and the communities with which they identify, have also added their ideas and given of their time to show what is possible when partnerships are established between homes and schools which are culturally quite different.

Nowadays, the health room is seen as too constricting an environment to hold the really important classes for language minority learners. They need to be where the real action is. Since language minority children can be any age when they arrive at school, it is also understood that, though there are some language items which all students need to learn – numbers, colours, greetings, phrases for expressing intentions, wishes, dislikes and so on – that does not necessarily imply extracting a common core of items and teaching them to all students in the same way, carrying the same concepts and using the same visual support. Numbers, for example, might well be introduced to 4-year-olds using lots of manipulatives and providing many opportunities for grouping and regrouping so that the concept of the number is taught at the same time as the linguistic label. Twelve-year-olds are unlikely to need such an approach. A game with dice, played with some peers who already know numbers in the target language, would guarantee proficiency in the numbers one to twelve in less than half an hour, and a few interesting problems involving large sums of money could introduce the larger numbers.

Viewing second language acquisition as a means to academic achievement and social integration rather than an end in itself also means that every content lesson and every school activity is a language lesson. Given an activity such as having children make a scale drawing of their classroom, a traditional approach to second language teaching would use that task as a vehicle for teaching vocabulary items such as "window", "bulletin board", "door", the unit of measurement – metre or yard – and numbers below twenty. This kind of language, however, while certainly appropriate, does not go nearly far enough when the goals of academic achievement and social integration are taken seriously. In this latter case, in addition to the relatively easy-to-teach vocabulary items mentioned above, learners have to demonstrate their understanding of the concept of "scale", make accurate measurements, and transfer those measurements correctly to a two-dimensional format. Often students are required to cooperate with a peer in completing the task, which might necessitate asking for help from their partner and will almost certainly involve negotiating who is going to do what parts of the task. They also need to be able to describe and answer questions about their completed drawing. This combination of conceptual, linguistic and social skills is a far cry from some superficial naming of parts.

The life, learning and school experiences which young second language learners bring to school are now recognized as constituting the foundation for all their future learning. If some teachers choose to remain ignorant of these formative experiences, or if they disregard or even worse discredit them, then a gap is created between children and teachers which is left up to the children to close. Hardly a fair task to add to all the others which they must engage in! A detailed assessment on entry into school in the new environment which records these experiences and recognises the children's accomplishments to date is now accepted as an essential starting point of any quality program. The next step is the creation of a program plan which builds on what they already know and allows them to use learning strategies with which they have already experienced success. Any subsequent assessment of their progress, as Cloud (Chapter 10) reminds us, will evaluate the learning environment (teacher expertise, curriculum, amount and nature of instruction provided) as much as the performance of the students.

A lot has been learned about educating language minority children in the past two decades. Undoubtedly we will learn as much again in the next two. It is disturbing, however, that the application of these insights to date is so uneven. Enough examples of exemplary practise exist to demonstrate that the ideas put forward in this volume are more than just theoretical constructs, but too few exist to ensure that most, if not all, minority students are receiving as good an education as we educators know how to provide (Ashworth, 1988: Bourne, 1989; National Coalition of Advocates for Students, 1991). The contributors to this volume hope that their words will provide helpful advice as to what needs to be done and useful arguments for persuading the reluctant that certain changes to present practise are required. Many young lives will be affected by the individual and collective action which we decide to take.

References

Ashworth, M. (1988). *Blessed with bilingual brains: Education of immigrant children with English as a second language.* Vancouver: Pacific Educational Press.

Bourne, J. (1989). *Moving into the mainstream.* Windsor, Berkshire: NFER-Nelson.

Churchill, S. (1986). *The education of linguistic and cultural minorities in OECD countries.* Clevedon, Avon: Multilingual Matters.

Collier, V. P. (1989). How long? A synthesis of research on academic achievement in a second language. *TESOL Quarterly, 23,* 3:509–531.

Commins, N. L. (1992). Parents and public schools. *Equity and Choice, 8,* 2: 40–45.

Corson, D. (1992a). Minority cultural values and discourse norms in majority culture classrooms. *Canadian Modern Language Review, 48,* 3: 472–496.

Corson, D. (1992b). Bilingual education policy and social justice. *Journal of Education Policy, 7,* 1: 45–69.

Ellis, R. (1984). *Classroom second language development.* Oxford: Pergamon Press.

Enright, D. S., & McCloskey, M. L. (1988). *Integrating English.* Reading, Massachusetts: Addison-Wesley.

Fullan, M. G., & Stiegelbauer, S. (1991). *The new meaning of educational change.* New York: Teacher's College Press.

Gardner, H. (1991). *The unschooled mind: How children think and how schools should teach.* New York: Basic Books.

Handscombe, J. (1989). A quality program for learners of English as a second language. In P. Rigg & V. G. Allen (Eds.), *When they don't all speak English* (pp. 1–14). Urbana, IL.: National Council of Teachers of English.

Heath, S. B. (1983). *Ways with words*. Cambridge, England: Cambridge University Press.

Kutz, E. (1992). Teacher research: Myths and realities. *Language Arts, 69,* March: 193–197.

Lambert, W. E. (1980). The social psychology of language: A perspective for the 1980s. In H. Giles, W. P. Robinson, & P. M. Smith (Eds.), *Language: Social psychological perspectives* (pp. 415–424). Oxford: Pergamon Press.

Lightfoot, S. L. (1978). *Worlds apart: Relationships between families and schools*. New York: Basic Books.

McDonald, J. P. (1986). Raising the teacher's voice and the ironic role of theory. *Harvard Educational Review, 56,* 4:355–378.

McGroarty, M. (1986). Educators' response to sociocultural diversity: Implications for practice. In Bilingual Education Office (Developer) *Beyond language: Social and cultural factors in schooling language minority students* (pp. 299–343). Los Angeles: Evaluation, Dissemination and Assessment Center, California State University.

Milner, D. (1983). *Children and race: Ten years on*. London: Wardlock Educational.

National Coalition of Advocates for Students (1991). *The good common school: Making the vision work for all children*. Boston: N.C.A.S.

Newman, J. M. (Ed.) (1990). Finding our own way: Teachers exploring their assumptions. Portsmouth, NH: Heinemann.

Ochs, E., & Schieffelin, B. B. (1984). Language acquisition and socialization: Three developmental stories and their implications. In R. Shweder & R. LeVine (Eds.) *Culture theory: Essays on mind, self and emotion* (pp. 276–320). Cambridge: Cambridge University Press.

Williams, J. E., & Morland, J. K. (1976). *Race, color and the young child*. Chapel Hill: The University of North Carolina Press.

Wong Fillmore, L. (1983). The language learner as an individual: Implications of research on individual differences for the ESL teacher (pp. 157–173). In M. A. Clarke & J. Handscombe (Eds.), *On TESOL '82: Pacific perspectives on language learning and teaching*. Washington DC: TESOL.

Wong Fillmore, L., & Meyer, L. M. (1992). The curriculum and linguistic minorities. In P. W. Jackson (Ed.), *Handbook on Research in Curriculum* (pp. 626–656). New York: Macmillan.

Author index

Subject index

academic language skills, 39, 41
activities, instructional, 164–5, 185–6, 189
  individual, 194–6
  large group, 193–4
  pair work, 196–8
  small group, 199–200
additive bilingualism, 8, 40, 340
assessment, 174–8, 204–6, 321–2
  checklists, 177, 233–6
  conferences, 176, 177, 225–7
  of content, 175–6, 220, 230
  cross-linguistic, 257–8
  definition, 215, 217
  of disabilities, 251–9
  ecological, 247, 255
  performance, 214
  planning, 218–23, 223, 226, 228
  prereferral of disabled students, 251–2, 254
  portfolios, 176, 231–2
  record keeping, 219, 225, 231–6
  teacher as researcher, 95–6, 204–5
  tests, 176, 184, 229–30, 256, 321, 322
  see also observation

big books, *see* reading
bilingual education, 37, 40, 133, 138, 185, 267–8
bilingualism, simultaneous, 61–2
  rate of, 68–70
bilingual mixing, 64–73

castelike minorities, 21–2, 28
checklists, *see* assessment
Chinese Americans, 20, 22
cognitive development, 3–4
collaborative learning, 141, 165, 170
  and literacy development, 141
common underlying proficiency, 39
community, 5–8, 94–9, 344–5, 347–9
  information about, 96–8
  language use in the, 8, 98
content-compatible language, *see* objectives

content-obligatory language, *see* objectives
context-embedded language, 23–4, 164–5, 333
context-reduced language, 24–5, 254, 334
cooperative learning, 28, 198–9, 262, 320
creative construction, 17
critical literacy, *see* literacy
cultural diversity, 8, 15–6, 44, 83, 166, 187–9, 261, 295, 310–1, 312, 341, 349
  and school personnel, 322, 346
curriculum, 8–11, 27, 42–3, 319–21
  hidden, 47, 206
  preschool, 121–2

decision making, *see* instruction
deficit hypothesis, 6, 7
dialogue journals, *see* journals
difference hypothesis, 6–7
disabled students, behavior management of, 265–6
  see also assessment; instruction; special education
drama, 201–2

Eastside, 83–5
environmental print, 131–2, 141, 281–2, 292
equity, 33–4, 37
experience, *see* instruction

families, *see* parents
first language acquisition, 16–8, 38–9, 104–5, 111, 248–9
funds of knowledge, 7, 95

heritage language programs, 323

identity, 40, 45–7, 54, 335–6
  see also language variation
immersion, 159, 160
immigration, 103
  rates of, 35–7